QuickBASIC:
The Complete Reference

QuickBASIC:
The Complete Reference

Steven Nameroff

Osborne **McGraw-Hill**

Berkeley   New York   St. Louis   San Francisco
Auckland   Bogotá   Hamburg   London   Madrid
Mexico City   Milan   Montreal   New Delhi   Panama City
Paris   São Paulo   Singapore   Sydney
Tokyo   Toronto

Osborne **McGraw-Hill**
2600 Tenth Street
Berkeley, California 94710
U.S.A.

For information on translations and book distributors outside of
the U.S.A., please write to Osborne **McGraw-Hill** at the above
address.

A complete list of trademarks appears on page 579.

QuickBASIC: The Complete Reference

234567890 DOCDOC 89

ISBN 0-07-881362-x

CONTENTS

"I love QuickBASIC, and I need a good desktop reference book."

"I bought QuickBASIC, but I really don't understand it. I need a book that will help me now and as I gain experience."

"I learned to program with BASIC, but switched to a more structured and versatile language."

"I started to learn to program using BASICA, but it confused me."

If your situation matches any of these, this book is for you. This really is a complete reference, covering subjects from binary arithmetic to activating DOS interrupts. It is written for both the novice programmer and the expert.

If you've never tried Microsoft's QuickBASIC versions 4.0 or 4.5, you don't know what has happened to BASIC. QuickBASIC is a far cry from older implementations. Maybe you learned BASIC several years ago, but were taught later that it wasn't structured enough. QuickBASIC combines the simplicity of the original BASIC language with statements that force structured programming. In addition, you will never need line numbers again.

Included with QuickBASIC is an environment that makes editing, running, and debugging programs almost a pleasure. It is menu-driven for the first-time user, yet includes many shortcuts for when you gain experience. It includes a full-screen editor that allows you to move around the program with ease.

If you have used QuickBASIC, you already know this. Now what you need is a book that explains the features of QuickBASIC in an orderly fashion. Unlike many references, you can read *QuickBASIC: The Complete Reference* page by page, as you would a book. The text flows smoothly from subject to subject, covering each one in depth. The entire book is permeated with hints and suggestions from an author that has years of experience writing application software. This means that you will not always get schoolbook answers — you will get tips with experience-backed reasons to support them.

Maybe you are an experienced programmer who occasionally needs to look up the syntax of a statement or the parameters of a QuickBASIC function. With a quick glance at the index and a quick flip to the proper page, you will find statement and function syntax with brief explanations and warnings enclosed in a box. If you need more information, start reading on that page until you find what you need.

This book is divided into four parts:

1. Getting Started with QuickBASIC

2. The QuickBASIC Language

3. The QuickBASIC Environment

4. QuickBASIC Applications

Part One is for the person who has little programming experience, or is somewhat "rusty" in BASIC programming. It starts with a discussion of the differences between QuickBASIC and most other versions of BASIC. In the rest of Part One you can review programming essentials, working with the Quick-BASIC environment, and writing simple programs.

Part Two contains the complete language reference. Every QuickBASIC statement and function is discussed in detail. You will learn when to use each one, or why you shouldn't use it. Part Two has ten chapters that take you from the simple to the complex. This is the area you'll be checking when you want to quickly find the syntax of a QuickBASIC statement.

Part Three covers the QuickBASIC environment. The editor and associated software is filled with commands that make your programming job easier. You will find hints and shortcuts that will be applicable when you gain experience. You will also find complete coverage of the DOS compiler and linker.

Part Four contains complete applications. You can use many of the routines in this part in other applications without modification. You will find routines for creating menus, performing error-free I/O, and some fancy graphics. As with the rest of the book, the routines in Part Four are superb examples of professional programming and documentation techniques.

In this book you'll find thousands of lines of useful Quick-BASIC code. Part Four especially has programs that are ready to run. If you want to use these routines and love to type, you can enter the code line by line. If you prefer to spend your time in more exciting activities, consider purchasing the author's diskette package.

For $19.95 plus $3.00 shipping and handling, you will receive a 5 1/4-inch floppy disk in MS-DOS format. On that disk are all the programs and subroutines found in this entire book. You'll also get a handy listing of the routine names for easy retrieval. Just fill in the order blank that follows and mail it with your payment to the address shown. Please allow four to six weeks for delivery.

— S.N.

Please send me the programs and subroutines from *Quick-BASIC: The Complete Reference* on a floppy disk. Enclosed is my check or money order for $19.95 plus $3.00 shipping and handling.

Name:_____

Address:_____

Phone:_____

Send payment to:
Starry Software
Box 131
Big Canoe, GA 30143

This is solely the offering of the author and Starry Software. Osborne **McGraw-Hill** takes no responsibility for the fulfillment of this order.

Getting Started with QuickBASIC

Many programmers learned a version of BASIC as their first programming language, but later switched to another language like Pascal or C. QuickBASIC lets you return to BASIC programming without losing capabilities. Part One is designed for programmers who are either new to QuickBASIC, or are very rusty. If you have already programmed in QuickBASIC you may want to just skim this part before starting with Part Two.

Chapter 1 is for readers who are familiar with older versions of BASIC, but are unsure of what QuickBASIC has to offer. This chapter shows you, in detail, how QuickBASIC's additional statements and data structures place it far above standard BASIC.

Chapter 2 teaches background information you need before starting to program in QuickBASIC. You will learn how to do binary arithmetic and how to read syntax descriptions. You will also learn the steps a programmer must go through to solve a problem.

Chapter 3 introduces you to the QuickBASIC environment. After covering installation procedures, this chapter gives you the basic commands to edit, load, save, and run programs.

Chapter 4 discusses some of the statements and concepts that are used in nearly all QuickBASIC programs. It covers variables, assignment statements, and simple input/output. This chapter contains a comprehensive example that uses the problem-solving sequence to go from a problem statement to a working program.

P
A
R
T

O
N
E

The QuickBASIC Advantage

ONE

The QuickBASIC Language Versus Standard BASIC
The QuickBASIC Environment Versus Standard BASIC

When BASIC was first introduced in the late 1970s, it was simple to learn but difficult to maintain. It was designed solely for beginners, so complex programs were nearly impossible to implement. Programmers who learned BASIC as a first language were later forced to learn a more advanced language to continue their programming efforts. The few that held on to BASIC wrote huge programs that no one else could interpret.

Today there is QuickBASIC 4.5, which includes all of the statements and functions found in earlier versions of BASIC and goes many steps further. QuickBASIC is an advanced language suited for all levels of programming, as well as an integrated programming environment that speeds up programming development tremendously. This chapter will introduce you to some of the many advanced features of QuickBASIC 4.5. It is intended for programmers familiar with BASIC, but not completely familiar with QuickBASIC.

The QuickBASIC Language Versus Standard BASIC

This section examines the differences between the QuickBASIC language and standard BASIC. It shows you the advanced features that are available with QuickBASIC 4.5 and demonstrates how they make BASIC programming easier.

Top-to-Bottom Versus Line Numbers

The most obvious difference between QuickBASIC and standard BASIC is the lack of line numbers. In QuickBASIC, statements are executed from the top of the program to the bottom, unless a control statement changes the order of execution. By contrast, many versions of standard BASIC require a line number for every statement.

Inserting a new line or several lines is much easier with QuickBASIC. In standard BASIC you have to enter the new lines with the proper line numbers. If you insert too many statements, you have to resequence the entire program. With QuickBASIC, you simply move the cursor to the proper line and start typing.

SELECT-END SELECT Versus IF-END IF

The IF-END IF structure allows you to execute one—and only one—statement block based on a series of conditions. This structure works well, but QuickBASIC's SELECT-END SELECT structure makes programs much more readable and easier to understand.

The following program fragment written in standard BASIC displays a comment based on a student's grade:

```
510  IF (grade$ = "A") OR (grade$ = "B") THEN
520      PRINT "You are doing fine."
530  ELSE
540      IF grade$ = "C" THEN
550         PRINT "You are doing average work."
560      ELSE
570         IF (grade$ = "D") OR (grade$ = "F") THEN
580            PRINT "You are doing poorly."
590         END IF
600      END IF
610  END IF
```

You can easily get confused trying to follow the logic of this fragment. Many versions of BASIC now include the ELSEIF clause, which helps somewhat. The SELECT-END SELECT structure in QuickBASIC, however, improves readability even more. Here is the same fragment rewritten in QuickBASIC:

```
SELECT CASE grade$
   CASE "A", "B"
      PRINT "You are doing fine."
   CASE "C"
      PRINT "You are doing average work."
   CASE "D", "F"
      PRINT "You are doing poorly."
   CASE ELSE
END SELECT
```

The SELECT CASE statement makes it obvious that all the decisions are based on the value of *grade$*.

DO-LOOP Versus WHILE-WEND

The WHILE-WEND loop in standard BASIC allows you to test a condition, then execute the loop as long as the condition is TRUE. Here is a loop that asks a question and waits for the correct response:

```
610   INPUT "What is 2 + 2 "; answer%
620   WHILE answer% <> 4
630      PRINT "Incorrect.  Try again."
640      INPUT "What is 2 + 2 "; answer%
650   WEND
660   PRINT "Correct!"
```

The DO-LOOP structure in QuickBASIC gives you much more flexibility. Here is the same loop rewritten in QuickBASIC:

```
DO
   INPUT "What is 2 + 2 "; answer%
   IF answer% <> 4 THEN
      PRINT "Incorrect.  Try again."
   END IF
```

```
LOOP UNTIL answer% = 4
PRINT "Correct!"
```

There are two things to notice in this loop: First, Quick-BASIC allows you to test the loop condition either at the beginning or end of the loop. In this case, you save having to repeat the INPUT statement by moving the test to the end. Second, QuickBASIC supports both a LOOP WHILE and a LOOP UNTIL statement. The LOOP UNTIL in this sample is slightly more readable than the LOOP WHILE would be.

EXIT Versus GOTO

Programming without GOTO has been a subject of debate for years. In standard BASIC, however, the only way to exit a loop without matching the exit condition is with a GOTO. Quick-BASIC provides the EXIT FOR and EXIT DO statements that make controlled, graceful exits from loops and keep you from having to use the ambiguous GOTO.

Here is an example of a loop written in standard BASIC that has an escape:

```
700   INPUT "How many scores"; total%
710   sum% = 0
720   FOR cnt% = 1 TO total%
730     INPUT "Enter score, or -1 to QUIT: ", score%
740     IF score% = -1 THEN GOTO 800
750     sum% = sum% + score%
760   NEXT
800   average! = sum% / cnt%
```

When you first see the GOTO 800, you really have no idea where the program is going. In QuickBASIC, to exit the loop you can use an EXIT FOR statement:

```
INPUT "How many scores"; total%
sum% = 0
FOR cnt% = 1 TO total%
   INPUT "Enter score, or -1 to QUIT: ", score%
   IF score% = -1 THEN EXIT FOR
   sum% = sum% + score%
NEXT
average! = sum% / cnt%
```

With the EXIT FOR statement, you leave no doubt in the reader's mind of where the program will branch.

SUB Versus GOSUB

The best advancement for QuickBASIC 4.5 is its handling of subroutines and functions. In standard BASIC, your entire program must be one long module that includes all the GOSUB subroutines. Every variable is a global variable, and there is plenty of room for side effects caused by changing the value of a variable at the wrong time or in the wrong place.

With QuickBASIC, you can divide your program into SUBs and FUNCTIONs. You can pass variables as parameters, declare local variables, and share global variables. In other words, you have much more control over which routines have access to which variables. The QuickBASIC environment automatically places each subprogram in a different window to help you recognize the vast difference between SUBs and GOSUBs. Chapter 10 of this book is devoted to explaining the details on writing QuickBASIC subprograms.

Records

One of the additions to the QuickBASIC language has no real counterpart in standard BASIC: records, or user-defined types. The closest structure to a record in standard BASIC is the field, a temporary set of strings that is used for I/O with random-access files. Before you can store an element of a field, you have to convert it to a fixed-length string. QuickBASIC supports the FIELD statement, as well as the other standard BASIC features discussed in this chapter, but it has become obsolete.

Records allow you to combine elements of different types and associate them with a common name. You can input and output records directly to a random-access file. With the SWAP statement you can exchange the elements of two records with a single statement. You can also pass records and arrays of records to SUBs and FUNCTIONs. The rules for records are discussed in Chapter 9.

The QuickBASIC Environment Versus Standard BASIC

In many versions of standard BASIC, the programming environment allows you to enter text with a line editor and run your program through an interpreter. The editing process is slow because you cannot edit using the entire screen. Often, the line editor is so crude that the most painless way to change a line is to retype it completely. The interpreter makes program execution slow since it must translate each line before executing it.

A few companies have solved these problems by writing BASIC compilers. With a BASIC compiler, you write the BASIC programs with the editor of your choice, exit the editor, compile the program, and run it. If you need to make a change, you return to the editor, make the change, leave the editor, rerun the compiler software, and finally rerun your program. Although program execution speed is much better, development time gets much worse.

The QuickBASIC programming environment combines the best elements of both of these options. You write your program with an advanced screen editor that makes making changes a breeze. As you write each line, the software translates that line into executable code. This means that at the same time you finish entering your program, it is translated and ready to run. Program execution goes much faster than traditional BASIC interpreters. After you run your program, you are automatically returned to the editor, where you can make any necessary changes.

When you finish debugging your program, you can invoke a separate compiler to make an .EXE version of the program. This version is run from the DOS command line, and it runs even faster than QuickBASIC's interpreted version. Thus, QuickBASIC gives you the ease of a screen editor, with the quick turnaround of an interpreter, and the execution speed of a compiler—all in a complete software package.

The rest of this section gives you more detail on what the QuickBASIC environment has to offer. It covers specifics on editing, debugging, and file-management features.

A Two-Tiered Environment

QuickBASIC 4.5 has introduced a *two-tiered environment:* one for the beginner and one for the advanced programmer. The beginner will use EasyMenus, the environment that displays only the menu options that apply to single-module programs. No advanced features clutter up these menus. Once you get more proficient in programming and more comfortable with the environment, just a few keystrokes can switch you to the FullMenus system. This system displays menus with every option available with the environment.

Figure 1-1 displays the File menu options with the Easy-Menus system: create a new program, load an existing program, save the current program, print the program, and exit the environment. Many programmers require only these options. The full menu is shown in Figure 1-2. It contains a total of 12 options, including three different save options and three options for multiple-module programs. The beginner might get confused with all of these options, which is why the EasyMenus system was developed.

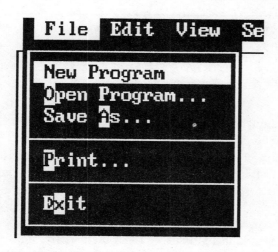

Figure 1-1.   File menu in EasyMenus

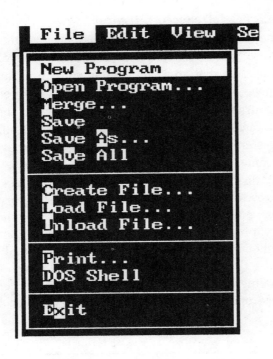

Figure 1-2.   File menu in FullMenus

The QuickBASIC Screen Editor

The editor in the QuickBASIC environment allows you to move the cursor to anywhere on the screen to enter, change, or delete text. It includes a *clipboard,* which is a section in memory where you can cut and paste blocks of text. You can also split the text window to edit two modules at the same time. The editor includes utilities to search for text, replace text, and merge files. In fact, the QuickBASIC editor can do everything you expect from a screen editor and more.

One of the unique features of the QuickBASIC editor is its automatic formatter. As you enter a line of text, the editor automatically capitalizes all reserved words. It also makes sure you have spaces between variable names and operators. It even keeps the capitalization of variable names consistent. If you change the case of a variable name, the editor changes the name in every other statement that uses that variable.

Watchpoints and Watch Expressions

The debugging tools in QuickBASIC 4.5 are superior to all other versions of BASIC. You can even set a flag that will highlight every line as the program is executed. This feature becomes indispensable when you are trying to find infinite loops. QuickBASIC makes TRACE statements obsolete.

Watchpoints in QuickBASIC allow you to write an expression so that program execution halts whenever the expression evaluates to TRUE. For example, you can set a watchpoint of **count% = 100** that will stop the program as soon as the variable *count%* has a value of 100. When this happens, QuickBASIC highlights the statement executed when the watchpoint was satisfied. You can then use another QuickBASIC tool to execute the program one step at a time to find your errors.

With *watch expressions,* you can constantly monitor the value of a variable or expression. These expressions appear in a special window on the screen, and they display the current value of the expression as long as you are in the right module or subprogram. You can observe the contents of each variable in the window and break the program when you notice a problem.

The Immediate Window

In standard BASIC, if you want to test a statement without having a program, you could write a statement without a line number. The statement

```
PRINT "This is the immediate mode."
```

will print the sentence immediately, instead of printing it when you run the program. This is known in standard BASIC as the immediate mode.

In QuickBASIC 4.5, program statements do not require line numbers, so there is no immediate mode. Instead, QuickBASIC provides something more powerful: the *immediate window*. When you move the cursor to the immediate window, it immediately runs any executable statement you type. Unlike immediate mode, you can use the immediate window to call your own subroutines.

You can also use the window to change the value of a variable. If you stop a program in the middle of its execution, you can move to the immediate window, write a LET statement to change the value, and restart the program where it left off. This can be very handy when you are debugging a program.

Modules and Libraries

If you have written many large programs in standard BASIC, you may have made several copies of subprograms that you used in more than one program. If you made a change to one of those routines, you had to track down the other copies and make the same changes. With QuickBASIC 4.5, you no longer have this problem because it allows you to use programs that have multiple files and to place commonly used routines into a *library*.

In QuickBASIC each file is called a *module*. QuickBASIC programs can span more than one module. This allows you to break a large program into smaller modules that are more manageable. When you load the program, QuickBASIC automatically loads all the modules the program requires. With modules, you can divide programs so that routines used by several programs can be placed in a module that the programs share.

If you have routines that are used by many programs, you can place them in a library. QuickBASIC has its own Quick libraries that include routines that are already translated. When you load a program that uses the library, the load is faster because the environment does not need to retranslate the routines in the Quick library.

This chapter has given you a brief look at some of the many features of QuickBASIC 4.5. The rest of the book is a complete reference, containing the details of these and the other features of the QuickBASIC language and environment.

Helpful Terms and Concepts

Programming Terms
Reading Syntax Descriptions
Problem Solving
Binary Arithmetic

If your only computer experience is in running interactive programs, you are considered a *user*. However, there is a big difference between using computers and programming them. If you have done very little programming recently (or at all), read this chapter for some essential concepts that you should master before writing QuickBASIC programs. After learning some programming terms, you will learn how to read syntax descriptions, how to convert a problem into a program, and how to do binary arithmetic.

Programming Terms

When a computer executes a program, it interprets a long series of ones and zeros written in *machine language*. If you had to write a program in machine language, you would see that it takes a long time and that it is easy to make mistakes. Unfortunately, languages like English are too unstructured for a computer to interpret. The word *run*, for example, can have many different meanings—from trotting, to a tear in a stocking, to a point in baseball.

QuickBASIC is one of many programming languages called *high-order languages*. These languages attempt to bridge the gap between human languages and machine language. High-order languages usually have less than two hundred words. Contrast this with spoken languages like English, most of which contain over 100,000 different words.

QuickBASIC is limited not only to a number of specific words, but also to the order in which the words can be used. The *syntax* of a language defines the words and the order in which the words can be used. *Semantics* define the meanings of the words and their relationships. QuickBASIC has strict semantic rules that further limit the types of words that you can use in various statements.

The *variable* is probably the most important concept to grasp before you start to program. In algebra you see variables in equations like these:

$$x + y = 15$$
$$x = 2y$$

Here, you use the letters x and y as variables because you did not know the value of each letter. Variables in math normally represent unknowns.

In QuickBASIC a variable has a slightly different meaning. A variable is a name you give to a memory location. You do not care which memory location the computer uses, as long as every time you use a variable name in your program, the computer uses the same memory location. Thus, a variable more often represents a "value that could be anything" rather than an "unknown." This will become clearer as you start using variables in Chapter 4.

Naturally, the computer cannot directly read programs written in QuickBASIC. To convert a program to machine code, older versions of BASIC used an *interpreter*, which is a program that converts a single line of code, executes it, and moves to the next line. Running a program with an interpreter allows you to begin execution right away, but program speed tends to be slower. When you work inside the QuickBASIC environment, your program is interpreted as you load it and as you enter each statement line. Thus, when you run the program it starts executing almost immediately.

QuickBASIC also includes a *compiler*, which is a program that converts an entire program from QuickBASIC to machine code. The output of the QuickBASIC compiler is an .OBJ file. To complete the conversion to an .EXE file you must use the *linker*. This program combines your .OBJ file with compiled code that is part of the QuickBASIC language.

Reading Syntax Descriptions

In this book, the discussion of each QuickBASIC statement includes a *syntax description*. This description is a line showing the proper syntax of the statement along with all of the options associated with that statement. All syntax descriptions in this book use certain symbols to represent variations in the syntax. This section will show you how to interpret those symbols.

The simplest of syntax descriptions contain no extra symbols. The syntax of the SWAP statement, for example, is this:

SWAP *variable1, variable2*

From this you can see that the SWAP statement begins with the word SWAP, followed by a variable, followed by a comma, followed by another variable. If a word is in italics, it is the name of an item you must provide. If the word is not in italics, you must use that exact word in the statement.

The square *brackets*, [and], surround part of a statement that is optional. In the syntax description for the DEF SEG statement,

DEF SEG [= *segmentaddress*]

the brackets indicate that you may include or omit the equal sign and address to make a valid statement.

Many statements have nested square brackets, making the interpretation more difficult. Consider the syntax description for the LOCATE statement on the following page.

LOCATE [*line*][,[*column*][,[*cursorflag*][,[*start*][,*stop*]]]]

From this description you can see that *column* is optional because it is enclosed in brackets. You should also see that you cannot include the column without preceding it with a comma. To include an item enclosed in more than one set of brackets, you must also include mandatory items inside the outer brackets. The following statements are all valid LOCATE statements:

```
LOCATE
LOCATE 3
LOCATE , 10
LOCATE 3, 10
LOCATE , , 1
LOCATE , , , 0, 6
LOCATE 3, 10, , 0, 6
```

The *braces*, { and }, enclose a set of items where you must choose one. These items are separated by vertical lines, |. In the syntax for a GOTO statement,

GOTO {*label* | *linenumber*}

you must include the word GOTO followed by either a label or a line number. If the braces are enclosed by brackets, as with the CLS statement

CLS [{0 | 1 | 2}]

you can include one or none of the items.

If you see three periods (called an *ellipsis*) following an item enclosed in brackets, you can include "zero or more occurrences" of that item. The syntax description of the PRINT statement includes an ellipsis:

PRINT [*expression* [{; | ,}]]. . .

From this description you know that the PRINT statement can have zero or more expressions followed by optional semicolons or commas.

In the designation of "one or more occurrences," you will see an item shown as mandatory, followed by the same item shown as "zero or more occurrences." Here is an example of this with the DATA statement:

DATA *constant* [,*constant*]. . .

From the syntax description you can see that the DATA statement must include at least one constant.

Problem Solving

Computer programming is both a science and an art. There are no specific or rigid rules for going from a problem to a computer program that solves the problem. In this section you will learn some general guidelines for solving problems.

There are seven basic steps to solving a problem with a program:

1. Define the problem.
2. Determine the inputs and the outputs.
3. Create a test case.
4. Write the high-level algorithm.
5. Refine the algorithm by getting more specific.
6. Convert the algorithm to a program.
7. Test the program.

The first step, defining the problem, is often the most difficult. In the classroom, a problem is given to you. In this case defining the problem is already done for you. In the real world, problems come from a user, often a person who has little or no computer background. In this case you may get a broad, open-ended statement like, "I need a program to keep track of my inventory."

When you define a problem you need to be specific. Seldom is a problem definition a single sentence. Occasionally, you may need to write an entire manual describing your interpretation of the problem. The more time you spend determining the problem the less time you will spend rewriting your programs. If you are working with a user, you will find that your first attempt at a problem definition will bring new requirements to the surface. Through repeated feedback from the user you should be able to create an accurate definition of the problem.

Suppose a user comes to you with a request for an inventory program. Your problem definition might start: "Write a program that tracks the inventory of the Ajax Auto Parts store. Stockroom workers must be able to see if a part is in stock and to remove a part from the inventory when sold. When a shipment comes in, a clerk must be able to update the inventory. The program must generate current inventory reports ..."

The second step in problem solving is determining the inputs and the outputs. The *inputs* are information that the user gives to the program. The *outputs* are the information that the program gives to the user. When you determine the inputs and outputs, give each one a meaningful name. These names could later be used as variable names in your program.

Consider a simple program that averages any three numbers. The following definitions would satisfy the second problem-solving step:

INPUTS: *firstnum*—the first number to average
               secondnum—the second number to average
               thirdnum—the third number to average
OUTPUT: *average*—the average of the three numbers

As you complete the rest of the problem-solving sequence you will continue to use these variable names.

In the third step you need to create some *test cases*. A test case is a set of actual inputs and their corresponding expected outputs. Test cases are the best way to determine whether your program meets the requirements of the problem. When you create the test cases, use several different ones, including both reasonable and extreme values. For simple programs like the one that computes averages, you can use a table like this:

Variables	Case 1	Case 2	Case 3
firstnum	2	2.1	0
secondnum	3	4.7	0
thirdnum	4	1.3	0
average	3	2.7	0

Notice that the table uses the input and output variables defined in the previous step.

For larger programs you will need a *test plan*. This plan will include sample files, databases, and user inputs. For output, a test plan often contains sample screen displays and report formats. All this work should be done before you begin writing any algorithms or code. If you spend a reasonable amount of time on the first problem-solving steps, you spend much less time debugging and rewriting your program.

Writing a high-level algorithm is the first problem-solving step. An *algorithm* is a step-by-step procedure for solving a problem. Algorithms are not supposed to be written in a programming language like QuickBASIC. Algorithms are written in English, programs are written in QuickBASIC. When you write an algorithm, limit the number of different words you use. The fewer number of words you use, the easier it will be to convert the algorithm to a program. (You may know a specific algorithm-writing language, like pseudocode or Structured English.)

From the definition, you know that an algorithm is a series of steps. A step might be defined as a single task. You should never have more than one task, or function, for a single step. When you write the steps of the high-level algorithm for your program, be general. If you get too specific right away the algorithm will be difficult to read. A high-level algorithm should give just enough information to explain the order of the steps leading to the solution. If your algorithm is more than 10 or 15 steps, it is probably too low-level.

As an example, suppose your problem is to write a program that takes a name in the form *lastname, firstname* and outputs it as *firstname lastname*. You determine that the input variable is *entirename* and the output variables are *firstname* and *lastname*. Here is a sample high-level algorithm:

1. Get *entirename* from the user.

2. Find the comma in *entirename*.

3. Define *lastname* as the first character up to the comma.

4. Define *firstname* as the first letter after the comma to the end of *entirename*.

5. Output *firstname*, a space, *lastname* to the screen.

Notice that the algorithm is written in English. The steps are clear, and each step accomplishes a single task. These guidelines will make writing the actual program easier.

The fifth step is the refinement of the high-level algorithm. Here is where you first start to mix English with QuickBASIC. The key word to the refinement process is *how*. At every step in your algorithm ask the question, "How?" Your answers to that question are the details for the algorithm. For example, study this simple high-level algorithm:

1. Input *num1, num2, num3*

2. Compute *average*

3. Output *average*

Steps 1 and 3 need no more refinement—you will be able to convert them directly to QuickBASIC statements. Step 2 requires more detail. You will need to add the actual equations:

2. Compute *average*

    a. *total = num1 + num2 + num3*

    b. *average = total* / 3

When you are designing larger programs, obviously this step is going to be more complex. Consider this high-level algorithm, which plays blackjack:

1. Place bets.

2. Shuffle cards.

3. Deal cards.

4. Display player cards.

5. Play player hand.

6. Display dealer cards.

7. Play dealer hand.

8. Determine winner and pay out.

Each step in this algorithm will break down into as many as 20 more steps. As you will see in Chapter 10, this high-level algorithm will become the main program, and each step will become a subroutine.

Do not feel that you must expand on every detail of every step. Keep in mind that this is an algorithm not necessarily tied to a computer program. Save details like prompts, colors, and other "bells and whistles" for the programming step. Most error checking can also wait. The reasoning behind this is that as you revise and update the algorithm, you want to avoid having to constantly change and rewrite these other details.

When you have finished writing and refining the algorithm, you are ready for Step 6, writing the computer program. You will spend much of the time translating your algorithm line-by-line into QuickBASIC. For larger programs, start with a small section, make sure it works, then move on to the next section.

The seventh step, testing the program, is actually combined into Step 6. In this step, you return to the test case you made in Step 3. Enter the test inputs into the program and make sure that you get the outputs you expected. If you get different results, you must start one of the toughest processes in programming: *debugging.* Debugging is the term for determining why you do not get the answers you expect, and fixing the problems. Debugging is discussed in Chapter 18.

One of the drawbacks to creating a step-by-step sequence is that it often implies that when you have finished all the steps, you will have a working program. Unfortunately, problem solving is far from being a sequential process. As you progress from one step to another you will find new problems, and with luck, new solutions. This may mean going back a few steps, even back to redefining the problem. Once you are finally finished, however, you have a program that does what the user wants, and does it correctly.

Binary Arithmetic

The computer does all of its calculations using only ones and zeros. Most programming languages allow you to manipulate those ones and zeros directly through *binary arithmetic.* In this section you will learn how to convert numbers to and from binary, how to represent negative numbers, and how to add and subtract binary numbers.

The numbers you use every day are decimal numbers. Also known as *base ten,* decimal numbers have digits that range from zero to nine. When you see the number "913" you read "nine hundred thirteen." Mathematically speaking, each digit of the number is multiplied by a power of ten:

$$913 = 9 \times 100 + 1 \times 10 + 3$$

Binary numbers are in *base two,* so their digits can only be zero or one. A typical binary number is 101101001b. This number is not 101 million, 101 thousand and 1. The "b" at the end of the number means it is binary. Binary numbers follow the same principles as decimal numbers, but their places are powers of two, not ten, as shown at the top of the next page.

$$101101001b = 1 \times 256 + 0 \times 128 + 1 \times 64 + 1 \times 32 +$$
$$0 \times 16 + 1 \times 8 + 0 \times 4 + 0 \times 2 + 1$$

You may have heard of decimals having a one's place, a ten's place, a hundred's place, and so on. Binary numbers have a one's place, a two's place, a four's place, and so on.

To convert a binary number to decimal, you first determine the places of the digits. It might help at first to write those values over their digits. To convert 101101001b, start by writing this:

256	128	64	32	16	8	4	2	1
1	0	1	1	0	1	0	0	1

Now add the numbers that have a one underneath:

$$101101001b = 256 + 64 + 32 + 8 + 1 = 361$$

Converting a number from decimal to binary is slightly more complicated. You must first find the largest power of two that is smaller than the number you are converting. For instance, if you want to convert 812 to binary, you start by going through the powers of two: 2, 4, 8, 16, 32, 64, 128, 256, 512, 1024. 1024 is too large, so 512 is the largest power of two that is less than 892. Once you have found the first number, write it down and subtract it from the original number:

$$892 = 512 + 380$$

Now take the new number, in this case 380, and repeat the same process. Eventually you will work your way down to a power of two (one is the zeroth power of two):

$$892 = 512 + 380$$
$$= 512 + 256 + 134$$
$$= 512 + 256 + 128 + 6$$
$$= 512 + 256 + 128 + 4 + 2$$

Once you have broken the number into powers of two, you can write the binary number. Again, it will help to write down all the powers of two. Then place a one under the numbers in your equation and a zero under the others:

$$892 = \frac{512 \quad 256 \quad 128 \quad 64 \quad 32 \quad 16 \quad 8 \quad 4 \quad 2 \quad 1}{1 \quad\quad 1 \quad\quad 1 \quad\quad 0 \quad\quad 0 \quad\quad 0 \quad 0 \quad 1 \quad 1 \quad 0}$$

Thus, 892 in binary is 1110000110b. As an exercise, try converting this binary number back to decimal to see if you get 892.

You can represent numbers less than zero in several different forms. The most common, and the one used internally in QuickBASIC, is called *two's complement*. Every INTEGER in QuickBASIC uses 2 memory locations (bytes), so there are 16 bits available for storage. In the two's complement representation, the sixteenth bit (the 32768's place) is used for the sign of the number: zero for positive and one for negative. In the computer, 892 is stored as 0000001110000110. The largest positive number is 0111111111111111, or 32767. To make the examples in this chapter easier to understand, you will learn two's complement with 8-bit numbers instead of 16. The largest positive number will be 127, stored as 01111111.

To represent a negative number in two's complement form, you first determine the binary equivalent of the same positive number. Then perform a *NOT function* on each bit; that is, change all the ones to zeros and the zeros to ones. Finally, you add one to the number. Here is the process for −92:

```
  92  =  01011100
 NOT     10100011
 + 1     10100100
```

Notice that the eighth bit automatically becomes a one, showing that it is a negative number.

If you follow the same process on the negative number, you will convert the number back to positive. To accomplish this, first perform the NOT function, then add one, as in the following example.

```
−92  =  10100100
NOT      01011011
+ 1      01011100
```

If you do everything properly, taking the two's complement of a number twice should give you the same number.

Addition of binary numbers follows all of the principles for adding decimals. In base ten you carry any values larger than nine to the next higher place. In base two you carry values bigger than one to the next place. Here is a simple example:

```
  00001100
+ 00001010
  ‾‾‾‾‾‾‾‾
  00010110
```

As with base ten addition, you start from the right side. From right to left:

$$0 + 0 = 1$$
$$0 + 1 = 1$$
$$1 + 0 = 1$$
$$\text{and } 1 + 1 = 0 \text{ carrying a } 1$$

These four equations represent the basic sums of binary addition.

For a slightly more complex equation, study this one:

```
  00000111
+ 00001011
  ‾‾‾‾‾‾‾‾
  00010010
```

Starting from the one's place, you add one and one. The sum is 10b, so you write the zero and carry the one. In the two's place, you add both ones and the one carried from the one's place. This gives you 11b, so you write a one and carry a one. In the four's place you have a one, a zero, and a carried one. This sum is 10b, so write the zero and carry the one. Finally, you have a one and a carried one, so you write 10. To check your answer, convert the addends to decimal:

$$7 + 11 = 18$$

When you convert 18 to binary you get 00010010b, so you know the addition worked.

You can add with negative numbers in two's complement form without doing any other conversions. For instance, here is the sum of 36 and −53:

$$
\begin{array}{r}
36 = 00100100 \\
+ \quad -53 = 11001011 \\
\hline
11101111
\end{array}
$$

Now you must convert 11101111b to decimal, taking the two's complement first:

$$11101111 = -00010001 = -17$$

You can subtract with two's complement binary by simply negating the minuend and adding. You already know that the two expressions

$$35 - 23$$
$$35 + (-23)$$

are the same. You will follow the same principle with binary numbers. For example, here is how the computer subtracts 36 from 53:

$$
\begin{array}{r}
53 - 36 = 53 + (-36) \\
53 = 00110101 \\
+ \quad -36 = 11011100 \\
\hline
00010001 = 17
\end{array}
$$

Again, notice that the sign bit came out positive automatically. The extra one that you would normally carry to the ninth bit is ignored, since the numbers can be only 8 bits long.

Getting Started in the QuickBASIC Environment

Environment Basics
Editing Commands
Saving a File
Loading a File

Until recently, language compilers were sold by themselves. You used your favorite editor or word processor to write the program, and you compiled the program from the DOS prompt. If you made any errors, you went back to the editor. Other languages supplied a line editor, like BASICA. With QuickBASIC you have a complete *programming environment*. In an environment you can edit, compile, run, and debug your programs with a single piece of software.

This chapter introduces you to the QuickBASIC environment, using version 4.5 and the EasyMenus system. If you have already used the environment, read Part Three of this book to get more complete coverage. If you have never used the environment, read this chapter to see how to use the menus and dialog boxes, and how to do simple editing commands. As you read this chapter, try each of the samples for yourself. By the end of the chapter you should be moving through the QuickBASIC environment with ease. If you have yet to install the system onto your hard disk or floppy disks, read Appendix C.

Environment Basics

Moving around in the QuickBASIC environment is quick and easy once you learn a few key concepts. If you have a hard disk, you invoke the environment with the following command.

C>QB

If you have two floppy-disk drives, move to disk drive B and type this command:

B>A:QB

This way, the files you save will be saved on the disk in drive B instead of the disk that has the QuickBASIC system files.

When you have entered the QB command from DOS, the screen will clear and you will see a screen similar to Figure 3-1. The top line of the screen is the *menu line*. The second line is the *title line*, which displays the name of the current text. Since you have not specified a name, this line should read "Untitled." The majority of the screen, from line 3 to line 20, is the *text window*. The shaded lines at the right side and on the bottom of the text window are *scroll bars*, which are useful only if you have a mouse. Lines 21 through 24 make up the *immediate window*. Finally, the bottom line is a *help line*.

Menus

When you first enter the QuickBASIC environment, you will see the text cursor at the top left of the text window. Press the ALT

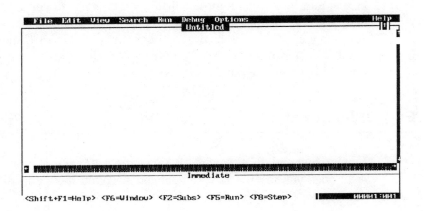

Figure 3-1.   The QuickBASIC environment screen

key to get to the menu line. You do not use this key in combination with other keys—simply press the ALT key and release it. The word "File" should be highlighted on the left side of the title line. The highlighted word shows the menu that will appear when you press ENTER. Although you will still see the text cursor in the text window, the highlighted word in the menu line tells you that the text window is inactive.

When you need to get to a specific menu, QuickBASIC offers three ways to get there. Keyboard and mouse operations can be intermixed.

- If you have a mouse, click the left button over the name of the menu you need.

- Move the highlighted word on the menu line with the LEFT and RIGHT ARROW keys and press ENTER.

- Type the different-colored letter of the name of the menu. For example, if you type the letter S you will find yourself in the Search menu.

Once you are in a specific menu, you can move to another menu with the LEFT and RIGHT ARROW keys. Notice that the entire menu is displayed as you pass through it. If you make a mistake and do not wish to be in any menu, press the ESC key. This will take you all the way back to the text window. If you have a mouse, click the left button anywhere in the text window.

To select a command from a menu, again you have three options:

- Use the mouse to move the pointer to the command and click the left button.

- Use the UP and DOWN ARROW keys to move the highlight to the desired command and press ENTER.

- Press the colored letter of the desired command.

Select the File menu from the menu line with one of these techniques. You will notice five different commands on this menu, which is shown in Figure 3-2. The commands that end in an ellipsis (. . .) will display a *dialog box* when you select them. The other commands, like Exit, will execute as soon as you select them.

Dialog Boxes

If you select the Save As command from the File menu you will see a typical dialog box, as shown in Figure 3-3. Dialog boxes display all of the possible options of a command to let you finalize a command before executing it. The most important keys in a dialog box for the keyboard user are TAB and SHIFT-TAB. These keys move you around inside the dialog box to all the inner boxes. The text cursor shows you the current inner box. Press the TAB key several times to see the cursor move through the inner boxes. The SHIFT-TAB combination will change boxes in the opposite direction.

Use the TAB key to get to the "Format" box in the "Save As" dialog box. This type of inner box acts very much like a menu. The dot inside the parentheses by the QuickBASIC Fast Load

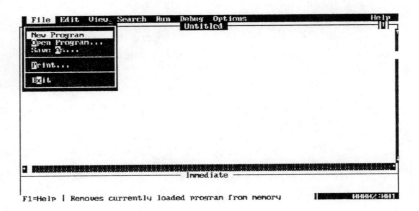

Figure 3-2.   The File menu

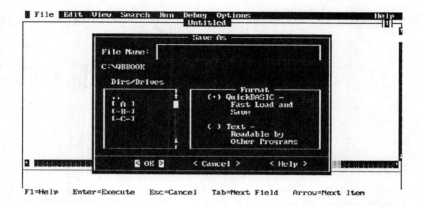

Figure 3-3.   The "Save As" dialog box

and Save option shows you that it is the current option. To change options, use the arrow keys or press the first letter ("Q" or "T").

In the "File Name" box you type the name of the file you are saving. If you have not selected all the options you want in the dialog box, do not finish entering text with the ENTER key. The ENTER key signals the end of the dialog, and the command will be executed. If you enter a filename, but still want to change the Format option, finish the text entry with the TAB key.

When you execute the command from a dialog box by pressing ENTER, QuickBASIC completes the command and returns you to the text window. If you decide you do not want to execute the command, you can either TAB over to the "Cancel" box, press the ESC key, or use the mouse. Selecting "Cancel" will also take you back to the text window.

For practice, save the blank text window as the text file BLANK.BAS.

1. Select the Save As command from the File menu.

2. Enter **BLANK.BAS** as the new filename.

3. Use the TAB key to get to the Format area.

4. With the arrow keys, move the dot next to the Text file type.

5. Press ENTER to complete the command.

If you have done everything properly, you should be in an empty text window with the title line showing "BLANK.BAS."

Editing Commands

You should now be familiar enough with the QuickBASIC environment to get to any menu and any menu command. Since you will not be writing a program, start by disabling the syntax checker. Select the Syntax Checking command from the Options menu. This will keep the QuickBASIC environment from trying to compile your text. You are now ready to start entering text. Try writing a letter or typing this page of the book.

When you get to the end of a line, press ENTER to get to the beginning of the next line. Use the BACKSPACE key (which is above the ENTER key) to correct errors. This key removes one character to the left of the text cursor. Continue typing until you have ten or more lines of text.

Cursor Movement

The QuickBASIC editor is known as a *screen editor* because you can move to any text in the text window. Once you have filled the screen with your text, move around the text window with the four arrow keys. Now move just to the right of any word on the screen, remove it with the BACKSPACE key, and then type a different word. If you chose a word in the middle of a line, you should have seen the text to the right of the cursor move left when you made the deletion, and back to the right when you typed the new text. Making that simple change is very cumber-some with a line editor, which often requires you to retype the entire line. Once you use a screen editor, you will never go back to anything else.

In addition to the arrow keys, there are a few other keys that move the cursor around in the text window. The HOME key takes you to the first column of the current line. If you need to get to the last character in the line, press the END key. These keys keep you from having to use the LEFT and RIGHT ARROW keys to get to these places. If you use the RIGHT ARROW key at the last position of a line, you will continue to move across the window.

The UP and DOWN ARROW keys also act as scrolling keys. The term *scroll* is used for when the window changes by one line. If you are at the bottom of the text window and you press the DOWN ARROW key, you will scroll down. This means that the top line of text will disappear and all other lines will move up one. A new line will appear at the bottom of the window where the cursor is. If you are at the top of the window and press the UP ARROW key, you will scroll up (as long as you are not at the top of the file). If you hold down one of these keys, you will see the entire file scroll by on the screen.

When you have a larger amount of text, there are a few simple commands that allow you to move freely throughout the file. The PGUP and PGDN keys move the text one page up or down. A *page* is the number of lines you can see in the window, normally 19 lines. When you first load a file into the window, you see the first page. Pressing PGDN several times takes you all the way through the file until you get to the end. Pressing PGUP several times brings you back to the first page of the file.

The QuickBASIC editor includes two other commands that move you to the end of your file more easily. The CTRL-HOME key combination moves the cursor to the top of the file. If the first page of the file is not already on the screen, this command will display it. The CTRL-END command takes you to the end of the file.

Deleting Text

If you are not an expert typist, you may be more interested in the various delete commands. If you need to delete the character directly above the cursor, press the DEL key on the numeric keypad. That character will disappear and all the characters to the right of the cursor will move left one column. An alternative way of doing the same thing is the CTRL-G combination.

If you mistype more than just one letter, you may want to use another delete command. The CTRL-T combination deletes one word to the right of the text cursor. Normally, this means you will lose all characters to the right (including the character above the cursor) until a space, then all spaces until a character. For example, if the cursor is under the "x" on this line,

```
an example of a delete
```

pressing CTRL-T leaves you with this line:

```
an eof a delete
```

To delete an entire line, use the CTRL-Y combination. This command will delete the entire line that includes the cursor, regardless of what column the cursor is on.

Searching for Text

Another handy function supported by the QuickBASIC environment is the Find function. This function is helpful when you have a large file and you want to see a specific area. Rather than paging through the entire file, you can search for a word or phrase that you know is near the area. If the word appears more than once, you can search again with one keystroke. As you go through the following tutorial, you will also learn a few more rules for QuickBASIC dialog boxes.

To start the search, move to the Search menu by pressing the ALT key, then **S** (or use one of the other methods you have learned). Now select the Find command from the Search menu. Here you should get a dialog box similar in format to the "Save As" dialog box. Enter a word in the "Find What" box that you know is in your file. When you press ENTER the dialog box will disappear, and the cursor will move to the end of the text you chose. The text itself should be highlighted.

To search for the next occurrence of the same phrase, press F3. This is a shortcut for going to the Search menu and selecting the Find command again. If you had more occurrences of the selected text string, the cursor should have moved to the next position. If you continue this process, the QuickBASIC editor will circle back to the front of the file to find the first occurrence.

Return to the "Find" dialog box and enter a word that you know does not appear in your file. When you press ENTER to finalize the command, you will get another dialog box in the center of the screen. This box should read "Does not match", and it should have two inner boxes: "OK" and "HELP". If you do not need help, you can eliminate the box by pressing ESC or ENTER. All other keys will either have no effect or will cause the computer to beep.

Once more, select the Find command from the Search menu. Press the TAB key several times until the cursor is next to the option "Match Upper/Lowercase." This small box is actually two brackets, []. This is called a *toggle option* because it can only be on or off. Use the SPACEBAR to toggle between matching and not matching. As you press the SPACEBAR, you should notice an "X" appearing and disappearing from the center of the box. If you do not have a mouse you will probably be tempted to try to toggle the option with the ENTER key. Unfortunately, the ENTER key starts the execution of the command with the options you had before you pressed it. Remember, never press the ENTER key while in a dialog box until you have finished entering all your text and selecting all your options.

There are many other editing commands in the Quick-BASIC environment. Part Three of this book covers each command in full detail. The commands you have learned in this chapter should be enough to allow you to enter and change text with relative ease. As you get more comfortable with moving around in your file, deleting characters and words, and searching for text, you might want to learn the shortcuts provided in Part Three.

Saving a File

Before you are ready to proceed with learning to program, you must be able to work with files. This section will teach you how to save files, name files, and load files back into the QuickBASIC environment.

If you have been following along in this chapter by doing everything on the computer, you may have a letter or other text that you want to keep. When you type something in the Quick-BASIC environment, it is not saved automatically. To save the text, press ALT to get you to the menu line, type **F** to get you to the File menu, and type **A** to save the file. You will see the "Save As" dialog box discussed previously. If you have already given your file a name (like BLANK.BAS), pressing ENTER will save your file and return you to the text window. If you have not named the file, or if you want to change the name, enter the new one in this inner box. Press ENTER to finalize the command and save the file.

To leave the QuickBASIC environment, select the exit command from the File menu. If you have saved your current file, the output screen will appear and you will return to the DOS prompt. If you have made a change to your file without saving it, or if you never saved your current file, the QuickBASIC environment will give you an opportunity. You will see a dialog box with this message: "One or more loaded files are not saved. Save them now?" Along with the message will be four inner boxes:

• The "Yes" box will save the file and get you out of the environment.

• The "No" box will leave the environment without saving the file.

• The "Cancel" box will cancel the exit command and return you to the text window.

• The "Help" box will give you information on this particular dialog box.

You should now be out of the QuickBASIC environment. To see if you really created a file, type DIR from the DOS prompt. Somewhere in the directory list you should find your new file.

Loading a File

Return to the QuickBASIC environment with the QB command. When the environment is loaded you will be in an empty text window with "Untitled" in the title line. Select the Open Program command from the File menu. A dialog box should appear with an inner box for the "File Name", a directory box, and an inner box for changing the directory. The "File Name" box should have the text "*.bas," and the directory box should have all the .BAS files in your current directory.

If you type the name of a file that is in the directory and press ENTER, that file will be loaded into the environment and will appear in the text window. If you are not sure of the name of your file, you can use this dialog box to see which files are in the directory. The "*" character is called the *wildcard character*. If you type ***.txt** in the "File Name" box, you will get a list of files that have the .TXT extension. Use ***.*** to get a complete directory listing.

Here is another way to load a file:

1. Use the TAB key to move the cursor to the inner box that contains all the filenames.

2. With the arrow keys, move the highlight to the name of the file you want to load.

3. Press ENTER to load that file.

If you have a mouse, you can move the pointer to the name of the file and double-click the left button.

Notice that this dialog box contains an exception to the rule that the ENTER key executes the command. If you enter a filename that includes the wildcard character, you use the ENTER key to initiate the directory search and list. If you type the name of a file that is not in your directory, you will see a small dialog box that reads "File not found." After pressing ENTER to acknowledge the message, you will be back in the text window. To load a file, you must return to the "Open Program" dialog box and type a correct filename.

If you have not done so already, load the text that you typed and saved earlier into the text window. Make sure you have turned off syntax checking so the environment does not think you are loading a BASIC program. Once you are back in the text window, practice the commands you learned in this chapter. When you are comfortable with loading, editing, and saving files, you are ready to learn how to create your first QuickBASIC program.

FOUR

QuickBASIC Fundamentals

A Very Simple Program
Data Types
Operators and Expressions
Assigning Variables
The PRINT Statement
The INPUT Statement
Using Problem-Solving Techniques

In Chapter 3 you studied the QuickBASIC environment without writing any programs. In this chapter you will study the Quick-BASIC language. You will get an overview of data types, expressions, screen output with the PRINT statement, and keyboard input with the INPUT statement. In the last section in this chapter you will use the problem-solving sequence from Chapter 2 to write a complete QuickBASIC program.

A Very Simple Program

You will get more benefit from this chapter if you input the QuickBASIC statements and execute the commands as you read about them. To start, invoke the QuickBASIC environment with the QB command. Once there, create a file called FIRST.BAS. If you need to, review Chapter 3 on how to create a file. If you have done everything properly, the title line above the text window should read "FIRST.BAS."

Enter the following simple program exactly as you see it:

```
PRINT "Hey, everyone!"
PRINT "This is my first QuickBASIC program."
```

The QuickBASIC editor will allow you to enter these two statements as long as you make no typing errors. If you get a dialog box with a message after entering a line, check your typing to make sure you entered the text exactly.

Before running your program, save it using the File menu and the Save command. Now press the F5 key to start the program. If you have done everything correctly, the screen should appear as it looked before you invoked the QuickBASIC environment. This is called the *output window*. You should see your QB command on the screen. Just below that command should be this:

```
Hey, everyone!
This is my first QuickBASIC program.
```

The bottom line on the screen should read "Press any key to continue." If you typed something improperly, you may instead get a dialog box. Check all your spelling and punctuation, and try again.

Congratulations! You have just run your first QuickBASIC program. To return to the QuickBASIC environment, press any key on the keyboard (the SPACEBAR is a good one). The output window should disappear and the editor screen should reappear.

Data Types

Before you can learn QuickBASIC statements, you need to understand how to describe the data you use. *Data* is simply another term for pieces of information. In this section you will learn what forms data can have in QuickBASIC programs.

Each piece of data in a QuickBASIC program has a specific *data type*. A data type first limits the set of the values the data can hold. INTEGER data, for example, cannot be numbers with decimal points. A data type also limits the set of operations you can perform on the data. For example, the expression

```
"HI" / "THERE"
```

is meaningless because the division operation is not valid for character data.

QuickBASIC uses six simple data types. *String data,* or character data, can be one of two types: variable-length STRING or fixed-length STRING. The INTEGER and LONG types are for numbers without decimal points. INTEGER data must be between −32,768 and +32,767. LONG integers can be as large as 2,147,483,647 ($2^{31} - 1$) or as small as −2,417,483,648. The SINGLE and DOUBLE data types are for numbers with decimal points. SINGLE numbers can have up to seven significant digits. If you need more accuracy, DOUBLE numbers are accurate to 15 significant digits.

All data in QuickBASIC is used as either a constant or a variable. A *variable* is a piece of data that can change. As you learned in Chapter 2, a variable points to a location in memory. What goes in that memory location depends on the program and the user. A *constant* is a piece of data that cannot change. The number 27 will always be 27, and you cannot write a statement to change the value of 27.

Data Types for Variables

Since the value of a variable can change, you must give the variable a name as well as a type. Variable names in Quick-BASIC can be up to 40 characters long, and must start with a letter, followed by any combination of letters and digits. When you assign a name to a variable, you should try to use one that explains how the variable is used. Try to avoid names with only one or two characters.

Once you determine the name of a variable, you give it a type by using a *type suffix.* A type suffix is one of five special characters that becomes the last character of a variable name. The following table shows the five types and their suffixes (fixed-length strings are defined separately and will have no suffix).

```
INTEGER    %
LONG       &
SINGLE     !
DOUBLE     #
STRING     $
```

If you see a variable name like *address$*, you know it is a string variable because it ends with the "$" character. If you have no suffix after a variable name, QuickBASIC normally makes it a SINGLE variable. You can change the default data type with the DEF*type* statement, covered in Chapter 5. To avoid confusion, however, the examples in this book include a suffix on almost every variable.

If you use a variable more than once in a program, as you usually will, make sure you spell it the same way each time. Every time you spell a different variable name, the QuickBASIC compiler will create a new memory location. You might be modifying a variable other than the one you expected.

The only real limitation on naming variables is that you cannot use a word reserved by the QuickBASIC language. Quick-BASIC defines over one hundred *reserved words*. If you use the type suffixes at the ends of your variable names, however, you will not have this problem. For instance, you cannot name a variable *print*, because PRINT is a reserved word, but you can name a string variable *print$*.

Data Types for Constants

The data type of a constant depends on the way that the constant is used. *String constants* are primarily characters enclosed in double quotes. You printed two string constants in the simple program given earlier. Here are examples of some other string constants:

```
"A"
"234"
"PRINT"
```

Notice that a string constant can be a number, too, as long as it is enclosed in quotes. The string constant "" is called the *null string;* it is a string with nothing in it.

By default, numeric constants take on the simplest possible type. The number 254 is the INTEGER type because it can fit into an INTEGER memory location. The number 35,000 is too large for the INTEGER data type, so it becomes type LONG. The number 3.3 has a decimal point, so it is a SINGLE constant. Often you will use a number without concern for the internal representation. When you need to specify a particular type, you must use the type suffix discussed earlier.

Operators and Expressions

When you combine constants and variables, as shown here,

```
2.3 * sum%
```

you create an *expression.* An expression can be a simple constant or variable, or a combination of variables and constants using operators.

Operators in QuickBASIC fall into five categories: arithmetic, relational, logical, string, and functional. The *arithmetic* operators are +, −, * for multiplication, / for division, and ˆ for exponentiation. For integer division you can also use \ for the integer quotient and MOD for the remainder.

The *relational* operators compare values to form a *Boolean expression,* an expression that evaluates to TRUE or FALSE. These operators are =, <, >, < = for less than or equal to, > = for greater than or equal to, and < > for not equal to. For instance, the expression in the statement

```
IF score% > 50 THEN
```

will evaluate to TRUE when the value of *score%* is 51 or more, and FALSE when the value of *score%* is 50 or less.

The *logical* operators in QuickBASIC are AND, OR, NOT, XOR, for exclusive "or," EQV for equivalence (or exclusive "nor"), and IMP for implication. Logical operators are primarily for combining Boolean expressions. For instance, if you need to know when a number is outside the range of 10 to 20, use

```
IF number% < 10 OR number% > 20 THEN
```

If the value of *number%* is 25, the expression evaluates to TRUE because of the OR operator. The expression will evaluate to FALSE only when both the left side and the right side of the expression are false.

Strings are much more limited in their available operators. You can use any relational operator on two strings, but logical operators are meaningless (and are not allowed). The + operator *concatenates*, or combines, two strings.

Functional operators make up the last class of operators. When you apply a function name as an operator, you are calling that function. These functions can be either the ones built into QuickBASIC, or those you define with a FUNCTION structure (see Chapter 10). A simple built-in function is ABS, which computes absolute value. When you want to take the absolute value of a number, you call the ABS function this way:

```
posnum% = ABS(mynum%)
```

Other common functions are SQR for square root; LOG for natural logarithm; and the trigonometric functions SIN, COS, and TAN.

Assigning Variables

Giving a value to a variable is known as *assignment*. The primary assignment statement in QuickBASIC is the LET statement. This statement assigns a value to a variable. The syntax of the LET statement is shown on the next page.

[LET] *variable* = *expression*

This is the interpretation of that description: "A LET statement optionally starts with the word LET, followed by a variable, followed by an equal sign, followed by an expression." Very few programmers still include the word LET.

In the LET statement, QuickBASIC evaluates the expression and places the final value in the memory location used by the variable. The simplest example of a LET statement has one variable and one constant:

```
count% = 0
```

This statement tells QuickBASIC to place the value 0 in the memory cell referenced by *count%*. Whatever used to be in *count%* is now lost forever, since a variable can only hold one value at a time.

If you do not give a variable a value, the QuickBASIC compiler will automatically initialize the variable. The initial value for all numeric variables is zero, and the initial value for all string variables is the null string. If you need to use any value other than these, you must use an assignment statement to assign new values.

The key to understanding the LET statement is realizing that the equal sign is not the same as the equal sign you remember from your high school algebra class. This equal sign is known as the *assignment operator*. You should read the statement

```
count% = count% + 1
```

as "assign the value *count%* plus one to *count%*," not "*count%* equals *count%* plus one." In other words, the expression to the right of the equal sign is evaluated before the assignment is made. If *count%* had a value of 2 before this statement, Quick-BASIC evaluates *count%* + 1 as 3, then assigns *count%* the value of 3.

The PRINT Statement

If you write a program that has only LET statements, you will run the program, watch the screen change to the output window, and see no results. A program will only do what it is told. If you want to write any data to the screen, you must use a Quick-BASIC statement to do so.

The primary QuickBASIC statement for displaying information on the screen is the PRINT statement. This is the syntax of the PRINT statement:

PRINT [*expression*[{;l,}]]. . .

When QuickBASIC executes a PRINT statement, it evaluates each expression and displays the value on the screen.

The PRINT statement can display the value of a variable or constant. Consider these two statements:

```
PRINT mystr$
PRINT "mystr$"
```

The first statement will print the value of the string variable and the second will print the actual letters "mystr$," without the quotation marks.

The semicolon or comma after the expression determines where the text cursor will go. If you end a PRINT statement with no punctuation mark, the text cursor will move to the beginning of the next line before executing the next PRINT statement. If you end a PRINT statement with a semicolon, the cursor stays at the end of the text just printed. The comma moves the cursor to the next TAB position, usually in 14-character columns. A PRINT statement with no expressions or punctuation skips a line on the screen.

When you print numeric data, QuickBASIC automatically adds a space in front of positive numbers. Thus, these two statements

```
PRINT 45
PRINT -45
```

would produce the following output:

```
 45
-45
```

You must be aware of this extra space when lining up columns of data. QuickBASIC also adds a space after each number, to keep you from writing two numbers next to each other.

When a PRINT statement has two strings separated by a semicolon, QuickBASIC prints the second string immediately after the first one. Since you need an extra space between the two strings, you must include a blank inside one of the strings:

```
PRINT "Your name is "; name$
```

QuickBASIC allows you to include an entire expression in a PRINT statement. The statements

```
LET sum% = a% + b% + c%
PRINT sum%
```

and the statement

```
PRINT a% + b% + c%
```

have the exact same output. The format you choose will usually depend on which is the most readable.

When you display a numeric variable, you should always include a description of that variable. For example, if your program prints the value of *sum%*, the statement

```
PRINT sum%
```

will print only a number, and someone using your program might have no idea what the number represents. A more appropriate display would be this:

```
PRINT "The sum is"; sum%
```

With this description, you have a better idea of what the number means.

The INPUT Statement

The primary statement for keyboard input is the INPUT statement. This statement allows the user to enter the value of a variable while the program is running. This way, your program can solve the same problem given different sets of inputs. Here is the syntax of the INPUT statement:

INPUT [;][*prompt* {;|,}] *variable* [,*variable*]. . .

The simplest INPUT statement will have the reserved word INPUT and a variable name. In this case QuickBASIC will display a question mark and flash the text cursor. The user must enter a value and press ENTER. This value becomes the new value for the input variable.

When you input numeric variables you must be careful about what you enter. Suppose you have this statement:

```
INPUT num%
```

QuickBASIC will not accept a letter instead of a number. If you enter a letter, you will see the error message "Redo from start" and another question mark. You must enter a valid number before the program can continue.

The optional string expression that you can place before the input variable name is called a *prompt*. The prompt tells the user what value is expected. The statement

```
INPUT "What is your name"; name$
```

will display the prompt and a question mark, followed by the flashing cursor. The user now knows what value to enter.

If you use a semicolon between the prompt and the input variable, QuickBASIC will add the question mark at the end of the prompt. If your prompt is not in the form of a question, use the comma after the prompt. The comma suppresses the added question mark. You might also add a colon inside the prompt string. For example:

```
INPUT "Please enter your name: ", name$
```

This format allows you to write the prompt that makes the most sense for the application.

Using Problem-Solving Techniques

Now that you have seen a few essential QuickBASIC statements, you are ready to design and write complete programs. In this section you will be using the problem-solving sequence from Chapter 2 in a QuickBASIC program.

The sample problem is to write a program that computes the average of any three numbers. Step 1 of the problem-solving sequence, the problem statement, is already done for you. It often helps to rewrite the problem in your own words. This problem statement helps to identify the inputs and outputs: "Write a program that inputs any three numbers and outputs their average."

The next step is to identify the inputs and the outputs. Since the problem says you must average any three numbers, these numbers must be inputs. Give each input a name, such as *firstnum!*, *secondnum!*, and *thirdnum!*. Each variable name has the "!" suffix because these are SINGLE numbers. Since the problem statement did not specify a type, you could have made these inputs INTEGER variables, depending on what you consider to be the most reasonable. The only output variable is *average!*, which must be real (SINGLE or DOUBLE) because you will be doing division.

Step 3 is to create test cases. Remember, you want to select some test inputs that are reasonable and some that are extreme. Here is a table for sample test cases:

Variable	Case 1	Case 2	Case 3
firstnum!	4	−2.1	0
secondnum!	2	4.6	0
thirdnum!	3	1.3	0
average!	3	1.266667	0

The high-level algorithm, Step 4, is rather simple in this case. You should come up with three steps:

1. Input *firstnum!*, *secondnum!*, and *thirdnum!*
2. Compute *average!*
3. Output *average!*

As this is a simple problem, you can go directly to Step 5, the refinement of the algorithm, and further specify the second step of the algorithm:

2. Compute *average!*
   a. *total!* = *firstnum!* + *secondnum!* + *thirdnum!*
   b. *average!* = *total!* / 3

Notice that you have introduced a new variable, *total!*, used as an intermediate value-holder in the program.

Now you must do Step 6, converting the algorithm to a program. Do not add bells and whistles yet; they will only clutter the program. Here is the simple program:

```
INPUT "Enter the first number:", firstnum!
INPUT "Enter the second number:", secondnum!
INPUT "Enter the third number:", thirdnum!

total! = firstnum! + secondnum! + thirdnum!
```

```
average! = total! / 3

PRINT "The average is"; average!
```

When you type this program into the computer, check your spelling and punctuation. Then complete Step 7 by running the program and trying the test cases.

Before you can call a program complete, you should include several other lines. The first set of lines is called *remarks*. These lines can be seen only when you list the program; they have no effect on program execution. Remarks are designed to help you remember key facts about the program. A remark line starts with an apostrophe or the reserved word "REM". The QuickBASIC compiler ignores all characters to the right of an apostrophe. Here is a sample of proper remark lines:

```
','','','','','','','','','','','','','','','','',
'   This program computes the average   '
'   of any three numbers.               '
'                                       '
','','','','','','','','','','','','','','','','',
```

If you place this remark box at the beginning of your program you will remember what the program does. You should also write remarks before each set of program lines, telling what each does.

You may want to also include a line or two that tells the user what the program does. This will keep the user from asking, "Enter the first number for what?" at your first prompt. Here is the final program with remarks and extra prompts:

```
','','','','','','','','','','','','','','','','',
'   This program computes the average   '
'   of any three numbers.               '
'                                       '
','','','','','','','','','','','','','','','','',
'  Introduce the program
CLS
PRINT
PRINT "      This program computes the average of";
PRINT " any three numbers."
PRINT
PRINT

'  Enter each of the three numbers
```

```
INPUT "Enter the first number: ", firstnum!
INPUT Enter the second number: ", secondnum!
INPUT "Enter the third number: ", thirdnum!

'  Compute the average
total! = firstnum! + secondnum! + thirdnum!
average! = total! / 3

'  Display the average
PRINT
PRINT "The average is"; average!
```

The QuickBASIC Language

When a language reference is in alphabetical order, you can skim through the book until you find a discussion of a particular statement or function. When the reference is in some other order, usually you can turn to the index, look up the name of the statement or function, and turn to that page. This will cost you only a few extra seconds.

If you are unsure of what you are looking for, however, you must peruse the entire book, hoping something will jump out at you. This language reference allows you to skim through a chapter, based on subject matter, looking for a statement that meets your needs. You can also read this reference, page by page, mastering one subject before moving to the next.

The chapters in Part Two are divided by subject. Each statement or function has its own syntax box that will be easily recognizable as you leaf through the pages.

Chapter 5 covers the pieces that make up each QuickBASIC statement: variables, constants, operators, and expressions. You will also study each of the standard types found in the language.

In Chapter 6 you will study the three types of statements that make up any QuickBASIC program: assignment, iterative, and conditional. Structured programming steps are stressed with each subject.

Chapter 7 describes basic input and output for the screen, the keyboard, and the printer. You will see how QuickBASIC allows you to create output that is pleasing to the eye. You will also find a discussion on idiot-proofing your input.

Chapter 8 covers string variables in full detail. Here you will find all of the intrinsic functions needed to create and manipulate strings.

Chapter 9 introduces arrays and records, and shows you how QuickBASIC implements each. You will learn the advantages and shortcomings of record structures in QuickBASIC.

Chapter 10 is a complete discussion on subroutines and functions. Modularity in creating your programs is stressed throughout the chapter. Also included are the standard mathematical functions.

Chapter 11 covers disk files and devices. After reading this chapter you will be able to use sequential, random-access, and binary files. You will also be able to make a device look like a file for easier input and output.

In Chapter 12 you will learn every QuickBASIC statement and function that deals with graphics and sound. The chapter separates the discussions of each graphics adapter type, so you need only study the capabilities of your machine.

Chapter 13 includes the statements and functions that access system resources. You will also get some background on what happens when you use each of these statements.

Finally, Chapter 14 is a compilation of all the statements that are obsolete or unnecessary. The statements and functions are often provided only to maintain compatibility with older versions of QuickBASIC and BASICA. This chapter will show you how to eliminate those statements from your programs.

Constants, Variables, and Expressions

Constants
Variables
Expressions
Type Conversion

A detailed study of the QuickBASIC language must begin with its simplest parts. These parts are constants, variables, and expressions. This chapter covers each of these parts in full detail, as well as discussing methods of type conversion. Chapter 4 introduced you to the six elementary data types, which are summarized in Table 5-1. If you are unfamiliar with the QuickBASIC data types, be sure to review the previous chapter before continuing with this one.

Constants

A *constant* is a value that does not change during program execution. In QuickBASIC, a constant can take one of two forms: literal or symbolic. This section will define and discuss both groups of constants.

Literal Constants

A *literal constant* is an actual number or string that is part of a QuickBASIC statement. The *type* of a literal constant must be a numeric type or a fixed-length string. Normally, the value of the literal constant defines its type.

Type	Suffix	Smallest Value	Largest Value
INTEGER	%	−32768	+32767
LONG	&	−2147483648	+2147483647
SINGLE	!	** 1.401298E −45	** 3.402823E +38
DOUBLE	#	** 4.940656458412465D −324	** 1.797693134862315D +308
STRING	$	0 characters	32767 characters
(fixed-length or variable-length)			

** Smallest and largest absolute values

Table 5-1.   Summary of QuickBASIC Data Types

QuickBASIC will allow you to write INTEGER and LONG constants as decimal numbers, hexadecimal numbers, or octal numbers. Therefore, the number 100 can be written in three ways:

```
100
&h64
&o144
```

QuickBASIC interprets the "&" without an "h" or "o" as an octal number. You will improve readability, however, if you include the "o" even though it is optional. If the number is larger than &hFFFF (or &o177777), add a trailing "&" to define the constant as a LONG integer (such as &hABCDE&). You cannot include commas anywhere in an integer constant.

If you use a constant with a decimal point (a real number), it will be of type SINGLE or DOUBLE. QuickBASIC provides a way to describe large (or very small) numbers through scientific notation. The constant 40E +5 is read, "Forty times ten to the fifth power." Use an "E" if the constant is SINGLE, and use a "D" for DOUBLE constants (such as 43.234D −9).

By default, numeric constants are stored in the simplest possible type. For instance, if you display a real number without a suffix, QuickBASIC will attempt to store it as a SINGLE constant. If it is too long to be stored in single precision accurately, it will be stored as double precision. If you want to specify a particular type for a constant, use a type character suffix, such as 45.23! or 45.231743#.

STRING constants are characters inside a set of double quotes. They can hold any of the 255 different characters in the ASCII character set, listed in Appendix B. Most strings are variable-length strings that can hold up to 32,767 characters. You can declare fixed-length strings that hold fewer characters. Fixed-length strings belong primarily in record structures and are covered in detail in Chapter 9.

Symbolic Constants

Symbolic constants are constants that a program refers to by name instead of by actual value. To determine that value, and to differentiate symbolic constants from variables, you must declare the constant with a CONST statement.

CONST   **statement**

Syntax: CONST *name* = *expression* [,*name* = *expression*]. . .

Purpose: Declares a symbolic constant

Note: The expression given in the syntax must be determinable at compilation time. You cannot include variables or function calls.

Sample use:

```
CONST errorMsg$ = "File not found"
```

Symbolic constants provide you with a way to use meaningful names to improve readability, and to make it easier to change widely used constants. For instance, suppose you write a program to determine the grades for a group of 20 students. As you go through the program, the number 20 may appear a dozen times. Instead, you can declare a symbolic constant,

```
CONST numStudents% = 20
```

and replace the number 20 with its equivalent, *numStudents%*. This dramatically improves program readability.

Now when a student drops the class, you have to change only the value of the symbolic constant. Without that definition, you would have to go through the program and replace every 20 representing class size with a 19. In a large program, there is a good possibility that other 20's will mean something besides the number of students, and you would create an error in the program by changing one of them.

Symbolic constants also provide a way to use names for values that should never change in the program. For example, given the previous definition of *numStudents%*, the compiler will generate an error if you try this statement:

```
numStudents% = numStudents% + 1
```

Using symbolic constants thus gives you a way of double checking your code.

Two of the most common symbolic constants are those that represent the Boolean values TRUE and FALSE. Here is a common declaration:

```
CONST false% = 0, true% = NOT false%
```

This declaration is consistent with QuickBASIC itself, which interprets any nonzero value as TRUE. The rest of this book relies heavily on this declaration.

Variables

Inside your computer, the central processing unit (CPU) has the primary function to manipulate the ones and zeroes stored in memory locations. There can be as many as 1,048,576 of these locations. If you had to, you could refer to each of these by number. However, when this approach was used in the early days of programming, the programs were practically impossible to read, understand, and maintain.

QuickBASIC allows you to refer to data by variable names, instead of memory locations. When you use a variable in a program, the QuickBASIC compiler selects a new memory location and uses that location every time you use that variable. Every variable has a name and a type. This section will cover the rules for both the name and the type of a variable.

The Name of a Variable

A variable name must start with a letter, and it may be followed by up to 39 more letters or digits. You cannot embed special characters like underscores (_) in variable names. You may have learned BASIC when you could use only one- or two-character variable names. With QuickBASIC, your limit is 40, which enables you to use more descriptive variable names. It is much easier to tell what the variable *Count* is for than the variable *I*. Using variable names that are five to fifteen characters long will make your programs much more readable and will make documentation easier.

The case (upper or lower) of a variable name is immaterial. QuickBASIC automatically capitalizes reserved words, so you should consider using lowercase letters for your variables. This will make them stand out, and therefore easier to find. The QuickBASIC environment automatically keeps track of the case of each variable. For example, if you use *anyint* as a variable name, then later use *AnyInt*, the environment will change all occurrences of *anyint* to *AnyInt*.

Almost any word can be a variable name. The only words that you cannot use for variable names are those that are already used as part of the QuickBASIC language, known as *reserved words* or *keywords*. Appendix A contains the complete list of QuickBASIC reserved words.

The Type of a Variable

The values a variable can hold are based on its type. For instance, a SINGLE variable can hold only the value of a valid single-precision number. This section will discuss variables that have elementary data types. You can read about array variables and record variables in Chapter 9.

Primarily, you set a variable's type by using the standard type character suffixes: %, &, !, #, and $. QuickBASIC considers variables that have the same name but different type character suffixes to be different variables. For instance, if your program uses the variables

```
mynum%
mynum!
mynum#
```

each variable uses a different location in memory. You should avoid using the same name for variables of different types because you can easily mistype a type character and produce unexpected results.

If you use a variable without the type character suffix, QuickBASIC will use a default type. Ordinarily, variables default to type SINGLE. You are able to change the default using the DEF*type* statement.

DEFtype   **statement**

Syntax: {DEFINT | DEFSNG | DEFDBL | DEFLNG |
        DEFSTR} *range*
    where *range* =>
        character[*−character*][*,character*[*−character*]]. . .

Purpose: Determines the default type of a variable that does
not have a type-declaration character

Note: This statement should precede all executable statements; placing it in the body of a program will not produce the
same result.

Sample use:

```
DEFINT A-Z
```

With the DEF*type* statement, you can have variables that
start with certain letters default to certain types. Consider the
following declarations:

```
DEFSNG A-H,Q-Y
DEFINT I-P
DEFLNG Z
```

If none of the variables in your program has a type character
suffix, all variables beginning with the letters "i" through "p"
will be type INTEGER. The variables that start with a "z" will
be LONG integers, and all others will be SINGLE. If you use a
variable with a type character suffix, the suffix will override the
default type. For example, given the defaults declared earlier,
the variable *count%* will be INTEGER, not SINGLE.

All variable names in this book use type character suffixes
whenever possible. The problem with using default starting letters is you tend to use variable names that either look strange
or that don't describe what the variable does. For instance, the
variable *count%* immediately tells you that the variable is an
INTEGER and it is used as a counter. Using the defaults, you

would either use *icount*, which looks strange, or a synonym that starts with "i" through "p", like *incr*. With this in mind, consider using type character suffixes whenever possible.

Another way to override the defaults without using a type character is with the DIM statement.

DIM (for standard types)   **statement**

Syntax: DIM [SHARED] *variable* [AS *type*][,*variable* [AS *type*]]. . .

Purpose: Declares a variable to be a certain type

Note: Nonarray variables in a DIM statement cannot have type-declaration characters (%, &, !, #, $).

Sample use:

```
DIM lastName as STRING
```

Declaring a variable with the DIM statement has the same drawback as using DEF*type*: the type of the variable is not as obvious when it is used in the program. When you use DIM, you must refer to the variable's declaration to determine its type. The DIM statement is primarily used to declare arrays, which you can read about in Chapter 9.

Expressions

An *expression* is a valid combination of constants and variables connected by operators. Chapter 4 introduced the five categories of operators, summarized in Table 5-2. In this section you will get more detail on the rules for operators and expressions.

Arithmetic	$+, -, *, /, \hat{}, \backslash,$ MOD
Logical	AND, OR, NOT, XOR, EQV, IMP
Relational	$<, >, =, <>, <=, >=$

Table 5-2.   Summary of QuickBASIC Operators

The truth tables for the less common logical operators are provided in Table 5-3. Logical operators are primarily for Boolean expressions that evaluate to TRUE or FALSE. However, they can also apply to INTEGER variables, one bit at a time. The computer stores integers as a set of 16 bits, each of which is a one or a zero. When you use a logical operator between two integers, QuickBASIC performs 16 operations, one on each set of bits. Consider the operation 300 OR 400. Convert each number to binary, then OR each bit:

```
   300 = 0000000100101100
OR 400 = 0000000110010000
         0000000110111100  = 444
```

The primary purpose for bitwise logical operations is *bit masking*. This means checking 1 bit (or several bits) of a number, then taking action based on that bit or those bits (called a *bit mask*). A simple application is checking to see whether a number is odd. All odd numbers have a 1 as their last bit, so you can use the logical operator AND to check for them, as shown on the next page.

x	y	x XOR y	x EQV y	x IMP y
0	0	0	−1	−1
0	−1	−1	0	−1
−1	0	−1	0	0
−1	−1	0	−1	−1

Table 5-3.   Truth Table for XOR, EQV, and IMP

```
IF (number% AND 1%) = 1% THEN...
```

Expressions are evaluated based on a particular hierarchy, known as the *order of precedence*. This order is displayed in Table 5-4. The QuickBASIC compiler looks for the operator highest in the order of precedence, completes that operation, looks for the next operator, and so on. If two operators in an expression are on the same level, the operations are completed left to right. If you need to override the order of precedence, you must use parentheses.

Another consideration for expressions is *type compatibility*. This concept means that operators in an expression must work on operands of the same type. For instance, the expression

```
23.4 + "dumb"
```

would generate a syntax error. In QuickBASIC, all numeric types are considered to be type compatible. If an expression has two operands of different numeric types, the result will be returned in the more precise type. In other words, if you add an INTEGER number with a SINGLE number, the compiler will convert the INTEGER to SINGLE before adding, so the sum will be SINGLE.

---

1. Parenthetic expressions ( )
2. Unary operators (NOT, −, +)
3. Exponentiation (^)
4. Multiplication, division (*, /, \, MOD)
5. Addition, subtraction (+, −)
6. Relational operators (=, <>, <, >, <=, >=)
7. Logical operators (AND, OR, XOR, EQV, IMP)

Table 5-4.   Order of Precedence in QuickBASIC

Type Conversion

Although QuickBASIC normally converts constants and variables to the proper type when evaluating expressions, there are circumstances where you need to override this. QuickBASIC includes several standard functions that convert expressions in one type to a value in another.

When QuickBASIC evaluates numeric expressions, it automatically converts each operand to the most precise type in the expression before computing. It also automatically converts the value of the expression to the type of the assigned variable. This feature limits the usefulness of the four numeric conversion functions CINT, CLNG, CDBL, and CSNG.

The CINT function rounds off numbers to INTEGER form.

CINT(expr)   **function**

Purpose: Converts an expression to type INTEGER by rounding off

Return type: INTEGER

Parameter: expr [any numeric type]—the expression to convert

Note: The expression must evaluate to a number in the range −32,768 to 32,767 or an overflow error occurs.

Sample call:

```
index% = CINT(realvar!) * 5
```

Look at the sample call for this function. If the value of *realvar!* is 2.41, the expression will evaluate to 10, since *realvar!* will be rounded down to 2 before multiplying. If the call to CINT is taken out, 2.41 times 5 is 12.05, so *index%* would become 12.

Occasionally, you might also need the CLNG function.

CLNG(expr)   **function**

Purpose: Converts an expression to LONG

Return type: LONG

Parameter: expr [any numeric type]—the expression to convert

Note: The expression must evaluate to a number between −2,147,483,648 and 2,147,483,647 or an overflow error occurs.

Sample call:

```
PRINT CLNG(bignum!)
```

The sample call is the same as the following two statements:

```
bigint& = bignum!
```
and `PRINT bigint&`

The CLNG function keeps you from having to introduce a new variable just to print out a number in integer form. If the value of *bignum!* was 123456.7, this code would display "1234568".

The CDBL function can force QuickBASIC to evaluate an expression with double precision.

CDBL(expr)   **function**

Purpose: Converts an expression to DOUBLE

Return type: DOUBLE

Parameter: expr [any numeric type]—the expression to convert

Sample call:

```
average# = totalscore! / CDBL(numscores%)
```

Normally, this expression would be evaluated in single precision, the more precise type between SINGLE and INTEGER. The call to CDBL converts the integer to DOUBLE, and therefore the entire expression will be evaluated in double precision.

CSNG converts expressions to type SINGLE.

CSNG(expr)   **function**

Purpose: Converts an expression to SINGLE, rounding off if necessary

Return type: SINGLE

Parameter: expr [any numeric type]—the expression to convert

Sample call:

```
average! = CSNG(sum#) / total!
```

Including the call to CSNG in this sample forces the expression to be evaluated with SINGLE precision numbers. Without that call, *total!* would automatically be converted to DOUBLE before dividing.

QuickBASIC also includes functions that convert characters to their ASCII codes and back.

ASC(expr)   **function**

Purpose: Converts the first character of a string to its numeric ASCII equivalent

Return type: INTEGER
Parameter: expr [STRING]—the string to convert
Note: A null string (" ") produces an error message.
Sample call:

```
asciiVal% = ASC(inStr$)
```

You could use the ASC function to check for *escape sequences*, which are strings that start with ASCII code 27. So if *asciiVal%* is 27, *inStr$* is an escape sequence.

The inverse of the ASC function is the CHR$ function.

CHR$(expr)   **function**

Purpose: Converts an ASCII code to its character equivalent
Return type: STRING
Parameter: expr [INTEGER]—an expression in the range of 0 to 255
Sample call:

```
PRINT CHR$(1)        'prints a happy face
```

Many characters in the ASCII set are not found on the keyboard. To use these characters you must use the CHR$ function. Another use of CHR$ is to put double quotes (" ") inside a string variable. To place the string constant "Hi!" in *mystr$*, including the double quotes, use the statement

```
mystr$ = CHR$(34) + "Hi!" + CHR$(34)
```

As you can check in Appendix B, 34 is the ASCII code for the double quote.

You can also convert entire strings to numbers and numbers to strings. (See the VAL and STR$ functions in Chapter 8.)

The final two functions convert decimal numbers to their hexadecimal and octal equivalents, respectively.

HEX$(expr)   **function**

Purpose: Converts an integer to its hexadecimal equivalent in string format

Return type: STRING

Parameter: expr [INTEGER or LONG]—the expression to convert

Sample call:

```
hexstr$ = HEX$(decnum%)
```

If the expression to convert is SINGLE or DOUBLE, Quick-BASIC will round the numbers to the nearest integer before converting.

OCT$(expr)   **function**

Purpose: Converts an integer to its octal equivalent in string format

Return type: STRING

Parameter: expr [INTEGER or LONG]—the expression to convert

Sample call:

```
octalstr$ = OCT$(decnum%)
```

Unfortunately, QuickBASIC does not include standard functions to convert these strings back to their decimal equivalents, but you can write them yourself, as you will see in the next chapter.

Assignment and Control Statements

Program Structure
Assignment Statements
Conditional Statements
Iterative Statements
Program Examples

In Chapter 5 you mastered the fundamental elements of any programming language: variables and constants. In this chapter you will see how these elements are manipulated. After a brief discussion of program structure, this chapter covers assignment statements and the two sets of control structures: conditional and iterative.

Program Structure

In any language, a *program* is a sequence of statements that "tells" the computer how to control locations in memory and auxiliary devices. A program is a combination of statement lines, remarks, and blank lines. This section will cover statement lines and remarks. Blank lines should need no further explanation.

Statement Lines

The *statement lines* are the lines in the program that give instructions. All statement lines follow this syntax:

[*label*] *statement* [: *statement*]. . . [*remark*]

Any statement line can start with an optional label; can include more than one QuickBASIC statement; and can include a remark at the end.

The *label* attaches a name to a statement line in case the program needs to jump there. The label can be either an integer constant, called a line number, or a word followed by a colon, like *MyLabel:*. In older versions of BASIC, labels in the form of line numbers are required on every statement line. In Quick-BASIC, line numbers are unnecessary. Statements are ordered from the beginning of the file to the end. In other words, your program will execute from top to bottom, except where control structures alter that order.

A statement line can include multiple statements if they are separated by colons. Like line numbers, this option is included in QuickBASIC principally for compatibility with older versions of BASIC, when multiple statements on a line saved valuable program space. You will be able to find statements more easily if you keep only one statement on a line.

Remarks

As you may recall from Chapter 4, you use *remarks* to explain sections of QuickBASIC code. The compiler ignores any line that begins with the word REM or an apostrophe (') (except for metacommands, covered later). The remarks in programs in this book follow the apostrophe syntax, since these tend to be easier to recognize.

Use remarks to outline the program. Well-written programs divide easily into logical groups of statements ranging from one to about twenty lines of code. Before each group, you should include a few lines explaining the statements that follow. Use proper English sentences in your remarks. You should be able to read only the remarks in a program and know exactly what the program does.

Be careful not to simply repeat what the QuickBASIC code already says. Remarks should enhance the code by giving information in addition to that which the code itself implies. For example, you should examine the remarks in the following program fragment.

```
'       Set the total to 0 and the counter to 1.
total%   = 0
counter% = 1

'       Loop until the counter is more than 5.
DO UNTIL counter% > 5

'       Add this score to the total.
   total% = total% + scores%(counter%)
LOOP
```

None of the remarks give any more insight on what is happening than the statements themselves. All this statement group needs is one simple remark:

```
'       Compute the sum of the first five scores.
total%   = 0
counter% = 1
DO UNTIL counter% > 5
   total% = total% + scores%(counter%)
LOOP
```

You can see how meaningful variable names make the rest of this code self-explanatory.

You can also include a remark as part of a statement line. If an apostrophe (or REM) appears after a legal QuickBASIC statement, the compiler ignores everything to the right of the apostrophe. This type of remark is especially useful in array declarations. You can give a brief description of each array when it is declared. Consider these lines of code:

```
DIM scores%(100,50)        'test scores for each
                           'student in the class
DIM students$(100)         'names of each student
```

The remarks at the end of each statement help clarify what the dimensioned array will be used for. See Chapter 9 for more information on arrays.

Assignment Statements

After reviewing the general syntax of a QuickBASIC program, this book will now cover syntax and usage of *every* statement found in the language. The first group of statements are known as *assignment statements* because they assign a value to a variable. QuickBASIC supports three different assignment statements: LET, READ, and SWAP.

The LET Statement

By far the most common assignment statement is the LET statement.

LET   **statement**

Syntax: [LET] *variable = expression*

Purpose: Gives a new value to a variable

Note: The value of the expression will be converted to the type of the variable, if possible.

Sample use:

```
LET count% = count% + 1    'these statements
count% = count% + 1        'are equivalent
```

As you can see from the syntax description, the word LET is optional. The compiler will recognize the LET statement from the equal sign.

In Chapter 5 it was mentioned that an expression evaluates to its most precise type. In a LET statement, the value is then converted to match the type of the variable on the left side of the assignment operator. If a statement reads

```
average! = total# / count% + curve!
```

the expression will be evaluated in double precision, then converted to SINGLE before assigning its value to *average!*. You can mix all of the numeric types in LET statements. This freedom is known as *loose type compatibility.* In other words, the type of the expression does not have to exactly match the type of the variable.

Type compatibility is more critical when using string variables and expressions. The QuickBASIC compiler will not allow you to assign a string expression to a numeric variable, or vice versa, in a LET statement—it will give you a "type mismatch" error. If you need to assign numbers to string variables or strings to numeric variables, you must use the string manipulation statements that will be described in Chapter 8.

If you use a variable before assigning a value to it, QuickBASIC will automatically initialize numeric variables to 0 and strings to the null string (" "). You might consider initializing variables even when the automatic initialization is valid. This often improves the readability of your code, and will help to guarantee that you are initializing at the proper time.

The READ and DATA Statements

Another way to assign values to variables is with the READ statement.

READ   **statement**

Syntax: READ *variable* [*,variable*]. . .

Purpose: Assigns the next value in a DATA statement to a variable

Sample use:

```
READ firstname$, lastname$
```

When QuickBASIC encounters a READ statement, it looks for the first DATA statement. A program that contains READ statements without at least one DATA statement will not run.

DATA   **statement**

Syntax: DATA *constant* [*,constant*]. . .

Purpose: Supplies values for READ statements

Note: String constants do not have to be in quotes.

Sample use:

```
DATA "John", "Smith", "Mary", "Jones"
```

or

```
DATA John, Smith, Mary, Jones
```

Often, your program will be more versatile if you input data from a file instead of using the READ statement. However, there are occasions where the READ and DATA combination is a better option. Consider this program fragment:

```
          get valid user names and passwords
FOR user% = 1 to 4
   READ username$(user%), password$(user%)
NEXT user%
DATA "ROGERS", "WIZARD", "MCCREADY", "SUZY"
DATA "KING", "COFFEE", "DRIEHORST", "MONGOOSE"
```

These statements are part of a program that only four people can use: Rogers, McCready, King, and Driehorst. Each user has a password that only they (and the programmer) know. Storing these passwords in a file makes them easily accessible to thievery. However, if the passwords are deeply nested in the DATA statements of an executable file, they are much safer. Only someone with programming expertise and the proper software tools would be able to find these. (If you needed more security, you would have to encrypt the names in a file.)

You can place DATA statements anywhere in the main module of your program. DATA statements are *nonexecutable.*

Whenever the QuickBASIC compiler encounters a DATA statement, it passes right over it. They can even be placed before the first READ statement. DATA statements are treated as though they are one group of statements. When the first READ statement is executed, QuickBASIC looks for the first DATA statement and reads the first value into the first READ variable. If you have too many READ statements for the amount of DATA statements, you will get an "Out of Data" error at run time. If you have too many DATA statements, the extra data will never get used. DATA statements cannot appear in subprograms.

Type compatibility is much looser for READ and DATA statements than for LET statements. Numbers can be read into string variables. You can even have two commas in a row in a DATA statement:

```
DATA  34, , 45.6, "Joe"
```

If the second variable in the READ statement is a string, the program will read the null string (" "). If the variable is numeric, it will read a 0.

The RESTORE Statement

The RESTORE statement enables you to reuse the values in the DATA statements.

RESTORE   **statement**

Syntax: RESTORE [*label*]
Purpose: Resets the pointer to the DATA statements
Sample use:

RESTORE

DATA statements can be implemented with an internal pointer. Before the first READ statement, this pointer is set to the first value in the first DATA statement. After each read, the pointer moves to the next value. The RESTORE statement with no label moves the pointer back to the first value in the first DATA statement. When RESTORE includes a label, the pointer moves to the first DATA statement at or after the label.

The SWAP Statement

The SWAP statement is a special kind of assignment statement.

SWAP   **statement**

Syntax: SWAP *variable, variable*
Purpose: Switches the values of two variables
Sample use:

```
SWAP first%, second%
```

Actually, the SWAP statement is the equivalent of three assignment statements. The sample statement is the same as these:

```
temp% = first%
first% = second%
second% = temp%
```

Both methods place the value in *first%* into the value in *second%*, and the value in *second%* into the value in *first%*.

The SWAP statement requires strict type compatibility. In other words, the type of the first and second variables must be exactly the same. The statement

```
SWAP first%, second!
```

will produce the "type mismatch" error. The variables in the SWAP statement can be of any type, as long as they are the same. This statement is especially useful for exchanging entire arrays or records without having to exchange each element. See Chapter 9 for a complete discussion of arrays and records.

From the syntax of the SWAP statement, notice that you cannot swap constants or expressions. The statement

```
SWAP myval%, a% + b%
```

will produce an "expression not allowed" compiler error. In this case the program has no memory destination for the value of *myval%*.

Conditional Statements

Normally, QuickBASIC will execute statements from top to bottom, one after the other. Often you will need to skip certain statements, or execute others more than once. The group of statements that determine which statements are executed and how often are known as *control statements*. This section will cover the control structures that enable you to skip certain statements, called *conditional statements*.

The structures in this section are considered conditional statements because they force execution of a statement block based on a condition. A condition is a Boolean expression—that is, an expression that evaluates to either TRUE or FALSE. When the condition is true, the program branches to one part of your code; when the condition is false, it branches to another. Each conditional statement follows this principle. Let's look at each statement individually.

The IF-END IF Structure

The most common conditional statement is the IF-END IF structure.

IF-END IF structure

Syntax:

    IF *expression* THEN
        statementblock
    [ELSEIF *expression* THEN
        statementblock]. . .
    [ELSE
        statementblock]
    END IF

Purpose: Controls which statement block gets executed

Note: See also the single-line IF statement.

Sample use:

```
IF numscores% > 0 THEN
    average! = total! / numscores%
ELSE
    PRINT "There are no scores"
END IF
```

The entire IF-END IF structure may look complicated, but it is rather simple when you break it down into parts. Let's start with its simplest form.

The following program fragment comes from a program that takes a survey or census:

```
INPUT "Are you married"; married$
INPUT "What is the name of your spouse"; spouse$
```

Obviously, you do not want to ask users the names of their spouses if they are not married. The IF-END IF construct singles out the second question so that a user sees it only if that user is married:

```
INPUT "Are you married"; married$
IF UCASE$(married$) = "YES" THEN
    INPUT "What is the name of your spouse"; spouse$
END IF
```

IF-END IF is called a structure because it contains several statements. Statements in QuickBASIC must fit on one—and only one—physical line. You cannot easily continue a statement on a second line. The IF-END IF structure is normally at least three lines: one for the IF statement, one or more for the statement block, and one for the END IF. You can have as many statements as you need between the IF statement and the END IF statement. None of these statements will be executed if the condition is not met.

Using ELSE

Suppose that in the survey example you want to know if an unmarried user is divorced. You can do this by adding an ELSE clause:

```
INPUT "Are you married"; married$
IF UCASE$(married$) = "YES" THEN
   INPUT "What is the name of your spouse"; spouse$
ELSE
   INPUT "Are you divorced"; divorced$
END IF
```

The statement block after the ELSE statement is executed only when the condition on the IF line is false. In this case, you will only ask the divorce question when the user is not married. The program does not ask if people are divorced if they respond that they are married. If the user answers "YES" to the marriage question, the program asks the spouse question and skips down to the END IF statement. Otherwise, the program asks the divorce question. In summary, for an IF-ELSE-END IF structure, only one group of statements will be executed: the statements before the ELSE if the condition is true, or the statements after the ELSE if the condition is false.

Using ELSEIF

The ELSEIF statement adds even more versatility to the IF-END IF structure. Consider the following statements, which are part of a grading program.

```
IF percent! > 89.5 THEN
   lettergrade$ = "A"
END IF
IF percent! > 79.5 AND percent! <= 89.5 THEN
   lettergrade$ = "B"
END IF
IF percent! > 69.5 AND percent! <= 79.5 THEN
   lettergrade$ = "C"
END IF
IF percent! > 59.5 AND percent! <= 69.5 THEN
   lettergrade$ = "D"
END IF
IF percent! <= 59.5 THEN
   lettergrade$ = "F"
END IF
```

After looking closely at these statements, you will see that you can only execute one statement block of the five. To make the code more readable, you can use statements. These statements enable you to execute one of several possible branches based on a series of conditions:

```
IF percent! > 89.5 THEN
   lettergrade$ = "A"
ELSEIF percent! > 79.5 THEN
   lettergrade$ = "B"
ELSEIF percent! > 69.5 THEN
   lettergrade$ = "C"
ELSEIF percent! > 59.5 THEN
   lettergrade$ = "D"
ELSE
   lettergrade$ = "F"
END IF
```

There are several advantages to this structure over five separate IF-END IF structures. First, it is more obvious that you will only assign a value to *lettergrade$* once. Only one branch of an IF-END IF structure can be executed. Second, your conditions are much simpler. When you get to an ELSE IF condition you know that all previous conditions have evaluated to FALSE. For instance, when you get to the third condition you know that *percent!* is less than or equal to 79.5 (otherwise, one of the first two conditions would have been true). The final condition is replaced by a simple ELSE statement, because if all the above conditions were false, then *percent!* must be less than or equal to 59.5, and the student fails.

You must be careful about the order of ELSEIF statements in an IF-END IF structure. The statement block that you expect to get executed will be skipped when an above condition evaluates to TRUE. For example, the following program fragment describes a number that the user enters:

```
INPUT "What is your number"; number%
IF number% < 50 THEN
    PRINT "Your number is smaller than 50"
ELSEIF number% < 20 THEN
    PRINT "Your number is smaller than 20"
ELSEIF number% < 10 THEN
    PRINT "Your number is smaller than 10"
ELSE
    PRINT "Your number is larger than 50"
END IF
```

If you run this program and enter the number 5, the program will tell you that your number is smaller than 50. If you want it to tell you that your number is smaller than 10, you have to change the order of the ELSEIF statements. The order of a large IF-END IF structure with many branches can often give you very different answers from what you expect. At first glance, the following program fragment assigns grades just like the previous one:

```
IF percent! > 89.5 THEN
    lettergrade$ = "A"
ELSEIF percent! <= 89.5 THEN
    lettergrade$ = "B"
ELSEIF percent! <= 79.5 THEN
    lettergrade$ = "C"
ELSEIF percent! <= 69.5 THEN
    lettergrade$ = "D"
ELSE
    lettergrade$ = "F"
END IF
```

If you look closer, however, you will see that the students in this class will all get either an "A" or a "B".

Nesting

You can also place an IF-END IF structure within another IF-END IF structure. This is known as *nesting*. Although you can nest conditional statements as much as you like, it is quite easy to get confused after two or three levels. Look at this expansion of the survey program fragment:

```
INPUT "Are you married"; married$
IF UCASE$(married$) = "YES" THEN
    INPUT "What is the name of your spouse"; spouse$
    INPUT "Do you have children"; children$
    IF UCASE$(children$) = "YES" THEN
        INPUT "How many children do you have"; numkids%
    ELSE
        numkids% = 0
    END IF
ELSE
    INPUT "Are you divorced"; divorced$
END IF
```

In this particular program, you only ask whether the user has children if that user is married. Therefore, you nest the questions about the children inside the IF-END IF structure on the marriage.

The Single-Line IF Statement

For short decisions and for compatibility, QuickBASIC includes a one-line IF statement.

IF (single line)   **statement**

Syntax: IF *expression* THEN *statements* [ELSE *statements*]
    where *statements* =>
statement [: *statement*]. . .

Purpose: Limits the execution of a statement based on a condition

Sample use:

```
IF choice% < 0 THEN PRINT "Choice too small."
```

In general, you want to keep your statement lines less than 80 characters in length so that you can see all of the code on the screen (or on the printer) at one time. Because of this, the IF-END IF structure in block form is usually preferred. Any code that uses the one-line form can easily be rewritten to the block form. The sample just given can be rewritten as

```
IF choice% < 0 THEN
    PRINT "Choice too small."
END IF
```

The SELECT-END SELECT Structure

QuickBASIC provides another conditional statement called the SELECT-END SELECT structure.

SELECT-END SELECT   **structure**

Syntax:
    SELECT CASE *expression*
        CASE *caseexpression* [, *caseexpression*]. . .
            statementblock
        [CASE *caseexpression* [, *caseexpression*]. . .
            statementblock]. . .
        [CASE ELSE
            statementblock]
    END SELECT

where *caseexpression* = >
    {*expression* [TO *expression*] | IS *operator expression*}

Purpose: Selects one of several statement blocks to execute

Note: The select expression must fit one of the case expressions, or the "CASE ELSE expected" error occurs.

Sample use:

```
SELECT CASE grade%
   CASE IS <= 6
      PRINT "elementary"
   CASE 7 TO 9
      PRINT "junior high"
   CASE 10 TO 12
      PRINT "high school"
   CASE ELSE
      PRINT "college"
END SELECT
```

When QuickBASIC encounters a SELECT-END SELECT structure, it evaluates the expression in the SELECT statement, known as the *select expression*. It then checks each of the CASE statements, looking for the first *case expression* that matches the select expression. When it finds one, it executes the statement block that follows. Finally, it skips down to the END SELECT statement. Thus, if more than one case expression matches the select expression, only the first one will be executed.

The case expression can have several forms, as shown by the syntax description. It can be a value, like 3; a range of values, like 5 TO 10; or relative to a value, like IS < 20. You can create a series of options by separating case expression by commas. The comma functions the same as the logical operator OR. For example, the CASE statement

```
CASE 1, 4, 6 TO 9
```

will cause execution of the statement block that follows when the select expression evaluates to 1, 4, or a number between 6 and 9.

There are a few case expressions that will not yield the results you expect. When you specify a range of values with the keyword TO, you must put the smaller value first. Also, be especially careful when you combine multiple ranges that use the keyword IS. The CASE statement

```
CASE IS > 8, IS < 12
```

is always true because the comma is like an OR.

Notice that SELECT-END SELECT structures are very similar to IF-END IF structures. The sample program fragment given earlier is the same as this one:

```
IF grade% <= 6 THEN
    PRINT "elementary"
ELSEIF grade% >= 7 AND grade% <= 9 THEN
    PRINT "junior high"
ELSEIF grade% >= 10 AND grade% <= 12 THEN
    PRINT "high school"
ELSE
    PRINT "college"
END IF
```

Whether you use SELECT-END SELECT or IF-END IF depends on the application. Often, SELECT-END SELECT is more readable when there are three or more choices involved.

Iterative Statements

The previous section discussed the control statements that determine whether a statement is executed once or never. This section will cover the statements that determine how many times a statement is executed. These are called *iterative statements* because they cause repetition. The primary iterative statements in QuickBASIC are the DO-LOOP structure and the FOR-NEXT structure. If you are accustomed to using WHILE-WEND, you will see that it has become obsolete with the addition of the DO-LOOP structure.

The Test-First DO-LOOP Structure

The DO-LOOP structure is the more versatile of the iterative statements. This structure has two different syntaxes, which need to be considered separately. The test-first DO-LOOP structure follows.

DO-LOOP (test first)   **structure**

Syntax:
> DO {WHILE | UNTIL} *expression*
>> *statementblock*
> LOOP

Purpose: Repeats a group of statements either as long as a condition holds true or until a condition becomes true

Note: See also the test-last syntax.

Sample use:

```
INPUT "What number"; usernum%
factorial% = 1
count% = 2
DO WHILE count% <= usernum%
   factorial% = factorial% * count%
   count% = count% + 1
LOOP
```

This small program fragment provides a review of how loops operate. The variable *count%* is the *control variable*. It determines how many times the program will execute the loop. The fragment computes the factorial (!) of a number, where you multiply a number by all numbers less than itself. For example:

$$6! = 6 * 5 * 4 * 3 * 2 = 720$$

At the start of the fragment, the program gets the number to compute, *usernum%*, from the user. Then *factorial%* is set to 1. The assignment statement

```
count% = 2
```

is the initialization for the loop.

The DO statement *tests* the control variable (*count%*) so that the statement block is executed while, or as long as, the value of *count%* is less than or equal to the value of *usernum%*.

The statement preceding the LOOP statement modifies the value of *count%* so it is ready for the next test. The LOOP statement marks the end of the loop structure. When the test expression evaluates to FALSE, the program will continue with the statement that follows the LOOP statement.

The statement

```
factorial% = factorial% * count%
```

constitutes the *body* of the loop. This is the statement that the program needs to execute more than once. Any statement can be in the body of a loop.

A DO UNTIL statement has the opposite effect as a DO WHILE statement. A DO WHILE loop will end when the condition on the DO WHILE statement is FALSE. A DO UNTIL loop will end when the condition on the DO UNTIL statement is TRUE. The DO statement in the previous example could also be written

```
DO UNTIL count% > usernum%
```

Whether you choose to use DO WHILE or DO UNTIL is up to you. In this case there is no advantage or disadvantage to either.

When you use the test-first DO-LOOP structure, the test is made before executing the body of the loop. This means that if a test condition evaluates to FALSE the first time, the program will never execute the statement block inside the loop. For instance, suppose a user enters a zero in the factorial program. Since the test

```
DO WHILE count% <= usernum%
```

is a test-first DO-LOOP, and since the test condition fails the first time (2 is greater than 0), the loop statement block is never executed. In this case, the variable *factorial%* will retain the value of 1, as it should.

The Test-Last DO-LOOP Structure

If you need to guarantee that a program executes a statement block at least once, you must use a test-last DO-LOOP structure.

DO-LOOP (test last)   **structure**

Syntax:

    DO
         statementblock
    LOOP [{WHILE | UNTIL} *expression*]

Purpose: Executes a statement block many times, and at least once

Note: See also the test-first DO-LOOP.

Sample use:

```
DO
    CALL PlayGame
    INPUT "Play again (Y/N)"; again$
LOOP WHILE again$ = "Y"
```

This example could be the main module for a game program. The program calls the *PlayGame* subroutine once, then asks users if they want to play again. The game repeats as long as the user answers with "Y."

Occasionally, you have a loop with an empty statement block; that is, there are no lines of code between the DO statement and the LOOP statement. A common example of this is the pause:

```
PRINT "Hit any key to continue: ";
DO
LOOP WHILE INKEY$ = ""
```

In this case the execute, modify, and initialize parts of the loop are all in the INKEY$ function, presented in Chapter 7.

The difference between LOOP UNTIL and LOOP WHILE is the same as with the test-first loop. LOOP UNTIL will iterate as long as the test condition is FALSE, and LOOP WHILE will iterate as long as the test condition is TRUE. Beware of subtle differences, as you can see here:

```
DO
    CALL PlayGame
    INPUT "Play again (Y/N)"; again$
LOOP UNTIL again$ = "N"
```

Suppose a user enters a strange character, like **B**. In the LOOP WHILE example, the game will quit. In the LOOP UNTIL example, the game will repeat. You need to make sure you use the statement that gives you the result you prefer.

Like IF-END IF structures, QuickBASIC allows you to nest DO-LOOP structures. The following program displays a simple multiplication table on the screen:

```
row% = 1
DO
    column% = 1
    DO
        PRINT USING "####"; row% * column%;
        column% = column% + 1
    LOOP UNTIL column% > 9
    PRINT
    row% = row% + 1
LOOP UNTIL row% > 9
```

Notice that the initialization statement for the inner loop (setting *column%* to one) is inside the outer loop. Try moving it up a line or two and see the result. This program is much simpler to understand when you use the FOR-NEXT structure, as you will see later in this chapter.

The EXIT DO Statement

If you look closely at the syntax of the DO-LOOP structure, you will notice that you can have a loop with no WHILE or UNTIL clause. At first glance you would expect this to form an infinite loop: there is no test of a control variable, and GOTO statements out of a DO-LOOP are not allowed. These particular loops require an EXIT DO statement in the statement block for proper execution.

EXIT DO   **statement**

Syntax: EXIT DO

Purpose: Causes the program to go to the statement following the next LOOP statement

Note: This statement must be part of the statement block inside a DO-LOOP structure.

Sample use:

```
DO
    INPUT "Enter name or QUIT to quit: ", newname$
    IF newname$ = "QUIT" THEN
        EXIT DO
    END IF
    CALL InsertName (newname$)
LOOP
```

Normally, EXIT DO statements are tucked inside IF-END IF structures, and thus provide control for getting out of an otherwise infinite loop. The experienced programmer knows that all loops in this form can be rewritten into a more conventional form, although occasionally the program loses readability. The program just given could be written this way:

```
DO
    INPUT "Enter name or QUIT to quit: ", newname$
    IF newname$ <> "QUIT" THEN
        CALL InsertName (newname$)
    END IF
LOOP UNTIL newname$ = "QUIT"
```

Here, you can see exactly what condition must be met to exit from the loop. Therefore, unless you have definite reason to use an EXIT DO statement, you should try to write your code without it.

The FOR-NEXT Structure

The FOR-NEXT structure is a much more specialized iterative statement.

FOR-NEXT   **structure**

Syntax:
    FOR *variable* = *expression* TO *expression* [STEP *expression*]
        statementblock
    NEXT [*variable*]

Purpose: Repeats execution of a statement block a specific number of times

Note: The STEP expression defaults to 1.

Sample use:

```
FOR count% = 1 TO 10
    PRINT
NEXT count%
```

The control variable is the key to the FOR-NEXT structure. This variable keeps track of the number of times the statement block is executed. In the sample fragment, the control variable *count%* will start with a value of one. When the program gets to the NEXT statement, it goes back to the FOR statement and increments *count%* to two. This continues until *count%* is incremented to ten. Then, when the program reaches the NEXT statement, it moves on to the statement following the loop structure. Thus the program skips ten lines on the screen.

For the most part, the FOR-NEXT structure is the compact version of a DO-LOOP. The PRINT example is the same as this fragment:

```
count% = 1
DO UNTIL count% > 10
    PRINT
```

```
        count% = count% + 1
    LOOP
```

The subtle difference is that QuickBASIC evaluates all expressions on the FOR statement when the program reaches it the first time. You might expect this fragment to skip eight lines instead of ten:

```
ten% = 10
FOR count% = 1 to ten%
    PRINT
    ten% = 8
NEXT count%
```

If you try to run this, however, you will see that you still get ten lines. If you need to change the value of a test expression inside a loop, use the DO-LOOP structure.

The STEP option of the FOR-NEXT structure enables you to modify the control variable by adding or subtracting any number. The following program uses a STEP 2 to output a series of odd numbers:

```
FOR odd% = 1 TO 15 STEP 2
    PRINT odd%;
NEXT odd%
PRINT
```

If you use a negative value for STEP, make sure the expression before the TO is larger than the expression after.

Normally, the control variable for the FOR-NEXT structure should be an INTEGER variable. If you use a SINGLE or DOUBLE control variable you will slow down program execution significantly. The values on either side of the reserved word TO should also be of the lowest numeric type that will support the requirements of the loop.

As with the other structures, QuickBASIC supports nesting of FOR-NEXT structures. Here is a rewrite of the multiplication table program you studied earlier in this chapter:

```
FOR row% = 1 TO 9
    FOR column% = 1 TO 9
        PRINT USING "####"; row% * column%;
```

```
      NEXT column%
      PRINT
   NEXT row%
```

If you flip between this example and the one with DO-LOOP structures, you will see how much simpler this one looks. You can see with little effort that the outer loop will execute nine times and the inner loop will execute nine times for every outer loop.

In QuickBASIC you cannot close an outer loop before closing the inner loop. Suppose you had this program fragment:

```
DO
   FOR count% = 1 TO 10
      PRINT count%
      INPUT "Do it again"; again$
LOOP UNTIL again$ = "N"
   NEXT count%
```

You should first notice the indentation. If you indent your programs correctly, you will never have a problem with improper nesting. Second, try to determine what this program would do, if the compiler somehow compiled it. It would cause the compiler error "LOOP without DO" because it must find the NEXT statement before the LOOP statement.

When using FOR-NEXT structures, you should avoid changing the value of a control variable inside the loop structure. QuickBASIC will allow it, but it is extremely poor programming practice. The following program demonstrates this:

```
FOR count% = 1 to 10
   PRINT count%;
   IF count% = 3 THEN
      count% = 8
   END IF
NEXT count%
```

The program displays the numbers

```
1  2  3  9  10
```

on the screen. If that is what you need you should not use the FOR-NEXT structure. Another programmer might glance at the loop and decide right away that the statement block will be executed ten times, and would never examine the logic to make sure. If you need to do fancy things with control variables, use DO-LOOP structures.

The EXIT FOR Statement

One way to work around the restriction on modifying control variables is with the EXIT FOR statement.

EXIT FOR   **statement**

Syntax: EXIT FOR

Purpose: Causes the program to go to the statement following the next NEXT statement

Note: This statement must be part of the statement block inside a FOR-NEXT structure.

Sample use:

```
INPUT "How many names will you enter"; numnames%
FOR name% = 1 TO numnames%
   INPUT "Enter name, or QUIT to quit:", anyname$
   IF anyname$ = "QUIT" THEN
      EXIT FOR
   END IF
   CALL AddName (anyname$)
NEXT name%
```

This provides an excellent example of how to write interactive programs. You ask the user how many names will be entered, and then you enter a loop expecting that many names. However, what if a user types the wrong number, or there is a fire and the

user needs to save the current list and get out? By adding the
option to type **QUIT**, you enable users to change their minds.
Your only sacrifice is losing the ability to add a person named
QUIT to the list.

Program Examples

In Chapter 5, you were challenged to write routines to convert
strings in hexadecimal or octal form back to decimal form. These
programs will combine the FOR-NEXT structure with the
SELECT-END SELECT structure, which you studied in this
chapter. Notice the documentation every few lines:

```
',',',',',',',',',',',',',',',',',',',',',',',',',',',',
'  hexadecimal to decimal routine        '
',',',',',',',',',',',',',',',',',',',',',',',',',',',',

'          get the requested number
INPUT "What is the number to convert"; hexstr$

'          make required initializations
decimal& = 0
exponent% = 0

'          go through each character, right to left
FOR position% = LEN(hexstr$) TO 1 STEP -1

'          isolate the character
   hexcode% = ASC(MID$(hexstr$, position%, 1))
   SELECT CASE hexcode%

'          if it's 0..9, convert this digit by
'          multiplying by the appropriate power
'          of 16.
      CASE 48 TO 57
         tempval& = (hexcode% - 48&) * 16& ^ exponent%

'          if it's A..F, convert to number first
      CASE 65 TO 70
         tempval& = (hexcode% - 55&) * 16& ^ exponent%
      CASE 97 TO 102
         tempval& = (hexcode% - 87&) * 16& ^ exponent%

'          otherwise, the character is invalid
      CASE ELSE
         PRINT "invalid character - "; CHR$(hexcode%)
```

```
            tempval& = 0
      END SELECT

            '      add current digit to the number
      decimal& = decimal& + tempval&
      exponent% = exponent% + 1
   NEXT position%

      '          display the final figure
   PRINT "Decimal equivalent is "; decimal&
```

Here is the routine to convert an octal string to a decimal number:

```
',',',',',',',',',',',',',',',',',',',',','
'    octal to decimal routine         '
',',',',',',',',',',',',',',',',',',',',','

'          get the requested number
INPUT "What is the number to convert"; octstr$

'          make required initializations
decimal& = 0
exponent% = 0

'          go through each character, right to left
FOR position% = LEN(octstr$) TO 1 STEP -1

   '          isolate the character
   octcode% = ASC(MID$(octstr$, position%, 1))

   '          if it's 0..7, convert this digit by
   '          multiplying by the appropriate power
   '          of 8.
   IF octcode% >= 48 AND octcode% <= 55 THEN
      tempval& = (octcode% - 48&) * 8& ^ exponent%

   '          otherwise, the character is invalid
   ELSE
      PRINT "invalid character - "; CHR$(octcode%)
      tempval& = 0
   END IF

   '          add current digit to the number
   decimal& = decimal& + tempval&
   exponent% = exponent% + 1
NEXT position%

   '          display the final figure
PRINT "Decimal equivalent is "; decimal&
```

Terminal Input and Output

Output to the Screen
Keyboard Input

When users run your program, they cannot see the hundreds of lines of QuickBASIC that it took to create the program. All they can see is what you display on the terminal screen or print on the printer. This is why the *user interface* is so important when you write a program for someone else. Your program may work perfectly, but may get rejected because of a poor user interface.

In this chapter you will see the functions and statements that QuickBASIC provides to help you create a good user interface. It will cover I/O through the screen, keyboard, and printer. You can read about special input devices like the light pen and joystick in Chapter 13.

Output to the Screen

Many novice programmers use the PRINT statement as their only method of displaying information on the terminal screen. The output starts at the top-left corner of the screen and works its way down, scrolling as necessary. A good user interface, however, requires effective use of the entire screen. This section provides the QuickBASIC statements and functions that are the building blocks for impressive screen displays.

The PRINT Statement

The most elementary statement for output to the screen is the PRINT statement. This statement was introduced in Chapter 4, but it is summarized here for continuity.

PRINT   **statement**

Syntax: PRINT [*expression* [{,|;}]]. . .

Purpose: Outputs information to the screen at the current cursor location

Sample use:

```
PRINT num1%; "plus"; num2%; "is"; num1% + num2%
```

If the values of *num1%* and *num2%* are 5 and 7, respectively, then the output from this statement will be

```
5 plus 7 is 12
```

Notice that when QuickBASIC prints a number, it automatically adds a space to the end of the number. If the number is positive, there is also an extra space before the number. If it is negative, there is a minus sign before the number. String expressions are printed just as they appear.

The comma and semicolon dictate where the cursor will go after the expression preceding them is printed. If a semicolon follows an expression, the cursor is moved to the position just to the right of the value. The comma forces the cursor to move to the first column of the next area of the screen, called a *print zone*. Normally, print zones start in columns 1, 15, 29, 43, and 57.

If you are in 40-column mode, only the first two print zones are valid. If the PRINT statement ends without a comma or semicolon, the cursor will go to the first column of the next line.

If an expression will not fit on a line, QuickBASIC will print the expression at the start of the next line. If a string is larger than the width of the screen, QuickBASIC will wrap the output to the next line — it will print as much as it can on the current line and the rest on the following line. For this reason, you should avoid working with strings longer than 79 characters.

When QuickBASIC prints a real number (SINGLE or DOUBLE), it displays as many digits as it has stored in memory without trailing zeros. For example, the statements

```
PRINT 5 / 7; 5# / 7#
PRINT 5 / 8; 5# / 8#
```

will give you the following output:

```
.7142857  .7142857142857143
.625  .625
```

Since five-eighths is exactly .625, QuickBASIC prints the same number in double precision as it does in single precision.

The PRINT USING Statement

Usually, you will want more control over how a number is displayed. To get around the defaults of the PRINT statement you can use the PRINT USING statement.

PRINT USING   **statement**

Syntax: PRINT USING *formatstring*; *expressions* [{,|;}]
where *expressions* =>

---

expression [; *expression*]. . .
Purpose: Prints an expression with a specific format
Sample use:

```
PRINT USING "#.###"; 5 / 7
```

If you use this sample statement, 5 / 7 will display as "0.714",
which is much more readable than .7142857 (assuming you do
not need the extra precision).

Formats for Integers

The format string in the PRINT USING statement consists of a
series of special symbols. For integers, the following symbols
can be part of the format string: The pound sign (#), the
comma, the plus sign, the minus sign, the asterisk (*), and the
dollar sign.

The pound sign in a format string is a *place holder*. In other
words, if you want to allow up to four places for an integer
display you use "####" as the format string. If the number
being displayed takes fewer than four digits, it is right-justified.
If it takes more than five digits, QuickBASIC will place a per-
cent sign (%) followed by the entire number. This output can be
confusing to users, so make sure you include enough place
holders in the format string for all reasonable values. ·

A comma in the format string tells the program to place
commas after every three digits. This makes larger numbers
easier to read. For program readability, you might want to
include a comma every place one might occur, such as

```
PRINT USING "#,###,###,###"; population%
```

The plus sign forces the sign of a number to appear. If the
symbol comes just before the place holders, QuickBASIC will

print the sign just before the number. If you place the plus sign after the number, the sign of the expression will be placed after the value. A minus sign at the end of a format string forces negative numbers to have a trailing minus sign and positive numbers to have a trailing space.

If you use two asterisks in place of the first two pound signs, leading spaces in front of the number will be replaced with asterisks. This will make a series of numbers appear to have the same number of digits. For instance, if *num%* in this statement

```
PRINT USING "**###"; num%
```

has a value of 4663, it will be output as "*4663." If the value of *num%* is 2, it will be displayed as "****2."

When you replace the first two pound signs with two dollar signs, a dollar sign will appear just to the left of the number. You can combine the effect of the dollar signs with the effect of the asterisks by using the **$ symbol combination. If the dollar figures you need to print are large, you might want to combine several of the PRINT USING formats, such as

```
PRINT USING "**$,###,###-"; balance%
```

In this case, you will display the value of *balance%* with leading asterisks, a dollar sign, commas every three places, and a trailing minus sign for negative balances.

Additional Formats for Real Numbers

All of the symbols available for integers (types INTEGER and LONG) are also usable for real numbers (types SINGLE and DOUBLE). In addition, real numbers can include a period and a series of carets (^).

The period shows where the decimal point of a real number will go. If you need to display a number with accuracy to the thousands place, use the statement

```
PRINT USING "####.###"; num!
```

QuickBASIC will always display at least one digit to the left of the decimal point, even if it is a zero. The places to the right of the period are always printed, even if they are all zeros.

For large real numbers you will probably need the exponent, or scientific notation, format. Most common numbers require four carets, as in this statement:

```
PRINT USING "##.###^^^^"; largenum!
```

The four carets hold places for the E, the sign of the exponent, and two digits. The number 123,456.7 in this case would be output as "1.234E+05". The first pound sign is reserved for either a space or a minus sign, unless you include a plus sign or minus sign in the format string. If the number is extremely large, or small, use five carets. This format will allow for 3-digit exponents.

Formats for Strings

You can use the PRINT USING statement to output both string constants and string variables. You can place a string constant inside the format string. The statement

```
PRINT USING "You have $$###.## in your account."; balance!
```

would be the same as these three statements:

```
PRINT "Your balance of ";
PRINT USING "$$###.##"; balance!;
PRINT " is over your limit."
```

Since you usually want to display the entire value of a string variable, the PRINT USING statement is not as useful for strings as for numbers. The following symbols can be used for string output:

• The exclamation point (!) prints only the first character of a string.

• The ampersand (&) prints the entire string as it is stored.

• Two backslashes (\) with spaces between limit the length of the string to two more than the number of spaces. All characters between the backslashes are ignored. For example, this statement could be used to limit the output of *lastname$* to twelve characters:

```
PRINT USING "\. . .5. . .10.\"; lastname$
```

The LOCATE Statement

Probably the most important key to making a presentable program is placing your output at the right place on the screen. Without cursor control, input and output occurs primarily at the bottom-left corner of the screen. This makes it impossible for users to anticipate future input. Moving the cursor to exactly the position on the screen where you need it is handled by the LOCATE statement.

LOCATE   **statement**

Syntax: LOCATE [*line*][,[*column*][,[*cursorinfo*]]]
   where *cursorinfo* = >
   [*cursorflag*][,[*top*][,*bottom*]]

Purpose: Moves the text cursor to a particular place on the screen and specifies the cursor type

Sample use:

```
LOCATE 13,40        'move to the center of the screen
```

As you can see from the description, the LOCATE statement serves two different functions. The primary purpose is to move the text cursor to a certain line and column. If you omit a line number or column number, that number does not change.

LOCATE can also be used to modify the cursor itself. The third argument of the LOCATE statement defines cursor visibility: 0 if invisible, any other number if visible. The fourth and fifth arguments allow you to alter the shape of the cursor. For most graphics devices, there are eight *scan lines* for every character, numbered 0-7. By default, the QuickBASIC cursor uses scan lines 5-7. If you want a smaller cursor that uses only the two bottom lines, use the statement

```
LOCATE , , , 6, 7
```

You can even make a two-part cursor by making the fourth number larger than the fifth.

The COLOR Statement

The COLOR statement enhances your displays by changing the color of future output text. This helps the user distinguish between important information and background information.

COLOR   **statement**

Syntax: COLOR [*foreground*][,[*background*][,*border*]]

Purpose: Sets the colors for the next PRINT statement

Note: There is also a COLOR statement in graphics mode (see Chapter 12).

Sample use:

```
COLOR 15, 6
```

The valid numbers for the COLOR statement depend on the type of graphics card you have in your computer. The 16 primary colors are given in Table 7-1. If you add 16 to any of the numbers, the color blinks.

0	Black	8	Dark gray
1	Blue	9	Bright blue
2	Green	10	Bright green
3	Cyan	11	Bright cyan
4	Red	12	Bright red
5	Magenta	13	Bright magenta
6	Brown	14	Yellow
7	Light gray	15	White

Table 7-1.   Color Table

There are three arguments in the COLOR statement, all optional:

• The foreground color, the color of the character itself (the default is light gray)

• The background color, the color of the area around the character (the default is black)

• The border color, the half-inch border around the entire screen

If you leave out an argument, that particular color does not change.

The CLS Statement

Another key to an attractive display is starting with a blank screen. You can clear the screen anywhere in your program with the CLS statement.

CLS   **statement**

Syntax: CLS [{0 | 1 | 2}]

Purpose: Clears the screen or the scrolling region

Note: CLS is also used to clear a graphics region (see Chapter 12).

Sample use:

```
CLS 0
```

The CLS statement can end with 0, 1, 2, or nothing. The 0 argument clears the entire screen and moves the cursor to the home position. The CLS 1 statement clears only the current graphics viewport (see Chapter 12). If you use CLS 2, you will clear only the current text viewport or scrolling region. If you have not set a scrolling region with the VIEW PRINT statement (covered later in this section), CLS 2 will also clear the entire screen. Finally, if you use CLS with no number, the current viewport will clear, whether it is a text viewport or a graphics viewport. Make a habit of using CLS as the first statement in all of your programs.

Other Statements and Functions

The rest of this section presents the less common QuickBASIC statements and functions for screen output. Many of these can be very useful at times, but are limited in their applications. You might consider skimming this section to become aware of a statement or function you might need in the future.

The TAB Function

The LOCATE statement can move the cursor to a specific column on the current line. Another method is to use the TAB function.

TAB(col)   **function**

Purpose: Moves the cursor to a particular column on the screen or printer

Return type: None

Parameter: col [INTEGER]—the column to move to

Note: This function is valid only in PRINT and LPRINT statements.

Sample call:

```
PRINT transamt!; TAB(50); balance!
```

In this sample, QuickBASIC will output the value of *transamt!*, then move the cursor to the 50th column before outputting the value of *balance!*. If the cursor is already past column 50, the function will place the cursor at column 50 on the next line.

The SPC Function

If you do not want to move to a specific column, but you want to add a certain number of blank spaces, you have two options. The first is to output a string constant that has that many blanks in it. The second is to use the SPC function.

SPC(num)   **function**

Purpose: Advances the cursor a given number of spaces

Return type: None

Parameters: num [INTEGER]—the number of spaces
Note: This function is valid only in PRINT and LPRINT statements.
Sample call:

```
PRINT num1%; SPC(10); num2%
```

The equivalent of the sample in the box is this statement:

```
PRINT num1%; "          "; num2%
```

The SPC function keeps you from having to count out spaces and makes programs more readable.

The VIEW PRINT Statement

Sometimes, you need to work with a portion of the text screen. You can create a text viewport for this with the VIEW PRINT statement.

VIEW PRINT   **statement**

Syntax: VIEW PRINT [*topline* TO *bottomline*]
Purpose: Limits the scrolling region of the screen
Sample use:

```
VIEW PRINT 5 TO 20
```

When you print something at the bottom of the screen, the text scrolls up, and the top line disappears. Thus, the entire screen is known as the *scrolling region*. If you need to keep certain information on the screen, but you don't mind scrolling others, you can use the VIEW PRINT statement. A VIEW PRINT statement with no arguments returns the scrolling region to be the entire screen. When QuickBASIC executes the VIEW PRINT statement, it moves the cursor to the first column of the first line of the region, known as the *home position*. The *scrolling region*, also called the *text viewport*, must be at least two lines.

The POS and CSRLIN Functions

QuickBASIC also includes two functions that tell you where the cursor is at the time the functions are called. If you create a user interface properly, however, you will usually know where the cursor is. The POS function identifies the current column number.

POS(0)   **function**

Purpose: Supplies the column that the text cursor is on

Return type: INTEGER

Parameters: 0—an unused parameter provided for compatibility only

Sample call:

```
LOCATE POS(0) -1            'move cursor left one column
```

The CSRLIN function provides the line number of the current cursor location.

CSRLIN   **function**

Purpose: Supplies the line that the text cursor is on
Return type: INTEGER
Parameters: none
Sample call:

```
LOCATE ,CSRLIN + 1          'move cursor down one line
```

The two samples given for these functions show you one way of moving the cursor to a relative location.

The WIDTH Statement

Normally, the screen dimensions are 25 lines of 80 characters each. Occasionally, you need to change these, for which Quick-BASIC provides the WIDTH statement.

WIDTH   **statement**

Syntax: WIDTH [*columns*][,*lines*]
Purpose: Changes the number of columns on the screen
Note: There is also a WIDTH statement for files and for the printer.
Sample use:

```
WIDTH 40
```

All IBM-PC compatibles support switching between 80 and 40 columns. If you have a CGA card in your computer, the only valid number of lines is 25. More advanced cards support 30, 43, 50, or even 60 lines. If you have one of these cards (EGA, VGA, or MCGA), see the SCREEN statement in Chapter 12.

Keyboard Input

The output statements covered in the previous section enable you to control screen displays. When you get input from the user, however, you have less control. To keep user input from destroying screen displays, you must "idiot-proof" the input by not allowing the user to create system errors. This section covers the QuickBASIC keyboard input statements as well as giving insight into idiot-proofing.

The simplest statement to use for keyboard input is the INPUT statement. This statement was covered in Chapter 4, but it is repeated here for continuity.

INPUT   **statement**

Syntax: INPUT[;] [*prompt* {;|,}] *variable* [, *variable*]. . .

Purpose: Assigns value(s) input from the user to the given variable(s)

Sample use:

```
INPUT "What is your name"; namestr$
```

When a program gets to an INPUT statement, it displays the text cursor and awaits user input. When the user enters the data, the values entered are assigned to the variable names in the INPUT statement.

ENTER	Terminates input
RIGHT	Moves cursor one character to the right
LEFT	Moves cursor one character to the left
BACKSPACE	Deletes character to the left of the cursor
DEL	Deletes character at the cursor
ESC	Deletes entire input line
END	Moves cursor to the end of the input line
HOME	Moves cursor to the start of the input line
INS	Toggles between insert and overstrike modes
CTRL-RIGHT	Moves cursor one word to the right
CTRL-LEFT	Moves cursor one word to the left
CTRL-END	Deletes all characters to the right of the cursor

Table 7-2.   Input Edit Keys

Prior to pressing ENTER to complete the input, the user can edit the data. The editing keys are summarized in Table 7-2. In many cases, they are similar to commands in the QuickBASIC environment.

The semicolon immediately following the word INPUT tells the program to leave the cursor on the current line after the input is completed. If you omit the semicolon, the cursor moves to the first column of the next line when the user presses ENTER.

The *prompt* is a string expression that can be in the form of a question or a command. QuickBASIC gives you the option of outputting a question mark to the left of the cursor or suppressing it. A semicolon after the prompt string, as in the sample just given, automatically adds a question mark after the prompt. The comma after the prompt string omits the added question mark. You will probably want to include a colon or similar character inside the prompt string to help users separate your command from the user's input.

QuickBASIC allows you to require multiple inputs with one INPUT statement. Too often, however, this leaves room for user error. Here is an example:

```
INPUT "Enter last name, first name: ", last$, first$
```

For multiple inputs, the user must separate the strings with a comma. If a user enters too many strings, or not enough, Quick-BASIC will display the "Redo from start" message. You will eliminate a lot of confusion by using one INPUT statement for each data item.

The type of the value entered by the user must match the type of the variable in the INPUT statement. If a user enters a string when the INPUT statement requires a number, Quick-BASIC displays a "Redo from start" error message. This kind of error message destroys your user interface. Obviously, this is a major drawback to using the INPUT statement. To work around this, you can write an error trap (see Chapter 13).

One way to avoid this problem is to use only string variables in your INPUT statements. You can then convert the strings that you need to assign to numeric variables with the VAL function. The check number example becomes this fragment:

```
INPUT "Enter the last check number: ", tempstr$
checknum% = VAL(tempstr$)
```

The VAL function, covered in detail in Chapter 8, converts the letters in *tempstr$* to digits until it reaches a character that is not a number. If the user enters a letter as the first character, *checknum%* will be assigned the value 0.

The INKEY$ Function

Because of the drawbacks just described, you should consider using the INPUT statement only when you are writing a quick program for yourself. When you write a program that someone else will use, it is preferable to have more control over user input. Also, you will often need to be able to determine when the user enters special keys, like HOME and PGDN. QuickBASIC provides the INKEY$ function to solve both of these problems.

INKEY$ **function**

Purpose: Supplies the key hit by the user, if any

Return type: STRING

Parameters: None

Note: Non-ASCII keys return CHR$(0) followed by the keyboard scan code; keys are not echoed.

Sample case:

```
DO
LOOP UNTIL INKEY$ <>""
```

The INKEY$ function is instantaneous—it does not wait for the user to press a key. For this reason, you need a DO-LOOP to wait for a key. If the user pressed a key, INKEY$ returns its value. If no key was pressed, INKEY$ returns the null string. This function neither displays a cursor nor echoes the character after the key is pressed.

You cannot use this loop when you need to evaluate the key pressed by the user. In order to save the value of the character you must assign the value returned by INKEY$ to a string variable. The following loop accomplishes this:

```
DO
   keyhit$ = INKEY$
LOOP WHILE keyhit$ = ""
```

Normally, the string returned by INKEY$ is one character in length, or zero if no key was pressed. Certain keys, such as the arrow keys and the function keys, return a 2-character string. The first character of this string is always CHR$(0). The second character is the scan code of the key pressed by the user. There are 83 keys on a standard keyboard, and each has its own scan code. These scan codes are listed in Appendix B. Here is a program fragment that checks for the LEFT and RIGHT ARROW keys.

```
DO
   keyhit$ = INKEY$
LOOP UNTIL keyhit$ <> ""

'     check for special keys
IF LEFT$(keyhit$, 1) = CHR$(0) THEN
   scancode% = ASC(RIGHT$(keyhit$, 1))

'     check for arrows
   IF scancode% = 75 THEN        'left arrow
      . . .
   ELSEIF scancode% = 77 THEN    'right arrow
      . . .
   END IF
END IF
```

In Chapter 8 you will see a complete numeric input routine that reads the characters one at a time and handles these special strings.

The KEY Statement

On the left side or the top of most keyboards is a set of ten function keys: F1 through F10. You have probably used these keys within the QuickBASIC environment to run your program, survey the output screen, or perform debug commands. In your own programs, you may choose to redefine the function keys to simplify input for your users. QuickBASIC includes the KEY statement to define these keys and others.

KEY   **statement**

Syntax: KEY *keynumber, definition*
        KEY ON
        KEY OFF
        KEY LIST
Purpose: Redefines a function key or a user-defined key

Note: Valid key numbers are 1-10 for function keys and 15-25 for user-defined keys.

Sample use:

```
KEY 2, "ADD" + CHR$(13)
KEY 3, "CHANGE" + CHR$(13)
KEY 4, "DELETE" + CHR$(13)
KEY 10, "QUIT" + CHR$(13)
```

When a user presses F2 during an INPUT statement, there is no response. During an INKEY$ loop, F2 returns "CHR$(0) + CHR$(60)". After the KEY statement redefines the F2 key, the INPUT statement returns "ADD". The INKEY$ loop will get four characters: A, D, D, and the carriage return.

The KEY ON statement refers to the display on line 25 of the screen. When the program executes this statement, it displays the numbers one through ten on line 25. If you have redefined any keys, it displays up to the first six characters of the key definition on the screen. You can turn this legend off with the KEY OFF statement. The KEY LIST statement displays a table of each key and its full definition. Unfortunately, there is no way to control the output of this statement, so by using it in your program you will spoil your user interface. Consider placing it in a text viewport or using it only for debugging purposes.

Trapping Special Keys

The input statements you have studied so far have given you the ability to read a key from the keyboard when the program reaches that statement. QuickBASIC also allows you to trap a key as soon as the user presses it. To do this you must define the key as an event and write an event handler. Before describing the statements that support key trapping, this section includes a brief introduction to event trapping in general.

Introduction to Event Trapping

An *event* is an action, normally caused by the user, that suspends normal program execution until a special series of statements is completed. In QuickBASIC, you can program events caused by keyboard keys, joystick triggers, light pens, COM port inputs, background music ending, and time running out. Each of these is covered in separate sections in this chapter and in Chapters 12 and 13.

When an event occurs during program execution, QuickBASIC follows this sequence:

1. Finishes executing the current line

2. Branches to the appropriate GOSUB subroutine, called the event handler

3. Executes the event handler

4. Returns to the next statement to be executed

Before an event trap can take place, you must place three things in your program: the event definition, the event handler, and the event enabler. The *event definition* tells the program what type of event to trap, and where to go when the event occurs. This definition will always include an ON *event* GOSUB statement. The *event handler* is the GOSUB subroutine that tells the program what to do when the event occurs. The *event enabler*, in the form of an *event* ON statement, tells the program to start checking for the event between program statements.

QuickBASIC also allows you to temporarily disable events. There will probably be times when you do not want a user to be able to interrupt the system. A common example of this is when you are updating a group of files all at once. If a user caused an event to occur in the middle of these updates, some would be done and some would not. To avoid this possible catastrophe, QuickBASIC provides the statements *event* STOP and *event* OFF. The *event* STOP statement places the event trap on hold. If the event occurs, the system will remember until the next *event* ON statement. The *event* OFF statement disables the event trap completely. If an event occurs after you turn it off with an *event* OFF, the system will not remember it.

When the system branches to an event handler, it implicitly executes an *event* STOP statement. This is to keep from having an event occur while the same event is being handled. The RETURN statement in the event handler implicitly executes an *event* ON statement. If you need to disable an event trap later in the program, you can use an *event* STOP or *event* OFF statement to override the automatic one at the RETURN statement.

It is important to note that when you get to an event handler, you have no way of querying the system to find out what event has occurred. For this reason, you must include a separate event handler for every event you define.

Whenever you enable an event, the program will check for that event after it executes each statement in the main part of the program. Therefore, program execution time gets much slower. When you choose to use an event trap, make sure that you are willing to make sacrifices in program speed.

The ON KEY and KEY ON/OFF/STOP Statements

The ON KEY statement and the KEY statement discussed earlier combine to form the event definition for special key events.

ON KEY   statement

Syntax: ON KEY(*keynum*) GOSUB *label*
Purpose: Defines the location of a specified key event handler

Note: The label must be in the module-level code.

Sample use:

```
ON KEY(10) GOSUB QuitProgram
```

With this statement, when the user presses F10, the program executes the statement block at *QuitProgram.* This assumes, of course, that the event has been enabled.

Enabling and disabling of a special key event is achieved with the KEY ON/OFF/STOP statement.

KEY ON/OFF/STOP   **statement**

Syntax: KEY(*keynum*) {ON | OFF | STOP}

Purpose: Enables or disables the trapping of a specific key or key combination

Note: See Table 7-3 for possible values of *keynum.*

Sample use:

```
KEY(10) ON
```

The KEY ON statement enables special key event trapping, the KEY OFF statement disables it, and the KEY STOP statement suppresses the event.

From Table 7-3, you can see that you can have up to 27 special key event traps at once. Eleven of these special keys you can define yourself. To define your own keys you must use a modification of the KEY statement described earlier. The first number in the KEY statement is an arbitrary number between 15 and 25 that you wish to use for the event. The string that

Key Codes	Keys
1-10	Function Keys: F1 - F10
11-14	Arrow keys: UP, LEFT, RIGHT, DOWN
15-25	User-defined keys
26-29	Not available
30-31	F11 and F12, not always available

Table 7-3.   Special Key Codes

follows is two characters. The first character is the keyboard flag, and it must have one of the values in Table 7-4. The second character is the keyboard scan code of the key the user must press. These codes are listed in Appendix B.

Suppose you need to trap the CTRL-BREAK combination so a user cannot break out of your program. You can define key 15 as a special key like this:

```
KEY 15, CHR$(&H4) + CHR$(70)
```

The entire program fragment that includes the event definition and event handler is shown here:

```
'       define CTRL-BREAK as an event
KEY 15, CHR$(&h04) + CHR$(70)
ON KEY(15) GOSUB OrderlyExit
KEY(15) ON
. . .

'       Event trap for CTRL-BREAK
OrderlyExit:
   LOCATE 25, 1
   PRINT "You have pressed CTRL-BREAK.   ";
   INPUT "Are you sure you want to quit"; quit$
   IF UPCASE$(LEFT$(quit$, 1)) = "Y" THEN
      CALL CloseFiles
      END
   END IF
   LOCATE 25, 1
   PRINT STRING$(40, " ");
RETURN
```

Keyboard Flag	Key
&H00	None
&H02	SHIFT
&H04	CTRL
&H08	ALT
&H20	NUMLOCK
&H40	CAPSLOCK

Table 7-4.   Keyboard Flag Values

In this program, when the user presses CTRL-BREAK, the program prints a message on line 25. If the user pressed the keys by accident, this event trap allows the user to return to where the program was when the event occurred.

Other Functions and Statements

The rest of this section summarizes the less used QuickBASIC statements and functions that read keyboard input. Since the applications for these statements and functions are limited, you may choose to skim these pages to familiarize yourself with their usage.

The INPUT$ Function

The INPUT$ function is primarily designed for file and device input, but you can also use it for keyboard input.

INPUT$(nchrs)   **function**

Purpose: Reads a certain number of characters from the keyboard without echoing them to the screen

---

Return type: STRING

Parameters: nchrs [INTEGER]—the number of characters to read

Note: This function also has a format for files and devices (see Chapter 11).

Sample call:

```
inchar$ = INPUT$(1)
```

This function has very limited use with the keyboard for several reasons. First, it does not echo the input to the screen. This means that if the argument to the function is anything other than one, you cannot give any feedback to your user. Second, it cannot read the special keys. To read these keys you would need an INPUT$(2) call, but this would only accept the "normal" keys in pairs. Finally, there is no cursor, so the user has no idea what to input unless the prompt is the only text on the screen. Both the INPUT$ and INKEY$ functions require a lot of special code to make them user friendly.

The LINE INPUT Statement

If you want to enable a user to enter a long string with quotes, commas, or leading spaces, you can use the LINE INPUT statement.

LINE INPUT   **statement**

Syntax: LINE INPUT [;] [*prompt*;] *stringvariable*

Purpose: Assigns entire user input to a string variable

Note: Does not automatically display a question mark after the prompt string.

Sample use:

```
LINE INPUT "Enter the full name: "; fullname$
```

With the LINE INPUT statement, a user can, for example, enter nicknames and titles in the same string:

```
Jack "The Ripper" Smith, Jr.
```

Notice that the LINE INPUT statement does not place a question mark immediately following the prompt. This is why you cannot use a comma between the prompt and the variable, as you can in the INPUT statement. The user edit keys in Table 7-2 are valid for the LINE INPUT statement.

Printer Output

The printer is your way of keeping paper copies of the work you do on the computer. Report generation and desktop publishing are becoming more popular as printers for personal computers improve in quality. QuickBASIC includes several statements that deal solely with printer output. As an alternative, you can use the printer as a file-like device ("LPT1:"), and output to the printer with the file output statement (see Chapter 11).

The LPRINT Statement

The LPRINT statement is a replica of the PRINT statement, except that the output goes to the printer.

LPRINT   **statement**

Syntax: LPRINT [*expression* [{,|;}]]. . .
Purpose: Prints a series of expressions to the printer
Note: See the text associated with the PRINT statement for more explanation.
Sample use:

```
LPRINT fullname$; TAB(30); phonenum$
```

The TAB and SPC functions work in LPRINT statements as well as PRINT statements.

The LPRINT USING Statement

To better format the printer output, QuickBASIC provides the LPRINT USING statement.

LPRINT USING   **statement**

Syntax: LPRINT USING *format*; *expressions* [{,|;}]
    where *expressions* = >
    expression [, *expression*]. . .
Purpose: Prints expressions with a specified format

Note: See the text associated with the PRINT USING statement for more explanation.

Sample use:

```
LPRINT USING "###.##"; INTEREST!
```

The same rules apply for this statement that apply for the PRINT USING statement, found earlier in this chapter.

The LPOS Function

QuickBASIC does not keep track of the printer line number automatically, but it does monitor the print-head column. You can determine the logical print-head position with the LPOS function.

LPOS(pnum)   **function**

Purpose: Supplies the logical print-head position
Return type: INTEGER
Parameter: pnum [INTEGER]—the printer number
Sample call:

```
IF LPOS(1) + LEN(mystr$) > 72 THEN
    LPRINT
END IF
```

This small fragment moves the print head to the next line if writing the string *mystr$* would put the end of the string past column 72.

The WIDTH LPRINT Statement

By default, QuickBASIC wraps the output to the printer at 80 characters. To change this, use the WIDTH LPRINT statement.

WIDTH LPRINT   **statement**

Syntax: WIDTH LPRINT *printerwidth*
Purpose: Changes the permitted width of the printer output
Sample use:

```
WIDTH LPRINT 132
```

You will need this statement primarily to take advantage of a wide-carriage printer. The WIDTH statement affects all future printer output.

String Manipulation

The ASCII Character Set
Substrings
Comparing Strings
String Conversion
Miscellaneous Functions and Statements
Strings and I/O

One of the fundamental advantages of a personal computer is its ability to process data in character form. This chapter shows you how to exploit QuickBASIC's powerful string-handling statements and functions. Also in this chapter are several complete subroutines for replacing strings, comparing strings, and performing idiot-proof numeric input.

The ASCII Character Set

Inside the computer a string is stored as a series of integer codes known as *ASCII codes*. There are 256 different ASCII codes, as shown in Appendix B. The ASCII characters numbered 32 through 126 are the characters you can type on the keyboard: 26 lowercase letters, 26 uppercase letters, 10 digits, and 33 symbols. Most of the other codes represent characters that you can display only by referring to their codes. These include letters with accents, Greek letters, and mathematical symbols.

To display an ASCII character that you cannot type, use the CHR$ function. For instance, you can place the proper accents on the word tête-à-tête with this string:

```
tete$ = "t" + CHR$(136) + "te"
privatetalk$ = tete$ + "-" + CHR$(133) + "-" + tete$
```

Unfortunately, these characters do not display well on a CGA or monochrome monitor.

Some of the most commonly needed ASCII characters, which are not found on the keyboard, are the ones that create boxes. These characters, numbered 179 through 218, give you single-line boxes, double-line boxes, and their various combinations. The following program creates a 12 × 42 single-line box in the center of the screen:

```
CLS
LOCATE 7, 1
PRINT TAB(19); CHR$(218); STRING$(40, 196); CHR$(191)
FOR count% = 1 TO 10
    PRINT TAB(19); CHR$(179); SPC(40); CHR$(179)
NEXT count%
PRINT TAB(19); CHR$(192); STRING$(40, 196); CHR$(217)
```

Chapter 19 includes a routine that displays this box in any size anywhere on the screen.

QuickBASIC uses some of the ASCII codes for controlling the screen display. These codes are summarized in Table 8-1. There is no way to print the characters that you see next to these codes in Appendix B. Instead, if you use one of these codes in a PRINT statement, you will get the effect listed in Table 8-1. For instance, the character next to ASCII code 13 is a musical note. However, the statement

```
PRINT CHR$(13);
```

will move the cursor to the next line instead of displaying the musical note. You can see how some of these codes are used for both input and output in the *GetInput* routine at the end of this chapter.

Substrings

Often you will need to examine a part of a string called a *substring*. QuickBASIC includes several functions that isolate a

ASCII Code	Meaning
7	Rings the bell
8	Deletes one character to the left of the cursor
9	Moves the cursor one tab position
10	Moves the cursor to the start of the next line
11	Moves the cursor to the home position
12	Clears the screen and moves the cursor to home; form-feeds printers
13	Moves the cursor to the start of the next line
28	Moves the cursor right one character
29	Moves the cursor left one character
30	Moves the cursor up one line
31	Moves the cursor down one line

Table 8-1.   CRT Control Characters

substring from a larger string. You can also search for substrings and replace them. This section covers these subjects.

The LEFT$ Function

When you ask a user to choose from a list of items, you can often examine only the first character of the input string. The LEFT$ function allows you to isolate the first character, or first *n* characters, of a string.

LEFT$(expr$, num)   **function**

Purpose: Supplies the first *num* characters of a string
Return type: STRING

Parameters: expr$ [STRING]—the string expression
num [INTEGER]—the number of characters
desired

Note: If *expr$* has less than *num* characters, LEFT$
supplies all of *expr$*.

Sample call:

```
firstchar$ = LEFT$(instr$, 1)
```

Besides picking off the first character of a string, another
common use of LEFT$ is to limit strings in table output. For
example, if you want to output a table of names and addresses,
you can keep the table neat by limiting the size of a string:

```
FOR count% = 1 to numnames%
    PRINT LEFT$(fullname$(count%), 29);
    PRINT TAB(31); address$(count%)
NEXT count%
```

This loop will create a table where only the first 29 characters of
each name are displayed. This keeps longer names from either
running into the addresses or forcing the address to print on the
next line.

The RIGHT$ Function

If you want only the last part of a string, you can use the
RIGHT$ function.

RIGHT$(expr$, num)   **function**

Purpose: Supplies the last *num* characters of a string

Return type: STRING

Parameters: expr$ [STRING]—the string expression
num [INTEGER]—the number of characters
desired

Note: If *expr$* has less than *num* characters, RIGHT$ returns all of *expr$*.

Sample call:

```
lastchar$ = RIGHT$(instr$, 1)
```

You might use the RIGHT$ function when you are checking for special characters from the INKEY$ function described in Chapter 7. This program fragment determines if the user pressed the HOME key:

```
DO
    inchar$ = INKEY$
LOOP UNTIL inchar$ <> ""
IF LEFT$(inchar$, 1) = CHR$(0) THEN
    scancode$ = RIGHT$(inchar$, 1)
    IF scancode$ = CHR$(71) THEN
        PRINT "You pressed the HOME key."
    END IF
END IF
```

The DO loop repeats until the user presses a key. If the key is a special character, INKEY$ returns a 2-character string. The first character is CHR$(0) and the second is the scan code of the key. The RIGHT$ function isolates this second character.

The MID$ Function

If you need a substring from the middle of a string, you will need the MID$ function.

MID$(expr$, start, num)   **function**

Purpose: Supplies *num* characters of a string, starting at a particular position in that string

Return type: STRING

Parameters: expr$ [STRING]—the string expression

start [INTEGER]—the location of the first character to extract

num [INTEGER]—the number of characters desired

Note: If *num* is omitted, MID$ returns all characters to the right of *start*.

Sample call:

```
substr$ = MID$(inputstring$, 3, 1)
```

This statement isolates the third character of the input string. If the input string is shorter than three characters, *substr$* will become the null string.

The MID$ function also supplies a substring that includes all characters to the right of a certain position. To make sure you get all the characters, omit the third parameter. Then the statement

```
shortstr$ = MID$("This is a long string.", 16)
```

will assign the substring "string." to *shortstr$*. This form of the MID$ function takes all characters starting with the *n*th position. Contrast this with the RIGHT$ function, which takes the last *n* characters of the string.

The LEN Function

Often, you will want to examine every character in a string. To make sure that you do not miss any characters, you can use the LEN function to determine the current length of the string.

LEN(expr$)   **function**

Purpose: Determines the length of a string
Return type: INTEGER

Parameter: expr$ [STRING]—the string to check

Note: There is also a LEN function for variable sizes (see Chapter 11).

Sample call:

```
numspaces% = 0
FOR count% = 1 TO LEN(mystr$)
   onechar$ = MID$(mystr$, count%, 1)
   IF onechar$ = " " THEN
      numspaces% = numspaces% + 1
   END IF
NEXT count%
```

This sample shows how you can use the MID$ and LEN functions to examine every character of a string. The loop counts the number of spaces in a string.

The MID$ Statement

QuickBASIC also provides a MID$ statement, which changes only part of a string.

MID$ **statement**

Syntax: MID$ (*stringvar, startpos, length*) = *expression*

Purpose: Replaces one substring with another

Note: If the *length* parameter is omitted, the entire source string is used; the length of the destination string will never change.

Sample use:

```
MID$(deststr$, 6, 4) = sourcestr$
```

The arguments to the MID$ statement are the same as those of the MID$ function. The string on the left side of the equal sign is the *destination substring;* the string on the right side is the *source string.* The MID$ statement takes the characters in the source string and replaces them one-for-one into the destination string. In the sample statement just discussed, the first character in *sourcestr$* will go into the sixth character in *deststr$.* The second character in *sourcestr$* will replace the seventh character in *deststr$.* This process will continue four times (as specified by the third parameter) or until the end of either string is reached, whichever happens first.

You cannot use the MID$ statement to insert a string, or to replace substrings of different lengths. For example, to replace the word "simple" with the word "good" in the sentence

```
wrong$ = "This is a simple example."
```

the MID$ statement

```
MID$(wrong$, 11, 6) = "good"
```

would give you this sentence:

```
This is a goodle example.
```

The easiest way to do this particular replacement properly is to break the string into pieces and recreate it. Examine these statements:

```
ok$ = "This is a simple example."
ok$ = LEFT$(ok$, 10) + "good" + MID$(ok$, 17)
```

The second statement takes the first ten characters of the string, then adds the new word, and finally adds all characters starting with the seventeenth.

The INSTR Function

In the previous example, a substring was replaced with another substring by counting to a specific location in the source string. If you do not know the location of the unwanted substring, you need the INSTR function.

INSTR(pos, bigstr$, substr$)   **function**

Purpose: Determines the first occurrence of a substring within another string

Return type: INTEGER

Parameters: pos [INTEGER]—the first position to check

   bigstr$ [STRING]—the string to search

   substr$ [STRING]—the substring for which you are searching

Note: If the substring is not found, INSTR returns 0;
   if *pos* is omitted, INSTR searches from the first character.

Sample call:

```
ok$ = "This is a simple example."
strloc% = INSTR(ok$, "simple")
ok$ = LEFT$(ok$, strloc%-1) + "good" +
MID$(ok$, strloc%+6)
```

This sample shows how to make a replacement without having to count the characters in the large string. In the second statement, INSTR will return the first occurrence of "simple", in this case 11. After the third statement, *ok$* will contain all characters to the left of the substring position, the new substring, and all characters to the right of the unwanted substring.

The following subprogram is a generic replace routine. It replaces the first occurrence of a particular substring with another string.

```
SUB StrReplace (start%, bigstr$, oldstr$, newstr$, ok%)

',',',',',',',',',',',',',',',',',',',',',',',',',',',',',','
'    StrReplace: this subroutine replaces    '
'    the first occurrence of one substring    '
'    with another. The original string is    '
'    bigstr$, and it becomes the new string.  '
'    start% is the first position to look     '
'    for the substring. If found, the         '
'    string oldstr$ will be replaced by the   '
'    string newstr$. If the oldstr$ is not    '
'    found in bigstr$, ok% will be set to     '
'    false (0). Otherwise, ok% will be set    '
'    to the position where oldstr$ was        '
'    found.                                   '
',',',',',',',',',',',',',',',',',',',',',',',',',',',',',','

'    search for the original substring
ok% = INSTR(start%, bigstr$, oldstr$)

'    if found, replace it
IF ok% THEN
    leftstr$ = LEFT$(bigstr$, ok% - 1)
    rightstr$ = MID$(bigstr$, ok% + LEN(oldstr$))

    '    use all characters left of the old string,
    '    the new string, and all characters to the
    '    right of the entire old string
    bigstr$ = leftstr$ + newstr$ + rightstr$
END IF

END SUB
```

The *StrReplace* routine can be called in a loop to replace all occurrences of one substring with another:

```
two$ = "This is a simple example of a simple concept."
start% = 1
DO
    CALL StrReplace (start%, two$, "simple", "good", ok%)
    IF ok% THEN
        start% = ok% + LEN("good")
    END IF
LOOP WHILE ok%
```

In this example, you want to replace every "simple" with "good". After the first call to *StrReplace*, the first "simple" will be "good", and *ok%* will be set to 11, the location of the old substring. The variable *start%* will then be set to 15, the new position to start checking. *StrReplace* will be called again, and this time *ok%* will become 29 and *start%* will become 33. On the third call the substring "simple" no longer exists, so *ok%* is set to 0, and the loop ends.

Comparing Strings

One of the most common operations on a series of strings is to place them in alphabetical order. In QuickBASIC, you use relational operators to compare two string expressions. When QuickBASIC executes the statement

```
IF firststr$ > secondstr$ THEN
```

it follows this sequence of rules:

1. If the first characters of both strings are different, QuickBASIC evaluates the condition based on the ASCII codes of those characters.

2. If the first character of each string is the same, QuickBASIC will examine the second character of each string. If these are different, it will evaluate the condition based on those characters.

3. This process will continue through both strings until a difference is found.

4. If all the characters of the two strings are the same, but one string is shorter than the other, the shorter string is considered less than the longer one.

5. If all the characters in the two strings are the same, and they have the same length, QuickBASIC considers the strings equal.

The UCASE$ and LCASE$ Functions

In the ASCII code system, lowercase letters have larger values than uppercase letters. Because of this, the string "BZ" is less than the string "Ba". Often, when putting strings in alphabetical order you want to ignore this subtlety. To make the case of two strings the same (even if only temporarily), you can use the UCASE$ or LCASE$ functions.

The UCASE$ function converts an entire string from lowercase to uppercase.

UCASE$(expr$)   **function**

Purpose: Changes all lowercase letters in a string to their uppercase equivalents

Return type: STRING

Parameter: expr$ [STRING]—the string to convert

Sample call:

```
IF UCASE$(firststr$) > UCASE$(secondstr$) THEN
```

The counterpart of UCASE$ is LCASE$, which converts an entire string to lowercase.

LCASE$(expr$)   **function**

Purpose: Changes all uppercase letters in a string to their lowercase equivalents

Return type: STRING

Parameter: expr$ [STRING] — the string to convert

Sample call:

```
IF LCASE$(firststr$) > LCASE$(secondstr$) THEN
```

Both of these samples are valid ways of comparing strings without being concerned with the case of each character.

These functions are also useful when you are checking user input. For example, the fragment

```
    INPUT "Would you like to play again"; again$
LOOP WHILE again$ = "Y"
```

allows users to play again only if they enter the capital letter "Y". To allow for small letters too, you can use the UCASE$ function:

```
    INPUT "Would you like to play again"; again$
LOOP WHILE UCASE$(again$) = "Y"
```

Now suppose a user enters the entire word "yes". To handle this, you could check only the first character of the input:

```
    INPUT "Would you like to play again"; again$
LOOP WHILE LEFT$(UCASE$(again$),1) = "Y"
```

Although this statement looks somewhat complicated, it makes the input much more idiot-proof.

The LTRIM$ and RTRIM$ Functions

Spaces in strings tend to create seemingly false comparisons of strings. For example, the string "abc " is greater than the string "abc", and the string " abc" is less than "abc". If you want to ignore leading or trailing blanks, you need the LTRIM$ or RTRIM$ functions.

The LTRIM$ function eliminates the spaces at the front of a string.

LTRIM$(expr$) function

Purpose: Trims any leading spaces from a string expression
Return type: STRING
Parameter: expr$ [STRING]—the string to trim
Sample call:

```
nolead$ = LTRIM$(anystr$)
```

The RTRIM$ function eliminates any spaces at the end of a string.

RTRIM$(expr$) function

Purpose: Trims any trailing spaces from a string expression
Return type: STRING
Parameter: expr$ [STRING]—the string to trim

Sample call:

```
notrail$ = RTRIM$(fixedstr)
```

You can combine the effects of LTRIM$, RTRIM$, and UCASE$ to do a more standard string comparison:

```
tempfirst$ = UCASE$(LTRIM$(RTRIM$(firststr$)))
tempsecond$ = UCASE$(LTRIM$(RTRIM$(secondstr$)))
IF tempfirst$ > tempsecond$ THEN
    PRINT "The first comes after the second"
ELSE
    PRINT "The first comes before the second"
END IF
```

Whether you do a strict comparison, or a comparison ignoring case or leading or trailing blanks, will depend on your particular application.

When you do string comparisons, knowing which string comes first in alphabetical order is often not enough information. You may also want to know which position makes the difference. QuickBASIC does not provide a routine to do this, but it does provide all the tools to create such a routine. The following function, *FirstDiff%*, returns an integer showing the position where two strings first differ:

```
FUNCTION FirstDiff% (str1$, str2$)

',','','','','','','','','','','','','','','','','','','','','
'     FirstDiff%:  this function determines   '
'     the position where two strings differ.  '
'     If the two strings are the same, it     '
'     returns 0, similar to INSTR.  If the     '
'     strings are the same except one is       '
'     longer than the other, it returns the    '
'     position that exceeds the length of      '
'     the smaller string.                       '
',','','','','','','','','','','','','','','','','','','','','
'     if the strings are the same, return 0
```

```
IF str1$ = str2$ THEN
   FirstDiff% = 0

'     otherwise, figure out where they differ
ELSE
   tempdiff% = 0
   strpos% = 1

   '    loop through each character until
   '    the difference is found
   DO

      '     isolate one character from each
      char1$ = MID$(str1$, strpos%, 1)
      char2$ = MID$(str2$, strpos%, 1)

      '     if at the end of either string,
      '     the difference is here
      IF char1$ = "" OR char2$ = "" THEN
         tempdiff% = strpos%

      '      if these characters are different,
      '      the difference is here
      ELSEIF char1$ <> char2$ THEN
         tempdiff% = strpos%
      END IF
      strpos% = strpos% + 1

      '     loop until the difference is found
   LOOP WHILE tempdiff% = 0
   FirstDiff% = tempdiff%
END IF

END FUNCTION
```

Notice that this routine compares the strings exactly as you supply them. If you need to ignore the case of the letters, use the function in a call like this:

```
diff% = FirstDiff%(UCASE$(strone$), UCASE$(strtwo$))
```

If you also want to ignore leading or trailing blanks, call *FirstDiff%* with strings that you have converted already:

```
temp1$ = UCASE$(LTRIM$(RTRIM$(firststr$)))
temp2$ = UCASE$(LTRIM$(RTRIM$(secondstr$)))
diff% = FirstDiff%(temp1$, temp2$)
```

String Conversion

For many applications you will need to convert numbers from numeric form to string form and vice versa. Chapter 5 covered the CHR$ and ASC functions, which convert single characters to their ASCII equivalents and back. With these functions, you could write your own routines to convert numbers to strings and vice versa. Fortunately, QuickBASIC already includes functions for this purpose as part of the language.

The STR$ Function

To assign a number to a string variable, QuickBASIC provides the STR$ function.

STR$(expr)   **function**

Purpose: Converts a numeric expression to a string

Return type: STRING

Parameter: expr [any numeric type] — the expression to convert

Sample call:

```
zipcode$ = STR$(60609)
```

The way in which QuickBASIC converts a number to a string is similar to the way in which it displays numbers with a PRINT statement. If the number is accurate to 15 places, the string will include all 15 places. For numbers of type INTEGER or LONG, this is exactly what you want. For SINGLE or DOUBLE numbers, you may choose to round off the number to a particular number of digits before using STR$.

The VAL Function

If a string contains a number, you must convert the string to its numeric equivalent before you can use it in calculations. This is done with the VAL function.

VAL(expr$) function

Purpose: Converts a string expression to a number

Return type: Dependent on the expression

Parameter: expr$ [STRING]—the expression to convert

Note: If the first nonblank character is invalid, VAL returns 0.

Sample call:

```
areacode% = VAL(LEFT$(phonenum$, 3))
```

This sample uses the VAL function and the LEFT$ function to isolate the area code and convert it to an INTEGER.

Miscellaneous Functions and Statements

This section contains two functions and two statements that fall into the miscellaneous category. The STRING$ and SPACE$ functions create strings of repeated characters, and the RSET and LSET statements right- and left-justify fixed-length strings.

The STRING$ Function

With the STRING$ function you can easily define certain strings that repeat a character.

STRING$ (len, expr)   **function**

Purpose: Creates a string that repeats a given character a
certain number of times

Return type: STRING

Parameters: len [INTEGER]—the length of the string to
create

expr [STRING or INTEGER]—the character to
repeat or its ASCII equivalent

Sample call:

```
splats$ = STRING$(40, '*')
```

In this sample, the STRING$ function creates a string that
contains 40 asterisks. This string is assigned to the variable
splats$. An equivalent statement would be

```
splats$ = "****************************************"
```

As you can see, the STRING$ function saves you from having to
count out the 40 asterisks. If the character you want to repeat is
not on the keyboard, you can use the character's numeric ASCII
equivalent.

The SPACE$ Function

If you need to create a string that contains a specific number of
spaces, you can use the SPACE$ function.

SPACE$(len)   **function**

Purpose: Creates a string that repeats the space character
a certain number of times

Return type: STRING

Parameter: len [INTEGER] — the length of the string to create

Sample call:

```
PRINT SPACE$(20); "Hi"
```

The SPACE$ function is actually a special case of the STRING$ function. In fact, all four of these statements

```
PRINT "                    "; "Hi"
PRINT SPC(20); "Hi"
PRINT SPACE$(20); "Hi"
PRINT STRING$(20, " "); "Hi"
```

do exactly the same thing: they print out twenty spaces followed by the word "Hi". Use whichever form you prefer.

The RSET Statement

Fixed-length strings are primarily for use in record structures, which are covered in Chapter 9. These strings always have the same length so that the size of a record remains fixed. Suppose you define a record called "address" that contains a 5-character, fixed-length string named *zipcode*. No matter what INPUT or LET statements assign new values to *zipcode*, the variable will always be five characters. If a user inputs less than five characters, QuickBASIC will pad the string with spaces.

If you need to pad spaces at the front of a fixed-length string instead of the back, use the RSET statement.

RSET statement

Syntax: RSET *stringvariable* = *expression*

Purpose: Right-justifies a string inside a fixed-length string

Sample use:

```
DIM testscore AS STRING * 4
RSET testscore = STR$(score%)
```

The DIM statement in this sample defines a 4-character, fixed-length string. If you want to store or display scores that are right-justified, one way to accomplish this is with the RSET statement. If *score%* is 95, *testscore* will become " 95".

The LSET Statement

The LSET statement left-justifies fixed-length strings. Since QuickBASIC does this automatically, this statement exists primarily for compatibility.

LSET   **statement**

Syntax: LSET *stringvariable = expression*

Purpose: Left-justifies a string inside a fixed-length string

Sample use:

```
DIM longzip AS STRING * 9
DIM shortzip AS STRING * 5
shortzip = "34301"
LSET longzip = shortzip
```

This program fragment illustrates one of the few remaining uses for the LSET statement. Since *longzip* and *shortzip* are not type-compatible, the statement

```
longzip = shortzip
```

would create a "Type Mismatch" error. LSET remedies this by
left-justifying the shorter string within the longer one.

Strings and I/O

This chapter has described the various QuickBASIC string-
manipulation statements and functions. This section provides an
application that uses most of these routines to help you determine which string routines you will need to satisfy your particular applications.

In Chapter 7, you learned that the INPUT statement allows
you to get a value for a string or numeric variable. When you
use an INPUT statement, however, QuickBASIC will allow a
user to enter more characters than you want to accept. If you
have a screen that displays a mailing address for making labels,
you want to keep users from entering names or addresses that
are longer than the labels. You could use an INKEY$ loop, but
then the user could not use the INPUT statement editing
commands.

The solution to this dilemma is to write your own input
routine. The *GetInput* routine looks long and complicated, but if
you break it up into its logical pieces, you will understand how it
works. Examine the routine thoroughly before reading about
what it does and how it works.

```
SUB GetInput (instr$, maxlen%)

    ',',',',',',',',',',',',',',',',',',',',',',','
    '    GetInput:  this subroutine allows   '
    '    the user to enter a string, but     '
    '    limits the length of the string.    '
    '    Most cursor movement commands are   '
    '    handled.  The cursor is imitated    '
    '    by highlighting the current posi-   '
    '    tion in red and blinking the text.  '
    '    The available string length is      '
    '    shown in blue.                      '
    ',',',',',',',',',',',',',',',',',',',',',',','
```

```
CONST insert% = 1, overstrike% = 2

'     make required initializations
firstcol% = POS(0)
insertmode% = overstrike%
curpos% = 1

'     display available length with a blue box
PRINT instr$;
COLOR , 1
PRINT SPACE$(maxlen% - LEN(instr$));
LOCATE , firstcol%

'     blink cursor
COLOR 23, 12
IF LEN(instr$) = 0 THEN
    PRINT " "; CHR$(29);
ELSE
    PRINT LEFT$(instr$, 1); CHR$(29);
END IF
COLOR 7, 0

'     get first character
DO
    onechar$ = INKEY$
LOOP WHILE onechar$ = ""

'     process characters one at a time
DO UNTIL onechar$ = CHR$(13)

    '     de-highlight current character
    IF curpos% > maxlen% THEN
        PRINT " "; CHR$(29);
    ELSEIF curpos% > LEN(instr$) THEN
        COLOR , 1
        PRINT " "; CHR$(29);
        COLOR , 0
    ELSE
        PRINT MID$(instr$, curpos%, 1); CHR$(29);
    END IF

    '     check for special characters
    IF LEFT$(onechar$, 1) = CHR$(0) THEN

        '     check for <RIGHT>
        IF RIGHT$(onechar$, 1) = CHR$(77) THEN

            '     if before last character, move right one
            IF curpos% <= LEN(instr$) THEN
                curpos% = curpos% + 1
            END IF

            '     check for <LEFT>
        ELSEIF RIGHT$(onechar$, 1) = CHR$(75) THEN
```

```
      '      if past first character, move left one
      IF curpos% > 1 THEN
         curpos% = curpos% - 1
      END IF

   '     check for <DEL>
   ELSEIF RIGHT$(onechar$, 1) = CHR$(83) THEN

      '      if before last character, remove one
      IF curpos% <= LEN(instr$) THEN
         instr$ = LEFT$(instr$, curpos% - 1) + _
                     MID$(instr$, curpos% + 1)
         PRINT MID$(instr$, curpos%); " ";
      END IF

   '     check for <INS>
   ELSEIF RIGHT$(onechar$, 1) = CHR$(82) THEN

      '     toggle insert mode
      IF insertmode% = overstrike% THEN
         insertmode% = insert%
      ELSE
         insertmode% = overstrike%
      END IF

   END IF

'     check for <BACKSPACE>
ELSEIF onechar$ = CHR$(8) THEN

   '     if past first character, remove one
   IF curpos% > 1 THEN
      IF curpos% > LEN(instr$) THEN
         PRINT CHR$(29); " ";
      ELSE
         PRINT CHR$(29); MID$(instr$, curpos%); " ";
      END IF
      instr$ = LEFT$(instr$, curpos% - 2) + _
               MID$(instr$, curpos%)
      curpos% = curpos% - 1
   END IF

'     no special character, so check for overstrike mode
ELSEIF insertmode% = overstrike% THEN

   '     if overstrike, replace that character
   '     or add it to the end
   IF curpos% <= LEN(instr$) THEN
      MID$(instr$, curpos%, 1) = onechar$
      PRINT onechar$;
      curpos% = curpos% + 1
   ELSEIF curpos% <= maxlen% THEN
      instr$ = instr$ + onechar$
      PRINT onechar$;
      curpos% = curpos% + 1
   ELSE
```

```
        BEEP
    END IF

'       insert mode must be in insert
ELSEIF curpos% <= maxlen% THEN

    '       insert character, move rest of string over
    instr$ = LEFT$(instr$, curpos% - 1) + onechar$ + _
                    MID$(instr$, curpos%)
    PRINT MID$(instr$, curpos%);
    curpos% = curpos% + 1
ELSE
    BEEP
END IF

'       highlight cursor position
COLOR 23, 12
LOCATE , firstcol% + curpos% - 1
IF curpos% > LEN(instr$) THEN
    PRINT " "; CHR$(29);
ELSE
    PRINT MID$(instr$, curpos%, 1); CHR$(29);
END IF
COLOR 7, 0

'       get another character
DO
    onechar$ = INKEY$
LOOP WHILE onechar$ = ""

LOOP

'   redisplay string without length display
LOCATE , firstcol%
PRINT instr$; SPACE$(maxlen% - LEN(instr$))

END SUB
```

The following fragment is a sample of how to call the *GetInput* routine:

```
PRINT "Enter your zip code: ";
CALL GetInput (zipcode$, 5)
```

This fragment displays a prompt and allows the user to enter up to five characters. The user input will be stored in the variable *zipcode$*.

When you first call the *GetInput* routine, it displays the current value of the string you want to change. There will be many times when the string will not have an initial value, so make sure that you blank it out before calling *GetInput* if you need to. The routine then creates a blue box that shows the user how large the string can be. A cursor is created by changing the background color of the current character and blinking the character. The user can then enter or change the string, using most of the editing commands available with the INPUT statement. When the user presses ENTER, the input is complete and the blue box disappears. If your screen is monochrome, you might display underscores to show the allowable length of the input.

Now that you know what the routine does, let's see how it works. The first task of the routine is to create the blue box. The maximum length of the input string, *maxlen%*, is passed as a parameter to *GetInput*. The routine changes the background color to blue, then prints one space for every character longer than the current length of the string, but shorter than or equal to the maximum length allowed. It uses the SPACE$ function to print the spaces, and the LEN function to determine the current length of the string.

The next task is to simulate a cursor, since INKEY$ does not include one. The routine changes the background color to red and the foreground color to blinking gray. If the current position is part of the string, the character at the "cursor" is highlighted in red. If the "cursor" is at the end of the string, the routine prints a space in red. CHR$(29) moves the actual cursor back one character to its original position. After the user presses a key, the routine dehighlights the current character by writing the character using gray on black.

Every time the user presses a key, that key is processed. It can be a printable character or a cursor-control character. The routine examines each character as it is input and processes it. The RIGHT ARROW, LEFT ARROW, DEL, INS, and BACKSPACE keys are all handled appropriately. These should be self-explanatory. In the DEL and BACKSPACE handlers, you can see a character deleted by using a combination of the LEFT$ function and the MID$ function. This is similar to the replace process discussed earlier in the chapter.

If no control characters were entered, the routine adds the character input to the string. Both the overstrike mode and the insert mode are handled. The overstrike handler needs only the MID$ statement to replace a character in the middle of the string. The insert handler must recreate the string to move the right part over. Both handlers beep if the user tries to enter a character past the maximum length of the string.

When the user presses ENTER, the routine displays the string to eliminate the red cursor, and it displays enough spaces to eliminate the blue box. Thus, the screen returns to all-grey on black.

NINE

Arrays and Records

Introduction to Arrays
Declaring and Using Arrays
Dynamic Arrays
Declaring and Using Records
Common Algorithms

Suppose that you have a list of ten names to alphabetize. If you could use only simple variables, you would have to use ten different string variables—for example, *student1$*, *student2$*, and so forth. The code to put these students in alphabetical order would be a nightmare. QuickBASIC simplifies this task with arrays. If you need to keep addresses or test scores along with the names, you can put all the information for one student in a record. This chapter shows you how QuickBASIC supports these versatile data structures.

Introduction to Arrays

If you have never used arrays, this section will help you understand what arrays do and how they work. If you are already familiar with arrays, skip to the next section.

When you use a simple variable in a program, like an INTEGER variable, QuickBASIC allocates a certain amount of memory to store the value of that variable. You can think of that memory location as a box:

mynum% | 6488 |

Every time you refer to the variable *mynum%*, the computer uses the value inside the box. If you needed a group of boxes together, you would use an array. An *array* is a group of values stored with a common variable name. With an array, you have the ability to refer to all the boxes at the same time, and to each individual box in the group.

Before you use an array you must define its name and its size. For example, if you needed an array for test scores for 20 students, you could declare the array with a DIM statement:

```
DIM scores%(1 TO 20)
```

This statement defines the variable *scores%* as an array with 20 memory boxes.

When you use an array, you must refer to the boxes one at a time. Each individual box is called an *element* of the array. To specify an array element, you use an array subscript. The *subscript*, or *index*, narrows down the array to a single element, pointing to the particular box on the stack you want. In QuickBASIC, subscripts are enclosed in parentheses. The first element of the test score array would be *scores%*(1). Figure 9-1 shows the array with the proper subscripts next to the memory boxes.

An array element will be a specific type, so QuickBASIC will treat it like a simple variable. You cannot assign a value to an entire array, such as

```
scores% = 100
```

but you can assign a value to an array element:

```
scores%(10) = 100
```

Similarly, you cannot use just the array name in a PRINT statement—you must print the elements one at a time.

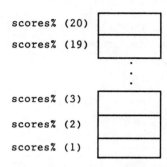

Figure 9-1.   Array subscripts for *scores%*

The most common way to assign values to array elements is with a FOR-NEXT loop. Consider this program fragment:

```
PRINT "Please enter the twenty scores."
FOR count% = 1 TO 20
   PRINT "Score"; count%;
   INPUT scores%(count%)
NEXT count%
```

In this loop, the user enters the 20 values one at a time. As the user enters a value, the INPUT statement places it immediately into an element of the array. At the end of the loop, each memory box will contain a value.

Now that you are familiar with the concepts and terms of arrays, study the rest of this chapter for details on declaring and using them.

Declaring and Using Arrays

An array is a group of values stored with a common variable name. Each element of an array must have the same type. This section will cover how to declare and use arrays and will point out some of their limitations.

The DIM Statement

In a few cases you can use an array variable without declaring it first. However, you are far better off always declaring arrays with the DIM statement.

DIM   **statement**

Syntax: DIM [SHARED] *variabledesc* [, *variabledesc*]. . .
where *variabledesc* = >
    variable [(*subscriptrange*)] [AS *type*]
where *subscriptrange* = >
    [lbound TO] ubound [, [lbound TO] ubound]. . .

Purpose: Declares the name and size of an array variable
Sample use:

```
DIM student$(1 TO 10)
```

DIM statements should precede all executable statements (like LET statements, loops, and subroutine calls). You must declare an array before you use it. If you attempt to place a DIM statement after a statement that uses that array, an "Array already dimensioned" error will result.

The optional word SHARED allows you to use the same array in all procedures and functions within the module. This concept is covered in detail in Chapter 10. If you want to declare an array to be of a specific type, use the AS clause:

```
DIM Student(1 TO 10) AS STRING * 30
```

This clause is primarily used for fixed-length strings and records. For simple types use the proper type suffix.

The *subscript range* is the number or numbers inside the parentheses that determine the bounds of the array. The first number is the lower bound and the second is the upper bound. You compute the total number of elements in the array with this equation:

$$\text{number of elements} = \text{upper bound} - \text{lower bound} + 1$$

QuickBASIC limits the available subscripts to INTEGER numbers, or numbers from −32,768 to 32,767. The lower bound is optional in the DIM statement and defaults to 0 unless you have an OPTION BASE statement (which will be covered later).

When you declare an array with a DIM statement, Quick-BASIC automatically initializes the array elements. Numeric arrays will contain all zeros, and string arrays will have null strings (""). You can reset an array to these values anywhere in your program with the ERASE statement, discussed later in this chapter.

Array Indices

Many programmers always declare arrays with a lower bound of 0 or 1. One key to becoming a better programmer is to use more meaningful array indices. For example, consider a program that counts the frequency of each alphabet letter in a string. The amateur programmer would declare this array:

```
DIM frequency%(1 TO 26)
```

At first this makes good sense since there are 26 letters in the alphabet. When you consider how the program will be implemented, however, you might change the indices to reflect the ASCII codes of the letters:

```
DIM frequency%(65 TO 90)
```

This subtle change can make a big difference in the final product. Here is the program fragment:

```
'         count values for each letter
FOR count% = 1 TO LEN(instr$)
   onechar% = ASC(UPCASE$(MID$(instr$, count%, 1)))
   IF onechar% >= 65 AND onechar% <= 90 THEN
      frequency%(onechar%) = frequency%(onechar%) + 1
   END IF
NEXT count%

'         print out occurences if > 0
FOR letter% = 65 TO 90
   IF frequency%(letter%) > 0 THEN
      PRINT "TOTAL FOR "; CHR$(letter%); ":";
      PRINT frequency%(letter%)
   END IF
NEXT letter%
```

If you rewrite this fragment using the first DIM statement, you will find yourself adding or subtracting 64 in every statement that uses the *frequency%* array.

In some applications, the actual size of an array used by the program varies with each user. For instance, a program that records grades for a class of 30 students could be declared with these statements:

```
DIM students$(1 TO 30)
DIM grades$(1 TO 30)
```

In this case, a fragment to print the names and grades would look like this:

```
FOR count% = 1 TO 30
   LPRINT students$(count%), grades$(count%)
NEXT count%
```

Think about what would happen if another user wanted to use the program, but had 35 students. You would have to change the number 30 to 35 everywhere in the program.

The solution to this situation was introduced in Chapter 5: symbolic constants. With a CONST declaration, the program is easier to maintain and easier to read. The revised declaration follows.

```
CONST numstud% = 30
DIM students$(1 TO numstud%)
DIM grades$(1 TO numstud%)
```

The print fragment is also changed slightly:

```
FOR count% = 1 TO numstud%
   LPRINT students$(count%), grades$(count%)
NEXT count%
```

As you can see, this second set of statements helps to identify the number of times the loop will execute—instead of a mystical number like 30, the upper bound is the number of students in the class.

Array Dimensions

The word *DIM* is short for *dimension.* In the physical world there are three dimensions: length, width, and height. For arrays, the dimension is the number of subscripts you must supply to specify an array element. All the arrays you have seen so far in this chapter have been one-dimensional. Just as you describe the size of a line with one number, so these arrays need only one subscript. A sheet of paper, on the other hand, is described with two numbers, such as 9 by 12. Likewise, a two-dimensional array requires two subscripts.

Suppose you want to write a program that uses a checkerboard. To model the board, you could use this declaration:

```
DIM board% (1 to 8, 1 to 8)
```

Each subscript range defines one dimension of the array. In this example the first subscript might represent the rows of the board, and the second the columns. Figure 9-2 shows the subscripts you need to access each element of the array (each square on the board).

```
board%
```

(1,1)	(2,1)	(3,1)	(4,1)	(5,1)	(6,1)	(7,1)	(8,1)
(1,2)	(2,2)	(3,2)	(4,2)	(5,2)	(6,2)	(7,2)	(8,2)
(1,3)	(2,3)	(3,3)	(4,3)	(5,3)	(6,3)	(7,3)	(8,3)
(1,4)	(2,4)	(3,4)	(4,4)	(5,4)	(6,4)	(7,4)	(8,4)
(1,5)	(2,5)	(3,5)	(4,5)	(5,5)	(6,5)	(7,5)	(8,5)
(1,6)	(2,6)	(3,6)	(4,6)	(5,6)	(6,6)	(7,6)	(8,6)
(1,7)	(2,7)	(3,7)	(4,7)	(5,7)	(6,7)	(7,7)	(8,7)
(1,8)	(2,8)	(3,8)	(4,8)	(5,8)	(6,8)	(7,8)	(8,8)

Figure 9-2.   Array subscripts for *board%*

In QuickBASIC an array can have up to 60 dimensions. However, arrays that are more than three or four dimensions are difficult to visualize and quickly become confusing. For example, visualize a program that keeps track of league bowling scores. The program would monitor eight leagues at once. Each league is broken into 20 or fewer teams, and each team has four or five bowlers. The bowling season last for 12 weeks, and every bowler bowls three games each week. To keep track of every game in a single array you need five dimensions:

```
DIM score% (1 TO 8, 1 TO 20, 1 TO 5, 1 TO 12, 1 TO 3)
```

You could think of this array as "(league, team, player, week, game)".

Using this large array would be very complicated. If people wanted to know how they did on a certain night, they would face this interrogation:

```
INPUT "League number" ; league%
INPUT "Team number"; team%
INPUT "Bowler number"; bowler%
```

```
INPUT "Week number"; week%
PRINT "On that week, that player bowled ";
PRINT score%(league%, team%, bowler%, week%, 1); ",";
PRINT score%(league%, team%, bowler%, week%, 2); ", and";
PRINT score%(league%, team%, bowler%, week%, 3);
```

As an exercise, you might try writing a subprogram that computes any team's average. By then you will realize how cumbersome this data structure is. You will find a more effective data structure later in this chapter.

Parallel Arrays

In many array applications, you will use several arrays at the same time that can use the same indices. For example, a database of address information could use these arrays:

```
CONST numpeople% = 200
DIM lastname$(1 TO numpeople%)
DIM firstname$(1 TO numpeople%)
DIM address$(1 TO numpeople%)
DIM city$(1 TO numpeople)
DIM state$(1 TO numpeople%)
DIM zipcode$(1 TO numpeople%)
```

Although there are six separate arrays, they all have corresponding indices. These are called *parallel arrays*. In parallel arrays, each element in one array relates to the same element in another array. In other words, this means that each array is ordered the same way.

The advantage of parallel arrays is that you can use the same control variable to access corresponding array elements. With the preceding declarations, you could use this program fragment to print labels on the printer:

```
FOR count% = 1 TO numpeople%
   LPRINT firstname$(count%); " "; lastname$(count%)
   LPRINT address$(count%)
```

```
   LPRINT city$(count%); ", "; state$(count%);
   LPRINT zipcode$(count%)
   LPRINT : LPRINT : LPRINT
NEXT count%
```

The only added complication with parallel arrays becomes evident when you attempt to sort the arrays, as you will see in the common algorithms section of this chapter.

The OPTION BASE Statement

The OPTION BASE statement changes the default lower bound for all array declarations.

OPTION BASE   **statement**

Syntax: OPTION BASE {0 | 1}

Purpose: Changes the default array lower bound

Note: This statement can be used only in module-level code.

Sample use:

OPTION BASE 1

This statement can be used only once in a program, and it must be placed before any DIM statements. Since the default lower bound is 0, the OPTION BASE 0 is meaningless. Your programs will be more readable if you specify the lower bound of each array you declare, instead of using OPTION BASE.

Dynamic Arrays

Normally, when the QuickBASIC compiler encounters a DIM statement it allocates enough memory space to hold all of the array elements. Since this amount of memory will not change anytime during program execution, the array is *static*. Static arrays are allocated at compilation time. In other words, the proper amount of memory for the array is laid aside before the program begins executing. If you need to be able to change the size of an array while the program is running, you need to use a *dynamic* array. The memory space for a dynamic array is allocated when QuickBASIC reaches the DIM statement during program execution.

There are two primary reasons for using dynamic arrays. The first is to make more efficient use of memory space. With a dynamic array you can declare an array to allocate the memory, use the array, then free the memory space taken by the array for other uses.

The second reason is to allow for larger arrays. Static arrays are limited in total size to 64K of memory (65,536 bytes). This means that an INTEGER array can only have 16K (16,384 elements), since each integer uses 4 bytes. For some applications this is not enough space. By making an array dynamic, you allow the array to be larger than 64K.

Before you can allocate a large dynamic array, you must invoke QuickBASIC with the /ah command option. This option is a signal to the compiler that you might have arrays larger than 64K. Internally, this tells the compiler to move dynamic arrays to a different location in memory. You need not concern yourself with the details on how QuickBASIC implements this—it has essentially no effect on program size or execution speed. If you have neglected to use /ah in the QB or BC command line, you will get a "subscript out of range" error. Without this option, dynamic arrays are also subject to the 64K limit.

The $DYNAMIC Metacommand

Before you can declare a dynamic array, you must include the $DYNAMIC metacommand.

$DYNAMIC metacommand

Syntax: {' | REM} $DYNAMIC
Purpose: Makes future DIM statements declare dynamic arrays
Sample use:

```
' $DYNAMIC
DIM myarray!(1 TO 1000)
```

A *metacommand* is a statement that is not part of the QuickBASIC language, but has special meaning to the compiler. The metacommand is actually hidden in a comment line. You must have at least one space between the comment indicator (' or REM) and the dollar sign. Also, be careful to spell the metacommand correctly. The compiler will not return an error if there is a wrong word in a metacommand.

To create a dynamic array, you need the $DYNAMIC metacommand followed by a DIM statement. Once declared, the dynamic array works exactly like a static array. Use the same rules for arrays that were discussed in the previous section.

The ERASE Statement

When you are finished using a dynamic array, you can eliminate it with the ERASE statement.

ERASE statement

Syntax: ERASE *variable* [, *variable*]. . .
Purpose: Frees memory allocated to dynamic arrays, or reinitializes static arrays

---

Sample use:

```
'  $DYNAMIC
DIM names$(1 TO 500)
CALL LoadArray (names$())
CALL SortArray (names$())
CALL StoreArray (names$())
ERASE names$
```

In this group of statements the array *names* is in memory only as long as it is needed. After the program stores the array on disk, the ERASE statement frees all the memory used by that array. If the array is static, the ERASE statement sets all values to 0 or null, depending on the element type.

The REDIM Statement

If you want to use a dynamic array more than once, you can change the size of the array with the REDIM statement.

REDIM   **statement**

Syntax: REDIM [SHARED] *variabledesc* [, *variabledesc*]. . .
    where *variabledesc* = >
        variable [(*subscriptrange*)] [AS   *type*]
    where *subscriptrange* = >
        [lbound TO] ubound [, [lbound TO] ubound]. . .

Purpose: Changes the size of a dynamic array

Note: You cannot change the number of dimensions with this statement.

Sample use:

```
' $DYNAMIC
INPUT "How many values"; arraysize%
REDIM uservals!(1 TO arraysize%)
```

Notice that with dynamic arrays, you can use variable names when defining the array subscripts.

One minor limitation of the REDIM statement is that you cannot change the number of dimensions of the array. Only the size can change. For instance, this fragment

```
' $DYNAMIC
DIM thisarray#(1 TO 9, 1 TO 15)
. . .
REDIM thisarray#(1 TO 145)
```

will produce an "Array already dimensioned" error.

The $STATIC Metacommand

To declare a static array after declaring a dynamic array, you need the $STATIC metacommand.

$STATIC   **metacommand**

Syntax: {' | REM} $STATIC
Purpose: Makes future DIM statements declare static arrays
Note: Arrays are declared static by default.

Sample use:

```
' $DYNAMIC
DIM first%(1 TO 1000)
' $STATIC
DIM second%(1 TO 1000)
```

In this program fragment, the array *first%* is a dynamic array and *second%* is a static array.

The LBOUND and UBOUND Functions

If you have a procedure that uses a dynamic array, the procedure may not know the dimensions of the array. To solve this problem, QuickBASIC includes the LBOUND and UBOUND functions. The LBOUND function returns the lower bound of the array.

LBOUND(arrayname, dimen)   **function**

Purpose: Supplies the lower bound of a given dimension for a particular array

Return type: INTEGER

Parameters: arrayname [any type]—the name of the array
                    dimen [INTEGER]—which dimension to check

Note: If *arrayname* is one-dimensional, the second parameter is optional.

Sample call:

```
FOR count% = LBOUND(myarray$) TO UBOUND(myarray$)
```

The UBOUND function is the counterpart to the LBOUND function, supplying the upper bound of a dimension of an array.

UBOUND(arrayname, dimen)   **function**

Purpose: Supplies the upper bound of a given dimension for a particular array
Return type: INTEGER
Parameters: arrayname [any type]—the name of the array
                      dimen [INTEGER]—which dimension to check
Note: If *arrayname* is one-dimensional, the second parameter is optional.
Sample call:

```
FOR count% = LBOUND(board%, 2) TO UBOUND(board%, 2)
```

The FOR statement under the LBOUND function shows the short form of the function call. If an array has one dimension you need only put the name of the array as a parameter. If the array is multidimensional, use the second parameter for the dimension you need.

The problem with using LBOUND and UBOUND is that too often you do not use all of the elements you declare. For example, suppose you write a program that keeps track of student names. Assuming that there will be no more than 50 students in a class, you declare this array:

```
DIM student$(1 TO 50)
```

For a class of 30 students, you could use the same array, but then store the number of students in a variable like *numstudents%*.

If you have a procedure sort that alphabetizes the array, the procedure needs to know the size of the array. If sort uses the UBOUND function, it will include 20 null strings in its sort. To avoid this, pass *numstudents%* as a parameter to the Sort function instead of using UBOUND.

Declaring and Using Records

If you have programmed with other implementations of BASIC for years but have never heard of records, do not be alarmed. Before QuickBASIC 4.0, records were available primarily in other languages like Pascal and C. These types are a long-awaited addition to BASIC.

A *record*, also called a *user-defined type*, is similar to an array, in that it is a collection of elements under a common name. Unlike arrays, however, record elements can have different types. You use a record whenever you want to group variables together. A common example is the date. A date is broken down into month, day, and year. Instead of using three separate variables to represent a single date, you can create a record that has these variables as record elements.

The TYPE-END TYPE Structure

To declare a record, you must first define the record type with a TYPE-END TYPE structure.

TYPE-END TYPE   **structure**

Syntax: TYPE *typename*
                variable AS *type*
                [*variable* AS *type*]. . .
            END TYPE

Purpose: Defines the name and elements of a record type

Sample use:

```
TYPE daterec
    month AS INTEGER
    day AS INTEGER
    year AS INTEGER
END TYPE
```

Inside the TYPE and END TYPE statements are one or more AS statements that define the elements of the record. Although an element name acts just like a variable name, you cannot use a type suffix in the element name. For instance, the statement

```
day% AS INTEGER
```

inside a TYPE-END TYPE structure will trigger an "identifier cannot end with %, &, !, #, or $" compiler error. Also, AS statements are invalid outside a TYPE-ENDTYPE structure.

A record element can be only of certain types. It can be a numeric type, a fixed-length string, or another record type. This means that you cannot have a variable-length string or an array as a record element. By restricting record elements to types that have a fixed number of bytes, the record becomes a perfect interface to random-access files (which will be covered in Chapter 11).

You cannot define a record type with a TYPE-END TYPE structure anywhere in a QuickBASIC program. You can use type definitions only in module-level code. In other words, you cannot have a TYPE-END TYPE structure inside a SUB or FUNCTION. You can declare records (with DIM statements) inside a subprogram, but you must have already defined its type in the main program.

Defining Record Variables

It is important to understand that the TYPE-END TYPE structure only defines a record type, not an actual record variable. Given the previous sample record definition, the *daterec* identifier cannot be used in the program as a variable name. Once you have declared a record type, you can then declare one or more record variables. You define record variables with a DIM statement:

```
DIM date AS daterec
```

The variable *date* is now a record variable. It has three elements: *month, day, and year.* In this particular record, all the elements are the same simple type, INTEGER. Often, elements will have different types.

Using Record Variables

As with arrays, you cannot use a record variable in a PRINT statement. You must work with each record element individually. To refer to a record element, use the record name, a period, and the element name. For example, these statements assign a value to each element of *date*:

```
date.month = 6
date.day   = 28
date.year  = 1961
```

With this syntax, you can use a record element in a QuickBASIC statement anywhere you could use a simple variable.

The exception to this rule is that with some statements you can replace one entire record with another. For example, if you have the declarations

```
DIM date1 AS daterec
DIM date2 AS daterec
```

then both of these statements are valid:

```
date1 = date2
SWAP date1, date2
```

However, any time you are doing input or output of records, you must do it one element at a time:

```
PRINT USING "##/##/##"; date1.month, date1.day, date1.year
```

Nested Records

There may be occasions when you want to have one record type as part of another. This process is called *nesting* records. Suppose you have a program that records bank transactions. A single transaction could be a record, like this:

```
TYPE transrec
    account AS LONG
    date AS daterec
    type AS STRING * 3
    amount AS DOUBLE
END TYPE
DIM trans AS transrec
```

To refer to an element in a nested record, you must use the first record name, the second record name, and the element name:

```
INPUT "Enter year:", trans.date.year
```

Arrays of Records

The real advantage of records comes in combining records with arrays. You studied parallel arrays earlier in this chapter. An array of records is similar to a set of parallel arrays in that the index of one part corresponds to the index of another. The advantage of the array of records is that all related data items are in the same data structure, and so are, easier to read. This greatly improves readability.

The discussion of parallel arrays included a personnel example. These arrays can be converted to this single array of records:

```
CONST numpeople% = 200
TYPE personnelrec
    lastname AS STRING * 30
    firstname AS STRING * 20
    address AS STRING * 50
    city AS STRING * 30
    state AS STRING * 2
    zipcode AS STRING * 5
END TYPE
DIM people(1 TO numpeople%) AS personnelrec
```

The type identifier in this DIM statement, *personnelrec,* is a
record type, thus creating an array of records.

As always, to use an array of records you must use each
element individually. Remember to use the array subscript before the record element name. For instance, the statement

```
people(3).lastname = "Sharp"
```

places the name "Sharp" in the *lastname* element of the third
record of the array. This fragment prints all records as labels:

```
FOR cnt% = 1 TO numpeople%
   LPRINT RTRIM$(people(cnt%).firstname); " ";
   LPRINT people(cnt%).lastname
   LPRINT people(cnt%).address
   LPRINT RTRIM$(people(cnt%).city); ", ";
   LPRINT people(cnt%).state; "    ";
   LPRINT people(cnt%).zipcode
   LPRINT : LPRINT : LPRINT
NEXT cnt%
```

The RTRIM$ function calls are included because record
elements that are strings are fixed-length. If you leave out the
RTRIM$ calls, you will have too many spaces between strings.

If you are a Pascal programmer looking for an equivalent to
the WITH statement, you will not find one. There are no short
forms for using record elements.

Common Algorithms

In this section you will find several algorithms that are frequently needed when using arrays. Naturally, you will need to
tailor these routines to fit your particular applications. In the
next chapter you will learn how to convert these routines into
more generic subroutines. All of the programs in this section use
the people array defined in the previous section.

Sequential Search

One of the most common algorithms with arrays is the *sequential search*. A search routine examines all the values of an array for a particular value. It starts with the first array element and checks one after another. If the value is not found, the routine must flag an error. If the value is found, the routine usually returns the index of the array where the value is located.

The following routine asks for a name to search. Then it searches the personnel array sequentially for the name. If it is found, the routine displays the rest of that record.

```
SUB SeqSearch

SHARED people1() AS personnelrec

    '     get the name to search
    INPUT "Enter name: ", desired$

    '     start with the first element
    check% = 1

    '     loop until the name is found or the entire list
    '     is checked
    found% = false%
    DO

        '     if this element is it, get out of the loop
        IF RTRIM$(people1(check%).lastname)=desired$ THEN
            found% = true%

        '     otherwise, get ready to check next element
        ELSE
            check% = check% + 1
        END IF
    LOOP UNTIL found% OR check% > numpeople%

    '     print out the entire found record, offsetting
    '     the desired information
    IF found% THEN
        PRINT "record found."
        PRINT people1(check%).lastname
        PRINT , people1(check%).firstname
        PRINT , people1(check%).address
        PRINT , people1(check%).city; ", ";
        PRINT people1(check%).state;
        PRINT " "; people1(check%).zipcode
    ELSE
        PRINT "record not found."
    END IF

END SUB
```

Binary Search

If you need to search a very large array, you will probably want to use a *binary search*. The prerequisite for a binary search is that the array must be sorted. In the binary search, the routine first examines the middle element of the array. If the desired value is greater than the element value, the routine can ignore the first half of the array. If the desired value is less than the element value, the routine eliminates the last half of the array. In the next iteration, the routine examines the middle value of the remaining half. This process will continue until the desired value can be found, or until the routine has narrowed down the search to one array element that does not match the desired value.

A common example of a binary search is the number-guessing game. Someone picks a number between 1 and 100 and asks you to guess it. You probably start with 50, halfway between 1 and 100. If 50 is too high, you know the right number will not be any number from 50 to 100. You would then guess 25, and continue to narrow the numbers down until you find the right one.

The advantage of the binary search comes in the number of comparisons it takes to search an array. If you have 100 array elements, a sequential search could make up to 100 comparisons, whereas the binary search will make a maximum of seven. For small arrays this will save you only fractions of a second, so you may choose to use the sequential search (especially if you would otherwise have to sort the array).

The next routine parallels the previous sequential search with a binary search:

```
SUB BinarySearch

SHARED people1() AS personnelrec

    '     get the name to search
    INPUT "Enter name: ", desired$

    '     make the entire list the first sublist
    low% = 1
    high% = numpeople%
```

```
'        loop until the name is found or there are no
'        more names to check
found% = false%
DO
'          check the middle element of the sublist
    check% = (high% + low%) \ 2

'          if name is found, stop!
    IF RTRIM$(peoplel(check%).lastname) = desired$ THEN
        found% = true%
'              if name checked is too high, eliminate the
'              top half of the sublist
    ELSEIF RTRIM$(peoplel(check%).lastname) > desired$ THEN
        high% = check% - 1

    ' if name checked is too low, eliminate the
    '        bottom half of the sublist
    ELSE
        low% = check% + 1
    END IF
'          high < low means the sublist has no elements
LOOP UNTIL found% OR high% < low%
'          print out the entire found record, offsetting
'          the desired information
IF found% THEN
    PRINT "record found."
    PRINT peoplel (check %).lastname
    PRINT , peoplel (check%).firstname
    PRINT , peoplel (check%). address
    PRINT , peoplel (check%) .city;";
    PRINT peoplel (check%) .state;
    PRINT " "; peoplel;peoplel (check%).zipcode
ELSE
    PRINT "record not found."
END IF
END SUB
```

Insertion Sort

Another common algorithm using arrays is the sort. There are
many different sort algorithms. A study of each one is a great
exercise in understanding algorithm development, but actually
has little practical value. After studying all those sort algorithms, you will find that you need only two: one for small arrays
and one for large arrays. For instance, there is only a slight
time difference between sorting a small array with a bubble sort
or an insertion sort.

The *insertion sort* is one of the best sorts for small arrays.
Unlike most other simple sort algorithms, the speed of the

insertion sort improves dramatically when you are sorting arrays that are already close to being in order. Conceptually, the insertion sort is similar to the way many people sort a hand of cards. They pick up the hand one card at a time, placing each card in the right spot in the hand.

Let's look at a specific example. The following list of names represents an array:

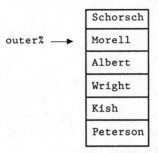

The *outer%* pointer starts at the second element of the array. At each iteration, *outer%* points to the element to be sorted. Everything before (above) the pointer is already in order.

In the first iteration, the first element moves down to the second position and the second element moves to the first position. Now the first two elements are in order:

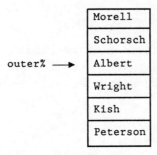

In the next iteration, *outer%* moves to the third element. The name "Albert" is saved temporarily, the first two names slide one position, and "Albert" becomes the new first element.

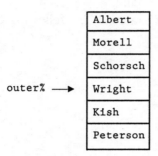

outer% ──▶

Albert
Morell
Schorsch
Wright
Kish
Peterson

In the third iteration, the first four elements are already in order, so the algorithm does nothing. In the fourth step, "Kish" moves to the second position after the second, third, and fourth elements slide down one:

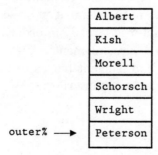

outer% ──▶

Albert
Kish
Morell
Schorsch
Wright
Peterson

Finally, "Peterson" finds its place in the fourth element after "Schorsch" and "Wright" move to the end of the array.

See if you can follow the logic in the actual algorithm:

```
SUB InsertSort

SHARED people1<> AS personnelrec
DIM temp AS personnelrec      'a temporary record
      '     the first element by itself is in order,
```

```
'      by definition
'      loop through the other elements
FOR outer% = 2 TO numpeople%

    '      preserve the current record
    temp = peoplel (outer%)

    '      start moving left
    inner% = outer% -1

    '      shift the records to the right until the
    '      current record is in its proper place
    DO WHILE temp.lastname < peoplel (inner%).lastname
        peoplel (inner% + 1) = peoplel (inner%)
        inner% = inner% - 1

        '      if the current record will be the new
        '      first record, get out of the loop
        IF inner% = 0 THEN EXIT DO
    LOOP

    '      restore the current record
    peoplel (inner% + 1) = temp

NEXT outer%
END SUB
```

If you had a set of parallel arrays instead of the array of records, you would have to replace each occurrence of the record with each array. Here is the same insertion sort using parallel arrays instead of the array of records. You can see how much more space and readability you have with records.

```
SUB InsertSortParallel

SHARED lastname$(), firstname$(), address$()
SHARED city$(), state$(), zipcode$()

    '      the first element by itself is sorted, by definition
    '      loop through the other elements
    FOR outer% = 2 TO numpeople%

        '      preserve the current elements
        templn$ = lastname$(outer%)
        tempfn$ = firstname$(outer%)
        tempad$ = address$(outer%)
        tempct$ = city$(outer%)
        tempst$ = state$(outer%)
        tempzp$ = zipcode$(outer%)

        '      start moving left
        inner% = outer% - 1
```

```
'      shift the elements to the right until the
'      current element is in its proper place
DO WHILE templn$ < lastname$(inner%)
    lastname$(inner% + 1) = lastname$(inner%)
    firstname$(inner% + 1) = firstname$(inner%)
    address$(inner% + 1) = address$(inner%)
    city$(inner% + 1) = city$(inner%)
    state$(inner% + 1) = state$(inner%)
    zipcode$(inner% + 1) = zipcode$(inner%)
    inner% = inner% - 1

    '      if the current record will be the new
    '      first record, get out of the loop
    IF inner% = 0 THEN EXIT DO
LOOP

'      restore the current record
people(inner% + 1) = temp
lastname$(inner% + 1) = templn$
firstname$(inner% + 1) = tempfn$
address$(inner% + 1) = tempad$
city$(inner% + 1) = tempct$
state$(inner% + 1) = tempst$
zipcode$(inner% + 1) = tempzp$

NEXT outer%

END SUB
```

Quick Sort

The *quick sort* is one of the fastest sorting algorithms for large arrays (arrays of more than 100 elements). Normally, you implement the quick sort with a recursive subroutine. (See Chapter 10 for a discussion of recursion.)

The quick sort orders a list by splitting it into a series of smaller lists. For example, the algorithm will start sorting the array

```
(1)  |  55  |
(2)  |  66  |
(3)  |  11  |
(4)  |  22  |
(5)  |  44  |  ←
(6)  |  33  |
(7)  |  99  |
(8)  |  88  |
(9)  |  77  |
```

by selecting the middle value—the fifth in this case—as a *separator value*. The array is then split into one list that contains values less than or equal to the separator value and one list that has the values greater than the separator value:

```
(1)  |  33  |        (5)  |  66  |
(2)  |  44  |        (6)  |  55  |
(3)  |  11  |        (7)  |  99  |
(4)  |  22  |        (8)  |  88  |
                     (9)  |  77  |
```

The quick sort then takes these two sublists and breaks each one down in the same fashion. This process continues until there is only one item in each sublist. At that point, the array will be sorted. Figure 9-3 gives you the final sublist breakdown.

The following is a quick sort for the last names of the personnel array:

```
SUB QuickSort (start%, finish%)

SHARED people1() AS personnelrec

    low% = start%
    high% = finish%

    '       split the current list in half
    middle% = (low% + high%) \ 2
    check$ = RTRIM$(people1(middle%).lastname)

    '       loop until all the records in the low "half"
    '       are less than the middle value and all the
    '       records in the high "half" are greater than
    '       the middle value
```

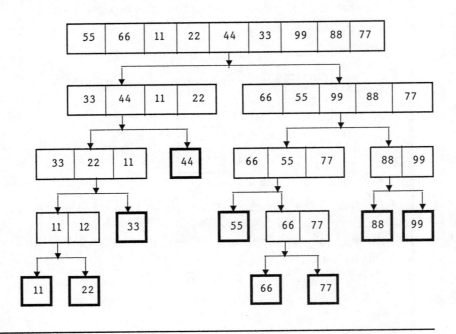

Figure 9-3.   Quick sort sublist breakdown

```
DO
    '        find the next record in the low half
    '        that belongs in the high half

    DO WHILE RTRIM$(people1(low%).lastname) < check$
      low% = low% + 1
    LOOP          '        find the next record in the high half
    '        that belongs in the low half
    DO WHILE RTRIM$(people1(high%).lastname) > check$
       high% = high% - 1
    LOOP

    '        unless the whole list is checked, switch the
    '        two records
    IF low% <= high% THEN
       SWAP people1(low%), people1(high%)
       low% = low% + 1
       high% = high% - 1
    END IF
LOOP UNTIL low% > high%

    '        if the low half has more than one element,
    '        sort the low half
IF start% < high% THEN
    CALL QuickSort(start%, high%)
END IF

    '        if the high half has more than one element,
    '        sort the high half
IF low% < finish% THEN
    CALL QuickSort(low%, finish%)
END IF

END SUB
```

Merge

The final array algorithm is a *merge*. As the name implies, the merge takes two sorted arrays and combines them into a third sorted array. The logic is straightforward: first the merge looks for the smaller of the first elements of both arrays. It takes the smaller value, adds it to the new array, and moves that array pointer down one. Then it compares the values at each pointer and follows the same logic. The merge is complete when both lists are exhausted. Here is the merge routine, which takes the arrays *people1* and *people2,* and merges them into *people3.*

```
SUB Merge (size1%, size2%)

SHARED people1() AS personnelrec
SHARED people2() AS personnelrec
SHARED people3() AS personnelrec

    '     start at the beginning of each list
    count1% = 1
    count2% = 1

    '     loop until the new list is filled
    FOR new% = 1 TO size1% + size2%

        '     if at the end of the first list, add record
        '     from the second list
        IF count1% > size1% THEN
            people3(new%) = people2(count2%)
            count2% = count2% + 1

        '     if at the end of the second list, add record
        '     from the first list
        ELSEIF count2% > size2% THEN
            people3(new%) = people1(count1%)
            count1% = count1% + 1

        '     if the value of current record of the first
        '     list should go next, add it
        ELSEIF people1(count1%).lastname <
                    people2(count2%).lastname THEN
            people3(new%) = people1(count1%)
            count1% = count1% + 1

        '     otherwise, add current record of the second
        '     list
        ELSE
            people3(new%) = people2(count2%)
            count2% = count2% + 1
        END IF

    NEXT new%
```

Subroutines and Functions

In Chapters 5 through 9 you have seen many sections of Quick-BASIC code, called *program fragments*. All of these examples were written at the *module level,* which is the highest statement level. Module-level code is normally reserved for type and array declarations, error and event handling, and the code for the main program. A large program written completely at the module level is usually difficult to read and debug.

If you have programmed in languages other than BASIC, you are probably familiar with subroutines. If BASIC has been your only language, however, you may be used to subroutines only in the form of GOSUB-RETURN. QuickBASIC makes GOSUB obsolete with its SUB and FUNCTION structures, as you saw in Chapter 1. In this chapter you'll learn about declaring and calling subroutines and functions; the scope of variables and subprograms; and the management of large programs.

Subroutines

Writing a program that contains a subroutine involves a three-step process. First you must define the subroutine, then you must declare it, and finally you must call it. This section discusses the details of each of these steps.

Defining a Subroutine

The first step in writing a subroutine is to define it. This definition must include both the statements to be executed and the information that must pass to and from the calling routine.

The SUB-END SUB Structure

The SUB-END SUB structure provides the skeleton for a subroutine definition.

SUB-END SUB   structure

Syntax: SUB *subname* [*parameters*] [STATIC]
             statementblock
        END SUB
where *parameters* =>
        (*variable* [( )][AS *type*] [, *variable* [( )][AS *type*]]. . .)

Purpose: Defines a subroutine

Sample use:

```
SUB InputInteger (anyint%, row%, col%)

LOCATE row%, col%
INPUT "", tempstr$
anyint% = VAL(tempstr$)

LOCATE row%, col%
PRINT STRING$(LEN(tempstr$), 32)
LOCATE row%, col%
PRINT anyint%

END SUB
```

The example in the box is a numeric input routine in generic form, as promised in Chapter 7. The code moves the cursor to the input location and waits for string input. When the string is entered, it is converted to an integer. Since the converted integer may not look exactly like the string (for example, if the user typed a letter by mistake), the subroutine erases the input string from the screen and displays the integer.

The statement block between the SUB statement line and the END SUB statement line comprises the body of the subroutine. Although the vast majority of QuickBASIC statements are allowed in a subroutine body, a few are illegal. For instance, subroutines and functions cannot be nested, so you must avoid SUB structures, FUNCTION structures, and DEF FN structures inside subroutine bodies. Also, you can use the COMMON, DECLARE, DIM SHARED, and OPTION BASE statements and the TYPE structure only in module-level code.

The Parameter List

The parameter list in the SUB statement definition is the set of variables that the subroutine either needs from the calling routine or provides to the calling routine. You must identify the type of each variable, with either a type character suffix or an AS clause. Array variables in the parameter list must include a set of parentheses. You cannot use a fixed-length string as a parameter.

Once you have written a subroutine, you should determine how the routine uses each parameter in the parameter list. If the parameter is not used at all, you should take it out of the list. If the subroutine uses the parameter but never changes its value, it is an *input parameter*. If the subroutine uses a parameter and changes its value, it is an *input/output parameter*. If the subroutine gives a value to a parameter but never uses its original value, it is an *output parameter*. In the subroutine *InputInteger*, the first parameter is an output parameter and the last two are input parameters. Study the body of the subroutine to verify this. These parameter types will become important when you want to call the subroutine. Also, be sure to document each parameter inside the subroutine so that when you call the subroutine you know which values will change and which values will not.

The DECLARE Statement

If you use the QuickBASIC environment to write a program and you save the program after defining and calling a subroutine or function, you may notice a new line created in the module-level code. This new line is a DECLARE statement, which becomes more important in multiple-module programs.

DECLARE   **statement**

Syntax:
DECLARE {FUNCTION | SUB} *subname* [*parameters*]
where *parameters* = >
    (*variable* [( )][AS *type*] [, *variable* [( )][AS *type*]]. . .)

Purpose: Defines the parameters of a subroutine or function for type checking

Sample use:

```
DECLARE SUB InputInteger (anyint%, row%, col%)
```

When you save the module containing the subroutine *InputInteger*—assuming that you call the routine somewhere in the module—the QuickBASIC environment adds this line. If you are using a different editor, you must add this line yourself. If you fail to add the DECLARE statements, you will not be able to use the BC command-line compiler. You must also type DECLARE statements for subroutines and functions that are in other modules, and for those in Quick libraries. Turn to the "Managing Large Programs" section of this chapter for more information.

Calling a Subroutine

The last step to writing a subroutine is to call that routine. A subroutine call is a statement that tells the program to execute that subroutine. Included in the call is an argument list. The CALL statement and the argument list are discussed here.

The CALL Statement

When you want to execute the body of a subroutine you must call that routine. The CALL statement initiates the execution of a subroutine.

CALL   **statement**

Syntax:
CALL *subname* [(*arguments*)]
   OR
subname [*arguments*]
where *arguments* = >
{*expression* | *variable*[( )]} [, {*expression* | *variable*[( )]}. . .

Purpose: Transfers program execution to a subroutine

Note: See Appendix D for CALL statement syntax to non-BASIC subroutines.

Sample use:

```
LOCATE 10, 1
PRINT "Enter your age: ";
CALL InputInteger (age%, 10, 17)
```

The three statements in the box display a prompt on the screen and call the input routine provided earlier in the chapter. Notice that the third parameter is the number of the column after the end of the prompt string. The actual input will occur just to the right of the prompt.

A subprogram can be called either in the module-level code or by another subprogram. The term *calling routine* refers to the routine that includes the call to the subprogram. A subroutine can even call itself, as you will see later in this chapter.

Note: In this book the term *subprogram* refers to a subroutine defined with a SUB structure or a function defined with a FUNCTION structure.

There are two separate syntaxes for calling a subroutine. The first syntax, which is used throughout this book, uses the reserved word CALL to distinguish it as a subroutine call. The second syntax makes your own subroutines look like actual QuickBASIC statements. Here is the same call to *InputInteger:*

```
LOCATE 10, 1
PRINT "Enter your age: "
InputInteger age%, 10, 17
```

You do not put the argument list in parentheses with this second syntax.

Argument Lists

A subroutine call includes an *argument list*, which lists the variables and expressions that the subroutine either requires from the calling routine or supplies to the calling routine. The argument list is similar to the parameter list in the SUB statement line.

When determining the arguments of a subroutine call you must refer to the parameters of the subroutine definition. Syntactically, the number of arguments and the type of each argument must match their respective parameters. Look again at the sample subroutine call and subroutine definition that follows.

```
CALL InputInteger (age%, 10, 17)
. . .

SUB InputInteger (anyint%, row%, col%)
```

There are three integer parameters in the subroutine definition. This definition requires all calls to *InputInteger* to include three INTEGER values in the argument list. This particular subroutine call has one INTEGER variable followed by two INTEGER constants.

When the call to *InputInteger* takes place, QuickBASIC associates, or matches, the calling arguments with the subroutine parameters. In the above example, the parameter *anyint%* will start with the value of the variable *age%*. The parameters *row%* and *col%* will start with 10 and 17, respectively. Program control will go from the CALL statement to the first statement after the SUB statement line in the subroutine. Any changes to *anyint%* within the subroutine will actually be changing the variable *age%*. Changes to *row%* and *col%* will have no effect on the calling routine, since you cannot change the value of a constant. When the program reaches the END SUB line, it returns to the calling routine and continues execution with the line after the CALL statement.

Variable Versus Value Arguments

In QuickBASIC all calling arguments are passed to a subroutine by reference. This means that the subroutine will receive only the memory address of the argument. There are two types of arguments in QuickBASIC: variable arguments and value arguments. *Variable arguments* are always variable names. A change in the subroutine to the associated parameter will change the value of the variable. For *value arguments,* QuickBASIC will create a temporary location and pass the address of that location to the subroutine. Thus, when the subroutine changes the value of the associated parameter, it will be changing only the value in the temporary location.

Whenever you use a variable name as a calling argument it becomes a variable argument. If you need to make a variable name a value argument you must convert the variable to an expression. One of the easiest ways to do this is to add zero to the variable. In this subroutine call

```
CALL InputInteger(age%, linenum% + 0, 17)
```

QuickBASIC must evaluate *linenum%* + 0 as an expression. The result of the addition is placed in a temporary location, and that address goes to the second parameter in *InputInteger*, creating a value argument. For string arguments, you can convert a variable to an expression by concatenating the null string ("") to the end of the string.

Choosing between a value argument and a variable argument depends on the subroutine. In general, output parameters and input/output parameters require variable arguments, and input parameters can be either value arguments or variable arguments. In the *InputInteger* subroutine it would be ridiculous to use a value argument as the first calling argument, because *anyint%* is an output parameter. If you had this program fragment

```
age% = 2
CALL InputInteger(age% + 0, 10, 17)
PRINT "Your age is"; age%
```

you would always get 2 as the value for *age%*. Even if the user entered another number within the *InputInteger* subroutine, the number would be placed in a temporary location because *age%* + 0 is a value argument.

The EXIT SUB Statement

If you are in the middle of a subroutine and need to return to the calling routine, you can use the EXIT SUB statement.

EXIT SUB   statement

Syntax: EXIT SUB

Purpose: Terminates a SUB before the END SUB statement line

Note: This statement is valid only in a subroutine body.

Sample use:

```
SUB FirstDiff (string1$, string2$, position%)

FOR cnt% = 1 TO LEN (string1$)
   IF cnt% > LEN (string2$) THEN
       position% = cnt%
       EXIT SUB
   ELSEIF MID$(string1$, cnt%, 1) <>
               MID$(string2$, cnt%, 1) THEN
       position% = cnt%
       EXIT SUB
   END IF
NEXT cnt%
position% = LEN (string1$) + 1

END SUB
```

The subroutine shown in the box determines the first position where two strings differ. As soon as that position is found, the routine executes an EXIT SUB statement to avoid looping through the rest of the first string.

Functions

A *function* is another type of subprogram. You have used functions defined by QuickBASIC already. These functions, sometimes called *intrinsic* functions, are listed as being part of the QuickBASIC language. The intrinsic function CINT is part of the expression in the following assignment statement.

```
myint% = 2 + CINT(realnum!)
```

Here, the variable *realnum!* is passed as an argument to the function CINT, which in turn returns a value to be used in the expression.

This section will show you how to define, declare, and call your own functions. You will see that a function is simply a special case of a subroutine. All of the rules and guidelines you just studied for subroutines also apply to functions. This section will cover the few exceptions.

From Subroutines to Functions

All functions should be written so that they have only one output parameter: the function name itself. However, QuickBASIC will allow you to have input/output and output parameters in function definitions. Unfortunately, this defeats the whole purpose of a function. When programmers see a function call in a program, they assume that the calling arguments never change value. If you write a function that does not follow these guidelines, you will confuse other programmers who might want to use your function. If you have a function that does not satisfy this criterion, consider converting it back to a subroutine.

If you have a subroutine that has only one output parameter and no input/output parameters, you should consider converting it to a function. By doing this you tell the readers of your program that the function name is the only output parameter, and that the rest of the parameters are input parameters.

The FUNCTION-END FUNCTION Structure

You start by defining the function with a FUNCTION-END FUNCTION structure.

FUNCTION-END FUNCTION   structure

Syntax: FUNCTION *funcname* [*parameters*] [STATIC]
              statementblock
         END FUNCTION
where *parameters* = >
(*variable* [( )][AS *type*] [, *variable* [( )][AS *type*]]. . .)

Purpose: Defines a function

Note: The function name must be assigned a value somewhere
within the body of the function.

Sample use:

```
FUNCTION Smaller! (firstnum!, secondnum!)

IF firstnum! > secondnum! THEN
    Smaller! = secondnum!
ELSE
    Smaller! = firstnum!
END IF

END FUNCTION
```

The function shown in the box determines the smaller of two
SINGLE values. It meets the requirements for a function because none of the input parameters change and there is one and
only one value returned by the function.

   Since the name of the function is actually a variable in the
function definition, you must give the name a type. If you do not
include a type character suffix showing the type of the function,
QuickBASIC will use the current default type.

Calling a Function

When you call a subroutine you use the CALL statement, which
is a statement by itself. A function call, on the other hand, can
only be part of another statement. The following loop calls the
function *Smaller!*.

```
FOR count% = 1 TO Smaller%(30, numstudents%)
```

This FOR statement means that the loop will execute at most 30 times. You would use this statement if, for example, your student arrays were only dimensioned to 30.

The EXIT FUNCTION Statement

If you need to terminate a function before the END FUNCTION statement line, use the EXIT FUNCTION statement.

EXIT FUNCTION   statement

Syntax: EXIT FUNCTION

Purpose: Terminates a FUNCTION before the END FUNCTION statement line

Note: This statement is valid only in a function body.

Sample use:

```
FUNCTION FirstDiff% (string1$, string2$)

FOR cnt% = 1 TO LEN (string1$)
   IF cnt% > LEN (string2$) THEN
      FirstDiff% = cnt%
      EXIT FUNCTION
   ELSEIF MID$(string1$, cnt%, 1)
             <> MID$(string2$, cnt%,1) THEN
      FirstDiff% = cnt%
      EXIT FUNCTION
   END IF
NEXT cnt%
FirstDiff% = LEN (string1$) + 1

END FUNCTION
```

The function shown in the box demonstrates how to convert a subroutine to a function. In the syntax box of the EXIT SUB statement given earlier in this chapter, you studied the SUB *FirstDiff*. Since the subroutine has one and only one output parameter, it becomes a perfect candidate for a function.

The Scope of Constants and Variables

In QuickBASIC there are two levels of statements: those in the main program that make up module-level code, and those in the subprograms that make up subprogram-level code. The *scope* of a variable or constant is the level or levels in which the variable or constant is defined. If you are unaware of the scope of each constant and variable in your program, you may accidentally refer to one memory location when you expect to refer to another. In this section you will learn how to define a constant or variable so that it has the proper scope.

Local and Global Constants

You have much less versatility with scope when you are defining constants than when you are defining variables. A *local* constant is one that is defined at the subprogram level. If you define a constant with the CONST statement inside a subroutine or function, that constant is understood by that subprogram only. A local constant is undefined in the main module and all other subprograms.

When you define a symbolic constant at the module level, you create a *global* constant. This means that the constant can be used by the module-level code and all subprograms. You cannot define a symbolic constant that is local only to the module-level code. The only way to override a global constant within a subprogram is to define a local constant with the same name. Study this simple program:

```
CONST numstudents% = 30
CALL Test
```

```
SUB Test
   CONST numstudents% = 25
   PRINT "The number of students is "; numstudents%
END SUB
```

Inside the *Test* subroutine the constant *numstudents%* has the value 25. In the main program and in all other subprograms, the value of the constant is 30, even after the subroutine is called. Since using the same name for two different constants can easily cause confusion, you are better off using a different name within the subprogram.

Local and Global Variables

The majority of variables that you use are never defined explicitly. These variables are automatically considered to be local variables. If you use a local variable in module-level code, its value is unknown to any of the subprograms. If you use a local variable in a subprogram, it is known to that subprogram only.

QuickBASIC also allows you to create global variables, which are variables that can be accessed by module-level code and by all subprograms. To define a global variable you use the SHARED attribute in a DIM, REDIM, or COMMON statement. The statement

```
DIM SHARED deck%(52)
```

defines an array *deck%* that is known to the module-level code and all subprograms. Remember that you can also use the DIM statement to declare variables of simple types.

If a subprogram requires a variable from the module-level code, you have three programming options to make that variable available. The first and best option is to include that variable in the argument list of the subprogram call. Using a parameter takes up only a few bytes of memory and only a few microseconds. For that cost you get self-documenting, easily maintainable code. The second option is to define the variable as a global variable. The third option is to share that variable using the SHARED statement.

The SHARED Statement

The SHARED statement turns a local variable into a hybrid of a global variable. In other words, the variable is global only to the subprogram that includes the SHARED statement.

SHARED   **statement**

Syntax:
SHARED *variable* [AS *type*] [, *variable* [AS *type*]]. . .

Purpose: Allows a subroutine or function to access a variable local to the module level

Note: This statement is valid only inside a subroutine or function body; it is invalid for subprograms within a separately compiled module or Quick library.

Sample use:

```
DIM testscores%(200)
. . .
FUNCTION Average!
SHARED testscores%(), totalscores%

   FOR cnt% = 1 to totalscores%
      sum% = sum% + testscores%(cnt%)
   NEXT cnt%
   Average! = sum% / totalscores%

END FUNCTION
```

The variable *testscores%* is defined as a local array in the main module. The SHARED statement allows the subroutine to access the array and the integer *totalscores%*, and to change their values. This method is preferred over making an array global, because it shows you which subprograms use the array.

The STATIC Statement

The STATIC statement has two separate functions: it allows you to retain the value of a local variable between subprogram calls, and it allows you to override a global variable to be a local variable.

STATIC   **statement**

Syntax:
STATIC *variable*[( )] [AS *type*] [, *variable*[( )] [AS *type*]]. . .

Purpose: Creates a local variable and preserves its value between subprogram calls

Note: This statement is valid only within the body of a subroutine or function.

Sample use:

```
FUNCTION GetCard% (Deck%())
STATIC cardnum%

cardnum% = cardnum% + 1
IF cardnum% > 52 THEN
    CALL Shuffle (Deck%())
    cardnum% = 1
END IF
GetCard% = Deck% (cardnum%)

END FUNCTION
```

If you had the statement

```
DIM SHARED cardnum%
```

in the main program, the STATIC statement in the function in the box allows you to use the same variable name for a different location in memory.

The main purpose of the STATIC statement, however, is to keep the value of a local variable between subprogram calls. Normally, when you call a subprogram QuickBASIC reinitializes its local variables. The STATIC statement maintains the memory location throughout a program run, so that the local variable keeps its value between subroutine calls. In the previous example, the function *GetCard%* supplies a new card from a deck. If it gets to the bottom of the deck, the function automatically shuffles the cards and takes the top card. If you did not use the STATIC definition, you would always get the same card (the top one). Your other option, of course, is to pass *cardnum%* as a parameter.

You may have noticed that the SUB and FUNCTION statement lines support an optional STATIC attribute at the end of the statement. Including this attribute is the equivalent of defining all local variables as STATIC. This option changes the way QuickBASIC treats the subroutine. When you call a subroutine without the STATIC attribute, it allocates space for the local variables and other parts of the routine, executes the routine, and then frees that memory space. With the STATIC attribute included, QuickBASIC reserves enough space in memory for each local variable at the start of the program. When you call this type of routine, the local variables maintain the value they had at the end of the last call. If you call a subroutine thousands of times you may choose to add the STATIC attribute to speed up the execution time. Otherwise, you will find a subroutine easier to maintain if you declare only the variables you need as STATIC with their own statements.

Make sure that you do not confuse the STATIC statement and the STATIC attribute with the $STATIC metacommand. In Chapter 9 you used the $STATIC metacommand to guarantee that an array was a static array or, in other words, always the same size. The word *"STATIC"* for local variables and subprograms means that memory will not be reallocated for new subroutine calls.

The Scope of a Subprogram

As stated earlier in this chapter, you cannot define a subroutine within another subroutine. This makes access available from any subroutine to any other subroutine. If you call a subroutine from another subroutine, you are nesting the call, or going one statement level deeper. Suppose you have a main program that calls a subroutine *GetData,* which in turn calls the subroutine *InputInteger.* Transfer of control will follow a stack (last in, first out), which means you will go from the CALL statement in the main program to the first statement in the body of the *GetData* subroutine. When you get to the CALL statement, you will transfer to the first statement in the body of *InputInteger.* When you reach the END SUB statement at *InputInteger,* you will go to the first statement after the CALL inside *GetData.* Finally, when you reach the END SUB statement in *GetData* you will go back to the main program to the statement following the call to *GetData.*

Recursion

If you have a subroutine that calls itself, you have a *recursive* subroutine. Most recursive subroutines are prone to errors and can be replaced easily by a loop. The most common example of a recursive routine is *Factorial,* which looks like this:

```
FUNCTION factorial# (expr%)

IF expr% <= 1 THEN
    factorial# = 1
ELSE
    factorial# = expr% * factorial#(expr% - 1)
END IF

END FUNCTION
```

You can rewrite this routine by taking out the recursion and adding a FOR-NEXT loop. The following is the new routine.

```
FUNCTION factorial2# (expr%)

fac# = 1
FOR cnt% = 1 TO expr%
   fac# = fac# * cnt%
NEXT cnt%

factorial2# = fac#

END FUNCTION
```

This second routine runs faster, looks simpler, and is less prone to bugs than the first routine. Therefore, even though Quick-BASIC supports recursion, you are often better off using other programming techniques.

Managing Large Programs

When you start creating large programs, you need to be concerned with file management and module management. Rather than placing all subroutines for a program in the same module, you should divide your subprograms into several modules. One module, the main module, will have the first statement to execute when you run the program. All other modules should have no executable statements at the module level.

If you are working on one module of a multiple-module program and you want to run the program, you may need to change the main module. You will see the name of the main module in the "SUBs" dialog box, as shown in Figure 10-1. If this is not where your program begins, select the Set Main Module command from the Run menu and change the name.

When you create a multiple-module program there are a few extra steps you must take to make the program work. Primarily, you must add DECLARE statements to any module that calls a subprogram in another module. The DECLARE statements help the compiler to match parameters with arguments. QuickBASIC cannot add these statements automatically. Also, you must remember that the DIM SHARED statement makes a variable global to all subprograms in the module in which it is defined, but not to the other modules.

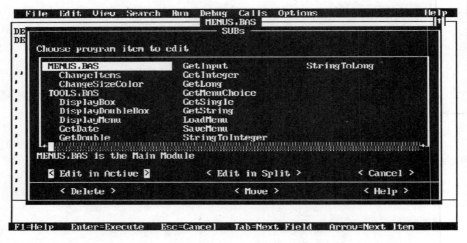

Figure 10-1. Main module in the "SUBs" dialog box

The COMMON Statement

To make a variable in one module accessible to subprograms in another module, you have two options. Usually, the better option—to keep the program maintainable—is to pass the variable as a parameter to all subprograms that need it. Alternatively, you can create a named common block with the COMMON statement.

COMMON **statement**

Syntax: COMMON [SHARED] [/*commonname*/] *variables*
where *variables* = >
variable[( )] [AS *type*] [, *variable*[( )] [AS *type*]]. . .

Purpose: Defines a series of variables that can be shared between modules or between chained programs

---

Note: Arrays in a common block must be dimensioned before the COMMON statement; common blocks must be defined before all executable statements.

Sample use:

```
DIM personnel(200) AS personnelrec
COMMON /database/ personnel() AS personnelrec
```

When a COMMON statement includes a name between slashes, such as */database/,* it is called a *named* common block. You use named common blocks when sharing variables among modules. The sample common block in the syntax box would contain all the personnel data used by many subprograms in a variety of modules.

The COMMON statement includes an optional SHARED attribute, which makes data available not only to all modules at the module level, but also to all subprograms within all modules that have the common block defined. Do not use DIM SHARED because by doing so you will create two sets of variables with the same name that refer to different locations in memory.

The $INCLUDE Metacommand

To avoid having to duplicate common block definitions, record definitions, and subprogram declarations, you should place all of these in a separate file called an *include file.* You access this file with the $INCLUDE metacommand.

$INCLUDE   **metacommand**

Syntax: {' | REM} $INCLUDE: *'filename'*

Purpose: Tells the compiler to read and compile the statements found in the include file

Note: Include files cannot contain SUB or FUNCTION definitions.

Sample use:

```
$INCLUDE: 'DATADEF.INC'
```

This sample metacommand assumes that you have taken TYPE, COMMON, and DECLARE statements and saved them in the file DATADEF.INC. If you include this metacommand as the first statement in each module of a multiple-module program, you will keep from typing things many times and lessen the risk of making typing errors.

Using Quick Libraries

When you develop a large program, you will probably have a set of subroutines that are generic enough to be used by more than one program. You might consider moving these routines to a Quick library. The subprograms in a Quick library cannot access global variables or have SHARED statements—you must pass all variables as parameters. The *InputInteger* routine shown earlier in this chapter is an excellent candidate for a Quick library subroutine.

The biggest advantage of the Quick library is that the code is already compiled. This means that when you load a large program you do not have to wait for all the code to compile. The major drawback of a Quick library is that there is very little debug information available for routines contained in Quick libraries. For this reason you should make sure that a subprogram works properly before inserting it into a Quick library.

The CHAIN Statement

If you write two separate programs but want to give one program access to another, you might want to connect them with a CHAIN statement.

CHAIN   **statement**

Syntax: CHAIN *filename*

Purpose: Changes program control from one program to the start of another

Note: When run inside the environment, a .BAS extension is assumed; when run outside the environment, an .EXE extension is assumed.

Sample use:

```
IF menuitem% = changedevicespecs% THEN
    CHAIN "DEVICES"
END IF
```

When QuickBASIC finds a CHAIN statement, it immediately goes to the first statement of the named program. There is no way to chain to the middle of a program and there is no way to return to the original CHAIN statement. Because of these disadvantages, consider combining the two programs by making one program a SUB that the other program can call.

Almost all data is lost when you chain from one program to another. The only data that is retained is the data in an unnamed common block. If you look back at the syntax of the COMMON statement, you will see that the common block name is optional. When you give a common block a name, you can use it for sharing data among various modules within a single program. Omit the common block name and you can use the common block to share the data among chained programs. You can have only one unnamed common block for all chained programs.

Standard Mathematical Functions

QuickBASIC includes several mathematical functions as part of the language. These functions follow the same rules as the functions that you write yourself. A brief description of each of the mathematical functions is included here.

The function called ABS determines the absolute value of an expression.

ABS(expr)   **function**

Purpose: Computes the absolute value of an expression
Return type: Same as the input parameter
Parameter: expr [any numeric type] — a numeric expression
Sample call:

```
posval% = ABS(anynum%)
```

The SGN function extracts the sign from a number.

SGN(expr)   **function**

Purpose: Determines the sign of an expression
Return type: INTEGER (−1, 0, 1)
Parameter: expr [any numeric type] — a numeric expression
Note: The sign is determined by expr / ABS(*expr*) and is zero if the expression evaluates to zero.
Sample call:

```
IF SGN(value!) = -1 THEN PRINT "No square root"
```

The SQR function takes the square root of a number. It cannot take square roots of negative numbers.

SQR(expr)   **function**

Purpose: Computes the square root of an expression

Return type: SINGLE (DOUBLE if the input parameter is DOUBLE)

Parameter: expr [any numeric type]—a numeric expression

Note: The expression must be greater than zero.

Sample call:

```
root! = SQR(posnum!)
```

The COS function determines the cosine of an angle given in radians.

COS(expr)   **function**

Purpose: Computes the cosine of a numeric expression

Return type: SINGLE (DOUBLE if the input parameter is DOUBLE)

Parameter: expr [any numeric type]—a numeric expression

Note: All angles are computed in radians.

Sample call:

```
cos60! = COS(60 * 3.1416 / 180)
```

The SIN function (in the following box) takes the sine of an angle given in radians.

SIN(expr)   **function**

Purpose: Computes the sine of an expression

Return type: SINGLE (DOUBLE if the input parameter is DOUBLE)

Parameter: expr [any numeric type] — a numeric expression

Note: Angles are assumed to be in radians.

Sample call:

```
sin60! = SIN(60 * 3.1416 / 180)
```

The TAN function takes the tangent of an angle given in radians.

TAN(expr)   **function**

Purpose: Computes the tangent of an expression

Return type: SINGLE (DOUBLE if the input parameter is DOUBLE)

Parameter: expr [any numeric type] — a numeric expression

Note: Angles are assumed to be in radians.

Sample call:

```
tan60! = TAN(60 * 3.1416 / 180)
```

The ATN function computes arctangents and can be used indirectly to compute arcsines and arccosines.

ATN(expr)   **function**

Purpose: Computes the arctangent of an expression

Return type: SINGLE (DOUBLE if the input parameter is DOUBLE)

Parameter: expr [any numeric type]—a numeric expression

Note: All angles are computed in radians.

Sample call:

```
angle! = ATN(1.0)          'angle! will be .7854
```

The EXP function is the exponent function, which determines the value of "e to the power of" an expression.

EXP(expr)   **function**

Purpose: Computes "e to the power of" an expression

Return type: SINGLE (DOUBLE if input parameter is DOUBLE)

Parameter: expr [any numeric type]—a numeric expression

Note: Expression must be less than 88.02969, or an overflow error occurs.

Sample call:

```
xcubed! = EXP(3 * LOG(x!))
```

The LOG function will take the natural log (base e) of an expression.

LOG(expr)   **function**

Purpose: Computes the natural logarithm of an expression
Return type: SINGLE (DOUBLE if the input parameter is DOUBLE)
Parameter: expr [any numeric type]—a numeric expression
Note: Expression must be greater than zero.
Sample call:

```
xtotheq! = EXP(q! * LOG(x!))
```

The FIX function converts a real number to an integer by truncating the number.

FIX(expr)   **function**

Purpose: Truncates an expression (removes all digits to the right of the decimal point)
Return type: INTEGER
Parameter: expr [any numeric type]—a numeric expression
Sample call:

```
truncnum% = FIX(realnum!)
```

The INT function finds the largest integer that is less than or equal to a number.

INT(expr)   function

Purpose: Computes the greatest integer less than or equal to the given expression

Return type: INTEGER or LONG

Parameter: expr [any numeric type]—a numeric expression

Sample call:

```
myint% = INT(realnum!)
```

The RND function will give you a number between zero and one.

RND(num)   function

Purpose: Generates a random number between zero and one

Return type: SINGLE

Parameter: num [any numeric type]—determines how the next number is generated: if num > 0, generates a new random number; if num = 0, provides the last random number generated; if num < 0, supplies the same random number every time (based on the value of num)

Note: The parameter is optional; if omitted, num is assumed to be greater than zero.

Sample call:

```
roll% = INT(6 * RND) + 1
```

If you want a different set of random numbers every time you run a program, then you must include a RANDOMIZE statement.

RANDOMIZE   statement

Syntax: RANDOMIZE [*seedvalue*]

Purpose: Provides a seed value to the random number generator

Note: If you do not include an expression, QuickBASIC will ask for one during program execution.

Sample use:

```
RANDOMIZE TIMER              'uses the system clock
```

File and Device I/O

QuickBASIC File Types
Opening and Closing Files
Random-Access Files
Sequential Files
Binary Files
File-Like Devices
Sharing Files
File Information
Error Handling
Subdirectories

When you work on a personal computer, you use disk files to save information that you need to carry from one work session to the next. Without disk files, you would have to keep everything in memory, which would be extremely impractical. In programming, you use files to store and retrieve any data that is not part of the program. Many programmers use data files, but they often use the wrong file type for their application. In this chapter you will learn how (and when) to use each of the file types that QuickBASIC supports.

This chapter begins by describing the three QuickBASIC file types. Then it covers the syntax for opening and closing files. The majority of the chapter discusses input and output for random-access files, sequential files, and binary files. You will also find sections on file information and error handling. In addition, there are brief sections on file-like devices, sharing files, and subdirectories.

QuickBASIC File Types

QuickBASIC supports three different types of files: random-access files, sequential files, and binary files. Which type you need is determined by the kind of data you will place in the file. This section will describe the three types of files and show you when to use each type.

When you are working with data using user-defined types, the best way to store the data is in a random-access file. A *random-access* file is a file where all records are the same length. If you defined the simple type

```
TYPE FullName
    firstname AS STRING * 15
    middlename AS STRING * 15
    lastname AS STRING * 30
END TYPE
```

you could place a list of names in a random-access file where each record had 60 bytes. A sample file would look like Figure 11-1. (A note on terminology. The word *record* has two different

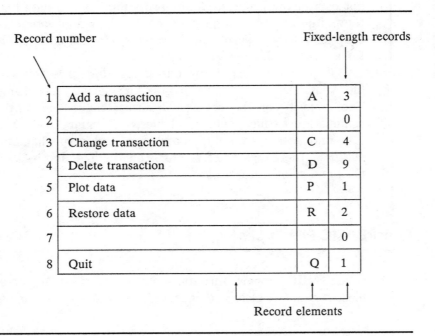

Figure 11-1.   A sample random-access file.

meanings: it is a synonym for user-defined type, which is a data structure discussed in Chapter 9; and it is an *element*, or "line," in a file. To avoid confusion, this chapter will use the word *record* when referring to the file element, and *user-defined type* when referring to the data structure.)

Because each record is the same size in a random-access file, a file pointer can move directly to any record in the file by counting the proper number of bytes. For instance, suppose the file pointer is at the start of a file that contains 40-byte records. If you want to read the tenth record, QuickBASIC will move 400 bytes (40 bytes per record times ten records) and input the next record.

When you need to store data of different types and sizes, you must use a sequential file. A *sequential file* is a file that can contain different size records. This type of file must be read in sequence—you cannot "jump" to a specific record in the middle of the file. Figure 11-2 depicts a sample sequential file.

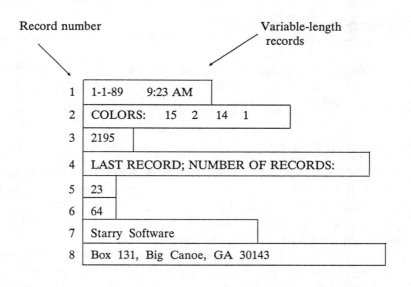

Figure 11-2.   A sample sequential file

One of the advantages of the sequential file is that it is stored in ASCII. This means you can read and edit the file with any text editor. In random-access files, data is stored exactly as it is stored in memory: INTEGER values use two bytes, LONG values use four, and so on. When you type or edit a random-access file you will see the ASCII equivalent of the internal representations in the numeric fields.

One of the biggest advantages of random-access files over sequential files is that you can read or write a single record in the middle of a file. With a sequential file you must read the entire file, change the record, then write out the entire file again.

The third file type that QuickBASIC supports is the binary file. A *binary file* is an unformatted, unstructured sequence of bytes. It is closely related to a random-access file in that you can read or write to a specific location in the file. When you read from or write to a binary file, however, you must specify the number of bytes to read or write. Binary files are not divided into records.

Opening and Closing Files

No matter what type of file you use, there are several steps that are common to all files: determining the file number, opening the file, and closing the file.

The FREEFILE Function

The first step in file manipulation is to determine a file number. You associate a number with every file you use so that you can later refer to the file by number instead of by name. The most common method of assigning file numbers is invention. This works well when you are working with only one or two files. However, as you start working with large programs that manipulate multiple files, you are more likely to accidentally use a wrong file number.

The better way to assign a file number is with the FREE-FILE function.

FREEFILE   **function**

Purpose: Supplies an unused file number

Return type: INTEGER

Parameters: None

Note: Even if there are too many open files, FREEFILE still returns the next number.

Sample call:

```
persfile% = FREEFILE
```

In this sample, the call to the FREEFILE function tells Quick-BASIC to find a file number. You do not care what number is chosen because you will be using the variable *persfile%* whenever you need to refer to that file.

In the syntax for many of the statements in this chapter, you will see an optional "#" sign before the file number. It is provided for compatibility, but it also acts as a signal. Whenever you see the "#" sign before a number or integer variable, you know it is a file number, and you know the statement that includes that number manipulates that particular file. All example statements dealing with files in this book include the optional "#" sign.

The OPEN Statement

Before you can do any input or output with a data file, you must open the file.

OPEN statement

First syntax: OPEN *filename* [FOR *filemode*] [*networkmode*]
        AS [#] *filenumber* [LEN = *recordlength*]
where *filemode* = >
    {RANDOM | OUTPUT | INPUT | APPEND | BINARY}
and where *networkmode* = >
    [ACCESS {READ | WRITE | READ WRITE}]
    [*lockmode*]
where *lockmode* = >
    {SHARED | LOCK READ | LOCK WRITE | LOCK
    READ   WRITE}
Second syntax:
    OPEN *filemode2*, [#] *filenumber*, *filename* [, *recordlen*]
where *filemode2* = >
    {"O" | "I" | "R" | "B" | "A"}

Purpose: Prepares a file for input and/or output and
assigns a file number

Note: The second syntax does not support many QuickBASIC
capabilities and is provided for compatibility only.

Sample use:

```
OPEN "personel.lis" FOR OUTPUT AS #persfile%
```

The string expression after the keyword OPEN is the name of
the DOS file. This can be a new file or an existing file, depending
on the application. The filename must conform to the DOS file-
naming conventions. The other options of the OPEN statement
will be covered for each file type in the appropriate section later
in this chapter.

The CLOSE Statement

After you open a file, you will perform one or many of the I/O
statements that are in this chapter. When you are finished with
file I/O, you must release the file with a CLOSE statement.

CLOSE   **statement**

Syntax: CLOSE [[#] *filenumber*] [, [#]*filenumber*]. . .

Purpose: Disassociates a file with its file number

Note: The following statements automatically execute
a CLOSE: CLEAR, END, RESET, RUN, and SYSTEM.

Sample use:

```
CLOSE #persfile%
```

Every time you find an OPEN statement, you should find the
associated CLOSE statement. QuickBASIC allows you to close
all open files by using the CLOSE statement with no arguments.
You can also close files automatically with the statements listed
in the box, or by leaving the QuickBASIC environment. You will
write much more readable programs, however, when you close
each file individually.

Random-Access Files

Before using a random-access file you must define the type that
the file uses. You studied user-defined types (records) in Chapter 9. The examples in this section will use this type:

```
TYPE ClassRec
    lastname AS STRING * 20
    firstname AS STRING * 10
    address AS STRING * 30
    city AS STRING * 20
    state AS STRING * 2
    zipcode AS LONG
END TYPE
DIM class(60) AS ClassRec
```

The DIM statement here defines a variable that can hold a single record from the file.

Opening a Random-Access File

To open a random-access file, you must know the name of the file, the file number you need, and the length of the records in the file. Here is a sample OPEN statement:

```
OPEN "class.fil" FOR RANDOM AS #classfile% LEN=LEN(class(1))
```

This statement searches the current directory for a file called *class.fil*. If no file exists, QuickBASIC creates one. The FOR RANDOM clause in the statement is used to define the file as random access. There is no need to open the file specifically for output or for input because you can do either with this file type. Since FOR RANDOM is the default file type, this statement is equivalent to the previous one:

```
OPEN "class.fil" AS #classfile% LEN=LEN(class(1))
```

The LEN clause in the OPEN statement defines the length of each record. QuickBASIC needs this information to be able to move instantly to a specific record. Instead of counting the bytes in the user-defined type *ClassRec*, you can use the LEN function and the name of a variable with that record type.

LEN(variable)   **function**

Purpose: Determines the length in bytes of a variable, usually a record variable

Return type: INTEGER

Parameters: variable [any type] — any variable

Note: There is also a LEN function for strings — see Chapter 8.

Sample call:

```
recsize% = LEN(myrecord)
```

When you use the LEN function as part of an OPEN statement, you eliminate the risk of forgetting to change a constant when you change the size of a record.

The following subroutine can be used to open any random-access file. The name of the file is provided by the user. If the file is empty, the user is allowed to create the file or select another.

```
SUB OpenRandomFile (recsize%, filename$, filenum%)

','','','','','','','','','','','','','','','','','','','','','','','
'
'   OpenRandomFile:  opens a random-acces file chosen
'       by the user.  The user can choose to leave
'       the program by typing "QUIT".  The parameter
'       filenum% is the number of the file.  The
'       parameter filename$ is the name of the file.
'
'
','','','','','','','','','','','','','','','','','','','','','','','
filenum% = FREEFILE

'  loop until user has entered a valid file name
DO
    openok% = -1

    '  get the name of the file
    CLS
    LOCATE 10, 10
    INPUT "Enter name of file or QUIT to quit: ", tempstr$
    IF tempstr$ <> "" THEN
        filename$ = tempstr$
    END IF

    '  if user wants out, get out
    IF filename$ = "QUIT" THEN END

    OPEN filename$ FOR RANDOM AS #filenum% LEN = recsize%

    '  if the file is empty, see if the user still wants
    '  to use it
    IF LOF(filenum%) = 0 THEN
        PRINT
        INPUT "File is empty.  Continue? (Y/N): ", answer$

        '  if the user made a mistake, delete the file
```

```
      IF UCASE$(answer$) = "N" THEN
         CLOSE #filenum%
         KILL filename$
         openok% = 0
      END IF
   END IF

LOOP UNTIL openok%

END SUB
```

The PUT# Statement

To write a record to a random-access file you must use the PUT# statement.

PUT#   **statement**

Syntax: PUT [#]*filenumber* [, [*recordnumber*] [, *variable*]]

Purpose: Outputs a record to a random-access file

Note: You can omit the variable name only when using a FIELD structure, now obsolete; this statement works only with files opened FOR RANDOM or FOR BINARY.

Sample use:

```
DO
   CALL InputPersData (personnel)
   PUT #persfile%, , personnel

   INPUT "Another record? (Y/N) ", yesno$
LOOP WHILE UCASE$ (LEFT$ (yesno$, 1)) = "Y"
```

This program fragment shows a sample sequence for writing a series of records to a random-access file. Assuming that the *InputPersData* subroutine gets values for the personnel record from the user, the PUT statement will add them to the end of the file.

The second argument of the PUT statement is the record number. With this argument you can specify where in the file to output a record. QuickBASIC maintains a *file pointer* that keeps track of the current record in a file. When you include a record number as part of a PUT statement, QuickBASIC moves the file pointer before outputting the record. The statement

```
PUT #persfile%, 1, personnel
```

moves the file pointer to the first record and replaces the data with the current values in the personnel record. If you omit the second argument, as in the previous example, the pointer will automatically go to the next higher number.

Normally, you will use a record number in a PUT# statement that is either part of a file or at the end of the file. If you use a nonpositive record number you will get a "Bad record number" error when you run the program. If you use a number that would place the pointer beyond the end of the file, Quick-BASIC will enter blank records in between the end of the file and the new record position, and then output the desired record to the file. Suppose you write a program that balances your checkbook. If your check numbers are sequential, starting with 101, you can determine that

```
recnum% = checknum% - 100
```

Now if you enter the checks when you get them back from the bank (because you never remember to do it when you write the checks), you do not need to worry about entering them in numerical order. The PUT# statement

```
PUT #checkfile%, checkrec.checknum - 100, checkrec
```

enters the data in the *checkrec* record into the proper location in the checkbook file.

The GET# Statement

When you need to input data from a random-access file, you must use the GET# statement.

GET#   **statement**

Syntax: GET [#]*filenumber* [, [*recordnumber*] [, *variable*]]

Purpose: Inputs a record from a random-access file

Note: You can omit the variable name only when using a FIELD structure, now obsolete; this statement works only with files opened FOR RANDOM or FOR BINARY.

Sample use:

```
DIM persdata(200) as personnelrec
. . .

cnt% = 0
DO WHILE NOT EOF(persfile%)
    cnt% = cnt% + 1
    GET #persfile%, , persdata(cnt%)
LOOP
```

This example requires the array of records *persdata( )*. In this case you are using a random-access file like a sequential file. The loop reads each record from the personnel file and places the records in the array. As with the PUT# statement, the GET# statement automatically moves the file pointer to the next record before getting input.

A random-access file is useful for updating a single record in the middle of the file. Study this program fragment, which continues the checkbook example:

```
INPUT "Change which check number"; checknum%
GET #checkfile%, checknum% - 100, checkrec
CALL ChangeCheck (checkrec)
PUT #checkfile%, checknum% - 100, checkrec
```

The INPUT statement gets a check number from the user, automatically determining the record number. Once the user enters the number, the GET# statement retrieves the data from the file. The *ChangeCheck* subroutine allows the user to change the current values of the record. Finally, the PUT# statement replaces the current record in the file.

The EOF Function

The loop in the GET# sample terminated when the file pointer reached the end of the file. To check for this it used Quick-BASIC's EOF function.

EOF(filenum%)   **function**

Purpose: Determines whether the file pointer is at the end of a file

Return type: −1 if true, 0 if false

Parameter: filenum% [INTEGER]—the number of the file to check

Note: This function works only with open files.

Sample call:

```
OPEN "myfile.dat" FOR RANDOM AS #filenum%
IF EOF (filenum%) THEN
    PRINT "New file created."
ELSE
    PRINT "Old file re-opened."
END IF
```

This sample uses the EOF function to see if there are any records in a file. The OPEN statement places the file pointer at the beginning of the file, and the EOF function checks for the end of the file. If EOF is true right after an OPEN statement, the file is empty.

A Random-Access Application

The following program maintains the names and addresses for a group of people. It is for a class of students, but it could be used for almost any group. The data is stored in a random-access file, maintained in alphabetical order. There are routines provided to add names, remove names, and display the names on the screen.

This program is provided to show you several examples of using random-access files. The program itself lacks many of the "bells and whistles" that make a program more professional. You are encouraged to make additions to the program to fit your particular application.

```
','','','','','','','','','','','','','','','','','','','','
'
'   CLASS.BAS:  This program maintains a list of
'       students for a class.  The user can add,
'       remove, and display records in the file.
'
'
','','','','','','','','','','','','','','','','','','','','
DECLARE SUB DisplayClassRecords (filenum%)
DECLARE SUB RemoveClassRecord (filenum%, classfile$)
DECLARE SUB OpenRandomFile (recsize%, filename$, filenum%)
DECLARE SUB AddClassRecord (filenum%)
DECLARE SUB DisplayClassIndex (filenum%)

TYPE ClassRec
    lastname AS STRING * 20
    firstname AS STRING * 10
    address AS STRING * 30
    city AS STRING * 20
    state AS STRING * 2
    zipcode AS LONG
END TYPE
DIM temprec AS ClassRec

','','','','','  executable code starts here   ','','','','','','','','
classfilename$ = "class.fil"
CALL OpenRandomFile(LEN(temprec), classfilename$, classfile%)

DO
    CALL DisplayClassIndex(classfile%)

    ' get a menu selection
    LOCATE 24, 3: PRINT SPACE$(60);
    LOCATE 24, 3
    INPUT ; "Add, Remove, Display or Quit: ", menu$

    ' call the appropriate subroutine
    SELECT CASE UCASE$(menu$)
```

```
        CASE "A"
           CALL AddClassRecord(classfile%)

        CASE "R"
           CALL RemoveClassRecord(classfile%, classfilename$)

        CASE "D"
           CALL DisplayClassRecords(classfile%)

        CASE "Q"

        CASE ELSE
           BEEP

     END SELECT

  LOOP UNTIL UCASE$(menu$) = "Q"
```

```
SUB DisplayClassIndex (filenum%)

',',',',',',',',',',',',',',',',',',',',',',',',',',',',
'
'    DisplayClassIndex:  displays the last names and
'       first initials of the students in the class.
'       The display can show up to sixty names.
'
'
',',',',',',',',',',',',',',',',',',',',',',',',',',',',',
DIM temprec AS ClassRec

CLS
LOCATE 1, 30
PRINT "Student Roster"

SEEK filenum%, 1

'   display names in three columns
FOR column% = 1 TO 3
   FOR row% = 1 TO 20
      GET #filenum%, , temprec
      IF EOF(filenum%) THEN
         EXIT SUB
      END IF

      LOCATE row% + 2, column% * 24 - 20
      PRINT USING "##"; (column% - 1) * 20 + row%;
      PRINT "   "; RTRIM$(temprec.lastname); ", ";
      PRINT LEFT$(temprec.firstname, 1)
   NEXT row%
NEXT column%

END SUB
```

```
SUB AddClassRecord (filenum%)

',',',',',',',',',',',',',',',',',',',',',',',',',',',',',',',',',',',',',',',
'
'   AddClassRecord:  allows the user to enter a new
'       name in the class file.  The names are kept
'       in alphabetical order by last name.  When a
'       record is added to the file, the records
'       after the new one are shifted down to make
'       room for the new record.
'
'
',',',',',',',',',',',',',',',',',',',',',',',',',',',',',',',',',',',',',','
DIM temprec AS ClassRec
DIM newrec AS ClassRec

CLS
LOCATE 5, 30
PRINT "Adding New Record"

'   get the student information
LOCATE 7, 1
INPUT "Last name: ", newrec.lastname
INPUT "First name: ", newrec.firstname
INPUT "Address: ", newrec.address
INPUT "City: ", newrec.city
INPUT "State: ", newrec.state
INPUT "Zip: ", tempstr$
newrec.zipcode = VAL(tempstr$)

filesize% = LOF(filenum%) / LEN(temprec)

'   determine where the new record will go
recnum% = 1
found% = 0
DO WHILE recnum% <= filesize% AND NOT found%
   GET #filenum%, recnum%, temprec
   IF temprec.lastname < newrec.lastname THEN
      recnum% = recnum% + 1
   ELSE
      found% = -1
   END IF
LOOP

'   move other records down
FOR rec% = filesize% TO recnum% STEP -1
   GET #filenum%, rec%, temprec
   PUT #filenum%, rec% + 1, temprec
NEXT rec%

PUT #filenum%, recnum%, newrec

END SUB
```

```
SUB DisplayClassRecords (filenum%)

',',',',',',',',',',',',',',',',',',',',',',',',',',',',',',',',',',
'
'   DisplayClassRecords:  displays each student
'       record on the screen, in groups of ten.
'
'
',',',',',',',',',',',',',',',',',',',',',',',',',',',',',',',',',','
DIM firstrec AS ClassRec, nextrec AS ClassRec

filesize% = LOF(filenum%) / LEN(firstrec)

CLS

'  display names in groups of two
FOR rec% = 1 TO filesize% STEP 2
    GET #filenum%, rec%, firstrec
    IF rec% + 1 <= filesize% THEN
        GET #filenum%, rec% + 1, nextrec
    END IF

    PRINT USING "## "; rec%;
    PRINT RTRIM$(firstrec.lastname); ", ";
    PRINT firstrec.firstname;

    IF rec% + 1 <= filesize% THEN
        PRINT TAB(39);
        PRINT USING "## "; rec% + 1;
        PRINT RTRIM$(nextrec.lastname); ", ";
        PRINT nextrec.firstname
    ELSE
        PRINT
    END IF

    PRINT "    "; firstrec.address;
    IF rec% + 1 <= filesize% THEN
        PRINT TAB(42);
        PRINT nextrec.address
    ELSE
        PRINT
    END IF

    PRINT "    "; RTRIM$(firstrec.city); ", ";
    PRINT firstrec.state; "  ";
    PRINT firstrec.zipcode;
    IF rec% + 1 <= filesize% THEN
        PRINT TAB(42);
        PRINT RTRIM$(nextrec.city); ", ";
        PRINT nextrec.state; "  ";
        PRINT nextrec.zipcode
    ELSE
        PRINT
    END IF

    '  after ten names, allow user to look, then
```

```
'   display the next ten
PRINT
IF rec% MOD 10 = 9 AND rec% + 2 <= filesize% THEN
    LOCATE 24, 3
    PRINT "Press any key to continue";
    DO
    LOOP WHILE INKEY$ = ""
    CLS
END IF

NEXT rec%

LOCATE 24, 3
PRINT "Press any key to continue";
DO
LOOP WHILE INKEY$ = ""

END SUB
```

```
SUB RemoveClassRecord (filenum%, classfile$)

','','','','','','','','','','','','','','','','','','','','','','','
'
'   RemoveClassRecord:  removes a student from the
'       class list.  Creates a new file so that the
'       file contains only valid student information.
'
'
','','','','','','','','','','','','','','','','','','','','','','','
DIM temprec AS ClassRec

'   get the record number
LOCATE 24, 3: PRINT SPACE$(60);
LOCATE 24, 3
PRINT "Enter the number to remove: ";
INPUT ; "", recnum%

filesize% = LOF(filenum%) / LEN(temprec)
IF recnum% > 0 AND recnum% <= filesize% THEN

    tempfile% = FREEFILE
    OPEN "temp.tmp" FOR RANDOM AS #tempfile% LEN = LEN(temprec)

    '   copy the records before the deleted one
    FOR rec% = 1 TO recnum% - 1
        GET #filenum%, rec%, temprec
        PUT #tempfile%, rec%, temprec
    NEXT rec%

    '   copy the records after the deleted one
    FOR rec% = recnum% + 1 TO filesize%
        GET #filenum%, rec%, temprec
        PUT #tempfile%, rec% - 1, temprec
    NEXT rec%
```

```
'   replace the old file with the new
CLOSE tempfile%, filenum%
KILL classfile$
NAME "temp.tmp" AS classfile$
OPEN classfile$ FOR RANDOM AS filenum% LEN = LEN(temprec)

ELSE
   BEEP
END IF

END SUB
```

Sequential Files

Working with sequential files is slightly more complicated than working with random-access files because you must open the file differently depending on what type of I/O you need to perform. This section will cover all the options for opening files and all the I/O statements that work on sequential files.

Opening a Sequential File

There are three different ways to open a sequential file. When you want to create a new file to store information, you open the file using FOR OUTPUT:

```
OPEN "defaults.dat" FOR OUTPUT AS #deffile%
```

If the file *defaults.dat* does not exist in the current directory, this OPEN statement will create a file with that name. If the file already exists, this statement will erase the file as it prepares to output the first record. Be sure that you no longer need the previous contents of the file, or that you have them stored elsewhere, before you execute this statement.

When you need to read the contents of a sequential file, you must open it using FOR INPUT:

```
OPEN "defaults.dat" FOR INPUT AS #deffile%
```

This statement places a file pointer at the beginning of a file and waits for file-input commands.

The third option, FOR APPEND, moves the file pointer to the end of a file before preparing it for output:

```
OPEN "notes.dat" FOR APPEND AS #notefile%
```

If the file *notes.dat* does not exist in the current directory, this OPEN statement will act exactly like the FOR OUTPUT option—it will create a new file.

The WRITE# Statement

When you need to output data to a sequential file, there are several statements to choose from. Most of the time the WRITE# statement will be the best one.

WRITE#   **statement**

Syntax: WRITE *#filenumber, expression* [*, expression*]. . .

Purpose: Outputs a record to a sequential file

Note: This statement works only with files opened FOR OUTPUT or FOR APPEND.

Sample use:

```
WRITE #deffile%, company$, forecolor%, backcolor%
```

If you were to sell a program to several different companies, you might consider customizing the program to allow each company to have its own name at the top of the screen with its own default colors. Part of the program would include a menu that would allow the user to change these things. The best way to store this data for future reference is with a sequential file.

After opening a file, executing this statement, and closing the file, you could type the file and see this record:

```
"Starry Software",15,2
```

The WRITE# statement is designed to be the exact complement of the INPUT# statement. In other words, whatever you output with a WRITE# statement, you can input with an equivalent INPUT# statement. The WRITE# statement automatically puts quotes around the strings and separates all data items with commas.

The PRINT# Statement

Another statement for sequential file output is the PRINT# statement.

PRINT#   **statement**

Syntax: PRINT #*filenumber*, [*expression* [{; | ,}]]. . .

Purpose: Outputs a record to a sequential file

Note: This statement works only with files opened FOR OUTPUT or FOR APPEND.

Sample use:

```
PRINT #deffile%, company$, forecolor%, backcolor%
```

The PRINT# statement works exactly like the PRINT statement except that the output goes to a disk file instead of to the screen. The problem with this statement is that what you output with the PRINT# statement is not necessarily what you input with the equivalent INPUT# statement. If the example PRINT# statement is executed in the proper context, the record in the file will look like this:

```
Starry Software        15          2
```

When you read this record with an INPUT# statement, the entire record will be the company name, because there are no commas or quotation marks separating the string from the integer. To keep this from happening, make each string variable a separate record in the file:

```
PRINT #deffile%, company$
PRINT #deffile%, forecolor%, backcolor%
```

The PRINT# USING Statement

QuickBASIC also provides a PRINT# USING statement, which is the file equivalent of the PRINT USING statement you learned about in Chapter 7.

PRINT# USING   **statement**

Syntax:
     PRINT #*filenumber*, USING *format*; *expressions* [{; | ,}]
where *expressions* =>
     expression [, *expression*]. . .

Purpose: Outputs a record to a sequential file with a specific format

Note: This statement works only with files opened FOR OUTPUT or FOR APPEND.

Sample use:

```
format$ = "&, ##, ##"
PRINT #deffile%, USING format$; company$, forecolor%, _
                          backcolor%
```

The function of each format string character is covered in Chapter 7. This PRINT# USING statement will produce a record that you can read with an INPUT# statement. If you have a comma as part of the company name, however, you must include quotation marks as part of the format string:

```
format$ = CHR$(34) + "&" + CHR$(34) + ", ## , ##"
```

This string guarantees that the INPUT# statement will read the data properly.

The INPUT# Statement

The primary statement for reading data from a sequential file is the INPUT# statement.

INPUT#   statement

Syntax: INPUT #*filenumber, variable* [, *variable*]. . .

Purpose: Inputs a record from a sequential file

Note: This statement works only with files opened FOR INPUT.

Sample use:

```
INPUT #deffile%, company$, forecolor%, backcolor%
```

When QuickBASIC executes an INPUT# statement, it searches for each item in the list one at a time. When searching

for a string variable, it will start with the first printable character and finish with a comma. If the first character is a quotation
mark, the string will extend until the next quotation mark. All
strings terminate with an end-of-line or end-of-file marker. When
the INPUT# statement searches for a numeric variable, it reads
in a set of characters until it finds a space, comma, or end-of-line
marker. It then converts the characters to the proper numeric
type, just as the VAL function does.

The LINE INPUT# Statement

The LINE INPUT# statement allows you to read an entire
record of a sequential file, regardless of its contents.

LINE INPUT#   **statement**

Syntax: LINE INPUT #*filenumber, stringvariable*

Purpose: Inputs a complete record from a sequential file

Note: This statement works only for files opened FOR
INPUT.

Sample use:

```
DO WHILE NOT EOF(echofile%)
    LINE INPUT #echofile%, textline$
    PRINT textline$
LOOP
```

You can use this DO-LOOP to echo a text file to the screen. The
LINE INPUT# statement ignores spaces, commas, and quotation marks when reading a record. This is the only statement
that will ensure you are getting the entire record.

Binary Files

Binary files are not used as often as sequential and random-access files. In this section you will see how to open a binary file, how to output to a binary file, and how to input from one.

Opening a Binary File

To use a binary file you must open the file FOR BINARY:

```
OPEN "password.dat" FOR BINARY AS #passfile%
```

As with a random-access file, this OPEN statement will search the current directory for the file *password.dat*. If it finds the file, it will place a file pointer at the first byte in the file. If the file does not exist, the OPEN statement will create one.

Output to a Binary File

The only statement that will output a series of bytes to a binary file is the PUT# statement. The second argument of this statement now represents the byte position instead of the record number. Here is a program that stores encrypted passwords in a binary file:

```
usernum% = LOF(passfile%) + 1
PRINT "Your user number will be"; usernum%
INPUT "Enter your password: ", password$

passwordsize$ = ASC(LEN(password$))
PUT #passfile%, usernum%, passwordsize$

'    encrypt each byte in the string
FOR cnt% = 1 TO LEN(password$)
   tempnum% = ASC(MID$(password$, cnt%, 1))
   tempnum% = tempnum% * 2 + 5
   MID$(password$, cnt%, 1) = CHR$(tempnum%)
NEXT cnt%

PUT #passfile%, , password$
```

The first PUT# statement in the program places the length of the password entered in the file. Since this length will be less than 80 characters, you can encrypt the length of the password in a single-character string variable. The second PUT# statement places the encoded password in the file.

The advantage of using a binary file in this case is that no one will be able to type the file and determine a person's password. First of all, most of the characters in the file will be the strange character set at the end of the ASCII table. Secondly, the file is one continuous string of characters with no breaks to show where one password ends and another begins. It would be extremely difficult for a person to decipher the passwords without seeing the source code that generated the file.

The INPUT$ Function

There are two methods of reading data stored in a binary file. The first is the INPUT$ function.

INPUT$(nchrs, filenum)   **function**

Purpose: Reads a set of characters from a file

Return type: STRING

Parameters: nchrs [INTEGER]—the number of characters to input

filenum [INTEGER]—the number of the open file

Note: The file number may be preceded by an optional # sign; this statement works only with open files.

Sample use:

```
DO
    onechar$ = INPUT$(1, #anyfile%)
    PRINT onechar$; " ";
    count% = count% + 1
```

```
    IF count% >= 900 THEN
        DO WHILE INKEY$ = ""
        LOOP
        count% = 1
        PRINT: PRINT
    END IF
LOOP WHILE NOT EOF(anyfile%)
```

The loop in the box displays each character in a file separated by a space. This would enable you to study the contents of a binary file more closely. If the characters appear to be gibberish, you may choose to display the ASCII equivalent of each character.

The SEEK Statement

To move to a specific record number before reading data from a binary file, QuickBASIC provides the SEEK statement.

SEEK   **statement**

Syntax: SEEK [#]*filenumber, recordnumber*

Purpose: Moves the file pointer to a specified byte position (or record number for RANDOM files)

Note: This statement works only with open files.

Sample use:

```
INPUT "What byte position"; bytenum#
SEEK #anyfile%, bytenum#
INPUT "How many characters to read"; numchars%
filechars$ = INPUT$(numchars%, #anyfile%)
```

The program fragment in the box displays the data from any part of an open file. The SEEK statement moves the file pointer, and the INPUT$ function reads the data.

The following program is the complement of the password program given earlier in this section.

```
INPUT "Enter your user number: ", usernum%
INPUT "Enter your password: ", password$

SEEK #passfile%, usernum%
passwordsize% = ASC(INPUT$(1, #passfile%))
checkpass$ = INPUT$(passwordsize%, #passfile%)

FOR cnt% = 1 TO LEN(password$)
   tempnum% = ASC(MID$(password$, cnt%, 1))
   tempnum% = tempnum% * 2 + 5
   MID$(password$, cnt%, 1) = CHR$(tempnum%)
NEXT cnt%

IF checkpass$ = password$ THEN
   PRINT "Password accepted."
ELSE
   PRINT "Password rejected."
END IF
```

In this program the user is asked for a number and a password. The password the user enters is encoded and compared to the one stored in the file. If they match, the password is accepted. Obviously some idiot-proofing should be done before you use these routines in an actual program.

File-Like Devices

QuickBASIC allows you to make a device act like a file. In this way you can use the same code to read from a disk file as you do for reading from the keyboard. Likewise, you could use the same subroutine to write a sentence to a disk file, to the screen, or to the printer. This section covers a few methods for using the file-like devices. The COM*n*: communications ports are discussed in Chapter 13.

There are a total of eight file-like devices. Only the communications ports COM1: and COM2: can be used for both input and output. The KYBD: file is the keyboard and can be used for input only. The valid output file-like devices are CONS: and SCRN: for the terminal screen, and LPT1:, LPT2:, and LPT3: for the printers.

You open a file-like device in the same way that you open a disk file. The statement

```
OPEN "LPT1:" FOR OUTPUT AS #outfile%
```

prepares the printer to accept sequential-file output commands. The statement

```
PRINT #outfile%, myname$
```

would print the value of *myname$* on the printer.

Using the keyboard as an input file is impractical in many ways. First of all, the INPUT# statement does not display a text cursor to indicate that it is waiting for input. Also, the characters you enter are not echoed to the screen automatically. In addition, the INPUT# statement does not allow you to edit your input with the DEL or BACKSPACE key.

The screen and the printer files work well together when you need to output the contents of another file. Study this subroutine:

```
SUB Echo(infilename$, outfilename$)

infile% = FREEFILE
OPEN infilename$ FOR INPUT AS #infile%
outfile% = FREEFILE
OPEN outfilename$ FOR OUTPUT AS #outfile%

DO WHILE NOT EOF(echofile%)
   LINE INPUT #infile%, textline$
   PRINT #outfile%, textline$
LOOP

CLOSE #infile%, #outfile%
END SUB
```

You could always use this subroutine to copy the contents of one file to another. A better use, however, would be to echo the contents of a file to either the screen or the printer:

```
INPUT "<T>ype or <P>rint"; display$
IF LEFT$(UCASE$(display$),1) = "P" THEN
   CALL Echo(myfile$, "LPT1:")
ELSE
```

```
    CALL Echo(myfile$, "SCRN:")
END IF
```

By calling the same routine with one of the two device names, you save yourself the trouble of writing one routine with PRINT statements and one with LPRINT statements.

Sharing Files

QuickBASIC includes several options and statements for sharing files among many processes. The setup of a multiuser environment is beyond the scope of this text. This section, however, will demonstrate how to use the access and lock commands in QuickBASIC.

Access Modes and Lock Modes

When you look at the syntax description for the OPEN statement, you will see a line for the network mode of the file being opened. There are three ways to access a file in a multiuser environment. You can open any file with ACCESS READ except a FOR OUTPUT sequential file. You can open any file with ACCESS WRITE except a FOR INPUT sequential file. Files opened using FOR RANDOM, FOR BINARY, and FOR APPEND can be opened with ACCESS READ WRITE. The statement

```
OPEN "persons.dat" ACCESS READ AS #filenum% LEN=34
```

opens a random-access file for reading only.

There are four lock options. The LOCK READ WRITE option gives your process exclusive access to the file. If you omit a written lock option, the LOCK READ WRITE option is the default. The SHARED option gives other processes the right to read or write to the file you are opening. The LOCK READ and

LOCK WRITE options keep others from reading and writing, respectively, to your file. LOCK WRITE is probably the most useful:

```
OPEN "persons.dat" FOR RANDOM ACCESS WRITE LOCK WRITE_
                        AS #filenum % LEN=34
```

With this statement, only you can write to *persons.dat* as long as the file is open. Also, because you specified ACCESS WRITE, you cannot read a record from the file.

The LOCK-UNLOCK Structure

The more common way to lock a person from using a file is with the LOCK-UNLOCK structure.

LOCK-UNLOCK   **structure**

Syntax: LOCK [#] *filenumber* [*recordrange*]
          statementblock
          UNLOCK [#] *filenumber* [*recordrange*]
where *recordrange* = >
          {*recordnumber* | *lowerbound* TO *upperbound*}

Purpose: Locks other processes from accessing all or part of an opened file

Note: The LOCK and UNLOCK statement lines must match *exactly;* this structure works only with open files.

Sample use:

```
OPEN "persons.dat" SHARED AS #filenum% LEN=34
. . .

LOCK #filenum%, recnum%
PUT #filenum%, recnum%, personnel
UNLOCK #filenum%, recnum%
```

The LOCK-UNLOCK structure allows you to lock a specific record or set of records in a file. Also, the lock holds only for the time you are making your change. This allows all other users access to the other records in your file while you are making changes to certain sections.

File Information

You have already used the EOF function to see if the file pointer is at the end of a file. QuickBASIC has a few other functions that give information about a file.

The LOF Function

To help determine the length of a file, QuickBASIC provides the LOF function.

LOF(filenum)   **function**

Purpose: Supplies the number of bytes in a file

Return type: LONG

Parameter: filenum [INTEGER]—the number of the file

Note: This function works only with open files.

Sample call:

```
OPEN "persons.dat" AS #fnum% LEN=LEN(personnel)
numrecords% = LOF(#fnum%) / LEN(personnel)
```

This sample call uses the LOF function to determine the number of records in a random-access file. When you divide the total number of bytes in the file by the length of each record, you have the length of the file in records. You cannot use LOF to determine the number of records in a sequential file.

The LOC and SEEK Functions

The LOC and SEEK functions provide positioning information on the file pointer. The LOC function will tell you where I/O last occurred.

LOC(filenum)   **function**

Purpose: Supplies the latest position of a file pointer

Return type: LONG

Parameters: filenum [INTEGER]—the number of the file

Note: The value returned by LOC depends on the file type: if the file is random-access, LOC gives the record number of the last record read or written; if it is binary, LOC gives the number of the last byte; if it is sequential, LOC divides the current byte position by 128; this function works only with open files.

Sample call:

```
curpos% = LOC(myfile%)
```

The SEEK function works slightly differently, telling you where I/O will occur next.

SEEK(filenum)   **function**

Purpose: Supplies the current position of the file pointer

Return type: LONG

Parameters: filenum [INTEGER]—the number of the file

Note: The value returned by SEEK depends on the file type: if the file is random-access, SEEK gives the record number of the file pointer; otherwise, SEEK gives the byte position. This function works only with open files.

Sample call:

```
curpos% = SEEK(myfile%)
```

SEEK and LOC differ in that SEEK tells you where the pointer is now, whereas LOC tells you where it performed the last I/O operation. Neither function is very helpful with sequential files.

The FILEATTR Function

The FILEATTR function gives you other key information about a file.

FILEATTR(filenum, key)   **function**

Purpose: Supplies a file's open mode or DOS handle

Return type: INTEGER

Parameters: filenum [INTEGER]—the number of the file
        key [1 or 2]—1 for the mode, 2 for the handle

Note: This function works only with open files.

Sample call:

```
openmode% = FILEATTR(myfile%, 1)
```

If you use the FILEATTR function to get the open mode, you will get one of the following values: 1 if FOR INPUT, 2 if

FOR OUTPUT, 4 if FOR RANDOM, 8 if FOR APPEND, or 32 if FOR BINARY. The file handle is used by certain DOS functions, some of which are covered in Chapter 13.

The WIDTH# Statement

The last three statements in this section change the attributes of a file, as opposed to getting them. The WIDTH# statement changes the width of a device, usually the printer.

WIDTH#   **statement**

Syntax: WIDTH {*devicename* | *#filenumber*}, *newwidth*

Purpose: Changes the width of a file-like device

Note: If the file is already open, you should use the file-number format; the device-name format defers the command until the file is opened.

Sample use:

```
WIDTH "LPT1:", 132
```

If you want to change the width of the screen, you may want to use the WIDTH statement described in Chapter 7.

The NAME Statement

The NAME statement and the DOS RENAME command will change the name of a file.

NAME **statement**

Syntax: NAME *oldfilename* AS *newfilename*

Purpose: Changes the name of a file

Note: You can rename a file across directories but not across disks; this statement works only with closed files.

Sample use:

```
NAME "myfile.dat" AS "oldstuff\myfile.old"
```

This sample statement moves the file *myfile.dat* into the subdirectory "oldstuff" with the name *myfile.old*.

The KILL Statement

The KILL statement is the same as the DOS ERASE command.

KILL **statement**

Syntax: KILL *filename*

Purpose: Deletes a file

Note: The file specification may include wildcards; this statement works only with closed files.

Sample use:

```
KILL "*.BAS"
```

Obviously, you need to use this statement with extreme caution.

Error Handling

The novice programmer will probably wonder why the section on error handling is in the file-manipulation chapter. A more experienced programmer, however, should realize that most errors are handled without special error traps. The only statements you cannot control are those that manipulate files. There is no convenient way, for example, to see if a file exists in your directory without using the OPEN statement. If you try to open a file that does not exist with FOR INPUT you will get an error. To keep from stopping the whole program when this type of error occurs, you use error-handling statements.

The ON ERROR Statement

The primary statement for error handling is the ON ERROR statement.

ON ERROR   **statement**

Syntax: ON ERROR GOTO *label*

Purpose: Enables error handling and identifies the error-handling section of the program

Note: The statement label must be in the module-level code; error handling does not occur in the error-handling section of the code.

Sample use:

```
myfile% = FREEFILE
ON ERROR GOTO GetFileError
DO
    openerror% = 0
    INPUT "What file do you want"; myfilename$
    OPEN myfilename$ FOR INPUT AS #myfile%
LOOP UNTIL NOT openerror
ON ERROR GOTO 0
```

```
PRINT "File opened successfully."
END

GetFileError:
    PRINT "Open error.  Please try again."
    openerror% = -1
    RESUME NEXT
```

The program in the box shows a simple error-handling technique. If there is an error in trying to find the file, QuickBASIC will jump to the *GetFileError* label. The PRINT statement will display the error message, the error flag will be set, and RESUME NEXT will send you back to get another filename. The ON ERROR GOTO 0 statement is QuickBASIC's method for disabling error handling.

This small program demonstrates a few important guidelines in using error-handling statements. Notice that error handling is set only for the statement area that might cause an error. This way you know what happened when you get to the *GetFileError* label. There is only one way to get to this label and one way back. If you have other file-manipulation statements elsewhere in the program, you should create a separate label and error handler.

You should also notice that very little is done inside the error handler except setting a flag. The flag is interpreted by the main area of code. The problem with getting another filename in the error handler is that a person reading the code has to search too much to find out how the error is handled. With the DO-LOOP in the main part of the code, the error handling is obvious. If you trap errors inside a subroutine or function, remember that your error flag must be a global variable.

The RESUME Statement

Once you are in an error handler, you need to find your way back to the area where the error occurred. In QuickBASIC you accomplish this with the RESUME statement.

RESUME   **statement**

Syntax: RESUME [{0 | NEXT | *label*}]

Purpose: Returns program control from an error handler to another area of the program, which may be a specific label, the error-causing statement, or the statement after it

Note: Any label must be defined at the module level.

Sample use:

```
ON ERROR GOTO FileProblem
OPEN "newfile.dat" FOR OUTPUT AS #myfile%
ON ERROR GOTO 0
. . .

FileProblem:
   PRINT "Error creating file."
   INPUT "<R>etry or <A>bort"; retry$
   IF LEFT$(UCASE$(retry$),1) = "R" THEN
      RESUME
   END IF
   END
```

When you open a file with FOR OUTPUT you do not expect to have an error. Errors usually mean that the disk is full or the drive is not ready. The RESUME statement returns program control to the OPEN statement, which attempts to create the file again. In the previous example you saw the RESUME NEXT statement. In that case you did not want to go right back to the OPEN statement because you would immediately get the same error over and over again.

If you write a program that uses error handling and you want to compile the program with the BC program, you must include one additional compiler option. If you are using ON ERROR with only the RESUME [label] format, add the /e option to the command line. If you have a RESUME or RESUME NEXT statement, add the /x option. These options will generate the proper code to keep track of where an error occurs.

The END Statement

In module-level code, you must keep from executing an error handler when the program finishes the main code. Therefore, you must include an END statement.

END   **statement**

Syntax: END

Purpose: Terminates program execution

Sample use:

```
CALL GetData
CALL ChangeData
CALL SaveData
END

ErrorHandler:
    PRINT "Error!"
    RESUME NEXT
```

This sample is a typical main module. It calls three subroutines and terminates. If you did not include the END statement, the program would call the three subroutines, then print the error message, then produce a "Resume without error" message.

The ERR Function

To help determine the exact cause of an error, you can use the ERR function.

ERR   **function**

Purpose: Supplies the error number of the last error

Return type: INTEGER

Parameters: None

Sample call:

```
OpenError:
  IF ERR=53 THEN
     "File is not in this directory."
  ELSEIF ERR=70 THEN
     "Another user has locked the file."
  ELSE
     "Error"; ERR; "trying to OPEN file."
  END IF
```

The ERR function allows you to better inform your user (and yourself) of what caused an error. In this sample the two most common error numbers are explained. If a different error occurs, the number is displayed. You can look up the number in your QuickBASIC reference book to determine how to correct the error.

The ERROR Statement

If you want to force program termination, you can create an error with the ERROR statement.

ERROR   **statement**

Syntax: ERROR *errornumber*

Purpose: Simulates a QuickBASIC error

Sample use:

```
INPUT "What record do you want displayed"; recnum%
IF recnum% <= 0 THEN ERROR 63
```

In this example, if the user enters a nonpositive record number, the code will simulate error number 63: "Bad record number." If there is no error handler for that error, or if error handling is disabled, the error message will appear and the program will terminate. The number of applications requiring this statement is extremely few.

Subdirectories

QuickBASIC includes three statements that work with subdirectories. Each statement works the same way that the equivalent DOS command does.

The CHDIR statement will change the current directory. There is no "CD" shortcut.

CHDIR   **statement**

Syntax: CHDIR *directoryname*
Purpose: Changes the current default directory
Sample use:

```
CHDIR "temp"
```

The MKDIR statement creates a new directory.

MKDIR   **statement**

Syntax: MKDIR *directoryname*
Purpose: Creates a new subdirectory
Sample use:

```
MKDIR "temp"
```

The RMDIR statement removes a directory, as long as the directory is empty.

RMDIR   **statement**

Syntax: RMDIR *directoryname*
Purpose: Removes a directory listing
Sample use:

```
RMDIR "temp"
```

Normally, there is little use for these statements inside small programs. If you need a working area, however, a temporary subdirectory keeps your other directories clean. Study this program skeleton:

```
MKDIR "temp"
CHDIR "temp"

'create temporary files and work with them here

KILL "*.*"
```

```
CHDIR ".."
RMDIR "temp"
```

In this fragment you create a subdirectory and do all your work there. When you are finished you can clean everything up easily by deleting each file, moving back to the parent directory, and deleting the temporary subdirectory.

TWELVE

Graphics and Sound

Graphics Devices
Changing Modes and Colors
Graphics Coordinates
Simple Graphics
More Complex Graphics
Sound and Music

Almost every business section in the local newpapers includes a plot showing a historical view of various stock averages. As an investor, you understand how the market is faring by looking at the graph, which is much easier than sifting through a set of numbers. The same theory holds true with computer applications: the more information you can display in a picture, the more easily the user will understand it.

This chapter covers the QuickBASIC statements and functions that support graphics and sound. It divides graphics capabilities by adapter type so you can easily find what screen modes and color options apply to your system. You will learn statements for producing simple lines and complex pictures. Finally, you will find out how to play music with your computer. Chapter 21 will develop complete subroutines that use these statements to make meaningful and colorful plots.

Graphics Devices

QuickBASIC includes graphics support for every major graphics adapter and display monitor. Unfortunately, most of the documentation you find is disorganized and confusing. This section will let you study the graphics capabilities that match your particular configuration.

If your system has no graphics adapter, you will not be able to use any of the graphics statements or functions in this chapter. You should consider purchasing a color card and color monitor. These allow you to run popular games and other software, and to create your own graphics.

The Color Graphics Adapter (CGA)

The CGA provides enough graphics capabilities for most typical users. It has three modes: one for text only that can display 16 colors at the same time, one for low-resolution graphics with three drawing colors, and one for medium-resolution graphics with one drawing color.

When you start any program you are in screen mode 0. This is commonly called text-only mode. None of the graphics statements or functions are valid in mode 0. The screen size defaults to 80 columns by 25 rows of characters (80×25). CGA owners can use the WIDTH statement from Chapter 7 to switch to 40×25 and back. Each character can be one of 16 different colors, which you define with the COLOR statement described later.

Screen mode 1 is for low-resolution graphics. The actual resolution is 320 pixels wide by 200 pixels high (320×200). A *pixel* is an individual dot on the screen and is the smallest graphics element you can modify. This mode has a palette size of four, which means that the screen can display four colors at once, with one color being the background color. Here are the default colors:

Color #	Default Color	Color Code
0	black	0
1	bright cyan	11
2	bright magenta	13
3	white	15

Color 0, the background color, can be one of 16 different colors. These colors, called the primary colors, are coded from 0

0 - Black	8 - Dark gray
1 - Blue	9 - Bright blue
2 - Green	10 - Bright green
3 - Cyan	11 - Bright cyan
4 - Red	12 - Bright red
5 - Magenta	13 - Bright magenta
6 - Brown	14 - Yellow
7 - Light gray	15 - White

Table 12-1.   Color Table

to 15 and are listed in Table 12-1. Colors 1 through 3 are the foreground colors. These belong to a palette and cannot be changed individually.

For the CGA you can specify one of two palettes. Palette 0 (or any even number from 0 to 254) is the default, with foreground color codes 11, 13, and 15. Palette 1 (or any odd number from 1 to 255) will give you color codes 10 (green), 12 (red), and 14 (yellow). You must use the COLOR statement to change palettes when you have a CGA.

The Enhanced Graphics Adapter (EGA)

The EGA provides better resolution and larger palette sizes than the CGA. The capabilities of your EGA will depend on the type of display monitor you have. This section covers all of the available screen modes for the EGA, for the color display monitor (CDM), the extended color display monitor (ECDM), and the monochrome display monitor (MDM).

When you start any program you are in screen mode 0, the text-only mode. None of the graphics statements or functions are valid in mode 0. The screen size defaults to 80 columns by 25 rows of characters (80×25). The WIDTH statement, shown in Chapter 7, enables you to change the size of all characters on the screen. With any monitor you can change between 80×25 and 40×25. The ECDM and MDM also support modes with 43 rows of text: 40×43 and 80×43. The color palette size for this mode is 16, so each character can be one of up to 16 different colors. CDM owners have only the 16 primary color codes to choose from, ECDM owners have 64 color codes, and MDM owners have three color codes.

Screen mode 1 is for low-resolution graphics: 320 pixels wide by 200 pixels high (320×200). This mode has a palette size of four, with one color being the background color. Each of these can be one of 16 different colors, coded with the numbers in Table 12-1. The default colors are these:

Color #	Default Color	Color Code
0	black	0
1	bright cyan	11
2	bright magenta	13
3	white	15

Screen mode 2 is for medium-resolution graphics, 640×200. The palette size in this mode is only two, since this mode is primarily for CGA users. With the EGA, you can use the PAL-ETTE statement to assign any of the 16 primary colors to either the foreground color or the background color.

Screen mode 7 is similar to mode 1—it gives you 320×200 low-resolution graphics. (*Note:* There are no screen modes 3 through 6 for any graphics adapter.) The palette size, however, increases from four colors to 16 colors. This means that you can see all 16 primary colors on the screen at the same time. Mode 7 is also the first mode that supports multiple graphics pages, which are discussed later in this chapter.

Screen mode 8 will give you the same 16-color palette size with medium-resolution graphics (640×200). It has the same resolution as mode 2, but it supports 16 colors instead of two. Modes 1, 2, 7, and 8 work the same for the CDM as they do for the ECDM.

Mode 9 takes full advantage of the EGA, but it requires the ECDM monitor. With mode 9 the number of color codes available increases from 16 to 64. If you want to change the color code for a certain color number you can use the PALETTE statement, which is covered later in this chapter.

Screen mode 10 is designed specifically for users with the EGA and the MDM (monochrome display monitor). It gives you the high resolution found in screen mode 9, but the palette is much smaller. In this mode you have a palette size of four. The possible "colors" are black, grey, blinking, and white.

The Video Graphics Array (VGA)

The VGA card is the most versatile—and the most expensive—graphics adapter supported by QuickBASIC. With the VGA you can use each of the ten screen modes, from low-resolution graphics to very high-resolution graphics. For screen modes 1, 2, 7, 8, 9, and 10, see the text in the EGA section.

When you start any program you are in screen mode 0, the text-only mode. You may not use any of the graphics statements or functions in mode 0. The screen size defaults to 80 columns by 25 rows of characters (80×25). With the VGA you can use the WIDTH statement to choose from any of the following sizes: 40×25, 40×43, 40×50, 80×25, 80×43, or 80×50.

Screen mode 11 gives you very-high-resolution graphics: 640 pixels wide by 480 pixels high (640×480). The palette size of this mode is only two, giving you a foreground color and a background color. Either color can be one of 262,143 different color codes. To change the color code for a color number, you need the PALETTE statement covered later in this chapter. The color codes are based on the following equation:

$$code = 65536 * blueint + 256 * greenint + redint$$

The values for blueint, greenint, and redint are integers from 0 for lowest intensity to 63 for highest intensity. For example, the number 256 * 63, or 16128, is high-intensity green. To change the foreground color to bright green use this statement:

```
PALETTE 1, 16128
```

When QuickBASIC executes this statement, everything currently drawn in color number 1 will change to green.

When you display text in mode 11 or 12, you have a choice of two screen sizes: 80×30 or 80×60. Obviously, the latter will give you twice as many characters on the screen, but each character will be half the size (and not as readable). Use the WIDTH statement to change these sizes.

Screen mode 12 takes more advantage of the VGA's capabilities. In this mode you still have very high resolution, but now you have a palette size of 16, instead of two. Again, each of the 16 color numbers can be one of 262,143 color codes.

Screen mode 13 sacrifices resolution for palette size. This mode gives you the same resolution as modes 1 and 7 (low), but has a palette size of 256. Use the PALETTE USING statement to change these colors.

The Multicolor Graphics Array (MCGA)

The MCGA is a cross between the CGA and the VGA. If you select screen mode 0, 1, or 2, the MCGA acts like a CGA. If you select mode 11 or 13, the MCGA will act like a VGA. All other modes are invalid for this card. The color codes of the MCGA are the same as those of the VGA. See the text in each respective section for the resolution and palette size of each mode.

Changing Modes and Colors

Now that you know the capabilities for your particular adapter, you can study the statements that alter the current graphics modes, colors, and palettes.

The SCREEN Statement

To change display modes with any graphics adapter you must use the SCREEN statement.

SCREEN   statement

Syntax:

SCREEN *mode* [, [*colorflag*] [, [*apage*] [, *vpage*]]]

Purpose: Changes the graphics display mode

Note: See the text for each graphics adapter for the valid screen modes.

Sample use:

```
SCREEN 1                          'set low-resolution graphics
```

There are four arguments to the SCREEN command. The first is the screen mode, which is a number from 0 to 13. The second argument is a *color flag*. If you have a monochrome monitor you should set this flag to 0 in screen mode 0 and 1 in screen mode 1. The color flag is ignored in all other modes. The third argument is the number of the *active page*, which is the page that future graphics commands will affect. The final argument is the *visual page*, which is the page that is displayed on the monitor. Working with pages is covered later in the chapter.

The COLOR Statement

To change the screen colors you need the COLOR statement.

COLOR   statement

Syntax: COLOR [*color1*] [, *color2*]

Purpose: Changes the display colors

Note: See the text for each graphics adapter for the valid Color options; for screen mode 0, see the entry for the COLOR statement in Chapter 7.

Sample use:

```
COLOR 2, 1
```

The purpose of each argument in the COLOR statement varies with the screen mode and the graphics adapter type. For screen mode 2, the COLOR statement is invalid. In mode 1, the first argument is the background color code and the second argument is the palette number. If you have a CGA, the COLOR statement in the box will set the background color to blue and the foreground colors to green, red, and yellow.

The PALETTE Statement

If you have an EGA or VGA, you can change the color code of a color in the palette with the PALETTE statement.

PALETTE   **statement**

Syntax: PALETTE [*colornumber, colorcode*]
Purpose: Changes a color in the current palette
Note: This statement is invalid for CGA users.
Sample use:

```
PALETTE 0, 1
PALETTE 3, 11
```

The first statement changes the background color to blue. The second statement changes color number 3 to cyan (color code

11). Anything displayed on the screen in color 3 will change immediately to cyan. If you use a PALETTE statement with no arguments you will return the palette to the default values.

The PALETTE USING Statement

To change the entire palette, QuickBASIC provides the PALETTE USING statement.

PALETTE USING   **statement**

Syntax: PALETTE USING *variable*[*(arrayindex)*]
Purpose: Changes all colors of the current palette
Note: This statement is invalid for CGA users.
Sample use:

```
FOR count% = 1 TO 16
    colors%(count%) = 17 - count%
NEXT count%
PALETTE USING color%
```

The program fragment in the box creates an array that reverses the color codes of the palette. When QuickBASIC executes the PALETTE USING statement, the screen immediately changes to reflect the new palette.

Graphics Coordinates

In the previous section you learned about each screen mode and its resolution. Before you can start executing graphics commands, however, you need to understand how to prepare a coordinate system for your pictures. In this section you will study screen- and world-coordinate systems, viewports, and windows. The examples in this section assume that you are in screen mode 1. Other modes have different screen limits, but the concepts are the same.

When you enter screen mode 1, QuickBASIC sets up the coordinate system shown in Figure 12-1. The resolution in this mode is 320×200, so the x-coordinates range from 0 to 319 and the y-coordinates range from 0 to 199. Unlike the Cartesian system you learned in school, the screen-coordinate system has its origin in the upper-left corner of the screen.

When you use the screen-coordinate system, the numbers in the graphics statements will be actual pixel numbers. Each pixel is defined by its coordinate pair. In mode 1, the coordinate pair (160, 100) in screen coordinates is a pixel in the center of the screen.

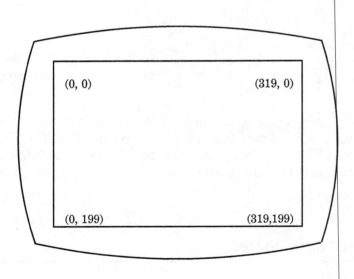

Figure 12-1.   Screen-coordinate system

Creating a Viewport

If you want to limit your output to a portion of the screen, you can create a *viewport* with the VIEW statement. A viewport is a section of the screen to which all future graphics output is limited.

VIEW   **statement**

Syntax:
    VIEW [[SCREEN] *coordpair-coordpair* [, *viewoptions*]]
where *viewoptions* = >
    [*fillcolor*] [, *bordercolor*]
and where *coordpair* = >
    (*xcoord, ycoord*)

Purpose: Limits graphics output to a specific viewport

Note: A VIEW statement with no arguments restores the viewport to the full screen; this statement is invalid in screen mode 0.

Sample use:

```
VIEW (160, 100)-(318, 198), 0, 3
```

The sample statement in the box moves the current viewport to the lower-right quarter of the screen. The new viewport will have a border drawn in color 3 and will be filled with the background color.

The two coordinate pairs in the VIEW statement are the opposite corners of an imaginary box. The order of the pairs is immaterial, and you can choose a lower-left/upper-right combination, or a lower-right/upper-left combination. The statements

```
VIEW (160, 100)-(318, 198)
VIEW (318, 100)-(160, 198)
VIEW (160, 198)-(318, 100)
```

all define the same viewport.

The option word SCREEN in the VIEW statement defines the new range of coordinates for the viewport. If you omit the word SCREEN, QuickBASIC redefines the origin to be the upper-left corner of the viewport. When you add the keyword SCREEN, the origin remains the upper-left corner of the screen. With the viewport definition given in the box, the statement

```
LINE (1, 1)-(10, 10)
```

will display a line inside the viewport. If you added the word SCREEN to the VIEW statement, however, this line would be outside the viewport and would not appear on the screen. The same line with the new viewport would be this statement:

```
LINE (160, 100)-(170, 110)
```

If you try to draw a shape that is partially inside the viewport and partially outside, the shape will be *clipped*. When a program clips an object, it displays only the part of the object that is inside the viewport. Given a viewport in the upper-left quarter of the screen, the statement

```
CIRCLE (160, 100), 50
```

would display only the quarter of the circle that is inside the viewport and would appear as shown in Figure 12-2.

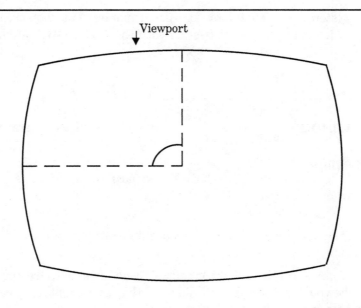

Figure 12-2.   Viewport example

The two optional arguments at the end of the VIEW statement are the *fill color* and the *border color*. If you include a fill color, the entire viewport will become that color when you create it. If you use the background color, color number 0, you will clear the viewport when you reach the VIEW statement. If you specify a border color, QuickBASIC will draw a box around the viewport in the desired color. If you do not specify a border color, no box will be displayed.

Defining a World-Coordinate System

In many programs you will want to display data that does not fit conveniently into the screen-coordinate system. QuickBASIC lets you create your own coordinate system called a *world-coordinate system*. The numeric limits of a world-coordinate system are defined by the programmer. You can create your own world-coordinate system with the WINDOW statement.

WINDOW   **statement**

Syntax:
     WINDOW [[SCREEN] *coordpair-coordpair*]
where *coordpair* = >
     (*xcoord, ycoord*)

Purpose: Defines a world-coordinate system for the current viewport

Note: A WINDOW statement with no arguments restores the viewport to screen coordinates; this statement is invalid in screen mode 0.

Sample use:

```
WINDOW (0, 0)-(50, 50)
```

This sample statement changes the limits of the viewport to 0 through 50 in both directions. All future graphics statements and functions must use world coordinates.

When you use the WINDOW statement, you reverse the y-axis so that the origin is the lower-left corner of the viewport instead of the upper-left corner. If you use the SCREEN keyword in the WINDOW statement, however, you will keep the origin in the upper-left corner. (The keyword SCREEN in the WINDOW statement has no relation to the keyword SCREEN in the VIEW statement.)

The set of coordinate pairs represents the diagonal limits of an imaginary box. The order of these pairs is immaterial. The statements

```
WINDOW (0, 50)-(50, 0)
WINDOW (50, 50)-(0, 0)
```

both represent the same window, as do these two:

```
WINDOW SCREEN (0, 50)-(50, 0)
WINDOW SCREEN (50, 50)-(0, 0)
```

In the first two statements, the point (0,0) will be in the lower-left corner of the viewport. In the second two statements, (0,0) will be in the upper-left corner.

Mapping Coordinates

If you need to convert from world coordinates to screen coordinates, or vice versa, you can use the PMAP function.

PMAP(expr, key%)   function

Purpose: Maps a point in world coordinates to screen coordinates, or maps a point in screen coordinates to world coordinates

Return type: SINGLE

Parameters: expr [any numeric type] — the coordinate to map
key% — specifies the conversion [0..3] -
        0 — converts x-world to x-screen
        1 — converts y-world to y-screen
        2 — converts x-screen to x-world
        3 — converts y-screen to y-world

Sample call:

```
LINE (PMAP(0, 2), PMAP(199, 3))-(PMAP(319, 2), PMAP(199, 3))
```

If you have defined a world-coordinate system, all future graphics statements will use world coordinates. If you have data in screen coordinates, you need to use PMAP to convert the data before you display it. The sample call in the box draws a line across the bottom of the screen regardless of the defined world-coordinate system.

The CLS Statement

You learned how to clear the screen with the CLS statement in Chapter 7. Now that you understand viewports you can see that this statement is more versatile than was previously described.

CLS   **statement**

Syntax: CLS [{0 | 1 | 2}]

Purpose: Clears the viewport or the entire screen

Note: Action depends on the argument: if 0, entire screen clears; if 1, graphics viewport clears; if 2, text viewport clears; if no argument, text viewport clears in screen mode 0, otherwise graphics viewport clears.

Sample use:

```
CLS 1
```

This statement introduces the concept of a *text viewport.* In QuickBASIC the text viewport is always the entire screen, except for the bottom line (where the KEY LIST might be). The CLS 2 statement will clear only the text viewport.

Simple Graphics

The QuickBASIC graphics statements are divided into two sections: simple and more complex. This division refers to the objects you can draw, not the statements themselves. As you shall see, many of the simple graphics statements have complicated options.

The PSET Statement

To display a single pixel on the screen, you use the PSET statement.

PSET   **statement**

Syntax: PSET [STEP] (*xcoord, ycoord*) [, *color*]

Purpose: Draws a pixel on the screen in the given color

Note: This statement is invalid in screen mode 0.

Sample use:

```
PSET (100, 100), 2
```

This sample statement plots the point (100,100) in color 2. If you have not defined a viewport or a world-coordinate system, this point will be in the middle-left section of the screen. Otherwise, the point could be anywhere. If the point is outside the current viewport, it will be clipped and not displayed.

The optional keyword STEP determines the action on the coordinate pair. Without this keyword, QuickBASIC will move directly to that location to plot the point. With STEP, QuickBASIC will move relative to the current cursor location. Consider the following two statements.

```
PSET (50, 50), 2
PSET STEP (10, 0), 2
```

The first PSET statement moves the graphics cursor to the point (50,50) and plots that point. The second PSET moves the cursor ten pixels to the right, and plots the point (60,50).

The last argument is an optional color number. This number can range from 0 to one less than the current palette size. If you are in screen modes 2 or 11, you might leave out the color, since there is only one foreground color. In all other modes, however, you will avoid confusion by including the color number.

The PRESET Statement

If you know you are plotting a point in the background color, you should use the PRESET statement.

PRESET   **statement**

Syntax: PRESET [STEP] (*xcoord, ycoord*) [, *color*]

Purpose: Draws a pixel on the screen in the given color

Note: This statement is invalid in screen mode 0.

Sample use:

```
PRESET (100, 100)
```

As you can see from the syntax charts, the PRESET statement can act the same as the PSET statement. The PRESET statement is designed to plot points in the background color, so that is the color you will get if you omit the color argument. Using any other color defeats the purpose of the statement, and you should consider using PSET instead.

The LINE Statement

The LINE statement plots lines and rectangles. Special options in the LINE statement allow you to draw dotted or dashed lines, or filled boxes.

LINE   **statement**

Syntax:
LINE [[STEP] *coordpair*] - [STEP] *coordpair* [, *lineoptions*]
where *lineoptions* =>
    [*color*] [, [B[F]] [, *linestyle*]]
and where *coordpair* =>
    (*xcoord, ycoord*)

Purpose: Plots a line or a box

Note: This statement is invalid in screen mode 0.

Sample use:

```
LINE (3.2, 2.7)-(3.8, 2.1), 1
```

Naturally, this LINE statement will have more meaning if you have used the WINDOW statement to define a world-coordinate system. It draws a diagonal line in color number 1.

You can think of the two coordinate pairs as a "move to" pair and a "draw to" pair. In the sample statement you move to (3.2,2.7) and then you draw to (3.8,2.1). You can omit the first coordinate pair, and QuickBASIC will draw from the graphics cursor location to the second coordinate pair. For example, when you execute these statements

```
PSET (35, 40), 1
LINE -(35, 80), 3
```

you will get a point in color number 1 and a horizontal line from (35,40) to (35,80) in color number 3.

The keyword STEP is valid before either coordinate pair to indicate points relative to the graphics cursor. Study this program fragment:

```
LINE (0, 0)-(100, 0), 2
LINE -STEP (0, 100), 2
LINE STEP (-100, 0)-STEP (100, 0), 2
LINE STEP (-100, 0)-(0, 0), 2
```

These four lines show the hard way to make a box. In the first statement you move to the origin and draw to (100,0). In the second statement you stay there and draw down 100 pixels. The third statement says to move left 100 pixels and draw right 100 pixels. Finally, the fourth statement says move left 100 pixels and draw to the point (0,0). As you can see, you can have a direct move, a relative move, a direct draw, and a relative draw.

The line options allow you to draw fancy lines, rectangles, and solid boxes. The first optional argument is the drawing color. As with the PSET statement, you should include the drawing color except when you are in screen mode 2 or 11. You can look directly at any program line to see what color a LINE statement draws in, and you do not lose any time during execution. You can "erase" a line by drawing it in color 0.

If you add the letter B as the second optional argument, you will draw a rectangle instead of a line. The two coordinate pairs form the diagonal vertices of the rectangle. The four statements just listed could be replaced with this statement:

```
LINE (0, 0)-(100, 100), 2, B
```

When you use the BF combination after the color number, QuickBASIC will fill the rectangle with the same color. This fill is more efficient than using the PAINT statement, which is described later in this chapter.

The final optional argument is the *line style*. This argument allows you to draw solid lines, dashed lines, dotted lines, and combinations of dots and dashes. This is an INTEGER number, normally represented in hexadecimal. When QuickBASIC plots a line or box and a style is selected, it will plot each set of pixels on the line, depending on the line style. For example, a line style argument of &HF0F0 will plot four pixels, skip four, plot four, skip four, and so on. If you use the BF filled rectangle option, this argument is ignored.

The CIRCLE Statement

To draw a circle or an arc, you use the CIRCLE statement.

CIRCLE   **statement**

Syntax:
    CIRCLE [STEP] *coordpair, radius* [, *circleoptions*]
where *circleoptions* = >
    [*color*] [, [*startangle*] [, [*endangle*] [, *aspectratio*]]]
and where *coordpair* = >
    (*xcoord, ycoord*)

Purpose: Plots a circle, ellipse, or arc

Note: This statement is invalid in screen mode 0.

Sample use:

```
CIRCLE (160, 100), 50, 2
```

Assuming that you have not set a viewport or window, this statement will draw a circle in the center of the screen (in mode 1), with a radius of 50 pixels in color number 2.

The coordinate pair in the CIRCLE statement represents the center of the circle. The graphics cursor will move to the new point before drawing the circle. This statement also includes a STEP option to make a relative move before drawing the circle. For instance, the statement

```
CIRCLE STEP (30, -20), 10, 1
```

will center a circle 30 pixels right and 20 pixels above the current cursor location.

The CIRCLE statement options allow for other colors, arcs, and ellipses. After the color argument are two arguments showing the start and end angles of the circle or ellipse. These angles are in radians, with the 0 angle pointing to the right and increasing angles moving counterclockwise. The start angle defaults to 0 and the end angle defaults to 2π. If the start angle is larger than the end angle, QuickBASIC will still draw counterclockwise, beginning with the start angle and drawing until it gets to the end angle. If an angle is negative, QuickBASIC will treat it as though it were positive, but will draw a radial from the center of the circle to the endpoint.

The following short program demonstrates typical circle applications. If you run this program you should get an output screen like the one shown in Figure 12-3.

```
SCREEN 1
pi# = 3.14159265
CIRCLE (160, 100), 30, 3
CIRCLE (80, 50), 30, 3, pi# / 2, pi#
CIRCLE (240, 50), 30, 3, pi#, pi# / 2
CIRCLE (80, 150), 30, 3, -pi# / 2, -pi#
CIRCLE (240, 150), 30, 3 -pi#, -pi# / 2
```

The last optional argument for the CIRCLE statement is the *aspect ratio*. This option allows you to draw ellipses and parts of ellipses. The aspect ratio defaults to the value that draws a perfect circle. This formula is

$$aspect = 4/3 * (height/width)$$

where height and width are the screen dimensions in pixels. For screen mode 1, the default aspect ratio is 5/6. Values larger than this default will be ellipses that are higher than they are wide.

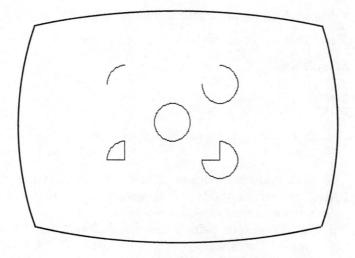

Figure 12-3.   Circles example

Values between 0 and the default aspect ratio will be wider than they are high. The radius argument for ellipses refers to the number of pixels in the shorter direction.

The PAINT Statement

There is no option in the CIRCLE statement to automatically fill the inside of the circle, ellipse, or arc. For these shapes and all others, QuickBASIC includes the PAINT statement.

PAINT   **statement**

Syntax:
  PAINT [STEP] *(xcoord, ycoord)* [, *paintoptions*]
where *paintoptions* = >

[colorORtile] [, *[bordercolor]* [, *skippattern]*]]

Purpose: Fills an area with a color or tile pattern

Note: This statement is invalid in screen mode 0.

Sample use:

```
CIRCLE (160, 100), 30, 2
PAINT (160, 100), 1, 2
```

The first statement draws a circle in color number 2. The PAINT statement starts at the center of the circle and fills with color number 1 until it finds color number 2.

The coordinate pair in the PAINT statement must be a point inside the shape you want to fill. If the point in the previous statement was (190,100), no painting would take place because the point would be on the circle (and already the stopping color). If the point was (200,100), QuickBASIC would fill the entire area outside the circle. The PAINT statement also supports the STEP keyword for points relative to the current cursor location.

The biggest problem you must watch out for when using the PAINT statement is called *spilling*. If you have a hole in the shape you are filling, the paint color will spill outside the shape and end up filling the rest of the screen. For example, the statement

```
CIRCLE (160, 100), 2, 0, 6
```

draws a large arc that is almost a complete circle, but has a gap in the right side. The statement

```
PAINT (160, 100), 3, 2
```

would end up filling almost the entire screen in color 3 because the paint would spill out of the shape.

The first paint option, the paint color, should be omitted only in screen mode 2 or 11. The next argument is the border color, which defaults to the paint color. If you draw a shape in cyan and fill it with magenta without specifying a border color, you will fill the entire viewport with magenta.

Tiling

QuickBASIC also supports a paint option called *tiling*. Tiling refers to filling a shape with a pattern instead of a solid color. If you want to fill with a tile pattern you must use a string expression for the paint color. The meaning of these expressions varies with the screen mode. In modes 7 through 13 the tiling process is extremely complicated, and you are probably better off finding an alternative way of filling shapes.

In screen mode 1, each byte in the string represents a piece of the pattern four pixels wide by one pixel high. If you have more than one byte in the string, each additional byte represents the line beneath the previous one—again, four pixels wide. Each byte is broken down into four sets of two bits each, with each set representing the color of the pixel. Consider this tile pattern:

```
tile$ = CHR$(&HF0) + CHR&(&HF0) + CHR$(&HF) + CHR$(&HF)
```

The first two rows of this pattern are two pixels of white (color 3) followed by two pixels of black (color 0). The second two rows are two pixels of black and two of white. The statement

```
PAINT (100, 100), tile$, 2
```

will fill a shape with this pattern, which looks like a small checkerboard.

Since screen mode 2 has only one drawing color, a byte in a tile pattern represents a block eight pixels wide by one pixel high. If you wanted to fill a shape with diagonal lines spread apart, you would make this pattern:

```
tile$ + CHR$(&H80) + CHR$(&H40) + CHR$(&H20) + CHR$(&H10) _
        + CHR$(&H8) + CHR$(&H4) + CHR$(&H2) + CHR$(&H1)
```

You should be able to see that each character moves a single pixel to the right. Given these two statements

```
CIRCLE (400, 100), , -0.0001, -3.14159
PAINT (400, 99), tile$
```

you would get the semicircle shown in Figure 12-4.

The final optional argument in the PAINT statement is a *skip pattern* for tiling. This argument is used so infrequently that it is difficult to create an example. Suppose that you fill a box with a thick-lined pattern using these statements:

```
LINE (0, 100)-(50, 150), 2, B
PAINT (1, 101), CHR$(&H5), 2
```

When you want to refill the box with this tile, which creates small boxes in the background color, use this statement.

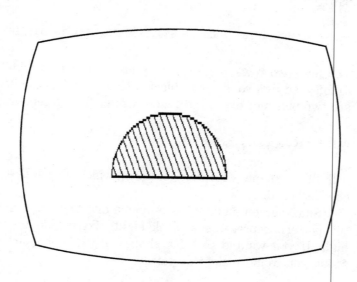

Figure 12-4.   Paint example

```
tile$ + CHR&(&H55) + CHR($H55) +CHR(&H5) + CHR$(&H5)
```

If you simply used the statement

```
PAINT (1, 101), tile$, 2
```

QuickBASIC would not finish the fill because it would see two rows of &H5 in the box that already matched the new pattern. To make sure that the box is filled properly, you must add this character as the skip pattern:

```
PAINT (1, 101), tile$, 2, CHR$(&H5)
```

This last argument tells QuickBASIC to ignore the vertical line pattern when filling the box with the new pattern.

The skip pattern argument cannot appear in the new pattern more than two consecutive times. If you attempt to do this, you will get an "Illegal function call" error. At this point you can see why it might be better just to clear the shape before filling in the new pattern:

```
PAINT (1, 101), 0, 2
PAINT (1, 101), tile$, 2
```

This alternative method takes twice as long (a few more milliseconds), but it will always work.

More Complex Graphics

You can draw anything with a series of lines and arcs created by LINE and CIRCLE statements. However, these can be slow and cumbersome with more complex shapes. In this section you will learn the rest of the graphics statements included in Quick-BASIC, including animation techniques.

The DRAW Statement

The DRAW statement provides a mini-language that gives you shortcuts from other graphics statements.

DRAW   **statement**

Syntax: DRAW *stringexpression*

Purpose: Draws specified shapes

Note: See Table 12-2 for a summary of commands.

Sample use:

```
star$ = "S30 TA-18 U5 TA18 D5 TA54 U5 TA-90 U5 TA-54 D5 TA0"
DRAW star$ + " BL10 " + star$
```

This sample defines a string *star$* that is a five-pointed star. The DRAW statement draws one star, moves left, and draws another star.

Command	Meaning
A n	Rotation angle (0-3)
B	Move only prefix
C n	Drawing color
D n	Draw down
E n	Draw up and right
F n	Draw down and right
G n	Draw down and left
H n	Draw up and left
M x,y	Move absolute or relative
N	Draw and return cursor prefix
P p,b	Paint out to border color
S n	Scale factor (1-255)
TA n	Rotation angle ($-360 - +360$)
X	Execute substring

Table 12-2.   DRAW Command Summary

The available commands for the DRAW statement can be divided into plotting commands and attribute commands. The plotting commands can plot lines or simply move the cursor. There is a different command for each plotting direction: U for up, D for down, R for right, and L for left. A number after the command specifies the number of pixels to move. The statement

```
DRAW "U5 R5 D5 L5"
```

draws a rectangle five pixels wide by five pixels high. Note that because of the aspect ratio of the screen, this will not be a square.

There are also diagonal-line commands: E for up and right, F for down and right, G for down and left, and H for up and left. A number after the command represents the number of pixels to move in both directions. In other words, the statement

```
DRAW  "R20 U20 G20"
```

will form a triangle with two legs 20 pixels long and one leg about 34 pixels long. Again, these commands reflect the aspect ratio of each screen mode, so they will not form 45-degree angles with the horizontal and vertical lines.

If you need to draw a line that is not in one of these eight directions, you need the M command. This command has two forms: an absolute move and a relative move. For an absolute move you specify the screen coordinates of the location you want to draw to. The statement

```
DRAW "M319,100"
```

draws a line from the current graphics cursor location to the coordinate (319,100). If you want to move a specific number of pixels from the current position, you use the relative move. For this you need to place a + or − sign in front of the relative x-coordinate. The statement

```
DRAW "M+5,10"
```

will draw a line from the cursor location to a point five pixels to the right and ten pixels down.

Any of the nine line-drawing commands can be preceded by a B or N prefix. The B prefix specifies a move without plotting the line. You need this command when you are finished with one shape and want to draw another. The sample statements for DRAW used the command BL10 to move the cursor left ten pixels without drawing a line. The statement

```
DRAW "BM0,0"
```

would move the cursor to the upper-left corner of the screen.

The N prefix tells QuickBASIC to draw the line and return the cursor to its original position. This is the same as drawing a line and using the complement command with the B prefix to return the cursor. For instance, these two statements

```
DRAW "NF100"
DRAW "F100 BH100"
```

accomplish the same task. The following statement uses this prefix to draw a box with its diagonals:

```
DRAW "E50 D50 L50 U50 NR50 F50"
```

The attribute commands of the DRAW statement modify the way the lines are drawn. The first of these is the C command. This command sets the current drawing color. It defaults to the foreground color, and its range depends on the current screen mode and graphics adapter. See the first section of this chapter for more information.

Another attribute command is S, for scaling factor. The number after the S is the number by which future drawing commands will be scaled. The default is S4, which corresponds to a 1:1 ratio of the number in the command to the number of pixels drawn. S8 will make objects twice as large, while S2 will make them half as large. The range of the S command is 1 to 255. The following fragment draws a series of different size boxes with the same centroid.

```
box$ = " M160,100 BE10 D20 L20 U20 R20"
DRAW "S2" + box$
DRAW "S4" + box$
DRAW "S6" + box$
DRAW "S8" + box$
DRAW "S10" + box$
```

Notice that the absolute M command is unaffected by the S command.

The P command is similar to the simplest versions of the PAINT statement. With this command you can specify the paint color and the border color. Be sure to move inside the object you want to paint before you include this command. Here is how to draw a painted box:

```
DRAW "C1 R20 U30 L20 D30 BE5 P2,1"
```

You need the BE5 command to move the cursor to the inside of the box before you fill it.

Unlike the LINE statement, the DRAW statement has the ability to rotate lines, automatically compensating for aspect ratio. The A command rotates lines through an angle of 0, 90, 180, or 270 degrees, using the numbers 0 through 3. For example, the A3 command makes all future commands rotate 270 degrees counterclockwise. This statement draws a perfect square without concern for the screen mode aspect ratio:

```
DRAW "U10 A1 U10 A2 U10 A3 U10 A0"
```

Be sure to return the rotation angle to 0 if you have future drawing commands.

The TA command is a more versatile way to rotate data. With this command you can specify any angle from −360 to +360. This statement plots a perfect equilateral triangle:

```
DRAW "L20 TA120 L20 TA240 L20 TA0"
```

Again, the rotation angle will remain in effect for the rest of the program, or until you reset with another TA or A command.

The VARPTR$ Function

The DRAW command becomes even more versatile with the ability to use variables in the command string. To accomplish this you must use the VARPTR$ function.

VARPTR$(variable)   **function**

Purpose: Converts the address of a variable to string form

Return type: STRING

Parameters: *variable* [any type]—the variable to use in the DRAW or PLAY statement

Sample call:

```
box$ = " M160,100 BE10 D20 L20 U20 R20"
FOR scale% = 2 TO 10 STEP 2
   DRAW "S=" + VARPTR$(scale%) + box$
NEXT scale%
```

The program fragment in the box does the same as the one shown when the S command was introduced.

When you use the VARPTR$ function with the DRAW statement you must include an equal sign between the command and the variable. The following program draws a flower by drawing one petal and rotating the petal 11 times:

```
SCREEN 2
petal$ = " s16 BM50,100 M-2,-7 E2 F2 M-2,7"
colr% = 1
FOR i% = 0 TO 330 STEP 30
   colr% = 3 - colr%
   DRAW "C=" + VARPTR$(colr%)
   DRAW "TA=" + VARPTR$(i%) + petal$
NEXT i%
```

The color of each petal alternates between color number 1 and color number 2. The drawing is shown in Figure 12-5.

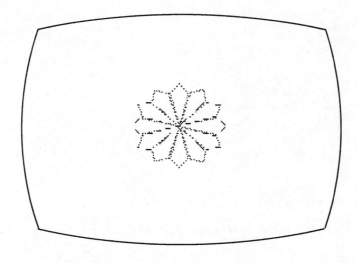

Figure 12-5.   Flower example

The final command in the DRAW statement is the X command. With the X command you can execute a string within another string. In QuickBASIC, you must use the VARPTR$ function with this command. You can often replace this command with a simple string concatenation. For instance, the following two statements draw the same object:

```
DRAW "M100,100 X" + VARPTR$(anyshape$)
DRAW "M100,100 " + anyshape$
```

The following listing is a program that allows the user to use the computer screen as a sketch pad. The user can draw a line, move the cursor without drawing, and change drawing colors. The program essentially uses one SELECT-END SELECT structure to determine what key the user has hit, and then sets up the appropriate DRAW command.

```
SCREEN 1
CLS

    initialize all variables
ypen% = 100
xpen% = 160
colr% = 2
DRAW "C2"
pendown% = -1
penstep% = 2

LOCATE 1, 3
PRINT "X:          Y:              STEP:  2"
LOCATE 25, 3
PRINT "PEN:  down              COLOR:  2";

DO
    LOCATE 1, 6
    PRINT USING "###"; xpen%
    LOCATE 1, 16
    PRINT USING "###"; ypen% - 10

    DO
        onekey$ = UCASE$(INKEY$)
    LOOP WHILE onekey$ = ""

    SELECT CASE onekey$

        CASE "C"                        ' change color
            IF colr% = 1 THEN
                colr% = 2
            ELSEIF colr% = 2 THEN
                colr% = 3
            ELSE
                colr% = 1
            END IF
            LOCATE 25, 34
            DRAW "C=" + VARPTR$(colr%)
            PRINT colr%;

        CASE "P"                        ' pen up/down
            LOCATE 25, 9
            IF pendown% THEN
                pendown% = 0
                PRINT "up   ";
            ELSE
                pendown% = -1
                PRINT "down";
            END IF

        CASE "S"                        ' change step
            LOCATE 1, 28
```

```
        INPUT ; "STEP"; penstep%
        LOCATE 1, 28
        PRINT USING "STEP: ##"; penstep%

   CASE CHR$(0) + CHR$(72)          ' up arrow
      IF ypen% - penstep% > 10 THEN
         ypen% = ypen% - penstep%
      ELSE
         ypen% = 11
      END IF

   CASE CHR$(0) + CHR$(80)          ' down arrow
      IF ypen% + penstep% < 190 THEN
         ypen% = ypen% + penstep%
      ELSE
         ypen% = 190
      END IF

   CASE CHR$(0) + CHR$(75)          ' left arrow
      IF xpen% - penstep% > 0 THEN
         xpen% = xpen% - penstep%
      ELSE
         xpen% = 1
      END IF

   CASE CHR$(0) + CHR$(77)          ' right arrow
      IF xpen% + penstep% < 320 THEN
         xpen% = xpen% + penstep%
      ELSE
         xpen% = 319
      END IF

END SELECT

' move to the new location
IF pendown% THEN
   DRAW "M=" + VARPTR$(xpen%) + ",=" + VARPTR$(ypen%)
ELSE
   DRAW "BM=" + VARPTR$(xpen%) + ",=" + VARPTR$(ypen%)
END IF

LOOP UNTIL onekey$ = CHR$(27)
```

The GET Statement

Once you have drawn an object, you can manipulate the object
with the GET and PUT statements. The GET statement is used
to save the contents of a portion of the screen.

GET   statement

Syntax:
    GET [STEP] *coordpair* - [STEP] *coordpair, getvariable*
where *getvariable* = >
    arrayvariable [*(arrayindex)*]
and where *coordpair* = >
    (xcoord, ycoord)

Purpose: Stores a screen image into an array

Note: This statement is invalid in screen mode 0.

Sample use:

```
DIM saveit%(88)
CALL DrawShape
GET (50, 80)-(75,100), saveit%
```

These three lines of code demonstrate the steps you need to take to save an image for future use. First you define an array large enough to handle the entire image. Then you draw the image on the screen. Finally, you use the GET statement to save the image into the array. In this example the image lies in a 21×26 box in the upper-left portion of the screen.

The two sets of coordinate pairs form a box similar to the boxes in the LINE statement. The STEP keyword before a coordinate pair signals a point relative to the current cursor location. If the keyword STEP is before the second coordinate pair it indicates a point relative to the first coordinate pair.

The final argument of the GET statement is the name of the array that will contain the image. Be sure to use only an INTE-GER or LONG array if you plan on doing any manipulation of the array elements. If you need to store the image starting with an index other than the first element, you can include the index as part of the argument. The statement

```
GET (0, 0)-(20, 20), saveit%(5)
```

stores the image starting with the fifth element of the array.

The most difficult part of using the GET statement is determining the size of the array. Most references include a long formula to help you calculate the exact minimum array size. Today, however, memory space is not as critical as it was, so a simpler formula is in order. You need these equations to determine an appropriate array size:

xrange = x2 − x1 + 1
yrange = y2 − y1 + 1
size = INT(**xrange**/8 + 1) * **yrange** * **colorbits** / **arraybits**
    + 4

The value of **arraybits** is 2 for INTEGER arrays and 4 for LONG arrays.

The value of **colorbits** depends on the screen mode. This value is the number of bits required to store the color of each pixel. The following table shows the value of **colorbits** for each screen mode:

Mode	Colorbits
2, 11	1
1, 10	2
7, 8, 12	4
13	8

For mode 9, **colorbits** will be 2 if you have less than 64K of screen memory; otherwise, **colorbits** will be 4.

Suppose you want to save the flower image shown in Figure 12-5. By drawing boxes around the flower with the LINE statement, through trial and error you determine that the entire image is within the coordinate pairs (6,62) and (94,138). If you are in screen mode 1 and you want to use an integer array, here are the calculations for the array size:

xrange = 94 − 6 + 1 = 89
yrange = 138 − 62 + 1 = 76
arraysize = INT(89/8 + 1) * 76 * 2 / 2 + 4 = 916

Assuming that you have an array *flower%* dimensioned to size 916, the statement

```
GET (6, 62)-(94, 138), flower%
```

will save the flower for future use.

The PUT Statement

Once you have an image in an array, you can redraw the image with the PUT statement.

PUT   **statement**

Syntax:
    PUT [STEP] *coordpair, arrayvar*[*(arrayindex)*]
    [, *putaction*]
where *putaction* = >
    {XOR | PSET | PRESET | AND | OR}
and where *coordpair* = >
    (*xcoord, ycoord*)

Purpose: Plots an array image on the screen

Note: This statement is invalid in screen mode 0.

Sample use:

```
PUT (200, 50), flower%, PSET
```

The statement in the box plots the flower saved with a GET statement on the right side of the screen.

The coordinate pair in the PUT statement represents the upper-left corner of the box formed by the array. You can use the keyword STEP before the coordinate pair to indicate a relative move from the current cursor location. The second argument is the name of the array used in the GET statement. You can include an array index if the image is stored in the middle of the array.

There are five different ways to place the image on the screen, as specified by the PUT actions listed in the syntax box. The first action, XOR, is primarily for animation. If you PUT an image on the screen in the same location twice, it will appear and disappear, leaving the current background intact. The problem with this mode is that the image you display will not be the same as the image in the array. For example, if you draw the flower partway inside a cyan box, the cyan petals will become black, and the magenta colors will become white. Since you can still see the image, many programmers consider this a small price to pay for simple animation.

The second action is PSET, which displays the image by replacing whatever is currently on the screen. If you have a background image, that image will be lost. This action will have the same effect no matter what the screen mode.

The third action, PRESET, inverts the image before placing it on the screen. In screen modes 2 and 11, the foreground color will become the background color and vice versa. In the other screen modes, the colors will switch around, which is not exactly an inverted image. If you PUT the flower from Figure 12-5 on the screen with the PRESET action and the default color palette, most of the box will be white, the petals that were cyan will be magenta, and the petals that were magenta will be cyan.

The AND action performs an and operation on each pixel as it draws the image. In screen modes 2 and 11, this means that only those pixels that are in the foreground color both on the screen and in the image will appear. In the other screen modes, like mode 2, the colors might also get degraded. For example, a cyan pixel AND a white pixel gives you a cyan pixel. A magenta pixel AND a cyan pixel leaves a dark pixel.

The final PUT action is OR. When you display an image over a background, this action will leave both images on top of each other. In multiple-color screen modes, the colors become upgraded. This means that in modes 1 and 10, any two non-black colors will become white.

The DEF SEG Statement

The rest of this section shows you how to load and save graphics images with the BLOAD and BSAVE statements. Since these statements must be used in conjunction with the DEF SEG statement and the VARSEG and VARPTR functions, it is important for you to understand these first.

The DEF SEG statement changes the current segment address.

DEF SEG   statement

Syntax: DEF SEG = *segaddress*

Purpose: Redefines the current segment address

Note: See Chapter 13 for a detailed explanation.

Sample use: See BSAVE and BLOAD

When using DEF SEG with BSAVE or BLOAD, you must first set the segment address to the address of the first element of the array you are going to save (or load). After completing the transfer, use the DEF SEG statement with no arguments to return the segment address to the QuickBASIC data segment.

The VARPTR and VARSEG Functions

The VARPTR and VARSEG functions are required to provide the system with the address of the array variable.

VARPTR(variable)   function

Purpose: Supplies the offset address of the variable

Return type: Memory address

Parameters: variable [any type]—the variable in question

Note: Since variables move around during program execution, use the address as soon as possible.

Sample call: See BSAVE and BLOAD

The VARPTR function supplies the offset address, and the VARSEG function provides the segment address.

VARSEG(variable)   **function**

Purpose: Supplies the segment address of the variable

Return type: memory address

Parameters: variable [any type] — the variable in question

Note: Since variables move around during program execution, use the address as soon as possible.

Sample call: See BSAVE and BLOAD

Both of these functions also have other uses, and they are covered in full detail in Chapter 13. For graphics purposes, you need only remember when you must use them.

The BSAVE Statement

If you want to save an image between sessions, you should write the image to a file using the BSAVE statement.

BSAVE   **statement**

Syntax: BSAVE *filename, offset, numbytes*

Purpose: Saves the contents of a memory area to a file

Sample use:

```
GET (6, 62)-(94, 138), flower%
DEF SEG = VARSEG(flower%(1))
BSAVE "flower.dat", VARPTR(flower%(1)), 1832
DEF SEG
```

The program fragment in the box saves the image of the flower to a file *flower.dat.*

There are three required arguments for the BSAVE statement. The first one is the name of the file. Do not use an OPEN or CLOSE statement for this file because BSAVE will do that automatically. The second argument is the starting address of the data being saved. Since addresses must include a segment and an offset, you must set the segment with the DEF SEG statement, and provide the offset as the second argument of BSAVE by using the VARPTR function. The final argument in the BSAVE statement is the number of bytes to be transferred. You compute this number by taking the number of array elements the image uses and multiplying by the number of bytes per element (two for INTEGER arrays, four for LONG arrays).

The BLOAD Statement

The BLOAD statement will load an image saved with the BSAVE statement into memory.

BLOAD   **statement**

Syntax: BLOAD *filename, offset, numbytes*

Purpose: Transfers an image from a file to an array

Sample use:

```
DEF SEG = VARSEG(flower%(1))
BSAVE "flower.dat", VARPTR(flower%(1)), 1832
DEF SEG
PUT (6, 62), flower%
```

Assuming that you executed the code associated with the BSAVE statement, the fragment in the box will retrieve the flower image from the file *flower.dat* and display it on the screen. The arguments to the BLOAD statement are exactly the same as those of the BSAVE statement.

The PCOPY Statement

The PCOPY statement copies the contents of one page to another page. This statement will help your EGA animations look smoother.

PCOPY   **statement**

Syntax: PCOPY *frompage, topage*

Purpose: Copies one screen page to another

Note: This statement is valid only for screen modes 0, 7, 8, 9, and 10.

Sample use:

```
SCREEN 7, , 0, 1
FOR fnum% = 1 to numframes%
   CALL DrawFrame (fnum%)
   PCOPY 0, 1
NEXT fnum%
```

The loop shown in the box would be used when you do not want the user to see the plotting commands. The SCREEN statement defines page 0 as the active page and page 1 as the visual page. This means that any graphics statements will be written to page 0, but the user will see only page 1. After drawing each frame, you call PCOPY to transfer the entire page to the screen.

The POINT Functions

The last two functions in this section actually have the same name, POINT. The only way to tell them apart is by the number of arguments.

The first POINT function returns the coordinates of the graphics cursor.

POINT(key)   function

Purpose: Supplies the current graphics cursor location

Return type: REAL or INTEGER

Parameters: key [INTEGER] — specifies which part to return
    0 — returns the x-location in screen coordinates
    1 — returns the y-location in screen coordinates
    2 — returns the x-location in world coordinates
    3 — returns the y-location in world coordinates

Sample call:

```
'draw a small circle around the cursor location
CIRCLE (POINT(2),POINT(3)), 3, 5
```

If you have not defined a world-coordinate system with the WINDOW statement, the values returned by POINT(2) and POINT(3) will be the same as those returned by POINT(0) and POINT(1), respectively.

The other POINT function reads a point from the screen.

POINT(xloc,yloc)   **function**

Purpose: Supplies the current color of a specific pixel

Return type: INTEGER

Parameters: xloc [REAL]—x-coordinate of the point
               yloc [REAL]—y-coordinate of the point

Note: If the coordinate pair is outside the screen coordinate system, POINT returns −1.

Sample call:

```
xpos% = 0
ypos% = 100
DO WHILE POINT(xpos%, ypos%) <> 0
    xpos% = xpos% + 1
LOOP
```

This loop travels across the middle of the screen searching for the first pixel that is not in the background color.

Sound and Music

In addition to very sophisticated graphics, QuickBASIC includes several not-so-sophisticated music capabilities. The limitations to sound are the computers, not the language, as you will see.

The BEEP Statement

The simplest of noises is the single beep, which is generated with the BEEP statement.

BEEP   **statement**

Syntax: BEEP

Purpose: Plays one note

Sample use:

```
IF ERR=64 THEN
    BEEP
    RESUME
END IF
```

The BEEP statement is commonly used in error-handling routines to inform the user that bad data has been entered. This statement is the equivalent of a PRINT CHR$(7) statement.

The SOUND Statement

There are two statements that generate actual musical notes. The simpler of these is the SOUND statement.

SOUND   **statement**

Syntax: SOUND *frequency, duration*

Purpose: Emits a specific sound for a given duration

Sample use:

```
FOR cnt% = 1 TO 100
    freq% = RND * 5000 + 37
    SOUND (freq%, 1)
NEXT cnt%
```

This program fragment plays a few seconds worth of random sounds and is good for little else besides getting someone's attention.

The first argument of the SOUND statement is the frequency in hertz. Although you can use any number between 37 and 32,767, frequencies above 5000 are difficult to hear and those above 15,000 are impossible. The second argument is the duration in clock cycles. One clock cycle is about 0.055 seconds, and the value of duration can be any number between 0 and 65,535.

The PLAY Statement

The primary statement for playing music, however, is the PLAY statement.

PLAY   **statement**

Syntax: PLAY *stringexpression*

Purpose: Plays specific notes for specific durations

Note: See Table 12-3 for available macros.

Sample use:

```
PLAY "O3 C D E F G A B >C C <B A G F E D C"
```

Like DRAW, the PLAY statement has its own mini-language. The statement in the box plays a simple C scale.

The first part of a PLAY statement string will usually be one or more setup commands. The T command sets the tempo, in number of quarter notes per minute. The default value is 120 and the possible range is 32 through 255. The larger the number, the faster the tempo. The other primary setup commands control the music style. MN, the default, stands for "music normal" and will pause for the last one-eighth of every note, giving the music some separation. ML (music legato) gives each note full value, thus giving no note separation. Finally, MS, or "music staccato," pauses for the final one-fourth of every note.

Two other setup commands determine how QuickBASIC will execute the PLAY statement. The MF command, for "music foreground," is the default and requires the computer to play out the entire PLAY statement before going to the next statement line. This makes the PLAY statement just like any other QuickBASIC statement. The MB, or "music background," command allows you to place up to 32 notes in a special buffer. QuickBASIC can then execute the next statement and play the music at the same time. This is very useful in games, where you want to play music while the user is playing the game.

There are 84 available tones with the PLAY statement. This gives you seven full octaves. To play a note you normally use the

Command	Meaning
A-G [n]	Play that note for that length
#, +	Sharp note suffix
−	Flat note suffix
.	Play note for 3/2 * length
>	Play one octave higher
<	Play one octave lower
L n	Note length (1-64)
MB	Music in background
MF	Music in foreground
ML	Music legato (full length)
MN	Music normal (7/8 length)
MS	Music staccato (3/4 length)
N n	Play this note (0-84)
O n	Change octave (0-6)
P n	Pause this length (1-64)
T n	Music tempo (32-255)
X	Execute substring

Table 12-3.   PLAY Command Summary

letter of the note: A through G. To make a note flat, you can add a "−" sign; to make a sharp, you can add a "#" sign or a "+" sign. Here is the beginning of "Flight of the Bumble Bee":

```
PLAY "G G- F E E- G# G G- G G- F E E- E F F# G"
```

IBM-PC compatibles can play only one note at a time, so Quick-BASIC does not support a way to play multiple notes.

The notes from C to B make up an octave. The default octave is O4. There are two ways to change the octave in the middle of a PLAY sequence. The first is to use the O command, with valid octaves being 0 through 6. The second way is to use ">" for down one octave or "<" for up one octave. Since the octave changes from B to C, the sample scale shown previously uses these two symbols to get to "high C" and back down.

The L command allows you to change the length of each note. The default is L4, which plays quarter notes. Its range is from 1 for whole notes to 64. If you have several quick length changes, you can use the alternative method of adding the length numeric to each note. Consider the start of the "Wedding March":

```
PLAY "O3 C4 F8. F16 F2 C4 G8. E16 F2"
```

The period after F8 means play a dotted-eighth note, or one-and-a-half times the normal length of an eighth note.

In some special circumstances you may want to refer to a note by its number. The N command plays a specific note, numbered 0 to 84. You must use the L command to specify the length of an N note—there is no short form. If you select N0, you will get a rest (no note). A better way to specify a rest is the P command. With this command you can select the length of the rest by using the same code as you use for the L command: 1 through 64 and an optional dot.

Like the DRAW statement, the PLAY statement allows you to refer to variables inside the command string. You must use the VARPTR$ function when you use this option. The following fragment plays the entire chromatic scale from bottom to top.

```
PLAY "L16"
FOR note% = 1 to 84
    PLAY "N=" + VARPTR$(note%)
NEXT note%
```

As with the DRAW statement, you need the equal sign to show
that the next part of the command string is a numeric variable.

The final command supported by the PLAY statement is the
X command, which is again similar to the one in the DRAW
statement. This small program allows users to try out their own
tunes, assuming that they understand the commands:

```
DO
    INPUT "Enter play sequence (Q to quit):", seq$
    IF UCASE$(seq$) <> "Q" THEN
        PLAY "X" + VARPTR$(seq$)
    END IF
LOOP UNTIL UCASE$(seq$) = "Q"
```

The following program uses graphics in combination with
music to simulate a piano on the keyboard:

```
'     main program of PIANO.BAS
DECLARE SUB TurnKeyOn (key$)
DECLARE SUB TurnKeyOff (key$)
DECLARE SUB DisplayPiano ()

PLAY "ML O2 T255 L64"

note$ = ""
octave$ = ""

SCREEN 1
CLS
CALL DisplayPiano

DO
    DO
        PLAY note$
        onechar$ = UCASE$(INKEY$)
    LOOP WHILE onechar$ = ""
    IF note$ <> "" THEN
        CALL TurnKeyOff(note$)
    END IF

    SELECT CASE onechar$

        CASE "A"
            note$ = "C"
        CASE "W"
```

```
                  note$ = "C#"
            CASE "S"
                  note$ = "D"
            CASE "E"
                  note$ = "D#"
            CASE "D"
                  note$ = "E"
            CASE "F"
                  note$ = "F"
            CASE "T"
                  note$ = "F#"
            CASE "G"
                  note$ = "G"
            CASE "Y"
                  note$ = "G#"
            CASE "H"
                  note$ = "A"
            CASE "U"
                  note$ = "A#"
            CASE "J"
                  note$ = "B"
            CASE "K"
                  note$ = ">C<"

            '  space bar for pause
            CASE " "
                  CALL TurnKeyOff(note$)
                  note$ = "P64"

      END SELECT
      CALL TurnKeyOn(note$)

      'up and down arrows to change octaves
      IF onechar$ = CHR$(0) + CHR$(72) THEN
            octave$ = octave$ + ">"
      ELSEIF onechar$ = CHR$(0) + CHR$(80) THEN
            octave$ = octave$ + "<"
      ELSEIF octave$ <> "" THEN
            PLAY octave$
            octave$ = ""
      END IF

LOOP UNTIL onechar$ = CHR$(27)


SUB DisplayPiano

'  draw white keys
FOR cnt% = 1 TO 8
      LINE (cnt% * 32 + 12, 42)-(cnt% * 32 + 42, 170), , BF
NEXT cnt%

'  draw black keys
FOR cnt% = 1 TO 6
```

```
        IF cnt% <> 3 THEN
            LINE (cnt% * 32 + 28, 43)-(cnt% * 32 + 58, 110), 0, BF
        END IF
NEXT cnt%

'  label the keys
LOCATE 23, 8
PRINT "C    D    E    F    G    A    B    C"
LOCATE 5, 10
PRINT "C#  D#        F#   G#   A#"

END SUB
```

```
SUB TurnKeyOn (key$)

IF LEFT$(key$, 1) = "P" THEN EXIT SUB

'  determine which key comes on
notenum% = ASC(key$) - 64
IF notenum% < 3 THEN
    notenum% = notenum% + 5
ELSE
    notenum% = notenum% - 2
END IF

'  turn on a white key
IF LEN(key$) = 1 THEN
    LINE (notenum% * 32+14, 120)-(notenum% * 32+40, 165), 2,BF

'  turn on a black key
ELSEIF LEN(key$) = 2 THEN
    LINE (notenum% * 32+30, 50)-(notenum% * 32+54, 95), 2, BF

'  turn on high C
ELSEIF LEN(key$) = 3 THEN
    LINE (270, 120)-(296, 165), 2, BF
END IF

END SUB
```

```
SUB TurnKeyOff (key$)

'  determine which key comes off
notenum% = ASC(key$) - 64
IF notenum% < 3 THEN
    notenum% = notenum% + 5
ELSE
    notenum% = notenum% - 2
END IF
```

```
'   turn off a white key
IF LEN(key$) = 1 THEN
    LINE (notenum% * 32+14, 120)-(notenum% * 32+40, 165), 3, BF

'   turn off a black key
ELSEIF LEN(key$) = 2 THEN
    LINE (notenum% * 32+30, 50)-(notenum% * 32+54, 95), 0, BF

'   turn off high C
ELSEIF LEN(key$) = 3 THEN
    LINE (270, 120)-(296, 165), 3, BF
END IF

END SUB
```

The ON PLAY Statement

In Chapter 7 you learned how to create a keyboard event trap with the ON KEY statement and the KEY ON/OFF/STOP statement. In a similar manner you can make a background music event trap with the ON PLAY and PLAY ON/OFF/STOP statements.

ON PLAY   **statement**

Syntax: ON PLAY (*queuelimit*) GOSUB *label*

Purpose: Defines a background music event trap

Notes: The event trap must be enabled with the PLAY ON statement; the statement label must be in the module-level code.

Sample use:

```
ON PLAY(2) GOSUB ReFill
PLAY ON
  . . .

ReFill:
   PLAY BackgroundMusic$
   RETURN
```

These sample statements provide the skeleton for a background music event trap. You define the GOSUB label with the ON PLAY statement. Then you enable the event trap with the PLAY ON statement. When the music buffer is left with one note, QuickBASIC will jump to the *ReFill* subroutine, refill the music buffer and return to wherever it was.

The number in parentheses in the ON PLAY statement represents the smallest number of notes in the music buffer before the event is trapped. In other words, ON PLAY(2) will trap the event when the music buffer size goes from two down to one. If you set the size to 0, you will never trap the event. Set it to 1, and you may get a pause before the buffer refills. If you set the number too high, you will trap the event too often, and thus slow program execution. Remember that QuickBASIC uses the music buffer only when the music is playing in background mode.

The PLAY ON/OFF/STOP Statement

The PLAY ON/OFF/STOP statement enables or disables the event trap.

PLAY ON/OFF/STOP   **statement**

Syntax: PLAY {ON | OFF | STOP}

Purpose: PLAY ON enables the music event trap, PLAY OFF disables it, and PLAY STOP inhibits the event

Note: There is an inherent PLAY STOP statement at the start of every music event handler.

Sample use:

```
PLAY OFF        'music stops when the buffer is empty
```

The PLAY ON and PLAY OFF statements are self-explanatory. The PLAY STOP statement temporarily disables the music event. If the buffer size goes below the number set by the ON PLAY statement, the event is remembered. When QuickBASIC encounters a PLAY ON statement, it will trap the event immediately. With the PLAY OFF statement, the events are ignored completely (and not remembered) until after the next PLAY ON statement.

The PLAY Function

The PLAY function has limited use in playing background music.

PLAY(dummy)   **function**

Purpose: Supplies the number of notes in the music buffer

Return type: INTEGER

Parameter: dummy [any numeric type]—a dummy variable

Note: If there is no music playing, or if the music is playing in foreground mode, PLAY will return 0.

Sample call:

```
PLAY OFF
DO
LOOP WHILE PLAY(0) > 0
```

Use these three statements when you need to wait until the music buffer is cleared. If you end a program without this loop the user may question why music is playing when the program is no longer running.

A Musical Application

The following program is a complete demonstration of background music and music event trapping. It draws random boxes on the screen while playing Beethoven in the background. Study the documentation to see the purpose of each statement.

```
'       define the music event
ON PLAY(2) GOSUB more
SCREEN 1

'       enable the music event
PLAY ON

'       load the music buffer with the first stanza
PLAY "T160 MB ML L8 O4 E E- E E- E <B >D C <A"
PLAY "O2 E A >C E A B"
PLAY "O2 E G# >E G# B >C"

PLAY "O2 E A >E"
stanza% = 1

'       draw random boxes on the screen
DO
    x1 = RND * 320
    x2 = RND * 320
    y1 = RND * 200
    y2 = RND * 200
    col = INT(RND * 4)
    LINE (x1, y1)-(x2, y2), col, B
LOOP WHILE INKEY$ = " "

'       when user presses a key, disable the music buffer,
'       and wait until the music stops before clearing the
'       screen
PLAY OFF
DO
LOOP WHILE PLAY(0) > 0
CLS

END

'       the event trap switches between playing the
'       first stanza and the second stanza
more:
    IF stanza% = 1 THEN
        stanza% = 2
        PLAY "MB ML L8 O4 E E- E E- E <B >D C <A"
        PLAY "O2 E A >C E A B"
        PLAY "O2 E G# >E >C <B A2. L8 NO"

    ELSE
        stanza% = 1
```

```
        PLAY "MB ML L8 O4 E E- E E- E <B >D C <A"
        PLAY "O2 E A >C E A B"
        PLAY "O2 E G# >E G# B >C"
        PLAY "O2 E A >E"
    END IF

RETURN
```

System Routines

Using the System Clock
Using Interrupts
Miscellaneous System Information
The Joystick
The Light Pen
I/O Ports
COM Ports

The majority of programs that you write will use only the statements and functions from the first twelve chapters of this book. There are, however, a series of other statements that can speed up program execution or make it look more professional. Most of these statements use system resources, or the internal software and hardware. You should be able to use these statements even if you are unfamiliar with the inner workings of your computer. In this chapter you will learn the statements and functions that use system resources, and you will get some background on how they work. Included are sections on using the system clock, triggering system interrupts, detecting joystick and light-pen input, using the communications ports, and getting system information.

Using the System Clock

Somewhere on one of the green cards in your computer lies a small circuit that does nothing but keep track of date and time. This is the *system clock*, and it is used whenever the operating system or a program needs the date or time. Normally, this clock resets automatically every time you turn the computer on or off. If you have a special battery-powered clock circuit, you can eliminate having to type in the new date and time every day.

The DATE$ and TIME$ Functions

Displaying the date and time on your program menus makes them look more professional. QuickBASIC allows you to get the current date with the DATE$ function.

DATE$ **function**

Purpose: Supplies the current date from the system clock

Return type: STRING

Parameters: None

Note: The date will always be in the form mm-dd-yyyy.

Sample call:

```
PRINT "Today is "; DATE$
```

The current time is obtained using the TIME$ function.

TIME$ **function**

Purpose: Supplies the current time from the system clock

Return type: STRING

Parameters: None

Note: The time will always be in the form hh:mm:ss, where hours are given in 24-hour format.

Sample call:

```
LOCATE 1, 71          'upper-right corner
PRINT TIME$;
```

The DATE$ and TIME$ Statements

If the date and time in the system are wrong, you can change them inside your program. The DATE$ statement sets a new date.

DATE$ statement

Syntax: DATE$ = *datestring*

Purpose: Sets the current date in the system clock

Note: The date must be in one of the following formats:
  mm-dd-yy   mm-dd-yyyy
  mm/dd/yy   mm/dd/yyyy

Sample use:

```
INPUT "Enter the current date (mm-dd-yy): ", newday$
DATE$ = newday$
```

The TIME$ statement sets a new time.

TIME$ statement

Syntax: TIME$ = *timestring*

Purpose: Sets the current time in the system clock

Note: The time must be in one of the following formats:
  hh hh:mm hh:mm:ss
  The hours (hh) must be 00 to 23

Sample use:

```
INPUT "Enter the current time (hh:mm): ", newtime$
TIME$ = newtime$
```

Both of these samples get the date or time from the user and pass the data to the system clock. To use these two statements more effectively, you must include code that validates the user's date and time before setting the system clock. An invalid date will cause an "Illegal function call" error.

Timer Event Trapping

If you want the system clock to trigger an event, you can use the TIMER ON and ON TIMER statements. The TIMER ON/OFF/STOP statement enables and disables the timer event trap.

TIMER ON/OFF/STOP   statement

Syntax: TIMER {ON | OFF | STOP}

Purpose: TIMER ON enables clock events; TIMER OFF disables them; TIMER STOP suppresses them

Sample use:

```
TIMER ON
```

The ON TIMER statement determines how long it will be until the event occurs, and what to do when the event occurs.

ON TIMER   statement

Syntax: ON TIMER (*seconds*) GOSUB *label*

Purpose: Defines the location of the clock event trap

Note: The expression in parentheses is the number of seconds since the ON TIMER statement was executed.

Sample use:

```
TIMER ON
ON TIMER(1) GOSUB ShowTime
. . .
ShowTime:
   LOCATE 1, 71
   PRINT TIME$
RETURN
```

If you have a program that displays a menu and waits for user input, you can use this fragment to constantly update the time in the upper-right corner of the screen until the user selects an option.

The TIMER Function

The last function that uses the system clock supplies the current time in seconds since midnight.

TIMER   **function**

Purpose: Supplies the time in seconds since midnight

Return type: SINGLE

Parameters: None

Sample call:

```
RANDOMIZE TIMER
```

This function is most often used to provide a seed for the RANDOMIZE statement, since it returns a different number every hundredth of a second.

Using Interrupts

QuickBASIC provides several statements that are equivalent to DOS commands for changing the directory, setting the system clock, and so on. There are, however, several actions that DOS does with regularity that cannot be accomplished through a specific QuickBASIC statement or function. This section will show you how to access system resources through software interrupts.

To understand interrupts you first need some understanding of the internal structure of the 8088 microprocessor, which contains a series of registers. Each register provides temporary storage for information needed to run a program.

When DOS needs to access a system resource it generates a software interrupt. With a software interrupt, the system stops whatever it is doing, places the current value of each register on the stack, and performs an interrupt service routine. When the routine is complete, the system restores the former values of the registers saved and continues execution where it left off.

The INTERRUPT and INTERRUPTX Subroutines

With the INTERRUPT and INTERRUPTX subroutines you have access to the same set of interrupt service routines that DOS has.

INTERRUPT(intnum%, invals, outvals)   subroutine
INTERRUPTX(intnum%, invals, outvals)   subroutine

Purpose: Generates a software interrupt

Parameters: intnum%
[INTEGER]—the interrupt number *invals*
[RegType]—the required inputs to the ISR
outvals [RegType]—the values of the registers after the ISR is performed

---

Note: The only difference between INTERRUPT and INTER-RUPTX is that INTERRUPTX allows you to set and retrieve the contents of the DS and ES registers.

Sample call:

```
' $INCLUDE: 'QB.BI'
DIM inregs AS RegType, outregs AS RegType

inregs.AX = &H1900
CALL INTERRUPT (33, inregs, outregs)

PRINT "The current default drive is ";
SELECT CASE outregs.AX MOD 256
    CASE 0
        PRINT "A:"
    CASE 1
        PRINT "B:"
    CASE 2
        PRINT "C:"
    CASE 3
        PRINT "D:"
END SELECT
```

This sample calls the INTERRUPT subroutine to get the current default disk drive. The drive comes back as a number, which is then converted to the proper letter.

All calls to INTERRUPT and INTERRUPTX follow the same basic format as this sample. You must first include the file QB.BI, which defines the subroutines and the types you need. The most important part of the file is the definition of the type RegType, which is similar to this:

```
TYPE RegType
    AX AS INTEGER
    BX AS INTEGER
    CX AS INTEGER
    DX AS INTEGER
    BP AS INTEGER
    DI AS INTEGER
    FLAGS AS INTEGER
END TYPE
```

Each register is represented by a 2-byte integer. To retrieve a value from half of a register you can use the following formulas.

```
IF outregs.ax < 0 THEN
    AX# = outregs.ax + 65536
ELSE
    AX# = outregs.ax
END IF
AXhi% = AX# \ 256
AXlo% = AX# MOD 256
```

Once you have the $INCLUDE directive you need to define two record variables: one for the input registers and one for the output registers.

Before you generate the interrupt you must set the required input registers. Then you can call the INTERRUPT subroutine and use the appropriate output register values. Table 13-1 provides a partial listing of the software interrupts, their required input values, and the locations of the output values. As you can see, most of these are already duplicated by a high-level QuickBASIC statement or function.

Applications Using Interrupts

The following subroutine determines if the user has pressed a key on the keyboard. It differs from QuickBASIC's INKEY$ function in that it does not retrieve the key from the keyboard buffer.

```
FUNCTION KeyPressed%

inregs.ax = &HB00
CALL interrupt(33, inregs, outregs)

IF outregs.ax MOD 256 <> 0 THEN
    KeyPressed% = -1
ELSE
    KeyPressed% = 0
END IF

END FUNCTION
```

The *KeyPressed%* function could be used to check for user interrupts during operations that take long periods of time. The following sample program displays a message in changing colors to simulate some sort of action, while it calls *KeyPressed%* to check the keyboard buffer.

Action	Required Inputs	Register Outputs
	INTERRUPT 5	
Print screen	None	None
	INTERRUPT 16	
Set video mode	AH: 0 AL: mode key— 0: BW 40×25 1: Color 40×25 2: BW 80×25 3: Color 80×25 4: Color 320×200 5: B/W 320×200	None
Set cursor size	AH: 1 CH: bottom scan line CL: top scan line	None
Set cursor position	AH: 2 BH: page number DH: text line DL: text column	None
Get cursor position	AH: 3 BH: page number	DH: text line DL: text column
Set page number	AH: 5 AL: page number	None
Get video attributes	AH: 16	AL: video mode BH: page number
Get character at cursor	AH: 8 BH: page number	AH: attribute AL: character
	INTERRUPT 18	
Get RAM size	None	AX: size in K

Table 13-1.   Partial List of Software Interrupts

Action	Required Inputs	Register Outputs
	INTERRUPT 20	
Get keyboard scan code	AH: 0	AH: scan code
		AL: ASCII code
	INTERRUPT 23	
Initialize printer	AH: 1	None
	DL: printer number	
	(0 if only one)	
	INTERRUPT 25	
Reboot system	None	None
	INTERRUPT 33	
Get keyboard status	AH:7	AL: &HFF if key hit
Set default drive	AH: 15	None
	DL: drive number	
	(0 = A, 1 = B,. . .)	
Get default drive	AH: 25	AL: drive number
Get free disk space	AH: 54	Space = AX ∗ BX ∗ CX
	DL: drive number	

Table 13-1. Partial List of Software Interrupts (*continued*)

```
'   code for CHECKKEY.BAS

DECLARE FUNCTION KeyPressed% ()

' $INCLUDE: 'QB.BI'

DIM SHARED inregs AS RegType, outregs AS RegType

CLS
DO
     COLOR i%
```

```
        LOCATE 2, 2
        PRINT "Press any key to quit"
        FOR cnt% = 1 TO 100
            j% = 3 - j%
        NEXT cnt%
        i% = (i% + 1) MOD 15
LOOP UNTIL KeyPressed%

LOCATE 5, 2
PRINT "Key was pressed"
```

The next program uses interrupts to allow you to change the date and time stamp for a file. If you ever wondered how all the files on a disk you bought in the store could have the same file dates and times, this is how.

When you change the date and time stamp for a file, you must open the file using an interrupt. This open differs from the OPEN statement in that it returns the number of the file handle, which is the number used internally by DOS to track open files. Later subroutines will use the handle to refer to the same file. Here are the routines to open and close a file:

```
SUB OpenFile (filename$, filemode%, handle%)

filename$ = filename$ + CHR$(0)
inregs.ax = &H3D00 + filemode%
inregs.dx = SADD(filename$)

CALL INTERRUPT(33, inregs, outregs)

IF outregs.flags AND &H1 THEN
    PRINT "error!"
    PRINT "status = "; outregs.ax MOD 256
    END
END IF

handle% = outregs.ax

END SUB
```

```
SUB CloseFile (handle%)

inregs.ax = &H3E00
inregs.bx = handle%
CALL INTERRUPT(33, inregs, outregs)

IF outregs.flags AND &H1 THEN
    PRINT "error!"
    PRINT "status = "; outregs.ax MOD 256
```

```
      END
 END IF

 END SUB
```

The following routines, *GetFileStamp* and *SetFileStamp*, call the INTERRUPT subroutine to retrieve and set the date and time stamp on an open file. The *GetFileStamp* routine must decode the date and time from the DX and CX registers. The *SetFileStamp* routine must encode the date and time into those registers.

```
SUB GetFileStamp (handle%, month%, day%, year%, _
                                   hour%, min%, sec%)

inregs.ax = &H5700
inregs.bx = handle%

CALL INTERRUPT(33, inregs, outregs)

IF outregs.flags AND &H1 THEN
    PRINT "error!"
    PRINT "status = "; outregs.ax MOD 256
    END
END IF

date# = outregs.dx
IF date# < 0 THEN date# = 65536# + date#

month% = (date# MOD 512) \ 32
day% = date# MOD 32
year% = date# \ 512 + 1980

time# = outregs.cx
IF time# < 0 THEN time# = 65536# + time#
hour% = time# \ 2048
min% = (time# MOD 2048) \ 32
sec% = (time# MOD 32) * 2

END SUB
```

```
SUB SetFileStamp (handle%, month%, day%, year%, _
                                   hour%, min%, sec%)

inregs.ax = &H5701
inregs.bx = handle%
time# = (CDBL(hour%) * 2048) + (min% * 32) + (sec% \ 2)
IF time# <= 32767 THEN
    inregs.cx = time#
ELSE
    inregs.cx = time# - 65536#
```

```
END IF

date# = (CDBL(year% - 1980) * 512) + (month% * 32) + day%
IF date# <= 32767 THEN
     inregs.dx = date#
ELSE
     inregs.dx = date# - 65536#
END IF

CALL INTERRUPT(33, inregs, outregs)

IF outregs.flags AND &H1 THEN
     PRINT "error!"
     PRINT "status = "; outregs.ax MOD 256
     END
END IF

END SUB
```

The module-level code given here shows the statements required to use *GetFileStamp* or *SetFileStamp*. This could easily be part of a larger program that maintains the files on your disk.

```
'  code for FILSTAMP.BAS

DECLARE SUB OpenFile (filename$, filemode%, handle%)
DECLARE SUB CloseFile (handle%)
DECLARE SUB SetFileStamp (handle%, month%, day%, year%, _
                          hour%, min%, sec%)
DECLARE SUB GetFileStamp (handle%, day%, month%, year%, _
                          hour%, min%, sec%)

' $INCLUDE: 'QB.BI'

DIM SHARED inregs AS RegType, outregs AS RegType

INPUT "file"; file$
CALL OpenFile(file$, 0, handle%)
CALL GetFileStamp(handle%, mon%, day%, year%, hr%, min%, sec%)
PRINT USING "file stamp: ##/##/####"; mon%; day%; year%;
PRINT USING "  ##:##:##"; hr%; min%; sec%

INPUT "new month"; mon%
INPUT "new day"; day%
INPUT "new year"; year%
INPUT "new hour"; hr%
INPUT "new min"; min%
INPUT "new sec"; sec%

CALL SetFileStamp(handle%, mon%, day%, year%, hr%, min%, sec%)

CALL GetFileStamp(handle%, mon%, day%, year%, hr%, min%, sec%)
PRINT
```

```
PRINT USING "new file stamp: ##/##/####"; mon%; day%; year%;
PRINT USING "  ##:##:##"; hr%; min%; sec%

CALL CloseFile(handle%)
```

Miscellaneous System Information

The functions and statements in this section either retrieve
information from the system or set system information. Several
of these statements allow you to manipulate parts of your system that can destroy your program and the operating system.
Therefore, you should use them only when you are sure you
understand their effects.

The COMMAND$ Function

To execute any program from DOS you type the program name.
If you type anything else on the same line as the program name,
that information is stored in memory. To access the data in
string form QuickBASIC includes the COMMAND$ function.

COMMAND$ **function**

Purpose: Supplies the command line entered by the user

Return type: STRING

Parameters: None

Note: All characters are automatically converted to uppercase.

Sample call:

```
IF COMMAND$ = "EXPERT" THEN
    PRINT "Expert user assumed. . ."
ELSE
    PRINT "Welcome to my program."
    CALL DisplayInstructions
END IF
```

Suppose that you create a program called MYPROG.EXE. The user will normally type

```
C>MYPROG
```

to execute the program. However, if the user types

```
C>MYPROG EXPERT
```

the sample fragment will skip display of the instructions.

If you are running a program from the QuickBASIC environment you can set the command string from the Modify COMMAND$ option on the Run menu. This is especially useful when you are testing your program for its ability to handle command-line parameters. You can also use the /cmd compiler option to set the initial command parameter string.

This next listing is the generic subroutine *GetCommandParams*. This routine parses the command string, returning the number of command-line parameters as well as each separate parameter in an array.

```
SUB GetCommandParams (paramcount%, paramstring$())

comstr$ = COMMAND$
strpos% = 1
strlen% = LEN(comstr$)
paramcount% = 0

DO WHILE strpos% <= strlen%

   token$ = ""
   DO WHILE MID$(comstr$, strpos%, 1) = " "_
      AND strpos% <= strlen%
      strpos% = strpos% + 1
   LOOP

   DO WHILE MID$(comstr$, strpos%, 1) <> " " _
                               AND strpos% <= strlen%
      token$ = token$ + MID$(comstr$, strpos%, 1)
      strpos% = strpos% + 1
   LOOP

   IF token$ <> "" AND paramcount% < MaxParams% THEN
      paramcount% = paramcount% + 1
      paramstring$(paramcount%) = token$
   END IF

LOOP

END SUB
```

To use *GetCommandParams* you must declare the constant *MaxParams%* in the module-level code. The following program shows how to call *GetCommandParams*. This program does nothing more than echo the parsed command line.

```
DECLARE SUB GetCommandParams (paramcount%, paramstring$())
CONST MaxParams% = 5
DIM params$(MaxParams%)

CALL GetCommandParams(numparams%, params$())

PRINT "num = "; numparams%
FOR cnt% = 1 TO numparams%
    PRINT params$(cnt%)
NEXT cnt%
```

The ENVIRON$ function

The ENVIRON$ function gets a value from the DOS environment table.

ENVIRON$(expr)   **function**

Purpose: Supplies an environment value from the DOS environment table

Return type: STRING

Parameter: expr [INTEGER or STRING]—the name or number of the environment variable

Note: If the name or number does not exist, ENVIRON$ returns the null string.

Sample call:

```
dirpath$ = ENVIRON$("PATH")
```

As you can see, there is a string form and a numeric form of this function. You should use the numeric form only when you need to see the values of all environment variables. Normally, you will use the string form.

The ENVIRON Statement

If you retrieve an environment variable and its value is not what you need, you can assign it a new value with the ENVIRON statement.

ENVIRON   **statement**

Syntax: ENVIRON *environstring*

Purpose: Assigns a new value to an environment variable

Note: The environment string must be in the form *variable=newvalue* or *variable newvalue*; if there is no *newvalue*, the variable is removed from the environment table.

Sample use:

```
ENVIRON "PATH=C:\QBASIC;\MYFILES"
```

The ENVIRON statement only modifies a copy of the DOS environment table. This means that when your program is finished the old environment table is restored.

The FRE Function

The FRE function gives you information about remaining memory space while your program is running.

FRE(expr)   **function**

Purpose: Supplies various information on free memory

Return type: LONG

Parameter: expr [INTEGER or STRING]—the key requesting information. These are the possible key values:

−1	The number of bytes in the largest memory block available for numeric data
−2	The number of free bytes in the stack
Any other number	The number of bytes in the largest memory block available for string data
Any string	The number of free bytes in the string data heap

Note: FRE will give inaccurate information when used in the immediate mode.

Sample call:

```
PRINT "You have room for"; FRE(-1); "bytes of data"
```

This function is useful when your program is using too much memory space, or when you want to allocate a dynamic array in a large database application.

The PEEK Function

The PEEK function will give you the value stored in any memory location.

PEEK(addr)   **function**

Purpose: Gives the value stored at a memory address

Return type: INTEGER

Parameter: addr [2 bytes]—the offset of the address in question (the segment is set by DEF SEG)

Sample call:

```
myval% = PEEK(&H00AF)
```

The POKE Statement

When you need to assign a value to a specific memory location, you need the POKE statement.

POKE   **statement**

Syntax: POKE *memaddress, databyte*

Purpose: Assigns a new value to a memory location

Note: The address in this statement is the offset of the address in question (the segment is set by DEF SEG).

Sample call:

```
POKE &H00AF, myval% + 1
```

Be extremely careful when you use the POKE statement because you can unintentionally overwrite the operating system or your own program.

The SHELL Statement

The final statement in this section allows you to execute a DOS command from within your program.

SHELL   **statement**

Syntax: SHELL *commandstring*

Purpose: Executes any DOS command, or creates a new DOS shell

> *Note:* Omitting the command string creates a new DOS shell;
> type EXIT to return to the program.
> *Sample use:*
>
> ```
> SHELL "DIR *.BAS"
> ```

The SHELL statement is useful for executing commands not
inherent to QuickBASIC, such as file copy commands.

The Joystick

The remainder of this chapter covers the QuickBASIC statements and functions that support less common I/O devices and
ports. In Chapter 7 you studied the three major I/O devices: the
screen, the keyboard, and the printer. Chapter 11 covered I/O
with your disk drives. In this chapter you will learn how to use
the light pen, the joystick, COM ports, and I/O ports.

Traditionally, the joystick has always been used for computer games. If you design a game using QuickBASIC, you can
allow for joysticks by using the statements and functions in this
section. QuickBASIC can read input from two joysticks simulta-
neously, allowing you to create games for two players.

The STICK Function

Each joystick has a stick to control movement and one or two
triggers to specify actions. To read the stick coordinates you
need the STICK function.

STICK(key%)   **function**

Purpose: Supplies the current coordinates of both joysticks

Return type: INTEGER

Parameter: key%—a key for the return value based on the following:

0	current x-coordinate of joystick A
1	current y-coordinate of joystick A
2	current x-coordinate of joystick B
3	current y-coordinate of joystick B

Note: STICK(0) stores the current coordinates of both joysticks in memory and must be called first; both x- and y-coordinates range from 1 to 200.

Sample call:

```
xlast% = STICK(0)
CALL DrawPaddle (xlast%)
DO
   xcur% = STICK(0)
   IF xcur% < xlast% THEN
      CALL MovePaddleLeft
   ELSE
      CALL MovePaddleRight
   END IF
   xlast% = xcur%
   CALL MoveBall
LOOP
```

Suppose you design a game that requires a simulated paddle to travel back and forth across the bottom of the screen. The loop in the box would serve as part of the main program for the game. The program detects joystick movement in the x direction and redraws the paddle on the screen (inside the subroutines).

The STRIG Function

If you want to see if the user presses one of the joystick triggers, you need the STRIG function.

STRIG(key%)   **function**

Purpose: Supplies the status of all joystick triggers

Return type: INTEGER (−1 if true; 0 if false)

Parameter: key% [INTEGER]—a key for the return value based on the following:

0	Has the lower button on stick A been pressed since the last call to STRIG(0)?
1	Is the lower button on stick A currently down?
2	Has the lower button on stick B been pressed since the last call to STRIG(2)?
3	Is the lower button on stick B currently down?
4	Has the upper button on stick A been pressed since the last call to STRIG(4)?
5	Is the upper button on stick A currently down?
6	Has the upper button on stick B been pressed since the last call to STRIG(6)?
7	Is the upper button on stick B currently down?

Sample call:

```
PRINT "Press lower trigger to continue"
DO
LOOP UNTIL STRIG(0)      'wait for the trigger
```

The even-numbered keys determine whether a trigger has been pressed since the last poll. Even if the user presses the trigger and releases it before the call to STRIG, QuickBASIC will remember the event and return the appropriate value. You can use the odd-numbered keys to execute an action as long as the user continues to hold down the trigger.

Joystick Event Trapping

QuickBASIC will support joystick event traps. The STRIG ON/OFF/STOP statement enables or disables the event.

STRIG ON/OFF/STOP   **statement**

Syntax: STRIG (*triggerid*) {ON | OFF | STOP}

Purpose: STRIG ON enables trigger trapping; STRIG OFF disables it; STRIG STOP suppresses it

Note: The trigger number in parentheses uses this key:
0	lower trigger on joystick A
1	lower trigger on joystick B
2	upper trigger on joystick A
3	upper trigger on joystick B

Sample use:

```
STRIG(0) ON
```

The ON STRIG statement will define which trigger is the event and the location of the event handler.

ON STRIG   **statement**

Syntax: ON STRIG (*triggerid*) GOSUB *label*

Purpose: Determines the location of the trigger event handler

Note: The trigger number in parentheses follows the same key as the one in the STRING ON/OFF/STOP statement.

Sample use:

```
ON STRIG(0) GOSUB FireMissile
ON STRIG(2) GOSUB DropBomb
```

When you use the STRIG function to check the trigger you must poll the joystick at regular intervals. The STRIG ON and

ON STRIG statements allow you to continue the program until the exact moment when the user presses the trigger.

The Light Pen

If you do not own a light pen, you need not run to your favorite computer store and buy one. Light pens have had very limited popularity, and only a few software applications support their use. If you happen to own a mouse and a light pen, you need to disable the mouse to use the light pen (see your mouse manual for details).

The PEN ON/OFF/STOP Statement

Before you can read light-pen values, you must enable light-pen input with the PEN ON statement.

PEN ON/OFF/STOP   **statement**

Syntax: PEN {ON | OFF | STOP}

Purpose: PEN ON enables light-pen input; PEN OFF disables input; PEN STOP suspends input

Note: Light-pen input is initially disabled by default.

Sample use:

```
PEN ON          'enable the light pen
. . .              'do light pen inputs
PEN OFF         'disable the light pen
```

Unlike most other event traps (for example, PLAY and KEY), the PEN ON/OFF/STOP statement does not have to be used in conjunction with the ON PEN statement. You use PEN ON before light-pen input, and PEN OFF afterwards.

The PEN Function

To determine the current status of the light pen, you must use the PEN function.

PEN(key%)   **function**

Purpose: Supplies current and recent light-pen information

Return type: INTEGER

Parameter: key%—a key for the return value based on the following:

0	pen-press flag (−1 if pressed since last call; 0 if not pressed)
1	x-coordinate when pen was last pressed
2	y-coordinate when pen was last pressed
3	current pen status (−1 if pressed, 0 if not)
4	current x-coordinate
5	current y-coordinate
6	text line number when pen was last pressed
7	text column number when pen was last pressed
8	current text line number
9	current text column number

Note: You must use PEN ON before using the PEN function.

Sample call:

```
DO
   penpressed% = PEN(0)
UNTIL penpressed%
LOCATE PEN(6), PEN(7)
PRINT "X";
```

This sample fragment waits until the light pen is pressed on the screen. Then it places an "X" in the text line and column where the pen was pressed.

The ON PEN Statement

If you want light-pen input as an event trap, you need the ON PEN statement.

ON PEN **statement**

Syntax: ON PEN GOSUB *label*

Purpose: Defines the location of the light-pen event handler

Sample use:

```
DIM SHARED penpressed%, menuinput%
ON PEN GOSUB PenHandler
. . .
PenHandler:
    penpressed% = -1
    xcoord% = PEN(1)
    ycoord% = PEN(2)
    CALL GetMenuItem (xcoord%, ycoord%, menuinput%)
RETURN
```

This program fragment could be part of a large program that handles input from several sources. If the user presses the light pen on the screen while the program is performing a calculation (or simply waiting for an event), this handler will set a global flag to inform the current routine that there is input from the light pen. Then the program determines which menu item was closest to the coordinates of the light pen when it was pressed, and sets another global variable.

I/O Ports

QuickBASIC allows you to manipulate your computer's I/O ports directly. If you are designing a security system or setting your computer to start your breakfast, you will probably use an interface card that you access through an open I/O port. Also, DOS uses I/O ports to access all I/O device drivers. You might speed up a program by doing the I/O yourself. Consult a system manual for information on which port controls which device.

The OUT Statement

To output data to a port you need the OUT statement.

OUT   **statement**

Syntax: OUT *portnum, databyte*

Purpose: Outputs a byte of information to an output port

Sample use:

```
FOR cnt% = 1 TO 25
   OUT 12, myarray%(cnt%) MOD 256
   OUT 12, myarray%(cnt%) \ 256
NEXT cnt%
```

Since the OUT statement can output data only one byte at a time, any data stored in a 2-byte integer must be sent in two parts. The sample loop outputs the lower byte and the upper byte of each of 25 elements of the *myarray%* integer array.

If you use the loop given with the OUT statement, the driver must be able to handle the data at the rate it is output by QuickBASIC. Since this is not normally the case, you must usually include two-way communication between the program and the device in the form of handshaking.

The INP Function

To get information from a device you need the INP function.

INP(port)   **function**

Purpose: Receives a byte from an input port
Return type: INTEGER
Parameter: port [LONG]—the port number
Sample call:

```
SUB Out1Byte (onebyte%)

'         send out data
OUT 12, onebyte%

'         send "data ready"
OUT 13, 1

'         wait for acknowledge
DO
LOOP UNTIL INP(11) > 0

'         reset "data ready"
OUT 13, 0

'         wait for acknowledge reset
DO
LOOP UNTIL INP(11) = 0

RETURN
```

This subroutine demonstrates one method of handshaking. Port 12 is used to send the data. Port 13 tells the device that valid data is waiting on port 12. The program now uses port 11 for the device to tell the program that it has received the data. The output loop for *myarray%* can now be changed to use the handshaking routine:

```
FOR cnt% = 1 TO 25
   Out1Byte (myarray%(cnt%) MOD 256)
   Out1Byte (myarray%(cnt%) \ 256)
NEXT cnt%
```

The WAIT Statement

The WAIT statement eliminates the need for the loops in *Out1Byte* that continue until an input condition is met.

WAIT   **statement**

Syntax: WAIT *portnum, andmask* [, *xormask*]
Purpose: Polls an input port until a set of conditions is met
Note: If the XOR condition is omitted, it is set to 0.
Sample use:

```
SUB Out1Byte (onebyte%)

OUT 12, onebyte%
OUT 13, 1
WAIT 11, 1
OUT 13, 0
WAIT 11, 1, 1

RETURN
```

The same subroutine is now rewritten to use WAIT statements instead of INP loops. The first WAIT statement checks port 11 until the data AND 1 is not zero. The second WAIT statement checks port 11, XORs it with one, and ANDs it with one; in other words, it waits until the data is zero again.

COM Ports

In addition to the I/O ports, the COM ports serve as a means of communication to the outside world. These ports use the RS-232 standard for asynchronous communication. If you have an application that requires the use of COM1: or COM2:, you can use QuickBASIC to write that application.

QuickBASIC treats the COM*n*: devices like files, which is similar to the way it treats KBD: and CONS:. Therefore, you must open the device and assign a file number to it. From then on you can use file I/O statements like INPUT# and PRINT#.

The OPEN COM Statement

The OPEN statement for COM ports is slightly different from the other OPEN statements and is referred to as the OPEN COM statement.

OPEN COM   **statement**

Syntax:
OPEN *comstring* FOR *openmode* AS [*#*]*filenum* [LEN = *reclen*]
where *openmode* =>
   {INPUT | OUTPUT | RANDOM}
and where *comstring* =>
   "{COM1: | COM2:} *comoptions*"
where *comoptions* =>
   [*baud*][,[*parity*][,[*size*][,[*stopbits*][,*others*]. . .]]]
Purpose: Prepares a COM port for asynchronous communication

Note: See Table 13-2 for other communications options.

Sample use:

```
comport% = FREEFILE
OPEN "COM1:1200,E,7,1,ASC,DS5000"
DO
    INPUT #comport%, onechar$
    PRINT onechar$;
LOOP UNTIL onechar$ = CHR$(26)
```

This sample echoes the input from COM1: to the screen. Since the device is in ASCII mode, the input stream should terminate with the CHR$(26) end-of-file marker.

Option	Meaning	Default [Range]
ASC	ASCII mode	Inactive
BIN	Binary mode	Active
LF	Line feed after carriage return	Inactive
RB n	Receiver buffer size	512 [1 − 32767]
TB n	Transmit buffer size	512 [1 − 32767]
DS n	DSR line timeout limit (in milliseconds)	1000 [0 − 65535]
CD n	DCD line timeout limit	1000 [0 − 65535]
OP n	Total timeout limit	10000 [1 − 65535]
RS	Suppress RTS request	n/a
CS n	CTS line timout limit	1000 [0 − 65535]

Table 13-2.   Other COM Options Summary

Most of the OPEN COM statement follows the same syntax as the OPEN statement from Chapter 11. When you specify the device name in the OPEN COM statement, however, you also have the option of setting various communications options. The first option is the baud rate, which is usually a number between 300 and 9600. The second is the type of parity checking you need: E for even, O for odd, S for space, or M for mark parity. The third option is the number of data bits: 5, 6, 7, or 8. If you need eight data bits you must select no parity since QuickBASIC stores the information in 8-bit memory locations. The fourth option is the number of stop bits: 1, 1.5, or 2. If you omit any of these first four options you must include commas as placeholders for them.

The rest of the options can be in any order and are summarized in Table 13-2. The ASC and BIN options define the device mode. In binary mode, all characters are transferred as they appear, without any interpretation. In ASCII mode, a CHR$(9) is treated as a tab character, CHR$(26) is the end-of-file, and carriage returns are forced at the end of each line. If you include the LF option with the ASC option, each carriage return will be followed by a line feed, CHR$(10). Normally, you use ASC when you open the port FOR INPUT or FOR OUTPUT, and you use BIN when you open the port FOR RANDOM. The default mode is BIN.

The RB and TB options set the receive and transmit buffer sizes. If you need to input large amounts of data quickly, you may need to set the receiver buffer size to something larger than 512. Similarly, for output to a slow device you may need to increase the size of the transmit buffer. Both options can have values from 1 to 32,767.

Before the device is considered open, there must be an established communications pattern. To generate this, Quick-BASIC sets the DTR (data terminal ready) line high and waits one second for the DSR (data set ready) to be set by the other device. If you want to wait longer (or not as long), use the DS option. If the given time expires without a DSR signal, a timeout occurs and the open fails. This signal is checked as long as the device is open. If you want to ignore the DSR line, use the DS0 option.

The DCD (data carrier detect) line normally shows that both devices are ready for communication. Unless you use the CD0 option, the open will be unsuccessful until this line goes high. If CD is greater than zero, QuickBASIC will wait the required amount of time for the line to go high before it generates a timeout.

The OP option specifies the total amount of time to wait before the open fails. If you use OP without a number, Quick-BASIC will wait indefinitely. This means that you will have to reset your computer if the open fails. If you omit the OP option completely, the system will automatically wait ten times the greater of the CD and DS option values before failing.

When you need to output data you can use a handshaking method with the RTS (ready to send) line and the CTS (clear to send) line. When you place data in the transmit buffer by using a PUT# or PRINT# statement, QuickBASIC sets the RTS line high and waits for the CTS line to go high before sending the data. If you select the RS option you can keep the system from setting that line. The CS option defines the amount of time to wait for the CTS signal before failing because of a timeout. You can set the CS option to wait longer than one second, or you can use CS0 to ignore the CTS line and just send the data.

COM Port Event Trapping

If you want to use the COM ports in an event trap, QuickBASIC provides the ON COM and COM ON/OFF/STOP statements. The COM ON/OFF/STOP statement enables or disables event traps for COM ports.

COM ON/OFF/STOP   **statement**

Syntax: COM (*portnum*) {ON | OFF | STOP}

Purpose: COM ON enables COM port event trapping for a specific port; COM OFF disables it; COM STOP suppresses it

Sample use:

```
COM(1) ON
```

The ON COM statement defines the port number and the event trap location.

ON COM   **statement**

Syntax: ON COM (*portnum*) GOSUB *label*

Purpose: Defines the location of the COM port event handler

Sample use:

```
COM(1) ON
ON COM(1) GOSUB GetData
. . .
GetData:
   GET #comport%, , MyRecord
   PRINT #infile%, , MyRecord
RETURN
```

In this sample, the program will run its normal course until a byte appears in the receive buffer. The program then branches immediately to the event handler, reads the data from the COM port, and stores it in a file.

Miscellaneous Functions and Statements

Compatibility with Older QuickBASIC Versions
Compatibility with BASICA
Other Miscellaneous Statements and Functions

If you are using a QuickBASIC statement or function that is not in the first 13 chapters of this book, you are not using Quick-BASIC as efficiently as you could. This chapter describes all the statements found in QuickBASIC that could, for the most part, be eliminated entirely from the language, and that should be eliminated from your programs.

After describing the syntax of each statement or function, this chapter will show you an alternative to that statement, explaining why the alternative is better. Many of the statements do not include a sample fragment because they have been replaced completely either by other statements or by the Quick-BASIC environment.

Compatibility with Older QuickBASIC Versions

The first group of statements and functions are those that provide compatibility with older versions of QuickBASIC.

The CVSMBF and CVDMBF Functions

Before QuickBASIC 4.0, real numbers were represented in a special form used only by Microsoft. With versions 4.0 and 4.5,

SINGLE and DOUBLE numbers are stored in the IEEE standard format. The CVSMBF and CVDMBF functions included in the current version of QuickBASIC simplify the transition from the old format to the new.

CVSMBF(oldnum$), CVDMBF(oldnum$)   functions

Purpose: Converts old-format real numbers into IEEE-format real numbers

Return type: SINGLE for CVSMBF; DOUBLE for CVDMBF

Parameter: oldnum$ [STRING]—a 4- or 8-byte string containing an old-format real number

Note: These functions should be used only in conversion programs.

Sample call:

```
TYPE NewRecType
   singlenum as SINGLE
   doublenum as DOUBLE
END TYPE

TYPE OldRecType
   oldsingle as STRING*4
   olddouble as STRING*8
END TYPE

DIM newrec AS NewRecType, oldrec AS OldRecType

OPEN "MYDATA.DAT" FOR RANDOM AS #1 LEN=LEN(oldrec)
OPEN "MYDATA.NEW" FOR RANDOM AS #2 LEN=LEN(newrec)

DO WHILE NOT EOF(1)
   GET #1, , oldrec
   newrec.singlenum = CVSMBF(oldrec.oldsingle)
   newrec.doublenum = CVDMBF(oldrec.olddouble)
   PUT #2, , newrec
LOOP

CLOSE #1, #2
```

This sample is a complete conversion program. It takes an old file that stores numbers in the old format and creates a new file that stores them in IEEE format. The alternative is to keep the old file and do the conversion every time you read from the file. The sample method is preferred because it keeps the main program updated and keeps it from doing unnecessary conversions forever.

The MKSMBF$ and MKDMBF$ Functions

The converse of CVSMBF and CVDMBF are the MKSMBF$ and MKDMBF$ functions. These two functions convert an IEEE-format real number into a string with the numbers in the old format. Again, you could include these as part of your program and convert everything before you store it. However, if you use the conversion program given earlier, these functions are completely useless.

MKSMBF$(singnum!), MKDMBF$(doubnum#)   functions

Purpose: Converts a SINGLE or DOUBLE number into a string with the number in the old Microsoft BASIC format

Return type: STRING

Parameter: singnum! [SINGLE]—the SINGLE number to convert

doubnum# [DOUBLE]—the DOUBLE number to convert

Note: If you need to convert a number to a string before storing it, use the STR$ function instead.

The TRON and TROFF Statements

Before the new QuickBASIC environment, debugging your program involved printing values at strategic locations and displaying line numbers with the TRON and TROFF statements. Now that you can set Trace On in the Debug menu and highlight each statement as you execute it, these statements have become obsolete. See Chapter 18 for a complete discussion of QuickBASIC's debugging features.

The TRON statement was used to turn on the old tracing mechanism.

TRON   **statement**

Syntax: TRON

Purpose: Enables line-number displays during program execution

Note: The TRON statement is obsolete in the QuickBASIC environment.

If you wanted to turn off the tracing mechanism somewhere in your program, you used the TROFF statement.

TROFF   **statement**

Syntax: TROFF

Purpose: Disables line-number displays during program execution

Note: The TROFF statement is obsolete in the QuickBASIC environment.

The FIELD Statement

QuickBASIC 4.0 introduced record structures to the BASIC language. Before this version, you stored data in random-access files using fields. Since the record structure is more versatile and easier to work with, you should convert your programs to use records instead of fields.

FIELD   **statement**

Syntax: FIELD [#]*filenum, fielddefinition* [, *fielddefinition*]
where *fielddefinition* =>
    fieldwidth AS *stringvariable*

Purpose: Defines the elements of a random-access file buffer

Note: You should replace all fields with records.

Sample use:

```
DIM lnames$(100), fnames$(100), ecodes$(100)

OPEN "PERSONNEL.LIS" FOR RANDOM AS #persfile% LEN=60
FIELD #persfile%, 30 AS lastname$, 20 AS firstname$, _
    10 AS employeecode$

cnt% = 0
DO WHILE NOT EOF(persfile%)
   GET #persfile%
   cnt% = cnt% + 1
   lnames$(cnt%) = lastname$
   fnames$(cnt%) = firstname$
   ecodes$(cnt%) = employeecode$
LOOP
Call SortByCode (cnt%, lnames$(), fnames$(), ecodes$())
```

The previous sample demonstrates how a random-access file was read and sorted under QuickBASIC 3.0. The following is the same code, converted to use records.

```
TYPE employeerec
   lastname AS STRING*30
   firstname AS STRING*20
   employeecode AS STRING*10
END TYPE
DIM people(100) AS employeerec

OPEN "PERSONNEL.LIS" FOR RANDOM AS #persfile% LEN=60

cnt% = 0
DO WHILE NOT EOF(persfile%)
   cnt% = cnt% + 1
   GET #persfile%, , people(cnt%)
LOOP
Call SortByCode (cnt%, people())
```

You'll notice that with the fields, you cannot place data from a random-access file directly into an array. Record structures have this capability built in.

The CVtype Functions

A major drawback of fields is their inability to store numbers directly. You must convert numbers to strings before storing them in a file, and you must convert them back after reading them. The CVI, CVS, CVL, and CVD functions are included in QuickBASIC to convert strings in a field to their respective numeric values. When you convert your programs to use record structures instead, these functions become useless.

CVtype(stringvar$)   **functions**

Purpose: Converts a string in a field

Return type: Depends on the function: an INTEGER (CVI), a SINGLE (CVS), a LONG (CVL), or a DOUBLE (CVD) variable

Parameter: *stringvar$* [STRING] — the string to convert

> *Note:* These functions are obsolete when you use records.

The MKtype$ Functions

The counterparts to the CVtype functions are the MKtype$ functions. These functions convert numeric variables to strings so they can be stored in the old random-access files. Again, now that you can use records you should have no use for these.

MKtype$(expr)   **functions**

Purpose: Converts an INTEGER (MKI$), SINGLE (MKS$), LONG (MKL$), or DOUBLE (MKD$) variable to a string

Return type: STRING

Parameter: expr [type based on the function]—the number to convert

Note: These functions are obsolete when you use records.

The INT86OLD and INT86XOLD Subroutines

The INTERRUPT and INTERRUPTX subroutines use records to pass information to the system software interrupts, as you studied in Chapter 13. Before QuickBASIC 4.0, when there were no records, this information had to be passed using integer arrays. The subroutines you called in older versions were INT86 and INT86X. In QuickBASIC 4.0 and 4.5, these subroutines are called INT86OLD and INT86XOLD.

INT86OLD(intnum%, invals%( ), outvals%( ))   subroutine
INT86XOLD(intnum%, invals%( ), outvals%( ))   subroutine

Purpose: Generates a software interrupt

Parameters: intnum% [INTEGER]—the interrupt number
    invals% [INTEGER]—an array containing the required inputs to the ISR
    outvals% [INTEGER]—an array containing the values of the registers after the ISR is performed

Sample call:

```
' $INCLUDE: 'QB.BI'

DIM invalsold%(1 TO 7), outvalsold%(1 TO 7)

invalsold%(1) = &H605
invalsold%(3) = &H0
invalsold%(4) = &H913

CALL INT86OLD(16, invalsold%(), outvalsold%())
```

This interrupt combination scrolls the first 20 characters of the first ten lines up five lines. The problem with this older form of the subroutine call is that you are not exactly sure which array element refers to which register. Use of records and subroutines handles this problem, because the register names are the names of the record elements. Here is the same interrupt converted to use records:

```
' $INCLUDE: 'QB.BI'

DIM invals AS RegType, outvals AS RegType

invals.ax = &H605
invals.cx = &H0
invals.dx = &H913

CALL INTERRUPT(16, invals, outvals)
```

The ABSOLUTE Subroutine

In Chapter 10 you can learn how to call a subroutine written in C or assembly language using the DECLARE and CALL (CALLS) statements. The ABSOLUTE subroutine was the former method of calling an assembly-language program.

ABSOLUTE([expr,expr,. . .,]address%)   subroutine

Purpose: Executes a set of machine-language instructions

Parameters: expr [any type]—optional arguments
address% [INTEGER]—the offset address of the start of the routine

Note: The new mixed-language capability avoids having to place the code in an array.

If you have a program that uses this subroutine, there is no reason to convert it. New assembly-language routines, however, should be written using the techniques given in Chapter 10.

Compatibility with BASICA

If you never used a version of QuickBASIC prior to the 4.0 release, the previous section probably made little sense to you. This section, however, is extremely useful to all programmers who learned some form of BASIC many years ago and are still doing things the old-fashioned way. Each of the following statements and functions is provided in QuickBASIC for compatibility with BASICA, but for the reasons given should be eliminated from your programming repertoire.

The GOSUB-RETURN Structure

The first is the GOSUB-RETURN structure, which was the standard way to modularize before you bought QuickBASIC.

GOSUB-RETURN   **structure**

Syntax:

    GOSUB *label*

    . . .

    label:

        statementblock
    RETURN [*nextlabel*]

Purpose: Calls and executes a subroutine

Note: The SUB-END SUB structure provides a better way to modularize your programs.

Sample use:

```
GOSUB GetData
GOSUB SortIt
. . .

GetData:
   myfile% = FREEFILE
   OPEN "names.dat" FOR INPUT AS #myfile%

   INPUT #myfile%, total%
   FOR i% = 1 TO total%
      INPUT #myfile%, names$(i%)
   NEXT i%
   CLOSE myfile%
RETURN

SortIt:
   FOR i% = 1 TO total% - 1
      FOR j% = i% + 1 TO total%
         IF names$(i%) > names$(j%) THEN
            SWAP names$(i%), names$(j%)
         END IF
      NEXT j%
   NEXT i%
RETURN
```

This program fragment includes two subroutines: one to read a list of names from a file, and one to put them in alphabetical order. The GOSUB method of partitioning, however, has a few disadvantages. First, all variables are global. If you use the variables *i%* and *j%* in the main program, their values will change when you call the subroutine. Second, the sort routine can be used for this program only.

If you convert this program so it uses SUBs instead of GOSUBs you eliminate these problems. The main program has no access to the local variables *i%* and *j%*. Also, the sort routine will sort any string array you pass to it. Here is the converted program:

```
CALL GetData (total%, names$())
CALL SortIt (total%, names$())
. . .

SUB GetData (filesize%, namearray$())

filenumber% = FREEFILE
OPEN "names.dat" FOR INPUT AS #filenumber%

INPUT #filenumber%, filesize%
FOR i% = 1 TO filesize%
   INPUT #filenumber%, namearray$(i%)
NEXT i%
CLOSE filenumber%

END SUB
. . .

SUB SortIt (arraysize%, strarray$())

FOR i% = 1 TO arraysize% - 1
   FOR j% = i% + 1 TO arraysize%
      IF strarray$(i%) > strarray$(j%) THEN
         SWAP strarray$(i%), strarray$(j%)
      END IF
   NEXT j%
NEXT i%

END SUB
```

The DEF FN Statement

Functions have evolved in a similar fashion to subroutines. The older versions of BASIC used DEF FN to define functions. Now you can use the FUNCTION structure covered in Chapter 10.

DEF FN   structure/statement

Syntax:

DEF FN*functionname* [*parameterlist*] = *expression*

OR,

DEF FN*functionname* [*parameterlist*]
    statementblock
END DEF

where *parameterlist* = >

variable [AS *type*] [, *variable* [AS *type*]]. . .

Purpose: Defines a function

Note: The identifier includes the letters FN as the first two letters of its name.

Sample use:

```
DEF FNSmaller (num1!, num2!)
   IF num1! < num2! THEN
      FNSmaller = num1!
   ELSE
      FNSmaller = num2!
   END IF
END DEF
```

The DEF FN structure is weaker than the FUNCTION-END FUNCTION structure because it is dependent on location. In other words, you must include the function in every module where it is needed. Also, you must define the function before you call it. You do not have these problems with a FUNCTION declaration. The conversion from DEF FN to FUNCTION usually requires only minor changes:

```
FUNCTION Smaller (num1!, num2!)
   IF num1! < num2! THEN
      Smaller = num1!
   ELSE
      Smaller = num2!
   END IF
END FUNCTION
```

As soon as you type the FUNCTION statement, the Quick-BASIC environment automatically places you in a new text window, keeping all subprograms separate.

The EXIT DEF Statement

Naturally, when you convert a DEF FN to a FUNCTION the EXIT DEF will become EXIT FUNCTION, as described in Chapter 10.

EXIT DEF   **statement**

Syntax: EXIT DEF

Purpose: Forces the immediate exit of a DEF FN structure

Note: This statement works the same way for DEF FN as EXIT FUNCTION does for a FUNCTION.

The ON GOSUB/GOTO Statement

The SELECT CASE statement is a versatile and convenient way to perform different operations based on a specific expression. The former way of doing this was with the ON GOSUB or ON GOTO statements.

ON GOSUB/GOTO   statement

Syntax: ON expression {GOSUB | GOTO} *label* [, *label*]. . .

Purpose: Calls one of many subroutines or jumps to one of many labels based on an expression

Note: If the expression is < 0 or > 255, an error occurs; if it is 0 or greater than the number of choices, QuickBASIC drops down to the next statement.

Sample use:

```
INPUT "Enter your yearly salary: ", salary!
salarycode% = salary! \ 10000 + 1
IF salarycode% > 7 THEN salarycode% = 7
ON salarycode% GOSUB Poverty, Low, Low, Middle, _
        Middle, Middle, High
```

This sample assumes that there are four subroutines elsewhere in the program: Poverty, Low, Middle, and High. Notice how cumbersome the ON GOSUB statement is. The biggest problem is that you have to coerce the number to be in the range from 1 to 7 (or another small number). By comparison this converted SELECT CASE structure is quite straightforward:

```
INPUT "Enter your yearly salary: ", salary!
SELECT CASE salary!
    CASE IS < 10000
       CALL Poverty(salary!)
    CASE 10000 TO 29999.99
       CALL Low(salary!)
    CASE 30000 TO 59999.99
       CALL Middle(salary!)
    CASE ELSE
       CALL High(salary!)
END SELECT
```

Now if you wanted to change the income levels so that they are not multiples of 10,000 you can do it painlessly.

The WHILE-WEND Structure

BASICA does not support the DO-LOOP structure. Its counterpart is the WHILE-WEND structure.

WHILE-WEND   **structure**

Syntax:

WHILE *expression*
    statementblock
WEND

Purpose: Executes a statement block while the condition is true

Sample use:

```
keyhit$ = INKEY$
WHILE keyhit$ = ""
   keyhit$ = INKEY$
WEND
```

The major deficiency of the WHILE-WEND structure is its inability to test the condition at the end of the loop. Notice in this sample that you must call INKEY$ before the loop and during the loop to make sure that you execute the loop. With QuickBASIC's DO-LOOP structure you can do the test at the very end.

```
DO
   keyhit$ = INKEY$
LOOP WHILE keyhit$ = " "
```

Although you need not convert all of your WHILE-WEND structures to DO-LOOPs, you should consider using the newer and more flexible structure from now on.

The STRIG Statement

In BASICA you have to enable joystick-trigger testing before you can use the STRIG function. For this you need the STRIG statement.

STRIG   **statement**

Syntax: STRIG {ON | OFF}

Purpose: STRIG ON enables all trigger testing; STRIG OFF disables it

Note: These statements are ignored by QuickBASIC.

When QuickBASIC encounters one of these statements, it simply ignores it. Do not confuse STRIG ON with STRIG(1) ON, a statement that enables a specific joystick trigger. These statements are still valid, as you learned in Chapter 13.

Other Miscellaneous Statements and Functions

The remaining statements and functions in this chapter complete the QuickBASIC language reference. These statements are all obsolete for the reasons given.

The SYSTEM Statement

The SYSTEM statement is primarily for BASICA, and you usually use it only in immediate mode. With the QuickBASIC environment you have no need for this statement.

SYSTEM   **statement**

Syntax: SYSTEM
Purpose: Returns a program to the QuickBASIC environment
Note: If you type SYSTEM in the immediate window, you will return to DOS.

The FILES Statement

The FILES statement is also obsolete in the immediate mode because the QuickBASIC environment provides directories when you need to load or open a file. If you want to provide a directory for the user in your program, use the SHELL statement; it supplies much more information.

FILES statement

Syntax: FILES *directorystring*
Purpose: Displays a list of files
Note: Wildcard characters are supported (*, ?).
Sample use:

```
FILES "B:*.DAT"
```

The STOP Statement

The STOP statement was used to temporarily halt a program to check values of program variables. Now that the QuickBASIC environment provides better debugging tools, this statement is no longer useful.

STOP statement

Syntax: STOP
Purpose: Halts program execution
Note: In a stand-alone program, STOP works the same as an END statement.

The RESET Statement

The RESET statement closes all open files. If you write your programs properly you will close each file when you are finished using it. Therefore, the RESET statement is unnecessary.

RESET   **statement**

Syntax: RESET
Purpose: Closes all open files
Note: Use the CLOSE statement to close each file.

The GOTO Statement

Some programmers will never get away from using GOTO statements to move around in a program. If you follow the programming practices discussed in this book, you should never need a GOTO statement.

GOTO   **statement**

Syntax: GOTO *label*
Purpose: Moves to a specified label
Note: The label must be in the same module and level.

The IOCTL Statement and IOCTL$ Function

The rest of the statements and functions in this chapter are not necessarily obsolete, but their functions are so limited that you probably will never use them. The IOCTL statement and the IOCTL$ function transmit and receive data from specific device drivers that support them. The device must be opened as a file-like device (see Chapter 11).

The IOCTL statement is used to output data to the device driver.

IOCTL statement

Syntax: IOCTL [#]*filenum, stringexpression*
Purpose: Outputs a control string to a device driver
Note: This statement works only on open files.

The IOCTL$ function is used to input data from the device driver.

IOCTL$(filenum%) function

Purpose: Inputs a control string from a device driver
Return type: STRING
Parameter: *filenum%* [INTEGER]—the number of the file
Note: This statement works only on open files.

The ERDEV and ERDEV$ Functions

ERDEV and ERDEV$ are two functions that provide device-specific information about an error. QuickBASIC itself normally provides very specific information with its error codes, so these functions seldom add any benefit.

The ERDEV function gives you an error number generated by the device.

ERDEV   **function**

Purpose: Supplies the device-specific error number

Return type: INTEGER

Parameters: None

Note: ERDEV also provides the device-attribute word as the upper byte of the integer.

The ERDEV$ function gives you the name of the device that caused the error.

ERDEV$ **function**

Purpose: Supplies the name of the device that generated an error

Return type: STRING

Parameters: None

The ERL Function

The ERL function tells you the last line number found before an error occurred. With the programming practices found in this book you should never have a line number. Therefore, this function will always return a 0.

ERL   **function**

Purpose: Supplies the line number before the last error
Return type: INTEGER
Parameters: None
Note: If no line numbers are present, ERL returns 0.

The CLEAR Statement

The CLEAR statement reinitializes all variables and can be used to change the stack size. Normally, you should reinitialize variables yourself so that you know which ones need to be reset. Also, there are very few times when you will need more stack space than is automatically provided.

CLEAR   **statement**

Syntax: CLEAR [, , *stacksize*]
Purpose: Reinitializes all variables and changes the stack size
Sample use:

```
CLEAR, , 4000
```

The QuickBASIC Environment

If you have been using a different editor to write your Quick-BASIC programs, you have no idea what you are missing with the QuickBASIC environment. This truly is a complete environment that lets you develop, debug, and manage any QuickBASIC program. Part Three is devoted to explaining how to use the many features of the QuickBASIC environment.

Chapter 15 gives you a complete listing of the editing commands, from cursor movement to cutting and pasting. It shows you why you should be using the QuickBASIC environment to create your programs.

Chapter 16 covers QuickBASIC file management. This chapter explains how to create programs that use multiple modules, how to create an include file, and how to turn a module into a Quick library.

Undoubtedly you will have run a program before reading Chapter 17. However, this chapter will show you the various options for running a program and invoking QuickBASIC. You will also find a description of the parameters and options for using the BC compiler and the LINK linker.

Chapter 18 begins with coverage of QuickBASIC 4.5's new on-line help system. It shows you how to move around in the many help screens. The rest of Chapter 18 deals with debugging. QuickBASIC has some of the most advanced debugging tools anywhere, and this chapter will show you how to use them.

Editing a Program

Special Features
Cursor Movement
Entering and Deleting Text
Using the Clipboard
Finding and Replacing Text
Using QuickBASIC Windows
Writing Subprograms

Computer software users usually fall into one of two categories. The first group tries to minimize the number of commands they need to learn. Once users in this group learn a certain command, they stick with it so they do not cloud their minds with useless alternatives or shortcuts. The other group tries to minimize keystrokes, constantly looking for new shortcuts. They attempt to avoid any activity that takes more than two keystrokes.

This chapter is primarily for those programmers who fit into the second group. It is filled with shortcuts and alternative methods to minimize the time it takes to edit programs. In this chapter you will discover the various ways to enter and delete text; how to move the cursor anywhere; how to find and replace text; how to use the clipboard and window features; and how to edit subprograms.

Special Features

After following the tutorial in Chapter 3 you have learned that the QuickBASIC editor works much like a fancy typewriter or word processor. There are some major differences, however, and these differences make clear why you should use the Quick-BASIC environment to write your programs. Thus, before discussing the text editing commands, this section explains some of the special features of the editor.

Syntax Checking

The primary advantage of using the QuickBASIC editor to write programs is its built-in *syntax checker*. As soon as you finish a line by pressing ENTER or by using an arrow key, QuickBASIC analyzes the syntax of the line. It automatically capitalizes the reserved words in the line and puts spaces between operators. If you skip a punctuation mark that the syntax checker can detect, it will add the comma or semicolon automatically. For instance, if you type this line:

```
print "the total is " total%
```

the syntax checker will rewrite the line as this:

```
PRINT "the total is "; total%
```

Notice the semicolon that has been placed between the two expressions.

When you are writing a program you should enter the reserved words in lowercase. After you press ENTER, look up at the screen and make sure the reserved words are now uppercase. If you make a spelling error that the syntax checker does not notice, the case of the letters will show the error.

If you make a syntax error on a line you type, a dialog box will appear telling you what the error is. Press ESC, ENTER, or SPACEBAR to remove the box. The box will disappear and the cursor will move to the location of the error. For example, suppose you type this line:

```
len% = 3
```

At first glance it looks syntactically correct, but a dialog box appears with the phrase "Expected: statement". The variable *len%* then appears in reverse video. You now realize that LEN is a reserved word, and that you cannot use it as a variable name. (If you did not realize it, you would select the Help option from the dialog box.) You could then change the name of the variable — perhaps to *length%* — and proceed with the program.

If you are using the EasyMenus system, syntax checking will always be enabled. In the FullMenus system, there are two ways to disable syntax checking. The first is to use the Create File or Load File command from the File menu and select the Document option. This option tells QuickBASIC that you are modifying a file other than a program; therefore, it disables syntax checking. The other way to disable syntax checking is to select the Syntax Checking option from the Options menu. To re-enable syntax checking, select the same option again.

Automatic Indentation

Another advantage of using the QuickBASIC editor to write your programs is the *automatic indentation* feature. When you indent a line a given number of spaces, pressing ENTER at the end of that line will move the cursor to the same column as the first character of the previous line. Thus, when you are writing a block of code that needs to be indented, you need to indent only the first line. The editor takes care of the remaining lines.

The most convenient way to indent a specific number of spaces is to use the TAB key. Normally, tab positions are spaced eight columns apart. Since indentation is most effective when you use two to four columns per level, QuickBASIC allows you to change the tab size through the Display Options command on the Options menu. Once you are in the Display Options dialog box, tab down to the Tab Stops option and enter the new value. When you press ENTER, you save this value in the QB.INI file so QuickBASIC will remember it in your next session.

If you have indented a set of lines and you need to back up the next line one level, press BACKSPACE after pressing ENTER.

Every time you press BACKSPACE you will move back one tab position. The HOME key will move you all the way back to the start of the line.

QuickBASIC also allows you to move a block of code to the left or right after you have entered it. If you need to indent some lines an additional tab position, select the block by using the SHIFT key and the arrow keys. (See the "Using the Clipboard" section of this chapter for more information.) When the entire block is highlighted, press the TAB key to move the block to the right. To move the block left, use the SHIFT-TAB key combination. Note that these commands will not work if you have used line numbers in the block.

Entering Special Characters

The QuickBASIC editor provides several methods for allowing you to enter ASCII characters that are not on the keyboard. Normally, if you are displaying these characters on the screen you should use the CHR$ function. However, occasionally you will improve the readability of your program by having the actual characters in the program. This is especially true with the characters that create boxes. To create a small box, you could use either of these two program fragments:

```
PRINT "┌───┐"
PRINT "│   │"
PRINT "│   │"
PRINT "└───┘"

PRINT CHR$(218); STRING$(3,196); CHR$(191)
PRINT CHR$(179); "   "; CHR$(179)
PRINT CHR$(179); "   "; CHR$(179)
PRINT CHR$(192); STRING$(3,196); CHR$(217)
```

Although the second set of statements is more portable, the first set is much more descriptive.

To create the characters corresponding to ASCII codes 128 through 255, you must follow a simple 3-step process.

1. Press the ALT key and hold it down. (If you do not hold it down, you will end up on the menu line.)

2. Use the keypad keys to enter the 3-digit ASCII code. (Here, you may use only the numeric keypad keys, not the numbers on the top row of the keyboard.)

3. Release the ALT key, and the character will appear.

See Appendix B for a table of ASCII codes and their associated characters.

QuickBASIC also gives you a way to display most of the special characters whose ASCII codes are 1 through 27. Normally, these characters are inaccessible because they are control characters. As with the high-order characters, you can always use the CHR$ function to display the character. If you want the character in the code, however, follow this 3-step process:

1. Hold down the CTRL key.

2. Type **P**.

3. Type the letter corresponding to the control character.

For instance, ASCII code 3 (a happy face) would be CTRL-P-C. The following characters will not display: G, I, J, K, L, M, and U.

Cursor Movement

If you have used a screen editor before, you will be familiar with using the four arrow keys to move to another area in your program. The QuickBASIC editor includes several other cursor-movement commands, which are summarized in Table 15-1. Most of these were introduced in the tutorial in Chapter 3.

Each table in Part Three provides a list of functions along with all the possible ways to accomplish the function. Most of the alternative methods are for users who learned an editor similar

Function	Primary Key(s)	Alternative Key(s)
Left one column	LEFT	CTRL-S
Right one column	RIGHT	CTRL-D
Left one word	CTRL-LEFT	CTRL-A
Right one word	CTRL-RIGHT	CTRL-F
Left 80 columns	CTRL-PGUP	
Right 80 columns	CTRL-PGDN	
Left to first column	HOME	CTRL-Q-S
Right to last column	END	CTRL-Q-D
Up one line	UP	CTRL-E
Down one line	DOWN	CTRL-X
Up one page	PGUP	CTRL-R
Down one page	PGDN	CTRL-C
Up to first line	CTRL-HOME	CTRL-Q-R
Down to last line	CTRL-END	CTRL-Q-C

Table 15-1.   Cursor-Movement Commands

to WordStar. If you can perform a function from the menus or by pressing a function key (like F2), the tables will show you those also.

When you need to work with a block of text, you first need to select that block. By holding down the SHIFT key and using any of the cursor-movement commands in Table 15-1, you will highlight a block of text. With the LEFT and RIGHT ARROW keys you can select a portion of a single line. However, when you use any other key to select more than one line, you will select the entire line. There is no way to select all of one line and only part of another.

If you no longer want to select a section of text, you can cancel the selection by releasing the SHIFT key and pressing any arrow key. Be sure that you do not simply start typing again — if you press a character instead of an arrow to cancel the text selection, you'll delete the entire section of highlighted text.

Entering and Deleting Text

Obviously, the primary way to enter text is to type it. The most common way to delete text is with the BACKSPACE key. You could write an entire program by typing the characters and erasing your mistakes with BACKSPACE. However, there are a few other methods that will save you time and effort under certain circumstances. Table 15-2 provides the commands that insert and delete text (other than those commands that use the clipboard).

You can enter text in one of two modes: insert mode or overstrike mode. When you first enter the QuickBASIC environment you are in insert mode. This means that if the cursor is under a character and you type another character, the current line will move right one space so that the new character can be inserted. Occasionally, you may want to switch to overstrike mode. In this mode, each character you type will replace any character that was at the current cursor location. Press the INS key to toggle between these two modes. If you are in overstrike mode, the cursor will appear as a block instead of as a line.

Function	Primary Key(s)	Alternative Key(s)
Change to insert mode	INS	CTRL-V
Delete character to the left	BACKSPACE	CTRL-H
Delete character to the right	DEL	CTRL-G
Delete word to the right	CTRL-T	
Delete all to the right of the cursor	CTRL-Q-Y	
Delete line	CTRL-Y	
Delete selected text	DEL	
Undo changes	ALT-BACKSPACE	

Table 15-2.   Insert and Delete Commands

If you are in the middle of changing a line of text and realize that you do not want to make the changes, you can restore that line with the Undo command. This command will work only if you have not left that line with any cursor-movement key. The shortcut command for Undo is the ALT-BACKSPACE combination.

As you can see from Table 15-2, there are many different commands to delete text. Most often, you will use the BACKSPACE key to delete characters to the left of the cursor that you have just typed. If you are in the middle of a line and want to delete a few characters to the right of the cursor, use the DEL key. This key actually deletes the character right above the cursor, but the characters to the right will move left one space. If you need to delete more characters, CTRL-T will delete characters until it finds a delimiter, like a space or an operator. CTRL-Q-Y will delete all of the line to the right of the cursor, and CTRL-Y will erase the entire line.

If you need to delete a series of lines, press CTRL-Y several times. However, this method is a little slow, and you might get ahead of the editor and end up deleting one line too many. The alternative is to select the block to delete using the SHIFT key as described in the previous section. Once you have highlighted all the text you need to remove, press the DEL key. The text is gone and irretrievable (it is *not* placed on the clipboard).

Using the Clipboard

The QuickBASIC editor reserves an area of memory for a text buffer called the *clipboard*. You can use the clipboard to move large (or small) sections of text from one part of your program to another, or from program to program. You may know the clipboard as a "cut and paste" buffer. The commands that use the clipboard are summarized in Table 15-3. As you can see, many of these commands are part of the Edit menu.

to search and allowing you to specify a few options. The first option reads Match Upper/Lowercase. If there is no dot next to this option, the editor will search for the word or phrase, ignoring the case of both the search text and the file text. This means, for example, that if you set the search text to *AnyVar,* the editor will find a match if it finds the word *ANYVAR.* If you want to search for only an exact match, select the Match Upper/Lowercase option.

The other option in the Find dialog box is the Whole Word option. If you search for the word *AS* in your program without this option selected, you will get a match with the word *TASTY.* When you select the Whole Word option you will get a match only if the text is surrounded by delimiters (spaces, operators, or punctuation marks).

If you are using the FullMenus you will also have the option to search the entire module, only the active window, or all of the modules you have loaded. This option is not available in the EasyMenus system because that system does not support multiple modules.

Once you have entered the text to find and selected all the options, press ENTER to initiate the search. The editor will search forward until it finds a match. If there is a match, the cursor will move to the beginning of the match and highlight the text. If there is no match, the editor will move to the start of the file and continue searching. If there is still no match, a "Match not found" message will appear.

If the editor has found a match, but it is not the one you are looking for, press F3. This function key causes the editor to search for the next appearance of the same text. If you are using the FullMenus system, you can also use the Repeat command from the Search menu. The third method is to select the Find command from the Search menu and press ENTER, keeping the same text and options.

The Selected Text and Label commands in the Search menu of the FullMenus are slightly altered methods of searching for text. Instead of entering a long word or phrase in the Find What section of the Find dialog box, you can select the text with the SHIFT and cursor-movement keys. Then use the Selected Text command or the CTRL-\ command to find the next occurrence of the same text. The Label command searches for the highlighted word followed by a colon.

Replacing Text

If you want to replace several appearances of a word with a different word—for example, to change a variable's name—you can use the Change command. This command dialog box, shown in Figure 15-2, looks like the Find command box, except that it allows you to enter the Change To text. When you have set all the text and options you need you can use either the Find and Verify command or the Change All command. The first command will stop at each occurrence of the search text and let you replace it and search again, skip it, or stop searching completely. The Change All command will complete the replacement without any confirmation.

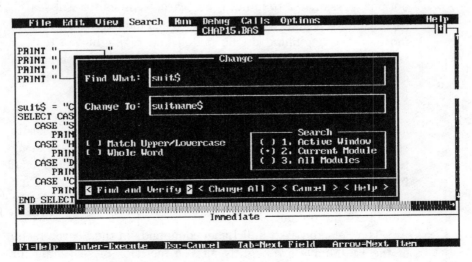

Figure 15-2. Change dialog box

Using QuickBASIC Windows

Depending on your definition of a window, there are up to five different windows that can appear on the screen. The first is the *Help window,* which will be on the screen any time you request help. You may consider this to be more of a dialog box than a window, however, because you cannot place the cursor inside the window and change anything. If you have a Help window on the screen and want to eliminate it, press ESC.

The *Watch window* will appear any time you create watch expressions or watchpoints. It will be in reverse video at the top of the screen. The term *window* is applied loosely here, too, since you cannot move to it. This window is covered in detail in Chapter 18.

The *Immediate window* is located near the bottom of the screen. In this window you can enter QuickBASIC statements that are executed immediately. The Immediate window is effective when you want to test a statement or subroutine without running the entire program. You can also halt execution of the program, use the Immediate window to change the value of a variable, and then continue program execution. You cannot load a file into this window.

The middle of the screen comprises the text window, or *View window.* This window is where you modify your programs. You can split the text window into two separate windows and see two different modules or two parts of the same module. To split the text window, select the Split command from the View menu. If you have a split screen and you want to restore the current window as the entire text window, select the Split command once again. This option is unavailable with the EasyMenus system.

There are several window commands, summarized in Table 15-4, that apply to the Immediate window and either of the text windows. Each command applies to the current window, which is the window that contains the cursor. The most useful command is CTRL-F10, which causes the current window to fill the entire

Function	Primary Key(s)	Alternate Key(s)
Copy text to clipboard	CTRL-INS	Edit Menu
Current window to full screen and back	CTRL-F10	
Move to next window	F6	
Move to previous window	SHIFT-F6	
Enlarge current window	ALT-PLUS	
Shrink current window	ALT-MINUS	
Display output window	F4	View Menu
Scroll window up one line	CTRL-W	
Scroll window down one line	CTRL-Z	

Table 15-4.   Window Commands

screen. This allows you to see more of your program at one time. Pressing CTRL-F10 again makes the other windows reappear.

The F6 and SHIFT-F6 commands move you from one window to another. When you press F6 you will move down one window. If you are at the lowest window—the Immediate window—you will move to the top window. When you press SHIFT-F6 you will move up one window. If you are at the top window, you will move to the bottom one.

Writing Subprograms

The QuickBASIC environment treats *subprograms*, or subroutines and functions, slightly differently than any other editor. Although the entire module is stored in the same physical file, the QuickBASIC editor separates them to help you maintain modularity. There are various ways to access, list, and create subprograms. This section describes how to work with subprograms when using the environment.

When you define a subprogram with a SUB or FUNCTION statement, the QuickBASIC editor automatically clears the text window and places the new subprogram in it. You will not be able to use any cursor-movement commands to return to the main module. You can create a new area for a subprogram by selecting the New SUB or New FUNCTION commands from the Edit menu (not available with the EasyMenus system). With these commands, the editor will display a dialog box in which you enter the name of the subprogram. When you use either the command or a statement, the editor will automatically add an END SUB statement in the new window.

When you need to move to a particular subprogram, or to the main program, you have two options. If your program is not too large, you can press SHIFT-F2. If you have the FullMenus system, you can also select the Next SUB command from the View menu. With either method, the current text window will become the next subprogram (or the main module). When you use this command repeatedly, you will see each subprogram in the current module that you have loaded in the environment.

The other way to move to another part of your program is to press F2, or use the SUBs command from the View menu. When you do either of these, a dialog box will appear with the names of all the modules and subprograms you have loaded in the system. You can use the arrow keys or the mouse to select which part of the module you want to edit. When the dialog box is erased, the text window will contain the selected subprogram.

The SUBs dialog box includes several other options. There is a Move option that allows you to move a subprogram from one file to another. You will also see a Delete option. If you highlight a module and select Delete, you will unload the module from the environment. If you select Delete when you have a subprogram highlighted you will completely delete that subprogram.

QuickBASIC File Management

Programs with One Module
Programs with Multiple Modules
Include Files
Quick Libraries
Stand-Alone Libraries

For many programmers, file management consists of loading a program, editing it, and saving it. In Chapter 3 you learned the simplest methods for loading and saving programs. As you write more programs, however, you will find your programs expanding. As they expand beyond reasonable size, you will need more file-management techniques for creating modules, include files, and libraries. This chapter describes in detail how to work with large programs and how to manage the files involved.

Programs with One Module

In QuickBASIC terminology a *module* corresponds to a disk file. If a program contains only one module, it is stored entirely in one file. You can write any program as a single module, unless it contains more than 64K bytes of code. There are several other reasons for dividing a program into multiple modules, and these are covered in the next section. This section will show you how to manage single-module programs.

Creating a New Program

The first time you use QuickBASIC you will not have a program, so you must create one. If you enter the environment with a simple QB command, the text window will be empty and the title line at the top of the window will read "Untitled." This means that no module name is associated with the text you type. When you save the program, QuickBASIC will prompt you for a module name.

The New Program command from the File menu will also create a module. More accurately, this is a "clear program" command, because its task is to clear any text that you have in the text window. If you have entered text that you have not saved, the editor will display a dialog box asking if you want to save your changes before clearing the window.

Saving the Program

Once you have created a module and entered the program statements, you need to save the module. If you leave the Quick-BASIC environment without saving the program you will lose any changes you made. In fact, if you attempt to use the Exit command from the File menu before saving your program, the editor will display a dialog box that asks if you want to save your program before leaving. If you answer Yes, the editor will save all modules where you have made changes.

The first time you save a module, you must give it a file name. These names follow the DOS rules for naming files, with an 8-character name and a 3-character extension. Normally, you will use the .BAS extension to distinguish the file as a Quick-BASIC program.

To enter a name for a module, you select the Save As command from the File menu. If you are using EasyMenus, this is the only command available for saving the file. This command displays the dialog box shown in Figure 16-1 for you to enter the new filename. You can also use this command to save an existing program under a new filename. In this dialog box you must also decide the internal format of the stored program. If you expect to edit the program with a different editor, or if you will be

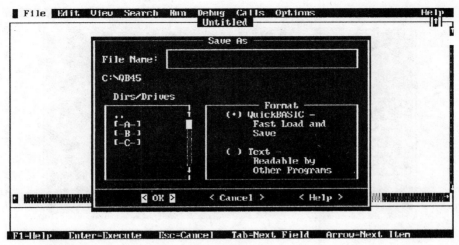

Figure 16-1.   "Save As" dialog box

compiling it with the BC compiler, select the Text (ASCII) format option. Otherwise, use the QuickBASIC (binary) format.

The Save command on the File menu (available only in the FullMenus) saves you an extra fraction of a second if you have already named your program. This command will save the current program with the same filename. If you try to use this command when your current program is "Untitled," Quick-BASIC will automatically display the "Save As" dialog box. When you save a file, the last copy of the file is deleted.

Loading a Program

If you want to load a program from disk, you need the Open Program command. This command displays the dialog box shown in Figure 16-2, which allows you to enter the name of the disk file. If you exclude a file extension, the default is .BAS. When you have entered the name of the program, QuickBASIC clears the text window of its contents and loads the new program. Again, if you failed to save the contents of the old text window QuickBASIC will give you the opportunity to do so.

Figure 16-2.   "Open Program" dialog box

The "Open Program" dialog box also includes an area that lists files and subdirectories of the default directory. When you first select the command, *.BAS appears as the filename and the list box shows you the names of all .BAS files. If you want to see a different directory listing, enter the directory name and wildcard specification in the "File Name" box.

The simplest way to load a file initially is to include the name of the program with the QB command. If you invoke the environment with the command

```
C>QB BUDGET
```

QuickBASIC will automatically load the file BUDGET.BAS into the text window. If the file does not exist, you will get an empty text window and the name BUDGET.BAS on the title line.

Merging Files

The Merge command on the File menu enables you to load the contents of a disk file into the program that is currently loaded in the text window. You need this command when you want to combine two programs into one larger program. To use the Merge command, first move the cursor to the line where you want the other file. Next, select the command. You will see a dialog box showing you the names of the .BAS files in the current directory. Type the name of the file you want, or use the TAB and arrow keys to highlight the name in the directory listing. The entire file will be loaded at the current cursor location.

If you want to load only part of one file into the current program, you must load the entire file and delete the parts you do not want. For instance, if you have a module with several subprograms, but you want to add just one to your program, use Merge to read the whole module. You will notice that the subprograms are moved into their own window, as you learned in Chapter 15. You can delete the unwanted subprograms by selecting the SUBs command from the View menu (or pressing F2), highlighting the subprogram name, and selecting the Delete option in that dialog box.

Programs with Multiple Modules

As your programs get bigger you may decide to split a large program into several modules. This section explains how to create a multiple-module program.

Creating the Program

To create a multiple-module program you first need to create an empty file. With the large program already in the text window, select the Create File option from the File menu. Then enter the name of a new module. When you use Create File to start a new program, the module that was in the text window stays loaded in memory. If you wanted to clear the other module you would use Open Program. Note that you must use FullMenus to edit a multiple-module program.

Once you have created an empty file, press F2 to get to the "SUBs" dialog box. Here you will see the original program with all its subroutines and functions, and the file you just created. Now use the arrow keys to highlight the subprogram you want to move from one module to the other. Then use the TAB key or the mouse to select the Move option. This command displays a small box, showing only the main module names. Use the arrow keys to highlight the new module name, and press ENTER. You will return to the "SUBs" dialog box, where you should see the new subprogram arrangement.

Setting the Main Module

Before you save your newly created program, make sure that the main module defined in the "SUBs" dialog box is the name of the module where you start execution. The "SUBs" dialog box displays a description of each entry at the bottom of the screen. Figure 16-3 shows a sample program with TEST.BAS described as "the Main Module."

All other modules besides the main module should have no executable statements at the module level (except for error

Figure 16-3.   "SUBs" dialog box

traps and event traps). If the wrong module name is displayed, select the Set Main Module command from the Run menu. The name of each module will appear in a dialog box. Use the arrow keys to highlight the main module, and press ENTER. The new main module name should appear at the bottom of the screen.

Saving the Program

The easiest way to save a multiple-module program is with the Save All command. This command saves every module that you have loaded in the environment. If you use just the Save command you will save only the module that is currently in the text window. No dialog boxes are associated with these commands.

When saving a program that has multiple files, the Quick-BASIC environment creates a .MAK file with the same name as the main module. The .MAK file contains a list of the filenames associated with your program. The next time you load the main module, QuickBASIC will use the .MAK file to load the rest of the required modules. If you have the wrong main module name, you'll create a .MAK file with the wrong name. This is why you should set the main module before saving the program.

Loading a Program

If you already have a module that you want to add to a program, use the Load File command. This command, located on the File menu, has a dialog box similar to the Open Program command. The Load File command, however, loads the file from disk without clearing any other files from the environment. If you use F2 to see the SUBs list, you should see the loaded module with all of its subprograms. Use the Save All command to update the .MAK file.

Considerations for Multiple-Module Programs

The QuickBASIC environment includes no logic to determine whether every module in your program is being used. You need to understand your program well enough to make sure that you are not wasting memory by loading unused modules. If you see that you have an unused module in your program, select the Unload File command from the File menu. This command will display a list of the module names for your program. Use the arrow keys to highlight the unwanted module, and press ENTER. Then use Save All to update the .MAK file. Note that the Unload File command removes a module from your program, but the module is still stored on disk.

When you have a large program with many modules, you will usually have to use the SUBs command or F2 to edit a particular subprogram. If you highlight a module name from this dialog box and press ENTER, you will load the module-level code of that module into the text window. If you select a subprogram, you will find that subprogram in the text window. Pressing SHIFT-F2 will move you only through subprograms within a single module. You cannot use SHIFT-F2 to change modules.

Although the editing commands to create and modify programs with multiple modules are straightforward, the syntax rules for variables are more complex. If you use only parameters to pass values to subprograms, you will have no problems when you split the program into modules. If you use SHARED or DIM SHARED statements you will have more work than simply breaking the program into its logical parts. Study Chapter 10 for complete details.

Include Files

Before QuickBASIC 4.0, the main purpose for *include files* was to keep your programs from getting too large. Multiple-module programs were unsupported, so include files were used in the same manner as a module is used today. Since you cannot have a

SUB or FUNCTION inside include files, their purpose has narrowed considerably. This section will discuss the primary uses for include files, as well as how to create and edit them.

You should use include files only with programs that have more than one module. You can then use the include file for statements that are required by several modules. The most common statements in an include file are TYPE-END TYPE structures, DECLARE statements, COMMON statements, and some DIM statements. The advantage of using an include file for these statements is that if you have to make a change, you only need to edit a single file.

Creating an Include File

Normally, you will use the same include file for each module of your program. If your main module is saved as BUDGET.BAS, create an include file called BUDGET.INC or BUDGET.BI. When you create an include file, use the Create File command. This command includes an option that lets you state that your new file will be an include file. If you fail to select this option, the include file will be added as a module in your program. It will be added to the .MAK file, and it will be loaded into memory uselessly every time you load the program.

Once you have created the file, use the Merge command to load the entire main module into the include file. Then delete all the subprograms and the statements that do not belong in the include file. When you save the file with the Save command, the file will automatically be saved in the text format. Finally, load the main module in the text window and replace the statements that are now in your include file with the $INCLUDE metacommand.

Viewing and Editing Include Files

The QuickBASIC environment provides a special method for viewing the contents of include files. Select the Included Lines command from the View menu. When you do this, the contents of each include file in the current module will appear in reverse video below their corresponding $INCLUDE metacommand. If you select Included Lines again, the lines will disappear.

When you display the contents of an include file with the Included Lines command, you cannot edit those lines. If you attempt to make a change to one of the highlighted lines, you will get a dialog box asking if you want to edit the file. If you do, QuickBASIC will load the file by itself into the text window so you can edit it.

You are also prohibited from editing lines in the module when you have displayed an include file with Include Lines. If you try to change a line in the module a dialog box will appear, asking if you want to eliminate the included lines from the window. If you select Yes, the window will return to its normal state with just the code from the module.

The Include File command provides another way to load and edit an include file. If you move the cursor to a line containing an $INCLUDE metacommand and select Include File, Quick-BASIC will load that file into the text window. This is the same as selecting Include Lines and starting to change a line in the include file. Include File is also the same as entering the name of the include file in the "Load File" dialog box.

Quick Libraries

After you write a series of large programs, you will probably find that you have a group of subprograms that you use in most of your software packages. Rather than always loading module source code when you need the routines, combine them into a Quick library. A *Quick library* is a series of compiled modules readable only by the QuickBASIC environment. When you load the library as you invoke the environment, you have almost immediate access to the object code of each module.

A major advantage of creating a Quick library is the ability to hide source code. Suppose you want to let another programmer use your menu package, but you do not want the other programmer to see how your package works. You can keep your trade secrets by placing all the routines in a Quick library. Other people can use the subprograms in the library, but they have no access to the source code.

Creating a Quick Library

By far the easiest way to create a Quick library is from within the QuickBASIC environment. The most difficult step in creating a Quick library is getting the right routines into the environment. If you have kept the amount of module-level code to a minimum and have divided your subprograms into meaningful modules, you will have no problem. Use the Load File command to load each module into the environment. A subprogram in a Quick library cannot call a subprogram that is outside the library. All routines called by other routines must be included as part of the Quick library.

If your code is not as well organized, you will end up with extraneous code in your Quick library. With smaller libraries this will be no problem, but as your libraries and programs grow, you will have to create "clean" Quick libraries. One way to accomplish this is to first create temporary copies of the modules you want to place in the Quick library. Then load them into the environment with the Load File command. From the "SUBs" dialog box you can remove unwanted subroutines and functions with the Delete subcommand. Since you are manipulating copies of your modules, you are in no danger of losing these subprograms. You can also use the editor to remove unnecessary module-level code from each module. Finally, you will be ready to create the Quick library.

The Make Library command is part of the Run menu and is not available with the EasyMenus system. When you select this command you will get the dialog box shown in Figure 16-4, where you enter the name of the new Quick library. The default file extension is .QLB. You can also choose to produce debug code, although this option normally costs more in size and execution time than it benefits in debug information. When you select Make Library, you will see the DOS commands that Quick-BASIC is using to create the Quick library. When the library is

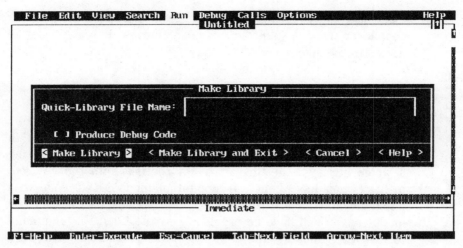

Figure 16-4. "Make Library" dialog box

created, you will be returned to the environment. There is also a Make Library and Exit option, which returns you to DOS when the library is created.

To include another Quick library as part of the new one, you must load the old library when you invoke the environment. If you want to create a Quick library that excludes the old library routines, make sure you do not load the old library. QuickBASIC provides a small Quick library called QB.QLB that includes the subprograms ABSOLUTE, INT86OLD, INTERRUPT, INT86XOLD, and INTERRUPTX. If you need any of these routines in your program, any Quick library you create should include them as well.

If the programs that use a Quick library use device inter-rupts—like ON KEY, ON STICK, and ON TIMER—the library itself must also contain at least one device statement. A simple statement like TIMER OFF in one subroutine will force the environment to produce the proper code for trapping device interrupts. If you fail to do this, an interrupt will not trigger until the program is executing code that is not contained in the Quick library.

You also have the option of using the LINK program directly from DOS without going through the QuickBASIC environment. The /Q option tells the linker to create a Quick library instead of an executable (.EXE) file. The first parameter in the command is for the object modules that will be placed in the new library. Since the linker expects .OBJ files, you must first compile each module with the BC program. The second parameter is the filename for the new Quick library, and the third parameter is the filename for a cross-reference listing. Use NUL if you do not want this file. The final parameter is the libraries that go into the new library. The library BQLB40.LIB must be included in this list. Here is a sample LINK command that creates a Quick library:

```
C>LINK MENUS+GRAPHICS,MYPROG.QLB,NUL,BQLB40.LIB /Q
```

See Chapter 17 for more details on the LINK program.

If you already have a Quick library, but are unsure of its contents, you can get a symbol listing with QLBDUMP.BAS. This program, included in the QuickBASIC package, displays the contents of any Quick library on the screen. Since it is a program, you must load QLBDUMP into the environment and run it. You may wish to modify the program to place subprogram names in a file for later use.

Before you place a routine in a Quick library, make sure you have debugged it as well as you can. Most of the advanced debugging features included in the QuickBASIC environment are unavailable if the error is in a subprogram contained in a Quick library. For example, if you run a program that has a "division by zero" error in a subroutine, the environment will place that subroutine in the text window, highlight the line where the error occurred, and explain the error. If the subroutine is contained in a Quick library, however, you will get a dialog box telling you only the error and the name of the module where the error occurred. If you run into this problem, the best way to debug is to reload the program using the original source code instead of the Quick library.

Using Quick Libraries

The first step to using a Quick library is to load it into the QuickBASIC environment. The only way to accomplish this is through the /l invocation option. When you use the QB command from DOS, the /l followed by the library name instructs the environment to load that Quick library. For example, the command

```
C>QB MYPROG /L MENULIB
```

loads the MENULIB.QLB Quick library as it is loading the MYPROG.BAS program. If you omit a library name, Quick-BASIC will load the QB.QLB library.

Once you have loaded a Quick library, your programs will have access to all the subprograms in that library. As with any subprogram, however, you must first use DECLARE statements to define the calling sequences. If you create an include file with all the necessary declarations for each Quick library, you will only have to do this once.

After you have defined the subprograms in the Quick library, you must remove these routines from your main program. Press F2 to see the "SUBs" dialog box. If you see any modules in your program that are part of the Quick library, remove them with the Delete option. If you attempt to run a program that has a routine in a loaded module and in a Quick library, you will get an error.

One minor drawback of Quick libraries is that you can use only one library at a time. This keeps you from dividing libraries by function: one for math functions, one for I/O, one for graphics, and so forth. Instead, you will more likely have a different Quick library for each large program. Use modules to store source code that is separated by function.

When you want to include a subprogram written in another language, you have to create the library from the DOS command line. First, compile the routines to create .OBJ files. Then use LINK to place them in a Quick library. Now you can add routines written in QuickBASIC by loading the library when you invoke the environment and creating a new library with the additional subprograms.

Stand-Alone Libraries

When you use the QuickBASIC environment to create a Quick library, you should notice that at the same time you create another library with the .LIB file extension. The .LIB file, or *stand-alone library*, is required by the LINK program to create an executable (.EXE) program. Unfortunately, the LINK program creates Quick libraries but cannot use them. To work around this problem you must maintain parallel libraries. Every time you make a change to a Quick library, you must make the same change to the stand-alone library.

If you create Quick libraries and executable programs only from the QuickBASIC environment, you need not worry about stand-alone libraries. If you use LINK to create a Quick library, however, you must also use LIB to create the stand-alone library. LIB.EXE is provided as part of the QuickBASIC package. This program was created for many uses other than with QuickBASIC, so there are several extraneous parameters and options beyond the context of QuickBASIC.

When using LIB to update stand-alone libraries for linking QuickBASIC programs, you need to provide only the library name and the names of the object files. The library name will be the first parameter and the object files will follow, separated by plus signs. The entire command should end with a semicolon. Earlier in this chapter you read an example LINK command to create a Quick library with the contents of two modules. The command

```
C>LIB MYPROG.LIB+MENUS+GRAPHICS;
```

would create the stand-alone library required to make an executable file.

If you are working with routines written in other languages, you must use LIB to place them in stand-alone libraries. The QuickBASIC environment cannot place non-QuickBASIC modules in either Quick libraries or stand-alone libraries.

Invoking, Compiling, and Running Programs

Invoking QuickBASIC
Running a Program in the Environment
Creating .EXE files from the Environment
Using BC to Compile
Using LINK

There is little chance that you are reading this chapter before running your first program. In fact, if you have yet to run a simple program you should read Chapter 4 and follow the tutorial. Then return to this chapter, which will show you all of the available options for invoking the QuickBASIC environment and running a program. Also included here are details on compiling and linking from the DOS command line.

Invoking QuickBASIC

When you type **QB** from the DOS command line you run the QB.EXE program, and thus invoke the QuickBASIC environment. When you first start using the environment, the only parameter you need add to the QB command line is the name of the QuickBASIC program to load. Table 17-1 shows all of the possible options available when you invoke QuickBASIC. The options may be in any order, except /run which must be first and /cmd which must be last. This section discusses each option.

   If you mistype an option on the QB command line, or if you try to use an option that no longer exists, QuickBASIC will display the list of valid options on the screen. You will be returned immediately to the DOS prompt, where you can enter the QB command correctly. This turns out to be a handy way to remind yourself of the command options: just type an option that you know does not exist (like /z).

The most common option you will use is the program name. If you include a program name as part of the QB command string, QuickBASIC will load all program modules as it initializes. This saves you from waiting for the initialization and then pressing ALT-F-L and the filename to load the program.

The /run option saves you a few keystrokes by automatically executing the file you specify. You must place the /run before the name of the file you are loading. If you type the line

```
C>QB MYPROG /RUN
```

Option	Function
/ah	Allows for $DYNAMIC arrays larger than 64K
/b	Forces a black-and-white display
/c:size	Sets the receive buffer size of the COMn: ports
/cmd string	Includes the rest of the command line as the COMMAND$ parameter string
/h	Sets the number of text lines to: 43 for EGA cards 50 for VGA cards
/l [library]	Loads the specified Quick library (default: QB.QLB)
/mbf	Assumes field conversion functions work with Microsoft Binary formatted numbers
/run	Loads and runs the specified program

Table 17-1. QB Command Options

the program will reject the command. You cannot use the /run option without a program name. Alternatively, you can load the file and press F5 to run the program.

You read about the /l option in the previous chapter. This option allows you to load a Quick library as you enter the QuickBASIC environment. If you omit the filename, Quick-BASIC will search for the standard Quick library, QB.QLB. Remember that this is the only way to load a Quick library—you cannot load one once you are in the QuickBASIC environment.

The /cmd option provides an initial parameter string that can be read by the COMMAND$ function. Everything to the right of the /cmd option is considered part of the string, which is why this option must be the last one on the QB command line. The QuickBASIC environment allows you to change this parameter string with the Modify COMMAND$ command from the Run menu.

The /ah option, covered in Chapter 9, enables dynamic arrays to be larger than 64K of total memory space. Without this option, each dynamic array must be smaller than 64K. Seldom will you need to use this option. If your arrays get this large, consider implementing your program using random-access files.

The /b option forces your color terminal to be black and white. If you do not have a color adapter, you do not need to use this option. The only time you should use /b is if you are writing a program for a system that has only a black-and-white terminal screen.

If you have a program that uses asynchronous communications, you might be tempted to use the /c option to set the receive buffer size. This option requires a colon and a number from 1 to 32,767. Unfortunately, if you use this QB command option to set the buffer size, it is undocumented in the program. Use the RB option with the OPEN COM statement instead (see Chapter 13).

If you are using a VGA or EGA card, you can choose the /h option to automatically increase the number of text lines to 50 or

43, respectively. This command modifies the text of the programming environment. If you need to modify the text of your program, use the WIDTH statement. If you do not have one of these cards, this option has no effect.

The /mbf option forces the field-related conversion routines (CVD, CVS, MKS$, and MKD$) to use QuickBASIC 3.0 Microsoft binary-format real numbers. If you are using fields to write to random-access files, read Chapter 14 to see how to convert your programs to use record structures.

Running a Program in the Environment

The simplest way to begin executing a program that is loaded in the environment is to press F5. Officially, the F5 function key is a shortcut for the Continue command on the Run menu. Most of the time, this means that program execution is started from the first program statement. If you run a program and an error occurs, this command continues execution where the program left off. The help line at the bottom of your screen will tell you if you are part way through a program.

To make sure you start at the beginning of the program, use the SHIFT-F5 key combination. This is the same as using the Start command on the Run menu. When you use either of these methods, you will start execution at the first program statement even if an error has suspended execution.

Creating .EXE Files from the Environment

When you have debugged your program and want to use it without going through the QuickBASIC environment, you can create an executable, or .EXE, file. The Make EXE File command is part of the Run menu. When you select this command you will get the dialog box shown in Figure 17-1, which allows you to change the name of the executable file. If you press ENTER, you will get an .EXE file with the same name as the associate .BAS file.

When you make an executable file, you also have a few decisions to make. First, you have the choice of creating one of two types of executable files. In the dialog box these types are labeled "EXE Requiring BRUN40.EXE" and "Stand-Alone EXE File." The default type is the .EXE file that must be run with a copy of BRUN40.EXE. The BRUN40.EXE file contains internal functions and subroutines required by the QuickBASIC language at runtime. When you make an .EXE file that requires BRUN40.EXE, the file is much smaller.

A stand-alone .EXE file includes all the internal functions and subroutines needed to run the program. It does not require the BRUN40.EXE file. This makes the file larger, but you will have only one file instead of two. If you expect to give (or sell) the program to a user, that user will probably be more comfortable copying a single file.

If you use an unnamed common block to pass data through the CHAIN statement, you must use the EXE that requires BRUN40.EXE. The stand-alone .EXE files do not preserve common block variables when you chain them together. If you still

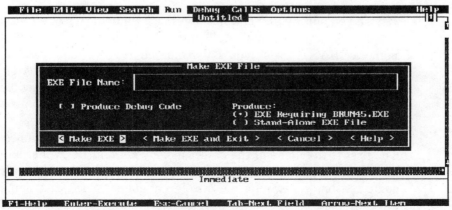

Figure 17-1.   "Make EXE File" dialog box

prefer to use stand-alone files, pass the data with a file instead of the common block.

The "Make EXE" dialog box also gives you the option to produce debug code inside the executable file. The debug code will check array bounds and arithmetic overflow when appropriate. You will also be able to press CTRL-BREAK to stop the program at any time. If you do not produce the debug code, you can only stop the program when the program pauses for user input. If execution speed is more important, however, do not select this option.

Using BC to Compile

Under most circumstances, you will save yourself plenty of time and keystrokes by making executable files from within the QuickBASIC environment. However, there are several options that are available only when you compile a program using the BC.EXE file. This section will discuss each parameter and each option in the BC command string.

BC Command Parameters

Before you specify any options, you must supply the name of the program you need compiled. The default extension for this filename is .BAS. If you type **BC** from the DOS prompt with no filename, the program will query you for the filename. If your program has multiple modules, you must compile each module separately. The linking process will combine the modules into a single executable file.

The BC program allows you to request two other filenames. The first is the name of the object file. By default, BC will create an .OBJ file that corresponds to your .BAS source file. If, for some reason, you would like a different name, place that name after the source file and a comma. For example, the command

```
C>BC CHEKBOOK,CHECK.OBJ;
```

will compile the file CHEKBOOK.BAS and place the object code in the file CHECK.OBJ, rather than CHEKBOOK.OBJ. The semicolon at the end signifies the end of the parameter list.

The other optional filename is the name of the source listing file. This file contains the original QuickBASIC code along with address offsets, error messages, and size information. By default, no source listing is created. If you want this file, you must specify the name of the file as the third parameter. If you want a source listing but do not want to change the name of the object file, use two commas in a row. Here is an example:

```
C>BC CHEKBOOK,,CHEKBOOK.LST
```

The .LST extension is the default.

BC Command Options

The options in Table 17-2 follow the command parameters. If you take the defaults for the object file and the list file, you do not place commas between the source file and the first option. Each of these options falls into one of three categories: those that match invocation options; those that the QuickBASIC environment handles automatically; and those that are available only with the BC command.

The /ah, /c, and /mbf options have corresponding invocation options (shown in Table 17-1). The /ah option allows you to have individual dynamic arrays that have more than 64K of total memory. The /c option sets the size of the receive buffer for the COM: ports. Finally, /mbf is for programmers who have yet to convert a program written with fields in version 3.0 to one that uses record structures. These options were covered in more detail earlier in this chapter.

The options in the second category are /x, /e, /v, /w, /d, and /o. These options specify things that the QuickBASIC environment detects automatically. The /x option indicates that your program contains an ON ERROR section that terminates with one of the following statements: RESUME, RESUME NEXT, or RESUME 0. If your program has an ON ERROR that ends with RESUME [label], you must use the /e option. The /v option indicates the presence of a device interrupt statement: ON COM, ON KEY, ON PEN, ON PLAY, ON STRIG, or ON TIMER. If you specify this option, QuickBASIC will check for a device interrupt after every program statement. The /w option is similar to /v, except that it checks for device interrupts after every statement in the object code. The /d option produces debug code, which is an option in the "Make EXE" dialog box. The /o option creates an object file that will create a stand-alone

Option	Function
/a	Produces a list file with the compiled assembly language statements
/ah	Allows for $DYNAMIC arrays larger than 64K
/c:size	Sets the receive buffer size of the COM*n*: ports
/d	Produces debug code
/e	Use if program has RESUME label statements
/mbf	Assumes field conversion functions work with Microsoft binary formatted numbers
/o	Produces a stand-alone executable file that does not need BRUN40.EXE
/r	Stores arrays in row order
/s	Places string constants in the code instead of in the symbol table
/v	Use if program has ON event statements
/w	Same as /v, but events are checked more often
/x	Use if program has RESUME, RESUME NEXT, or RESUME 0 statements
/zd	Places line numbers in the object code
/zi	Generates debugging information for use with the CodeView symbolic debugger

Table 17-2.   BC Command Options

executable file. Without this option you will create a file that requires BRUN40.EXE to run.

The third group of options represents the only good reasons for using the BC command instead of the QuickBASIC environment to compile a program. These options—/s, /r, /a, /zd, and /zi—are unavailable through the environment. If you get an "Out of memory" error when compiling, you might try including the /s option. This error often occurs when you have many string constants. If you include the /s option, the string constants will move from the symbol table to part of the object code itself. If you compile your program without getting that error, the /s option is not useful.

The /r option changes the internal storage of multidimensional arrays. Some languages other than QuickBASIC require these arrays in row (columns within rows) order. If you are writing a program in several different languages, you may need this option to make sure all routines use an array the same way. If you omit this option, the program will store multidimensional arrays in column order.

The /a, /zd, and /zi options provide additional debugging tools. When you include /a, you will get a source listing file that includes the actual assembly language statements created by the compiler. After every QuickBASIC statement in the file, you will be able to see the line (or lines) of compiled code. If you use the /zd option, the compiler will place line numbers inside the object code. If you plan to use Microsoft's Symbolic Debug Utility (SYMDEB), this option may be useful. Finally, /zd will tell the compiler to generate code that is compatible with Microsoft's CodeView debugger. If your program is written in several languages, this option will make it easier for you to find errors in the non-QuickBASIC subprograms.

Using LINK

When you compile a program you create an .OBJ file. Before you can run the program, you must link that file to any other object files and libraries to create an .EXE file. The LINK.EXE program, or LINK command, is provided for this purpose. When you create an executable file from the QuickBASIC environment, the LINK program is called automatically. If you compile with BC.EXE, you must call LINK explicitly. In this section, you will see the parameters and options associated with linking a QuickBASIC .OBJ file.

If you need to compile and link from DOS because you always need to include additional options, consider placing the BC and LINK commands in a batch (.BAT) file. You can run the batch file simply by typing its name. You will see the two commands being executed as the batch file calls each program. Since the batch file will likely have the program name throughout, you will need a separate batch file for each program.

LINK Command Parameters

The only required parameter for the LINK command is the list of object files. You must include the name of every .OBJ file required by the program, separating each by plus signs. Failure to include all the required files will cause the link process to fail. Make sure that the main module is the first file in this list. If you execute the LINK.EXE program with no parameters, the software will ask you to supply each parameter.

The second parameter is the name of the executable file. If you omit this parameter, the LINK program will use the name of the main module with the .EXE extension.

After the executable filename is an optional map filename. By default, LINK will not create a map file. If you need one for debugging purposes, you can specify the filename here or use the /m option. If you specify a name with no extension, you will get a .MAP file, which contains a list of all global symbols linked into the .EXE file. The symbols in uppercase letters are the modules and subprograms that you specified. The rest of the list contains internal symbols and segment information. Ignore symbols ending with "QQ" or starting with "B$".

The libraries to be linked comprise the fourth parameter to the LINK command. You do not need to include the default libraries BRUN40.LIB or BCOM40.LIB as parameters; these files are searched automatically. Any other libraries should be listed as part of the fourth parameter. To link a simple program that uses the INTERRUPT subroutine from the QB.LIB library, you would use this command:

```
C>LINK MYPROG,,,QB;
```

LINK Command Options

The LINK.EXE program is designed to link object files for many different languages. It includes 24 different options, most of which are ignored or unnecessary when linking QuickBASIC programs. If you feel you need one of these options, check the program documentation. To avoid unnecessary confusion, this book discusses only those options pertinent to QuickBASIC. These eight options are summarized in Table 17-3.

You studied the /q option in Chapter 16. When you specify this option, the linker creates a Quick library out of the list of modules, instead of an executable file. Also, you must include the BQLB40.LIB file as one of the libraries being linked. An easier way to create a Quick library is to select the Make Library command from the Run menu in the QuickBASIC environment.

Option	Function
/co	Creates an executable file compatible with CodeView
/e	Packs repeated strings in the executable file
/he	Displays a list of the available LINK options
/i	Displays the names of the object files as they are linked
/li	Includes object-code line numbers in the map file
/m	Creates a map file with the default name
/pau	Pauses before writing the final executable file
/q	Creates a Quick library instead of an executable file

Table 17-3.   LINK Command Options

If you want a map file with the default name, the easiest way to request it is with the /m option. The command

```
C>LINK MYPROG,,MYPROG;
```

creates the same map file as this command:

```
C>LINK MYPROG /M;
```

If you also include the /li option, you will see the source-code line numbers in the map file. You can use /li only when you compiled your modules with the /zd option.

When you use the /e option, you will get an executable file that is slightly smaller. The "e" is short for *exepack*, which tells the linker to pack the file, eliminating large sequences of repeated bytes. The linking time takes slightly longer, but packing tends to make the executable file load faster when you run the program.

If you think you may be entering a bad LINK command, but the link still completes, add the /i option to the command string. This option tells the linker to display the names of the object files as they are linked. You may find that you need to specify a different path to link the proper files.

When you write a program that uses subroutines written in other languages, you may need Microsoft's CodeView debugger to find an error. To make the files readable by CodeView, you must first compile with BC using the /zi option. Then when you link, you must also specify the /co option. This option ensures that the executable file supports the CodeView debugger in symbolic mode.

The /pau option should be used only with a floppy-disk system, where you may find that you do not have enough room to write the executable file on the same disk as the object modules. When you include the /pau option, the linker will pause prior to writing the file, enabling you to insert a different disk.

The final useful option is /he. This option displays the entire option list on the screen. When you use this option, all other options and parameters are ignored. The resulting display of all options includes those that are not applicable to QuickBASIC programming.

Help and Debugging

The On-Line Help System
Controlling Program Execution
Getting Variable Information
Putting the Tools Together

The term *software crisis* has been used in recent years to describe the fact that although hardware is making computers smaller and faster, programming time is getting longer and large programs have more errors. Debugging programs appears to be taking more time than writing them. The QuickBASIC tools that help you write and debug programs set this environment apart from all others. This chapter describes both the on-line help system and the available debugging commands.

The On-Line Help System

QuickBASIC 4.5 includes an on-line help system that is easy to learn and places a wealth of information at your fingertips. This section discusses how to get around in the help system, and how to use the system for help with keywords and program variable names.

When you select the Help menu you see four options: Index, Contents, Topic, and Help On Help. The Index section is a complete listing of every keyword in the QuickBASIC language. Because the list takes several pages, the system allows you to type the first letter of the keyword you need. Then you can use the DOWN ARROW key to get to the word. Once the cursor is on the same line as the word you want, press F1 to get help specific to that keyword. Keyword help is covered in detail later in this section.

The Contents section is a set of help screens that offer more general information. One of these screens appears in Figure 18-1. The Topic section can be reached only when the cursor in the text window is under a keyword or variable name. You can select this option much quicker with the F1 function key. Details on Topic help are covered later in this section. The Help on Help screen gives you a few lines on how to move through the help system.

Getting Around in the Help System

Table 18-1 summarizes the keys available to move you through the QuickBASIC help system. The best way to learn this system is to enter the environment and play with it. If you spend half an hour browsing through all the help screens, you will save yourself many hours of work later on.

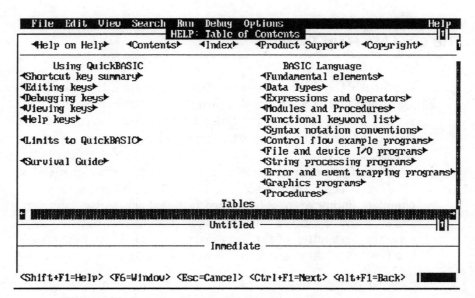

Figure 18-1.   Table of Contents help window

Function	Primary Key(s)	Alternative Keys
Help on Help	SHIFT-F1	Help menu
Context-sensitive help	F1	Help menu
Previous help screen	ALT-F1	
Next help screen in help file	CTRL-F1	
Previous help screen in help file	SHIFT-CTRL-F1	
Erase the help window	ESC	
Move to next hyperlink	TAB	
Move to previous hyperlink	SHIFT-TAB	

Table 18-1.   Help Commands

Once you are in the help system, QuickBASIC allows you to move from one topic to another of several related topics. These topics are referred to as *Hyper Links*. The available Hyper Links for a given screen are enclosed in green (or highlighted) triangles. For the keyboard user, the easiest way to choose a topic is to use the TAB key. Press TAB until the cursor is under the topic you want, and then press F1. If you have a mouse, the right button defaults to the F1 key. Simply move the mouse pointer to the topic you want and click the right button.

Often, the help for a particular topic takes more than one screen page. Since the help window is similar to the text window, you can use the PGUP and PGDN keys to browse through the text.

The ALT-F1 key combination allows you to return to the previous help topic. For example, if you select a topic from the Contents screen, you can return to the Contents screen by pressing ALT-F1. QuickBASIC remembers the last 20 help screens you were in, and you can use ALT-F1 to look back through them.

The CTRL-F1 key combination moves you through the Quick-BASIC help files sequentially. Often, this screen order is somewhat unpredictable. For instance, the next screen after the copyright information is the description of the QuickBASIC meta-commands. CTRL-F1 is particularly useful if you just want to explore the help files.

You can leave the help system at any time by pressing ESC. If you want the current help screen to remain, press F6 to move to the text window and continue editing. From the text window, the ESC key will eliminate the help window.

Help with Keywords

Suppose that you are writing a program in the QuickBASIC environment and you need to write a CIRCLE statement. You realize that the syntax of the statement is quite complex, and you do not have your *QuickBASIC 4.5, The Complete Reference* handy. To get help on the CIRCLE statement, type **CIRCLE** and press F1. You should get the screen shown in Figure 18-2. This screen gives you the exact syntax of the statement you need. Press ESC to eliminate the help window, and continue writing your program.

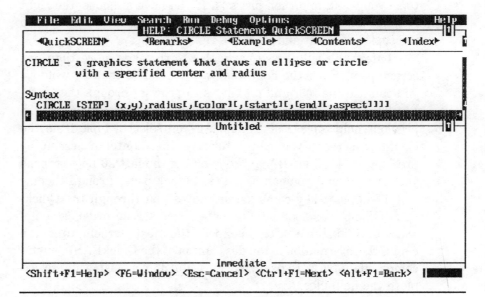

Figure 18-2.   CIRCLE QuickSCREEN help window

For most QuickBASIC statements, there are three separate help screens. The first is the QuickSCREEN, a small summary of the statement and its syntax. This is the same screen you will see if you select the Index option from the Help menu, move the cursor to the CIRCLE keyword, and press F1.

If the QuickSCREEN does not provide enough information, you can go to Remarks Hyper Link. This screen will give you more details on the options and restrictions of that particular statement. The first page of the Remarks for the CIRCLE statement is shown in Figure 18-3.

The third help screen available for most keywords is an Example screen. Figure 18-4 shows the Example screen for the CIRCLE statement. You can move an example to the text window by following this sequence:

1. Make sure that the current window is the help window. If not, press F6 until the title line of the help window is in reverse video.

2. Move the cursor to the first line of the text you are moving.

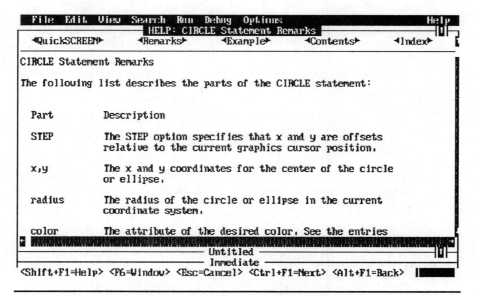

Figure 18-3.   CIRCLE Remarks help window

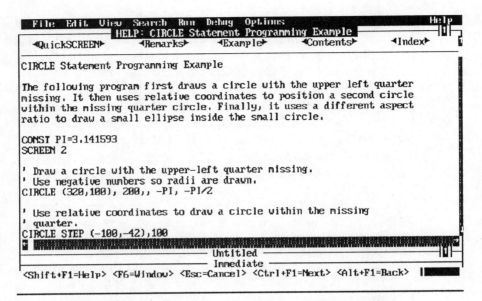

Figure 18-4.   CIRCLE Examples help window

3. Select the example by holding down the SHIFT key and moving the cursor to the bottom line of the example.

4. Copy the example onto the clipboard by pressing CTRL-INS, or by selecting the Copy command from the Edit menu.

5. Press ESC to eliminate the help window and return to the text window.

6. Move the cursor to the line where the example will go, and press SHIFT-INS or select Paste from the Edit menu.

Once the text is in the text window, it becomes part of your program. You can change variable names and expressions to fit your application.

Help with Variable Names

One feature of the QuickBASIC 4.5 help system is particularly useful for debugging. This feature gives you information on any variable name or subprogram name. To use this subset of Topic help, move the cursor to a variable name in your program and press F1. The help window will tell you which subprograms use the name, and how each name is defined.

To demonstrate how this feature can help, type the following program in the QuickBASIC environment:

```
mychar$ = CHAR$(65)
PRINT mychar$
```

At first glance, you might expect this program to type a letter "A" (ASCII code 65) on the screen. However, when you try to run the program, you get a "Subscript out of range" error. If you place the cursor under the word *CHAR$* and press F1, the screen shown in Figure 18-5 will appear, telling you that CHAR is an array variable. Since you want to use the function that converts an ASCII code to a character, you need the function named CHR$. (See Chapter 8 of this book.)

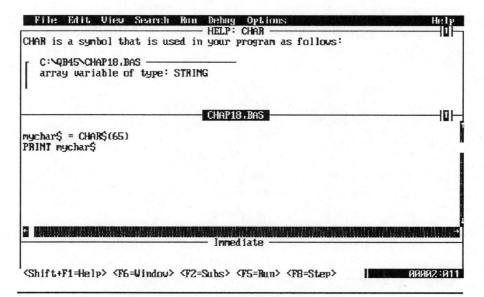

Figure 18-5.   Variable help for CHAR

Controlling Program Execution

The debugging tools that are part of the QuickBASIC environment can help you quickly determine both the location and the cause of the bug. This section will cover those features that determine (and change) the order of your program's execution summarized in Table 18-2. The following section will discuss how QuickBASIC simplifies getting variable information.

Function	Primary Key(s)	Alternative Key(s)
Start Program	SHIFT-F5	Run menu
Continue run	F5	Run menu
Execute to cursor	F7	
Execute one statement (single step)	F8	
Procedure step	F10	
Toggle breakpoint	F9	Debug menu
Add watchpoint	Debug menu (Full Menus only)	
Animate execution (Trace on)	Debug menu (Full Menus only)	
Toggle output screen	F4	
History on	Debug menu (Full Menus only)	
History backward	SHIFT-F8	
History forward	SHIFT-F10	
Break On Error	Debug menu (Full Menus only)	
Set next statement	Debug menu (FullMenus only)	

Table 18-2.   Execution Control Commands

Stopping the Program

When you are debugging a program, you will often want to stop the program somewhere in the middle and be able to continue later. QuickBASIC gives you several methods for doing this.

Most BASIC users are familiar with the "panic button:" the CTRL-BREAK key combination. While in the QuickBASIC environment, pressing these keys will immediately halt program execution. If you use BC to compile the program, you may be able to halt the program only when it is waiting for user input (see Chapter 16). When you press CTRL-BREAK in the environment, QuickBASIC displays the text window and highlights the statement it would execute next.

The F7 key gives you more control over where execution halts. This key will start or continue the current program, stopping when it gets to the line that the cursor is on. There is no menu equivalent to this function key.

Once you stop the program, you can use any of the variable help tools covered in the next section. You can also change statements in the program. If you want to continue program execution after that, press F5. If you want to restart the program from the beginning, press SHIFT-F5.

Breakpoints

Another way to stop your program is to define a breakpoint. A *breakpoint* is a specific line where you want a program to stop. With breakpoints you do not have to worry about moving the cursor, as you do with F7. To establish a breakpoint, you first move the cursor to the line containing the statement of interest. Then you can either press F9 or use the Debug menu. When you set a breakpoint, that line will be highlighted in a different color. You can set as many breakpoints as you need.

Once you set a breakpoint, it is valid until you reset it, clear the program from memory, or leave the programming environment. If you need to reset a breakpoint, the F9 key acts as a

toggle. This means that you can move the cursor to the breakpoint line and use F9 to remove the breakpoint. The Debug menu
includes a command to clear all of the breakpoints in your
program.

Watchpoints

The final way to stop a program is to use a watchpoint. A
watchpoint is an expression you create that will halt the program the first time the expression evaluates to TRUE. To define
a watchpoint, you use the Watchpoint command from the Debug
menu. When you select this command you will see the dialog box
shown in Figure 18-6. When you enter the watchpoint expression, the environment will display the expression in a Watch
window, along with its current value (TRUE or FALSE).

    After you define a watchpoint, run the program. As soon as
the watchpoint expression evaluates to TRUE, the program will

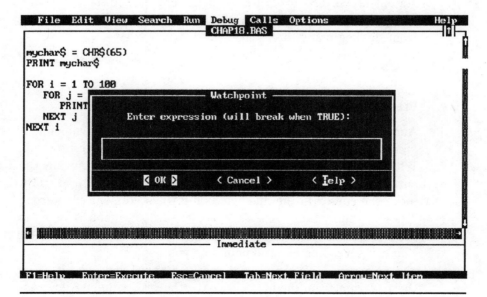

Figure 18-6.   Watchpoint dialog box

halt. QuickBASIC highlights the next statement that will execute. Therefore, the statement that caused the expression value to change is the one previous to the highlighted one. Once you find the problem related to that watchpoint, you can remove the watchpoint with the Delete Watch command.

Stepping Through the Program

Once you stop the program near the location that caused the error, QuickBASIC allows you to step through the program, one statement at a time. The F8 key will execute one statement. If that statement is a subprogram call, the text window will change to that subprogram and execute its first statement. Pressing F10 instead of F8 will execute an entire subprogram without stepping through each statement. (There are no equivalent menu options for these function keys.)

If the statement executed by F8 provides any screen output, the environment quickly displays the output screen and returns to the text window. If you need to see the results of that output, use F4 to toggle between the output screen and the text window.

Using the Trace Feature

The traditional method of *tracing* in BASIC is to use the TRON and TROFF statements. While the trace is active, each line number is displayed on the screen as it is executed. Although QuickBASIC supports TRON and TROFF, the QuickBASIC environment includes a much more effective method of tracing: *animation.*

In the FullMenus system, you can select the Trace On command from the Debug menu. This is a toggle command; a dot appears to the left of the command when the option is active. Now when you press F5 to start (or continue) your program, you will trace the program as it runs. Each time the program executes a statement, it highlights that statement in the text window. The program speed is slow enough that you can see each statement as it is executed.

When you combine the trace feature with watch expressions (covered later in this chapter), you can determine the cause of an infinite loop quickly and easily. Consider this simple loop:

```
DO WHILE cnt% <= 10
    sum% = sum% + values%(cnt%)
LOOP
```

When you run this program with Trace on, the program will execute the same statements again and again. You will soon realize that the program neglects to modify *cnt%* inside the loop.

As with the Single Step command, if a statement outputs data to the screen, you will see a quick flash of the output screen before it is replaced by the text window. If you want to see the output screen, stop the program with CTRL-BREAK, use F4 to toggle between screens, and continue to run the program with F5.

Using the History Feature

The *history feature* of the QuickBASIC environment allows you to see what statements were executed just before you halted your program. When you suspend the program with CTRL-BREAK, a watchpoint, or a breakpoint you can step back through the last 20 statements.

To use the history feature, you select History On from the Debug menu (in the FullMenus system only). The history feature slows program execution, so you will want to enable it only when you need it. When you halt the program, use SHIFT-F8 to step back through the last 20 statements. SHIFT-F10 is a History Forward key combination, which will step you forward after you have stepped back.

Breaking on Errors

The Break On Error command is an advanced feature found only in the FullMenus system. When you enable this feature, you create a breakpoint at the label of every error handler in your program. This command automatically enables the history feature. Break On Error is especially helpful when you are unsure of what caused a specific error to occur.

Using the Set Next Statement

The final command in this section allows you to change where a program will continue. When you select the Set Next Statement command, you tell QuickBASIC that you want to continue program execution with the statement that contains the cursor. This command will not restart the program — use F5 for that.

Do not confuse the Set Next Statement command with the Next Statement command. Set Next Statement is located on the Debug menu, and it will change program sequence. Next Statement is on the View menu, and it will move the cursor to the statement scheduled to be executed next.

Getting Variable Information

Before QuickBASIC, the most common way to find out the value of a variable at a given location in a BASIC program was to use the PRINT statement. You often had to fill the program with PRINT statements, find where the variable went bad, fix the problem, then try to remove the right PRINT statements. The features in the QuickBASIC environment for getting variable information are much neater and easier to use. These features — watch expressions and instant watch — are discussed in this section. The command that gets variable information is summarized in Table 18-3.

Watch Expressions

Watch expressions are variables or expressions that you can watch as their values change when you trace or step through a program. If you suspect a problem with a variable, you can place

Function	Primary Key(s)	Alternative Key(s)
Current value (Instant watch)	SHIFT-F9	Debug menu
Variable usage (Topic help)	F1	Help menu
Add watch expression	Debug menu	
Delete watch expression	Debug menu	
Delete all watch	Debug menu (Full Menus only)	

Table 18-3.   Variable Information Commands

it in the Watch window with the Add Watch command. The current value of that variable will be displayed whenever the Watch window is on the screen. Do not confuse watch expressions with watchpoints: the first displays a value in the Watch windows whenever possible, whereas the second stops the program when the expression evaluates to a specific value. When you are finished with the watch expression, use the Delete Watch command or the Delete All Watch command to remove that expression from the Watch window.

When you place a variable in the Watch window, the value of that variable can be displayed only when you are in a module or procedure that uses that particular variable. In other words, if you place the variable *mynum%* in the Watch window while you are in the *DoIt* subroutine, you will get the message "Not watchable" next to *mynum%* when you are in any other subprogram. If you had the same *mynum%* variable in another subprogram, you would have to add it to the Watch window separately. Only SHARED or COMMON variables can be accessed in multiple areas of your program.

The Watch window is most useful when you use the other debugging tools discussed in this chapter. If you add a watch expression to the Watch window and select Trace On, you will see the value of the expression change as you see the sequence of statements being executed. Also, you can set multiple breakpoints in the program, and see the watch expression's value at every breakpoint.

Instant Variable Information

After halting program execution with CTRL-BREAK or a breakpoint, you will often want to find out the current value of a given variable. The easiest way to do this in the QuickBASIC environment is to use the Instant Watch command. You can select this command from the Debug menu, or you can use SHIFT-F9.

To use the Instant Watch command, you must first move the cursor to the variable in which you are interested. Once the cursor is in place, pressing SHIFT-F9 (or selecting the Instant Watch command) will display a dialog box giving you the current value of the variable. If you want to see the value of an entire expression, use the SHIFT key with the LEFT and RIGHT ARROW keys to highlight the expression, and then press SHIFT-F9.

When you see the value of an instant watch, the dialog box gives you the opportunity to add that variable or expression to the Watch window. Once in the Watch window, it becomes a watch expression, just as though you had used the Add Watch command.

Putting the Tools Together

There are many advanced debugging features that are part of the QuickBASIC environment. This section works through a debugging example to help you gain familiarity with using various features concurrently.

Using Breakpoints and Watch Expressions

Here is a typical scenario that uses breakpoints and the instant watch feature to help solve a program bug:

1. In a particular array processing program, you notice that the following loop is being executed only once:

```
FOR cnt% = 1 TO 10
    CALL Sub1(myarray!(), cnt%)
    CALL Sub2(myarray!(), cnt%)
    CALL Sub3(myarray!(), cnt%)
    CALL Sub4(myarray!(), cnt%)
NEXT cnt%
```

You predict that one of the subprograms is modifying the value of *cnt%* when it should not. Since each subprogram is long, you decide it would take too much time to search the entire program for the bug.

2. You set a breakpoint at each subroutine call and at the NEXT statement by moving the cursor to each line and pressing F9.

3. You place *cnt%* in the Watch window by selecting the Add Watch command.

4. You restart the program with SHIFT-F5. The program starts, then halts at the first CALL statement. The value of *cnt%* in the Watch window is 1, as it should be.

5. You continue program execution by pressing F5. The program stops at the next statement, after it executes the first subroutine. Again you check the value of *cnt%* and continue.

6. When the program stops at the call to *Sub4*, the value of *cnt%* becomes 10. This means that the value of *cnt%* changes from 1 to 10 somewhere in the *Sub3* subroutine.

In this particular example, you could also have used the Procedure Step key, F10, to execute one subroutine at a time. If there are many statements between subroutine calls, however, you are better off using breakpoints.

Using Watchpoints and History

Once you decide that the error is somewhere in *Sub3*, clear all the breakpoints and delete the watch expression. Then use SHIFT-F2 to change the text window until it displays *Sub3*. Place the cursor on the first line of the subroutine, create a breakpoint there, and restart the program with SHIFT-F5. The program should stop automatically at the start of *Sub3*.

You then continue your search for the bug:

1. From the Debug menu, select the History On feature. This allows you to see the previous 20 statements executed by the program.

2. You notice that the subroutine call looks like this:

```
SUB Sub3 (AnyArray!(), arrayindex%)
```

You observe that the variable *arrayindex%* is the corresponding parameter to *cnt%* in the subroutine call. Thus, you realize that a change in *arrayindex%* in *Sub3* would change the value of *cnt%* in the module-level code.

3. Since *cnt%* and *arrayindex%* are supposed to maintain the value of 1 throughout the subroutine (in this case), you create the watchpoint *arrayindex%* <> 1. This means that the program will stop when the value of *arrayindex%* becomes any number besides 1.

4. You press SHIFT-F5 to restart the program. A few moments later, it stops somewhere in *Sub3* and "<TRUE>" appears next to the watchpoint in the Watch window.

5. You use SHIFT-F8 to back up one statement to see which statement caused the watchpoint expression to become TRUE. You correct the statement.

With the advanced debugging tools from the QuickBASIC environment you have just seen how you can solve a problem in a few moments, in what could have taken hours with another system. Use these features frequently to become familiar enough with them that they become second nature. By doing so, you can cut your programming time in half.

QuickBASIC Applications

Part Four is devoted to showing you the proper use of many of QuickBASIC's advanced features. You can study the programs to see proper modularization and documentation, as well as complete examples written entirely in QuickBASIC. If you like what you see, you can either type the programs from the source code provided, or send away for the diskette (see the Preface).

Chapter 19 is filled with software tools that can be used by any program. The emphasis is on I/O and the user interface, with routines for obtaining error-free user input and displaying menus. The last section of Chapter 19 is an interactive menu-editing program that lets you see your menus as you create them.

In Chapter 20 you will see a good example of screen management. This chapter contains a checkbook program that lets you throw away your current checkbook register. The entire source code is provided, including complete documentation and detailed explanations.

Chapter 21 gives you a useful data-plotting package while demonstrating the use of QuickBASIC graphics statements. Again you get the entire program, including a program description and documented source code.

P
A
R
T

F
O
U
R

I/O and Menus

User Input
Menus
The Menu Maintenance Program

In the days of standard BASIC, large programs had to fit into a single file. If you wanted to use a GOSUB subroutine from one program in another program, you had to search the original program to find the routine. Then you had to copy the routine into the new program and update the variable names to fit the new application.

When QuickBASIC added SUBs, FUNCTIONs, and modules to the BASIC language, there were several consequences. First of all, these additions allowed QuickBASIC programmers to separate large programs into many smaller and more manageable modules. Also, programmers could place subprograms used by several programs into one common module.

This chapter contains subprograms that can be used by many applications. The routines themselves are written with the author's personal style and preferences. When you type them into your computer (or when you purchase the disk from the author), feel free to change them to better satisfy your own needs. Programming is somewhat of an art, because there is rarely one proper way to do anything.

You may notice that some lines in these chapters have an underscore (_) as the last character. This is a *continuation character,* which is not allowed by the QuickBASIC environment but is accepted by the compiler. A few program lines have been split to fit printing requirements. When typing them into your computer, place the entire statement on one line.

User Input

Chapter 8 included the *GetInput* routine, which is preferred over the INPUT statement because it limits total characters. It displays the number of characters allowed for input, and beeps if the user tries to enter more. This keeps a user from entering 40 characters, for example, even though the program will store only 30.

The routines in this section build on the *GetInput* routine. There is an additional subroutine for string input, as well as separate routines for integer input and real-number input. Finally, there is a routine that demonstrates special-case input, in this case entering dates.

String Input

The programs in Part Five use the *GetString* subroutine for string input instead of *GetInput*. There is one subtle difference between the two. If the string variable being entered has an initial value, the *GetInput* subroutine will display that value and allow the user to edit it. At first, this ability appears to be beneficial, but it has one major side effect: If the new string entered is shorter than the initial value, the user must use the SPACEBAR to eliminate the rest of the unwanted string.

For instance, suppose that you are asking for a filename, and you want the initial, or default, value to be anyfile.dat. When you call *GetInput* with the statements

```
filename$ = "anyfile.dat"
CALL GetInput (filename$, 12)
```

the default filename will appear on the screen with the cursor on the first character. If the file the user needs is *mine.dat*, the user will type the filename and see "mine.datdat" on the screen. If the user presses ENTER to complete the input, the variable *filename$* will get "mine.datdat". To enter "mine.dat", the user must space over the last three characters before pressing ENTER.

The *GetString* routine, in contrast, creates a temporary string initialized to the null string. Thus, when it calls *GetInput* there is no default value displayed. If the user enters a new string, the old one is replaced. If the user presses only the ENTER key, the default value is used. This way the user can use a default value but does not need to space through a string to complete an entry. On the other hand, the user cannot edit the default string but must instead re-enter the entire string with any changes.

Whether you choose to use *GetString* or *GetInput* depends on personal preference. You may even choose to write a third routine that does not have these shortcomings. The routines in this book, however, will use *GetString* for string input.

Here is the *GetString* subroutine:

```
SUB GetString (stringvar$, numchars%)

',',',',',',',',',',',',',',',',',',',',',',',',',',',',',',',',',',',',',',',','
'
'   Purpose:  input a STRING variable from the
'       user, echoing the actual stored value.
'       If the user presses ENTER only, the initial
'       value is restored.
'
'   Parameters:
'       stringvar$ (in/out) - the default value (in),
'           and the value input (out)
'       numchars% (in) - the total number of digits
'           allowed
'
'   Other routines called:
'       GetInput - gets a string from the user
'
'   Local variables:
'       tempstr$ - string to hold user input
'       linenum% - line where user input starts
'       colnum% - column where user input starts
'
',',',',',',',',',',',',',',',',',',',',',',',',',',',',',',',',',',',',',',',','
'   save the current cursor location
tempstr$ = ""
linenum% = CSRLIN
colnum% = POS(0)

'   get a string from the user
CALL GetInput(tempstr$, numchars%)
IF tempstr$ <> "" THEN
    stringvar$ = tempstr$
END IF
```

```
'   display the actual stored value
LOCATE linenum%, colnum%
PRINT LEFT$(stringvar$, numchars%);

END SUB
```

Integer Input

When you need to get an INTEGER or LONG value from the user you have additional concerns. First, you want to make sure that there is no way for the user to cause an error that would stop the program. Also, you want to make sure that the user enters a value that will fit within the limits of the data type.

The simplest way to implement a nearly error-proof integer input routine would be to get the input data as a string and convert the string to an integer using VAL. Unfortunately, VAL has two drawbacks:

- If the string converts to a number that will not fit in the data type (such as 40000 into an INTEGER), VAL will produce an "Overflow" error.

- If the string contains a non-numeric character (such as 34s5), VAL will convert the string as though it stopped just before the invalid character (in this example, 34), but will not signal an error.

To get around these drawbacks, *GetInteger* calls its own version of the VAL function: *StringToInteger*. This routine sets an error flag if an overflow would have occurred, or if an invalid character is anywhere in the input string. When *GetInteger* sees the error flag, it beeps and forces the user to re-enter the data.

```
SUB GetInteger (intvar%, numchars%)

',',',',',',',',',',',',',',',',',',',',',',',',',',',',',',',',',',
'
'   Purpose:  input an INTEGER variable from the
'       user, echoing the actual stored value.
'       If the user presses ENTER only, the initial
'       value is restored.
'
```

```
'   Parameters:
'       intvar% (in/out) - the default value (in),
'           and the value input (out)
'       numchars% (in) - the total number of digits
'           allowed
'
'   Other routines called:
'       GetInput - gets a string from the user
'       StringToInteger - converts the string to
'           an INTEGER value
'
'   Local variables:
'       tempstr$ - string to hold user input
'       linenum% - line where user input starts
'       colnum% - column where user input starts
'       valerror% - error in converting to integer
'
','','','','','','','','','','','','','','','','','','','','
'   save the current cursor location
linenum% = CSRLIN
colnum% = POS(0)

DO
        valerror% = False%

        '   get a string from the user
        LOCATE linenum%, colnum%
        tempstr$ = ""
        CALL GetInput(tempstr$, numchars%)

        '   convert the string to INTEGER
        IF tempstr$ <> "" THEN
            CALL StringToInteger(tempstr$, intvar%, valerror%)
            IF valerror% THEN BEEP
        END IF
LOOP WHILE valerror%

'   display the actual stored value
LOCATE linenum%, colnum%
tempstr$ = STR$(intvar%)
PRINT tempstr$; SPACE$(numchars% - LEN(tempstr$))

END SUB
```

```
SUB StringToInteger (anystr$, intvar%, badnum%)

','','','','','','','','','','','','','','','','','','','','
'
'   Purpose:  convert a string variable to an
'       INTEGER variable.  Similar to the VAL
'       function, except it sets an error flag
'       when any character in the string is
'       invalid. (VAL returns as much of the
'       number as could be converted.)
'
```

```
'   Parameters:
'       anystr$ (in) - the string to convert
'       intvar% (out) - the converted value
'       badnum% (out) - error flag (TRUE if error)
'
'   Local variables:
'       negative% - flag to show if negative number
'       cnt% - loop counter
'       onechar$ - a single character in anystr$
'       digit% - one character converted to integer
'
',',',',',',',',',',',',',',',',',',',',',',',',',',',','
intvar% = 0
badnum% = False%
negative% = False%
anystr$ = LTRIM$(RTRIM$(anystr$))

'   loop through each character in the string
FOR cnt% = 1 TO LEN(anystr$)
    onechar$ = MID$(anystr$, cnt%, 1)

    '   see if the number is negative
    IF cnt% = 1 AND onechar$ = "-" THEN
        negative% = True%

    '   see if the character is not a number
    ELSEIF onechar$ < "0" OR onechar$ > "9" THEN
        badnum% = True%
        EXIT SUB

    ELSE
        digit% = VAL(onechar$)

        'see if the number is too large or too small
        IF intvar% > 3276 OR intvar% < -3276 THEN
            badnum% = True%
            EXIT SUB
        ELSEIF intvar% = 3276 AND digit% > 7 THEN
            badnum% = True%
            EXIT SUB
        ELSEIF intvar% = -3276 AND digit% = 9 THEN
            badnum% = True%
            EXIT SUB

        '   add the current digit to the number
        ELSEIF negative% THEN
            intvar% = intvar% * 10 - digit%

        ELSE
            intvar% = intvar% * 10 + digit%
        END IF
    END IF
NEXT cnt%

END SUB
```

The *GetLong* and *StringToLong* subroutines are the same as *GetInteger* and *StringToInteger,* except that they work with the LONG data type.

```
SUB GetLong (longvar&, numchars%)

',',',',',',',',',',',',',',',',',',',',',',',',',',',',',',','
'
'   Purpose:  input a LONG variable from the
'       user, echoing the actual stored value.
'       If the user presses ENTER only, the initial
'       value is restored.
'
'   Parameters:
'       longvar& (in/out) - the default value (in),
'           and the value input (out)
'       numchars% (in) - the total number of digits
'           allowed
'
'   Other routines called:
'       GetInput - gets a string from the user
'       StringToLong - converts a string to a LONG number
'
'   Local variables:
'       tempstr$ - string to hold user input
'       linenum% - line where user input starts
'       colnum% - column where user input starts
'       valerror% - error in converting to integer
'
',',',',',',',',',',',',',',',',',',',',',',',',',',',',',',',
'   save the current cursor location
linenum% = CSRLIN
colnum% = POS(0)

DO
        valerror% = False%

        '   get a string from the user
        LOCATE linenum%, colnum%
        tempstr$ = ""
        CALL GetInput(tempstr$, numchars%)

        '   convert the string to LONG
        IF tempstr$ <> "" THEN
            CALL StringToLong(tempstr$, longvar&, valerror%)
            IF valerror% THEN BEEP
        END IF
LOOP WHILE valerror%

'   display the actual stored value
LOCATE linenum%, colnum%
```

```
12tempstr$ = STR$(intvar&)
PRINT tempstr$; SPACE$(numchars% - LEN(tempstr$))
END SUB
```

```
SUB StringToLong (anystr$, longvar&, badnum%)

',',',',',',',',',',',',',',',',',',',',',',',',',',',',',',',',',',',',',
'
'   Purpose:  convert a string variable to a
'       LONG variable.  Similar to the VAL
'       function, except it sets an error flag
'       when any character in the string is
'       invalid. (VAL returns as much of the
'       number as could be converted.)
'
'   Parameters:
'       anystr$ (in) - the string to convert
'       longvar& (out) - the converted value
'       badnum% (out) - error flag (TRUE if error)
'
'   Local variables:
'       negative% - flag to show if negative number
'       cnt% - loop counter
'       onechar$ - a single character in anystr$
'       digit% - one character converted to integer
'
',',',',',',',',',',',',',',',',',',',',',',',',',',',',',',',',',',',',',
longvar& = 0
badnum% = False%
negative% = False%
anystr$ = LTRIM$(RTRIM$(anystr$))

'   loop through each character in the string
FOR cnt% = 1 TO LEN(anystr$)
    onechar$ = MID$(anystr$, cnt%, 1)

    '   see if the number is negative
    IF cnt% = 1 AND onechar$ = "-" THEN
        negative% = True%

    '   see if the character is not a number
    ELSEIF onechar$ < "0" OR onechar$ > "9" THEN
        badnum% = True%
        EXIT SUB

    ELSE
        digit% = VAL(onechar$)

        'see if the number is too large or too small
        IF longvar& > 214748364 OR longvar& < -214748364 _
                                                    THEN
            badnum% = True%
            EXIT SUB
        ELSEIF longvar& = 214748364 AND digit% > 7 THEN
            badnum% = True%
            EXIT SUB
```

```
            ELSEIF longvar& = -214748364 AND digit% = 9 THEN
                  badnum% = True%
                  EXIT SUB

              add the current digit to the number
            ELSEIF negative% THEN
                  longvar& = longvar& * 10 - digit%

            ELSE
                  longvar& = longvar& * 10 + digit%
            END IF
      END IF
NEXT cnt%

END SUB
```

Real-Number Input

When performing I/O on real numbers (SINGLE and DOUBLE), there is one dimension over integer I/O: the decimal places. There are many applications where you want to display only numbers with a limited number of digits after the decimal point. For this reason the *GetSingle* and *GetDouble* routines require a third argument: the number of places after the decimal point. For scientific applications, you would probably choose to eliminate this parameter and store the numbers exactly as they are entered.

In the *GetSingle* and *GetDouble* routines, the string entered by the user is rounded to the requested number of places before it is redisplayed and stored in memory. The rationale behind this is that you usually want to display the same number as you have in memory. In other words, if you output a number with only two places after the decimal point, the internal representation should not have more than two.

Since real numbers can be entered in scientific notation, a routine to replace VAL for real numbers would be much more complicated than *StringToInteger* is for integers. For this reason, the *GetSingle* and *GetDouble* subroutines use VAL but surround the function call with appropriate error handling. This prevents an error occurring if the user tries to enter a number such as 34E+65432, which is much too large to fit in any QuickBASIC data type.

The error trap for these routines requires some code at the module level. The following statements are necessary to make *GetSingle* and *GetDouble* work properly:

```
DIM SHARED converterror%

'  main program code here
END

ValError:
      converterror% = True%
      RESUME NEXT
```

The DIM SHARED statement defines *converterror%* to be a global variable. This way the error flag can be set by the module-level code and checked by the subroutine. The END statement prevents the program from executing the error handler without the error occurring. The error handler itself does nothing except set the error flag and return to the statement after the one that caused the error.

If you look now at the code for *GetSingle,* you will see how the error trap works. Just before the call to the VAL function, the error handler is enabled and the error flag is initialized. After the call to VAL, the error handler is disabled and the flag is checked. If the call to VAL is successful, the *converterror%* flag will never get set to TRUE, so the routine will return the new value. If VAL causes an "Overflow" error, the program will go to the *ValError* label in the module-level code, set the error flag, and return. The subroutine sees that the flag was set, beeps, and forces the user to re-enter the data.

These are the *GetSingle* and *GetDouble* routines:

```
SUB GetSingle (singlevar!, numchars%, places%)

','','','','','','','','','','','','','','','','','','','','','
'
'    Purpose:  input a SINGLE variable from the user,
'        echoing the actual stored value.
'        If the user presses ENTER only, the initial
'        value is restored.
'
'    Parameters:
'        singlevar! (in/out) - the default value (in),
'            and the value input (out)
'        numchars% (in) - the total number of digits
```

```basic
'        allowed
'      places% (in) - the number of decimal places
'         to store and display
'
'   Global variables used:
'      converterror% - flag set by error handler
'
'   Other routines called:
'      GetInput - gets a string from the user
'
'   Local variables:
'      tempstr$ - string to hold user input
'      linenum% - line where user input starts
'      colnum% - column where user input starts
',',',',',',',',',',',',',',',',',',',',',',',',',',',',',',
'   save the current cursor location
linenum% = CSRLIN
colnum% = POS(0)

DO

      '   get a string from the user
      LOCATE linenum%, colnum%
      tempstr$ = ""
      CALL GetInput(tempstr$, numchars%)

      '   convert the string to SINGLE
      IF tempstr$ <> "" THEN
            converterror% = False%
            ON ERROR GOTO ValError
            singlevar! = VAL(tempstr$)
            ON ERROR GOTO 0

            IF converterror% THEN
                  BEEP
            ELSE

                  '   round to the desired number of places
                  IF places% > 0 THEN
                      singlevar! = INT(singlevar! * 10 ^ _
                                    places%) / 10 ^ places%
                  ELSE
                      singlevar! = INT(singlevar!)
                  END IF
            END IF
      END IF
LOOP WHILE converterror%

'   display the actual stored value
LOCATE linenum%, colnum%
tempstr$ = STR$(singlevar!)
PRINT tempstr$; SPACE$(numchars% - LEN(tempstr$))

END SUB
```

```
SUB GetDouble (doublevar#, numchars%, places%)

',',',',',',',',',',',',',',',',',',',',',',',',',',',',',',',',',',',',',',',',',',',',',
'
'   Purpose:  input a DOUBLE variable from the user,
'       echoing the actual stored value.
'       If the user presses ENTER only, the initial
'       value is restored.
'
'   Parameters:
'       doublevar# (in/out) - the default value (in),
'           and the value input (out)
'       numchars% (in) - the total number of digits
'           allowed
'       places% (in) - the number of decimal places
'           to store and display
'
'   Global variables used:
'       converterror% - flag set by error handler
'
'   Other routines called:
'       GetInput - gets a string from the user
'
'   Local variables:
'       tempstr$ - string to hold user input
'       linenum% - line where user input starts
'       colnum% - column where user input starts
'
',',',',',',',',',',',',',',',',',',',',',',',',',',',',',',',',',',',',',',',',',',',',',
'   save the current cursor location
linenum% = CSRLIN
colnum% = POS(0)

DO

        '   get a string from the user
        LOCATE linenum%, colnum%
        tempstr$ = ""
        CALL GetInput(tempstr$, numchars%)

        '   convert the string to DOUBLE
        IF tempstr$ <> "" THEN
            converterror% = False%
            ON ERROR GOTO ValError
            doublevar# = VAL(tempstr$)
            ON ERROR GOTO 0

            IF converterror% THEN
                BEEP
            ELSE

                '   round to the desired number of places
                IF places% > 0 THEN
                    doublevar# = INT(doublevar# * 10 ^ _
                            places%) / 10 ^ places%
                ELSE
```

```
                    doublevar# = INT(doublevar#)
                END IF
            END IF
      END IF
LOOP WHILE converterror%

'  display the actual stored value
LOCATE linenum%, colnum%
tempstr$ = STR$(doublevar#)
PRINT tempstr$; SPACE$(numchars% - LEN(tempstr$))

END SUB
```

Date Input

There are some strings that you want the user to enter in a consistent manner. Probably the most common example of this kind of data is the date. If you need to sort records by date, you cannot have the user enter **1-1-89** one time and **01/01/89** another time. To force the user to be consistent you can write a special input routine.

The *GetDate* subroutine performs several functions. First, it allows the user to enter abbreviated dates. Users often have to search for keys such as "-" or "/", so *GetDate* lets the user enter the date without the separators. *GetDate* also allows the user to omit the first leading zero for months earlier than October. However, the user must enter 2-digit days (such as 01). If the user enters the string **31289**, *GetDate* will store it as "03-12-89". *GetDate* also performs limited error checking on the date itself: it does not allow month values greater than 12 or day values greater than 31. *GetDate* will, however, accept nonsense dates such as "02-31-89". You might consider adding the necessary logic to prohibit these dates.

```
SUB GetDate (datevar$)

',',',',',',',',',',',',',',',',',',',',',',',',',',',',',',',',',',','
'
'  Purpose:  get a valid date from the user, echoing
'     it in mm-dd-yy form
'
'  Parameters:
'     datevar$ (in/out) - the default value (in), and
'        the date entered, if valid
'
```

```
'    Other routines called:
'        GetInput - gets a string from the user
'
'    Local variables:
'        tempstr$ - string to hold user input
'        linenum% - line where user input starts
'        colnum% - column where user input starts
'        month% - the month entered by user
'        day% - the day entered by user
'
',',',',',',',',',',',',',',',',',',',',',',',',',',',',',',',',
'    store the current cursor location
tempstr$ = ""
linenum% = CSRLIN
colnum% = POS(0)

'    get a string from the user
CALL GetInput(tempstr$, 8)

'    if the user entered anything, see if valid
IF tempstr$ <> "" THEN

    '    add a leading zero to month, if necessary
    IF LEN(tempstr$) = 5 THEN
        tempstr$ = "0" + tempstr$
    END IF

    '    add date separators, if necessary
    IF LEN(tempstr$) = 6 THEN
        tempstr$ = LEFT$(tempstr$, 2) + "-" + _
                                    MID$(tempstr$, 3)
        tempstr$ = LEFT$(tempstr$, 5) + "-" + _
                                    RIGHT$(tempstr$, 2)
    ELSEIF LEN(tempstr$) = 8 THEN
        MID$(tempstr$, 3, 1) = "-"
        MID$(tempstr$, 6, 1) = "-"
    END IF

    '    see if month is valid
    month% = VAL(LEFT$(tempstr$, 2))
    IF month% >= 1 OR month <= 12 THEN

        '    see if day is valid (not exact)
        day% = VAL(MID$(tempstr$, 4, 2))
        IF day% >= 1 OR day% <= 31 THEN
            datevar$ = tempstr$
        ELSE
            BEEP
        END IF
    ELSE
        BEEP
    END IF
END IF

'    display actual date stored
LOCATE linenum%, colnum%
```

```
PRINT datevar$;

END SUB
```

Menus

When you need a user to choose among a group of options, you can simply list the options and ask the user to choose one. However, this query method leaves plenty of room for user error. A menu, on the other hand, if designed properly, forces the user to choose an option without room for error. This section will create a system for displaying menus and getting menu options.

Defining a Menu

The first step in creating a menu system is to determine what elements will form a complete menu. Once you finish this step, you can define records, or user-defined types, that define a menu. In QuickBASIC, you will need two separate records: one to define attributes that refer to the entire menu, and one to define the names and attributes of the individual menu items.

The first record is *MenuInfoRec*, which gives information on the entire menu:

```
TYPE MenuInfoRec
    menutitle AS STRING * 30
    numitems AS INTEGER
    topline AS INTEGER
    leftcol AS INTEGER
    rightcol AS INTEGER
    normfore AS INTEGER
    normback AS INTEGER
    highfore AS INTEGER
    highback AS INTEGER
END TYPE
```

In order, the elements of this record represent the title line of the menu, the size of the menu, the location of the top line of the menu, the left column of the menu, the right column of the menu, and the menu colors. There are four menu colors: foreground and background colors for the box and the menu items, and foreground and background colors for the highlighted letters and current menu item.

The second record definition, *MenuItemsRec*, gives information on each menu item:

```
TYPE MenuItemsRec
    itemname AS STRING * 40
    cmdkey AS STRING * 1
    cmdcol AS INTEGER
END TYPE
```

For each item, you have the item description, the letter that will be highlighted, and the column that is highlighted. All of these record elements will become more clear when you see a menu displayed.

The TYPE-END TYPE structures define the records, but declare no variables. The variable declarations are accomplished with DIM statements. These statements define a sample menu:

```
DIM mainmenu AS MenuInfoRec
DIM mainitems(5) AS MenuItemsRec
```

The variable *mainitems* is an array of records, so that each menu item has its own record.

The most tedious task in defining a menu is to assign values to all the elements of the record structure. The following listing is a set of LET statements that complete the sample menu definition:

```
mainmenu.menutitle = "Main Menu"
mainmenu.numitems = 5
mainmenu.topline = 8
mainmenu.leftcol = 26
mainmenu.rightcol = 54
mainmenu.normfore = 14
mainmenu.normback = 1
mainmenu.highfore = 15
mainmenu.highback = 3

mainitems(1).itemname = "Add a transaction"
mainitems(1).cmdkey = "A"
mainitems(1).cmdcol = 1
```

```
mainitems(2).itemname = "Change a transaction"
mainitems(2).cmdkey = "C"
mainitems(2).cmdcol = 1
mainitems(3).itemname = "Delete a transaction"
mainitems(3).cmdkey = "D"
mainitems(3).cmdcol = 1
mainitems(4).itemname = " "
mainitems(4).cmdkey = " "
mainitems(4).cmdcol = 0
mainitems(5).itemname = "Quit program"
mainitems(5).cmdkey = "Q"
mainitems(5).cmdcol = 1
```

Fortunately, you will never need to define a menu in this manner. Later in this chapter you will find a program that lets you define menus interactively.

Drawing a Menu

Once you have defined a menu, you are ready to display it on the screen. The *DisplayMenu* subroutine draws the menu according to the menu records passed as parameters. It includes a call to *DisplayBox*, a subroutine that draws a box using the special ASCII codes. The *DisplayDoubleBox* routine given here could also be used. Either of these works well to set off the menu and give it boundaries. Here are the three routines:

```
SUB DisplayBox (topline%, leftcol%, bottomline%, rightcol%)

',',',',',',',',',',',',',',',',',',',',',',',',',',',',',',',',',',',',',',',',','
  '
  '  Purpose:  draws a box on the screen with the
  '     current colors
  '
  '  Parameters:
  '     topline% (in) - top line of box
  '     leftcol% (in) - left column of box
  '     bottomline% (in) - bottom line of box
  '     rightcol% (in) - right column of box
  '
  '  Local variables:
  '     innerlen% - inside width of the box
  '     curline% - counter for each line
  '
',',',',',',',',',',',',',',',',',',',',',',',',',',',',',',',',',',',',',',',',',',',',',
  '  draw the top line
innerlen% = rightcol% - leftcol% - 1
LOCATE topline%, leftcol%
```

```
PRINT "Z"; STRING$(innerlen%, "D"); "?"

'   draw the middle lines
FOR curline% = topline% + 1 TO bottomline% - 1
    LOCATE curline%, leftcol%
    PRINT "3"; STRING$(innerlen%, " "); "3"
NEXT curline%

'   draw the bottom line
LOCATE bottomline%, leftcol%
PRINT "a"; STRING$(innerlen%, "D"); "Y"

END SUB
```

```
SUB DisplayDoubleBox (topline%, leftcol%, bottomline%, _
                                            rightcol%)

',',',',',',',',',',',',',',',',',',',',',',',',',',',',',',
'
'   Purpose:  draws a double-width box on the screen
'       with the current colors
'
'   Parameters:
'       topline% (in) - top line of box
'       leftcol% (in) - left column of box
'       bottomline% (in) - bottom line of box
'       rightcol% (in) - right column of box
'
'   Local variables:
'       innerlen% - inside width of the box
'       curline% - counter for each line
'
',',',',',',',',',',',',',',',',',',',',',',',',',',',',',',',
'   draw the top line
innerlen% = rightcol% - leftcol% - 1
LOCATE topline%, leftcol%
PRINT "I"; STRING$(innerlen%, "M"); ";"

'   draw the middle lines
FOR curline% = topline% + 1 TO bottomline% - 1
    LOCATE curline%, leftcol%
    PRINT ":"; STRING$(innerlen%, " "); ":"
NEXT curline%

'   draw the bottom line
LOCATE bottomline%, leftcol%
PRINT "H"; STRING$(innerlen%, "M"); "<"

END SUB
```

```
SUB DisplayMenu (menu AS MenuInfoRec, items() AS MenuItemsRec)

',',',',',',',',',',',',',',',',',',',',',',',',',',',',',',
'
'   Purpose:  displays a menu according to the
```

```
'       menu record specifications
'
'    Parameters:
'       menu (in) - the dimensions, size, title, and
'          colors of the menu
'       items (in) - the individual menu items
'
'    Other routines called:
'       DisplayBox - to display a box around the menu
'
'    Local variables:
'       bottom% - the bottom line of the menu
'       length% - title length (for centering)
'       col% - left column of title
'       cnt% - loop counter
'
',',',',',',',',',',',',',',',',',',',',',',',',',',',',',',',',',',',',',',
'    draw a box around the menu items
COLOR menu.normfore, menu.normback
bottom% = menu.topline + menu.numitems + 1
CALL DisplayBox(menu.topline, menu.leftcol, bottom%,-
'    menu.rightcol)

'    place the title above the menu box
IF menu.menutitle <> "" THEN

      '    draw a box for the title
      length% = LEN(RTRIM$(menu.menutitle))
      col% = (menu.rightcol + menu.leftcol) \ 2 - length% \ 2
      CALL DisplayBox(menu.topline - 2, col% - 2, _
                            menu.topline, col% + length% + 1)
      LOCATE menu.topline - 1, col%
      PRINT RTRIM$(menu.menutitle)

      '    connect the title box with the items box
      LOCATE menu.topline, col% - 2: PRINT "A";
      LOCATE , col% + length% + 1: PRINT "A"
END IF

'    display each menu item
FOR cnt% = 1 TO menu.numitems
      COLOR menu.normfore, menu.normback
      LOCATE menu.topline + cnt%, menu.leftcol + 3
      PRINT RTRIM$(items(cnt%).itemname)

      '    highlight the shortcut letter for each item
      IF LEFT$(items(cnt%).itemname, 1) <> " " THEN
            LOCATE menu.topline + cnt%, menu.leftcol + 2 + _
                                      items(cnt%).cmdcol
            COLOR menu.highfore, menu.highback
            PRINT items(cnt%).cmdkey
      END IF
NEXT cnt%
COLOR 7, 0

END SUB
```

Assuming that you have defined the records *mainmenu* and *mainitems* as shown earlier in this chapter, the following call will display the menu on the screen:

```
CALL DisplayMenu(mainmenu, mainitems())
```

This call produces the menu shown in Figure 19-1.

Using the Menu

Once you have displayed the menu, you must allow the user to select one of the items. The *GetMenuChoice* subroutine enables the user to make a selection in one of two ways:

• By using the UP and DOWN ARROW keys to move the highlighting to the item needed, and then pressing ENTER.

• By pressing the highlighted letter of the desired item, regardless of which item is highlighted completely.

This versatility satisfies both the user who wants to minimize keystrokes and the user who is more comfortable using the arrow keys.

Study the comments and the code in the *GetMenuChoice* subroutine to understand how this subprogram works.

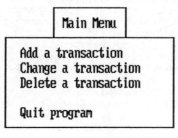

Figure 19-1.   Sample menu

```
SUB GetMenuChoice (menu AS MenuInfoRec, items() AS _
                                  MenuItemsRec, choice$)

',',',',',',',',',',',',',',',',',',',',',',',',',',',',',',',',',',',',',',',',',',',',',',',',',',',',',',',','
'
'  Purpose:  gets a menu item from the user.  User
'     can use the arrow keys to change the highlighted
'     item and press ENTER, or press the highlighted
'     letter of the desired item.
'
'  Parameters:
'     menu (in) - the dimensions, size, title, and
'        colors of the menu
'     items (in) - the individual menu items
'     choice$ (in/out) - the default choice (in), and
'        the item chosen (out)
'
'  Local variables:
'     choiceline% - the current highlighted line
'     choiceidx% - the current array index
'     cnt% - loop counter
'     inchar$ - the key pressed by user
'
',',',',',',',',',',',',',',',',',',',',',',',',',',',',',',',',',',',',',',',',',',',',',',',',',',',',',',','
'  determine default choice
choiceline% = menu.topline + menu.numitems
choiceidx% = menu.numitems
FOR cnt% = 1 TO menu.numitems - 1
    IF items(cnt%).cmdcol > 0 THEN
        IF choice$ = items(cnt%).cmdkey THEN
            choiceidx% = cnt%
            choiceline% = menu.topline + cnt%
            EXIT FOR
        END IF
    END IF
NEXT cnt%
choice$ = ""

'  highlight current choice
COLOR menu.highfore, menu.highback
LOCATE choiceline%, menu.leftcol + 3
PRINT RTRIM$(items(choiceidx%).itemname)

'  loop until a choice is selected
DO

    '  get a key
    DO
        inchar$ = INKEY$
    LOOP WHILE inchar$ = ""

    '  de-highlight current choice
    COLOR menu.normfore, menu.normback
    LOCATE choiceline%, menu.leftcol + 3
    PRINT RTRIM$(items(choiceidx%).itemname)
    COLOR menu.highfore, menu.highback
```

```
                LOCATE choiceline%, menu.leftcol + 2 + _
                                        items(choiceidx%).cmdcol
                PRINT items(choiceidx%).cmdkey

                '  check for special keys
                IF LEFT$(inchar$, 1) = CHR$(0) THEN

                     '  process <UP>
                     IF RIGHT$(inchar$, 1) = CHR$(72) THEN
                         IF choiceidx% > 1 THEN
                             choiceidx% = choiceidx% - 1
                         ELSE
                             choiceidx% = menu.numitems
                         END IF
                         DO UNTIL (items(choiceidx%).cmdcol <> 0) _
                                           OR (choiceidx% = 1)
                             choiceidx% = choiceidx% - 1
                         LOOP
                         choiceline% = menu.topline + choiceidx%

                     '  process <DOWN>
                     ELSEIF RIGHT$(inchar$, 1) = CHR$(80) THEN
                         IF choiceidx% < menu.numitems THEN
                             choiceidx% = choiceidx% + 1
                         ELSE
                             choiceidx% = 1
                         END IF
                         DO UNTIL (items(choiceidx%).cmdcol <> 0) _
                                       OR (choiceidx% = menu.numitems)
                             choiceidx% = choiceidx% + 1
                         LOOP
                         choiceline% = menu.topline + choiceidx%

                     '  all other special keys invalid
                     ELSE
                         BEEP
                     END IF

                '  check for valid characters
                ELSE
                     IF inchar$ = CHR$(13) THEN
                         choice$ = items(choiceidx%).cmdkey

                     ELSE
                         inchar$ = UCASE$(inchar$)
                         FOR cnt% = 1 TO menu.numitems
                             IF items(cnt%).cmdcol > 0 THEN
                                 IF inchar$ = items(cnt%).cmdkey THEN
                                     choiceidx% = cnt%
                                     choiceline% = menu.topline + cnt%
                                     choice$ = inchar$
                                     EXIT FOR
                                 END IF
                             END IF
                         NEXT cnt%

                         IF choice$ = "" THEN BEEP
```

```
        END IF

        '  otherwise, BEEP

      END IF

      '  re-highlight current choice
      COLOR menu.highfore, menu.highback
      LOCATE choiceline%, menu.leftcol + 3
      PRINT RTRIM$(items(choiceidx%).itemname)

LOOP UNTIL choice$ <> ""

COLOR 7, 0

END SUB
```

When you are using these menu routines, you will often want to place the menu display and selection in a loop. Study this skeleton, which is a sample of how to use the menus defined earlier:

```
DO
    CALL DisplayMenu(mainmenu, mainitems())
    CALL GetMenuChoice(mainmenu, mainitems(), mainchoice$)

    SELECT CASE mainchoice$
       CASE "A"
          CALL AddTransaction

       CASE "C"
          CALL ChangeTransaction

       CASE "D"
          CALL DeleteTransaction

       CASE "Q"
    END SELECT

LOOP UNTIL mainchoice$ = "Q"
```

This fragment displays the menu and forces the user to select an item. The *GetMenuChoice* subroutine returns the highlighted letter associated with the selected item. The SELECT-END SELECT structure evaluates the letter and calls a different subroutine based on that value.

The Menu Maintenance Program

The remainder of this chapter is a program that will allow you to develop and maintain menus. The program is not designed for a user, but for a programmer. Thus, there is not all of the error checking and idiot-proofing that would be done if the program were written for a user. This section will describe what the program does, then show you the QuickBASIC code. The documentation inside the program describes how the program works.

The program starts by asking you to enter a filename that contains a menu. The first time you run this program, you will have no menus on disk except for the default menu, default.mnu. You can modify this default menu to create your own menus. Once you select the filename, you will see two menus on the screen, as shown in Figure 19-2. The menu on the upper-right portion of the screen is the menu you are modifying, called the user menu. The menu on the lower-left portion is the main menu of the program, the "Menu Maker" menu.

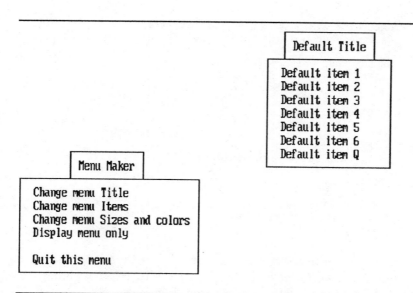

Figure 19-2.   Main menu of menus program

The "Menu Maker" menu has 5 items:

- "Change menu Title" allows you to change the title of the user menu.

- "Change menu Items" allows you to add, change, and delete items from the user menu.

- "Change menu Sizes and colors" lets you change the overall attributes of the user menu.

- "Display menu only" displays the user menu, alone, on the screen, in case the "Menu Maker" menu is in the way.

- "Quit this menu" leaves the program, allowing the user to save changes.

Whenever the user menu appears on the screen, it appears exactly as you would see it in a program. Occasionally, this means that the current program menu overlaps the user menu. If you need to see the user menu by itself, select the "Display menu only" item from the "Menu Maker" menu.

When you select "Change menu Items", you will see the "Menu Items" menu in the lower-left corner of the screen. This menu lets you change, add, and delete menu items. When you select "Change an item", the program will ask you the number of the item you want to change. Then you will be asked to enter the new item description and the new column number to highlight. Once you enter this information, the revised menu is immediately displayed on the screen. Figure 19-3 shows the screen after Item 1 was changed to "Add a transaction" with Column 1 highlighted.

The other menu in this program, the "Menu Sizes and Colors" menu, is shown in Figure 19-4. This menu has seven numbers that you can change, each corresponding to an element in the *MenuInfoRec* record. As with the previous menu, as soon as you make a change to a menu attribute, the menu is redrawn to reflect the change.

When you have finished modifying the menu, the program displays the menu and asks if you want to save it. If you do, the

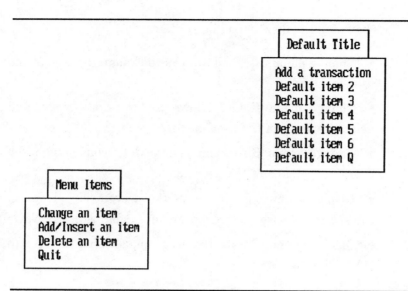

Figure 19-3.   Items menu of menus program

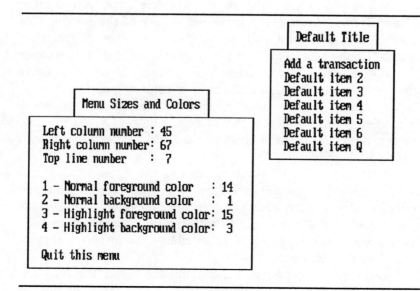

Figure 19-4.   Sizes and colors menu of menus program

program will prompt you for a filename. After saving the file, the program clears the screen and ends.

To avoid having to type required statements more than once, you should consider placing all the DECLARE statements, CONST statements, and record definitions associated with the routines given earlier in this chapter into an include file. This program assumes that such a file exists and that it is named TOOLS.INC.

```
DECLARE SUB ChangeSizeColor (scmenu AS ANY, scitems() AS ANY)
DECLARE SUB ChangeItems (itemsmenu AS ANY, _
                              itemsitems() AS ANY)

' $INCLUDE: 'TOOLS.INC'

','','','','','','','','','','','','','','','','','','','','','
'
'  Program:  MENUS.BAS
'
'  Required module:  TOOLS.BAS
'
'  Purpose:  This program allows a user to design
'     and modify menus that will later be used in
'     other programs.  Each menu is stored in a
'     disk file.  The user can start with an
'     existing menu, or use a default menu.  The
'     location, size, colors, title, and items
'     can all be modified.
'
'  Routines called:
'     LoadMenu - loads the user's menu and the menus
'        used by this program
'     GetString - gets a string from the user
'     DisplayMenu - displays a menu
'     GetMenuChoice - gets a menu item from the user
'     ChangeItems - allows the user to change the
'        items in the user's menu
'     ChangeSizeColor - allows the user to change the
'        sizes and colors of the user's menu
'     SaveMenu - saves the user's menu after the
'        changes are made
'
'  Local variables:
'     mainmenu, mainitems - main menu information
'     itemsmenu, itemsitems - ChangeItems menu
'        information
'     sizecolormenu, sizecoloritems - ChangeSizeColor
'        menu information
'     usermenu, useritems (GLOBAL) - user menu
'        information
'     filename$ - name of user menu file
'     mainchoice$ - selected main menu item
```

```
'       saveit$ - answer from user on whether to
'          save the changes
'
',','','','','','','','','','','','','','','','','','','','','','
DIM mainmenu AS MenuInfoRec
DIM mainitems(10) AS MenuItemsRec
DIM itemsmenu AS MenuInfoRec
DIM itemsitems(10) AS MenuItemsRec
DIM sizecolormenu AS MenuInfoRec
DIM sizecoloritems(10)  AS MenuItemsRec
DIM SHARED usermenu AS MenuInfoRec
DIM SHARED useritems(20) AS MenuItemsRec

' load all internal menus from their files
CALL LoadMenu(mainmenu, mainitems(), "menus.mnu")
CALL LoadMenu(sizecolormenu, sizecoloritems(), "sizeclr.mnu")
CALL LoadMenu(itemsmenu, itemsitems(), "items.mnu")

' get the name of the menu to change from the user
' (the default is default.mnu)
CLS
filename$ = "default.mnu"
LOCATE 10, 5
PRINT "Enter filename of menu to edit: ";
CALL GetString(filename$, 12)

' load the user's menu into memory
CALL LoadMenu(usermenu, useritems(), filename$)

mainchoice$ = "Q"
DO

    ' display both the user's menu and the main menu
    CLS
    CALL DisplayMenu(usermenu, useritems())
    CALL DisplayMenu(mainmenu, mainitems())

    ' get a menu selection from the user
    CALL GetMenuChoice(mainmenu, mainitems(), mainchoice$)
    SELECT CASE mainchoice$

        ' allow user to change the menu title
        CASE "T"
            LOCATE 23, 39: PRINT "Enter new title: "
            LOCATE 24, 39
            CALL GetString(usermenu.menutitle, 30)

        ' allow user to change menu items
        CASE "I"
            CALL ChangeItems(itemsmenu, itemsitems())

        ' allow user to change menu attributes
        CASE "S"
            CALL ChangeSizeColor(sizecolormenu, sizecoloritems())

        ' allow user to display the user's menu alone,
```

```
           '  in case the main menu is in the way
          CASE "D"
             CLS
             CALL DisplayMenu(usermenu, useritems())
             LOCATE 24, 20
             PRINT "Press any key to continue";
             DO
             LOOP WHILE INKEY$ = ""

          CASE ELSE

       END SELECT

    LOOP UNTIL mainchoice$ = "Q"

    '  display the user's menu with all changes
    CLS
    CALL DisplayMenu(usermenu, useritems())

    '  allow the user to save the changes
    LOCATE 23, 5
    PRINT "Save this menu? (Y/N): ";
    saveit$ = "Y"
    CALL GetString(saveit$, 1)

    '  save the menu under the new filename
    IF UCASE$(saveit$) = "Y" THEN
       LOCATE 24, 5
       PRINT "Enter filename or ENTER for "; filename$; ": ";
       CALL GetString(filename$, 12)
       CALL SaveMenu(usermenu, useritems(), filename$)
    END IF

    CLS
```

```
SUB ChangeItems (itemsmenu AS MenuInfoRec, _
                            itemsitems() AS MenuItemsRec)

',','','','','','','','','','','','','','','','','','','','','','','
'
'  Purpose:  allows the user to add, change, and
'     delete items from the menu.
'
'  Parameters:
'     itemsmenu (in) - items menu information
'     itemsitems (in) - the individual menu items
'        for the ChangeItems menu
'
'  Global variables used:
'     usermenu (in/out) - the dimensions, size,
'        title, and colors of the user's menu
'     items (in/out) - the individual menu items
'        for the user's menu
'
'  Other routines called:
```

```
'      DisplayMenu - displays a menu on the screen
'      GetMenuChoice - gets a selected item from the user
'      GetString - gets a string value from the user
'      GetInteger - gets an INTEGER value from the user
'
'  Local variables:
'     itemschoice$ - the selected Items menu item
'     item% - the item that the user wants to
'        work with (add, change, delete)
'     cnt% - loop counter
'     col% - column number to highlight
'
',',',',',',',',',',',',',',',',',',',',',',',',',',',',
itemschoice$ = "Q"

DO

    ' display both the user's menu and the Items menu
    CLS
    CALL DisplayMenu(usermenu, useritems())
    CALL DisplayMenu(itemsmenu, itemsitems())

    CALL GetMenuChoice(itemsmenu, itemsitems(), itemschoice$)

    SELECT CASE itemschoice$

        ' allow the user to change a menu item
        CASE "C"

            ' get the number of the item to change
            LOCATE 22, 24
            PRINT "Enter item number to change: ";
            item% = 0
            CALL GetInteger(item%, 2)

            IF item% > 0 AND item% <= usermenu.numitems THEN

                ' if valid item number, get new item name
                LOCATE 23, 24
                PRINT "Enter new item: ";
                CALL GetString(useritems(item%).itemname, 40)

                ' a blank in the first letter blanks out the
                ' entire menu item.  If the item is not blank,
                ' get the column of the letter to highlight
                IF LEFT$(useritems(item%).itemname, 1) <> " " THEN
                    LOCATE 24, 24
                    PRINT "Enter column number to highlight: ";
                    CALL GetInteger(col%, 2)
                    useritems(item%).cmdcol = col%

                    ' store the letter associated with the
                    ' highlighted column
                    IF col% > 0 THEN
                        ltr$ = MID$(useritems(item%).itemname, _
                                                        col%, 1)
```

```
                      useritems(item%).cmdkey = ltr$
              END IF
          END IF
      ELSE
          BEEP
      END IF


'   allow the user to add or insert a new item
CASE "A"

      '   find out where to insert the new item
      LOCATE 22, 24
      PRINT "Insert AFTER which item (0- ";
      PRINT USING "##)?"; usermenu.numitems;
      item% = 0
      CALL GetInteger(item%, 2)

      '   if valid location, add the new item
      IF item% >= 0 AND item% <= usermenu.numitems THEN
          usermenu.numitems = usermenu.numitems + 1

          '   shift the lower items down one
          FOR cnt% = usermenu.numitems TO item% + 2 STEP -1
              useritems(cnt%) = useritems(cnt% - 1)
          NEXT cnt%

          '   add a blank item
          useritems(item% + 1).itemname = " "
          useritems(item% + 1).cmdkey = " "
          useritems(item% + 1).cmdcol = 0
      ELSE
          BEEP
      END IF

'   allow the user to delete a menu item
CASE "D"

      '   get the number of the item to delete
      LOCATE 22, 24
      PRINT "Enter item number to delete: ";
      item% = 0
      CALL GetInteger(item%, 2)

      '   if valid number, delete that item
      IF item% > 0 AND item% <= usermenu.numitems THEN
          usermenu.numitems = usermenu.numitems - 1

          '   shift lower items up one
          FOR cnt% = item% TO usermenu.numitems
              useritems(cnt%) = useritems(cnt% + 1)
          NEXT cnt%
      ELSE
          BEEP
      END IF

CASE ELSE
```

```
    END SELECT

LOOP UNTIL itemschoice$ = "Q"

END SUB


SUB ChangeSizeColor (scmenu AS MenuInfoRec, _
                            scitems() AS MenuItemsRec)

','','','','','','','','','','','','','','','','','','','','','','','','',
'
'   Purpose:  allows the user to change the
'      location, width, and colors of the
'      user's menu
'
'   Parameters:
'      scmenu (in) - SizeColor menu information
'      scitems (in) - the individual menu items
'          for the SizeColor menu
'
'   Global variables used:
'      usermenu (in/out) - the dimensions, size,
'          title, and colors of the user's menu
'      items (in/out) - the individual menu items
'          for the user's menu
'
'   Other routines called:
'      DisplayMenu - displays a menu on the screen
'      GetMenuChoice - gets a selected item from the user
'      GetInteger - gets an INTEGER value from the user
'
'   Local variables:
'      scchoice$ - the selected SizeColor menu item
'
','','','','','','','','','','','','','','','','','','','','','','',
scchoice$ = "Q"

DO
    CLS
    CALL DisplayMenu(usermenu, useritems())
    CALL DisplayMenu(scmenu, scitems())

    LOCATE scmenu.topline + 1, scmenu.leftcol + 24
    PRINT USING "##"; usermenu.leftcol
    LOCATE scmenu.topline + 2, scmenu.leftcol + 24
    PRINT USING "##"; usermenu.rightcol
    LOCATE scmenu.topline + 3, scmenu.leftcol + 24
    PRINT USING "##"; usermenu.topline
    LOCATE scmenu.topline + 5, scmenu.leftcol + 35
    PRINT USING "##"; usermenu.normfore
    LOCATE scmenu.topline + 6, scmenu.leftcol + 35
    PRINT USING "##"; usermenu.normback
    LOCATE scmenu.topline + 7, scmenu.leftcol + 35
    PRINT USING "##"; usermenu.highfore
```

```
    LOCATE scmenu.topline + 8, scmenu.leftcol + 35
    PRINT USING "##"; usermenu.highback

    CALL GetMenuChoice(scmenu, scitems(), scchoice$)

    SELECT CASE scchoice$

        CASE "L"
            LOCATE 24, 24: PRINT "Enter new left column:";
            LOCATE scmenu.topline + 1, scmenu.leftcol + 24
            CALL GetInteger(usermenu.leftcol, 2)

        CASE "R"
            LOCATE 24, 24: PRINT "Enter new right column:";
            LOCATE scmenu.topline + 2, scmenu.leftcol + 24
            CALL GetInteger(usermenu.rightcol, 2)

        CASE "T"
            LOCATE 24, 24: PRINT "Enter new top line:";
            LOCATE scmenu.topline + 3, scmenu.leftcol + 24
            CALL GetInteger(usermenu.topline, 2)

        CASE "1"
            LOCATE 24, 24
            PRINT "Enter normal foreground color:";
            LOCATE scmenu.topline + 5, scmenu.leftcol + 35
            CALL GetInteger(usermenu.normfore, 2)

        CASE "2"
            LOCATE 24, 24
            PRINT "Enter normal background color:";
            LOCATE scmenu.topline + 6, scmenu.leftcol + 35
            CALL GetInteger(usermenu.normback, 2)

        CASE "3"
            LOCATE 24, 24
            PRINT "Enter highlight foreground color:";
            LOCATE scmenu.topline + 7, scmenu.leftcol + 35
            CALL GetInteger(usermenu.highfore, 2)

        CASE "4"
            LOCATE 24, 24
            PRINT "Enter highlight background color:";
            LOCATE scmenu.topline + 8, scmenu.leftcol + 35
            CALL GetInteger(usermenu.highback, 2)

        CASE ELSE

    END SELECT

LOOP UNTIL scchoice$ = "Q"

END SUB
```

```
SUB LoadMenu (menu AS MenuInfoRec, items() AS MenuItemsRec, _
                                                    filename$)

';';';';';';';';';';';';';';';';';';';';';';';';';';';';';';';';
'
'   Purpose:  loads a menu from the file given.
'       File is in random access format, stored by
'       the SaveMenu subroutine.  To ensure valid
'       file records, much of the menu information
'       in the file is encoded in character form.
'
'   Parameters:
'       menu (out) - the dimensions, size, title, and
'           colors of the menu
'       items (out) - the individual menu items
'       filename$ (in) - the name of the file to load
'
'   Local variables:
'       tempitem - a temporary record read from the
'           menu file
'       filenum% - the number assigned to the menu file
'       cnt% - loop counter
'
';';';';';';';';';';';';';';';';';';';';';';';';';';';';';';';',
DIM tempitem AS MenuItemsRec

'   open the existing menu file
filenum% = FREEFILE
OPEN filename$ FOR RANDOM AS #filenum% LEN = LEN(tempitem)

'   if the file does exist, get out
IF LOF(filenum%) / LEN(tempitem) <= 1 THEN
    PRINT "File "; filename$; " does not exist."
    EXIT SUB
END IF

'   first record contains title, number of items,
'   and top line location
GET #filenum%, , tempitem
menu.menutitle = tempitem.itemname
menu.numitems = ASC(tempitem.cmdkey)
menu.topline = tempitem.cmdcol

'   second record contains left column number,
'   right column number, and normal foreground color
GET #filenum%, , tempitem
menu.leftcol = ASC(tempitem.itemname)
menu.rightcol = ASC(tempitem.cmdkey)
menu.normfore = tempitem.cmdcol

'   third record contains remaining menu colors
GET #filenum%, , tempitem
menu.normback = ASC(tempitem.itemname)
menu.highfore = ASC(tempitem.cmdkey)
menu.highback = tempitem.cmdcol
```

```
'   read the menu items
FOR cnt% = 1 TO menu.numitems
     GET #filenum%, , items(cnt%)
NEXT cnt%

CLOSE #filenum%

END SUB
```

```
SUB SaveMenu (menu AS MenuInfoRec, items() AS MenuItemsRec, _
                                           filename$)

',',',',',',',',',',',',',',',',',',',',',',',',',',',',',',',',',',',',',',',',',','
'
'   Purpose:  saves a menu into the file given.
'      File is in random access format, each file
'      record being the length of one MenuItemsRec
'      record.  To ensure valid file records, much
'      of the menu information must be put into
'      character form before saving to the file.
'
'   Parameters:
'      menu (in) - the dimensions, size, title, and
'         colors of the menu
'      items (in) - the individual menu items
'      filename$ (in) - the name of the file to save
'
'   Local variables:
'      tempitem - a record that temporarily holds menu
'         menu data before storing to the file
'      filenum% - the number assigned to the menu file
'      cnt% - loop counter
',',',',',',',',',',',',',',',',',',',',',',',',',',',',',',',',',',',',',',',',',',','
DIM tempitem AS MenuItemsRec

'   open a new or existing file
filenum% = FREEFILE
OPEN filename$ FOR RANDOM AS #filenum% LEN = LEN(tempitem)

'   first record will contain title, number of items,
'   and top line location
tempitem.itemname = menu.menutitle
tempitem.cmdkey = CHR$(menu.numitems)
tempitem.cmdcol = menu.topline
PUT #filenum%, , tempitem

'   second record will contain left column number,
'   right column number, and normal foreground color
tempitem.itemname = CHR$(menu.leftcol)
tempitem.cmdkey = CHR$(menu.rightcol)
tempitem.cmdcol = menu.normfore
PUT #filenum%, , tempitem
```

```
'   third record will contain remaining menu colors
tempitem.itemname = CHR$(menu.normback)
tempitem.cmdkey = CHR$(menu.highfore)
tempitem.cmdcol = menu.highback
PUT #filenum%, , tempitem

'   place each menu item in the file
FOR cnt% = 1 TO menu.numitems
     PUT #filenum%, , items(cnt%)
NEXT cnt%

CLOSE #filenum%

END SUB
```

TWENTY

An Electronic Checkbook

What the Program Does
How the Program Works
Possible Enhancements

In Chapter 19, you studied many subprograms that were designed strictly to improve the user interface—the screens that the user sees. This chapter shows how many of these routines can be combined to create a professional-looking program. The chapter begins by describing what the program can do, and then provides the entire documented source code for making the program work.

What the Program Does

The Checkbook Deluxe program is designed to replace the checkbook register you use to keep track of checks, deposits, withdrawals, and so on. Your only additional task is to remember who you wrote checks to (and for how much) when you write checks while away from the computer. You might consider switching to checks that have carbon copies.

This section will describe what you as a user will see when you run this program. It shows you samples of each screen and describes how to use the program. Consider this section a user manual for the program.

Starting Out

The name of this program is *check.exe*, so you run the program by entering the word **CHECK** at the DOS prompt. When you do this, the screen will clear, and you will see this prompt in the center of the screen:

```
Enter the name of check file or QUIT to quit
```

The prompt is asking for the checkbook file you wish to work with. If this is your first time using the program, you will have no file. Select a filename that meets DOS requirements, and that will help you distinguish this account file from any others you might use. When you enter a new filename, you will see the statement shown in Figure 20-1. This will give you the opportunity to select another filename, in case you simply misspelled the name. If you entered the program by accident, type the word **QUIT** to exit the program.

Once you select a valid filename, you will move to the Checkbook Deluxe screen. This screen has two windows: a *data window*, which encompasses the majority of the screen; and a

---

```
        Enter name of check file or QUIT to quit: sample.fil
File does not exist.  Create one? (Y/N):
```

Figure 20-1.   Screen for selecting a file

mini-menu window, which is at the bottom of the screen. Appearing in the latter window will be the Edit Entries mini-menu. This menu displays the options available from this particular screen.

If you have entered an existing filename, you will see in the data window the last page of entries in the file. If you have just created a new file, you will see one entry: the initial file balance. Use this line if you are starting a file with an existing checking account. When you learn to use the system, you will want to enter the initial balance in the Amount column of the first entry.

To leave the program, you must press **Q** from the Edit Entries mini-menu. You must confirm your intention to exit by pressing **Y** and ENTER when asked "Are you sure?" This keeps you from leaving the program when you press **Q** by accident.

Moving Around the File

One of the lines in the data window will appear in reverse video (black on white). This line is called the *selected entry*. All commands execute based on the selected entry. To change the selected entry, you can use any of four keys on the keypad: UP ARROW, DOWN ARROW, PGUP, and PGDN.

The UP and DOWN ARROW keys will make the line above or below the selected entry become the new selected entry. If you press UP ARROW while at the top of the data window, the window will scroll down, so that a new entry appears at the top and all others move down one line. If you are at the bottom of the window and press DOWN ARROW, the window will scroll up to display a new entry at the bottom. You cannot move down past the "bottom of file" line, and you cannot move up beyond the first entry in the file.

The PGUP and PGDN keys display the previous page or the next page of entries. When a new page is displayed in the data window, the selected entry will be the entry on the same line as the previous selected entry. If you are on the first page and press PGUP, the top line will become the selected entry. If you press PGUP from there, the terminal will beep. If you press PGDN from the last page of entries, the "bottom of file" line will become the new selected entry. You cannot page down past the "bottom of file" line.

Adding Entries

When you want to add an entry to the end of the checkbook file, move the selected entry to the "bottom of file" line. If you just entered the program, this line should already be selected. Now press the **I** key to choose the Insert command. This command inserts a new item just before the selected entry. In this case you want to add the entry to the bottom of the file, so you choose the command from the "bottom of file" line.

Once you choose the Insert command, you must enter values for each field of the new entry. The first field is for the Transaction Type. For this field you will see a menu appear in the middle of the data window, as shown in Figure 20-2. You may select any of the six available transaction types. The first four types are *debits,* or entries that decrease the account balance. The last two types are *credits,* which will increase the account balance.

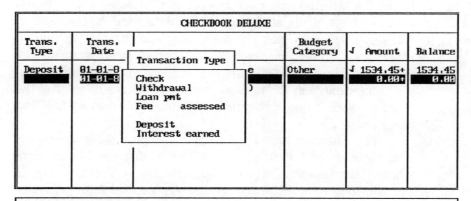

Figure 20-2.   The Transaction Type menu

You can select an item from this menu (or any menu in the program) with either of two methods:

- Use the UP and DOWN ARROW keys to change the highlighted menu item to the item you want; then press ENTER.

- Press the highlighted letter of the item you want.

If you select Check, the program will ask you for a check number of up to five digits. You will see the letter "C" and the "#" sign along with the check number. If you select any other Transaction Type, you will see the first eight letters of that type displayed in the field.

After selecting a Transaction Type, you will be asked to enter the Transaction Date. This date will default to the date from the previous entry. You may enter the date without dashes, because the program will add those automatically. You may also omit leading zeros from the month (but not the day). If the date of the entry is June 4, 1988, you could enter the date in any of these fashions:

```
06-04-88
060488
60488
06 04 88
```

If you enter a date improperly, the terminal will beep, and you must re-enter a valid date.

The third field is for a Memo. This is normally the person to whom you wrote the check, where the deposit came from, or why you made the withdrawal. The Memo can contain up to 25 characters.

When you finish typing the Memo by pressing ENTER, you will see another menu in the data window listing Budget Categories. These categories, shown in Figure 20-3, allow you to group your expenses. With one glance through each page of the file, you will see where the majority of your money goes. (*Note:* The program can easily be enhanced to create reports showing this

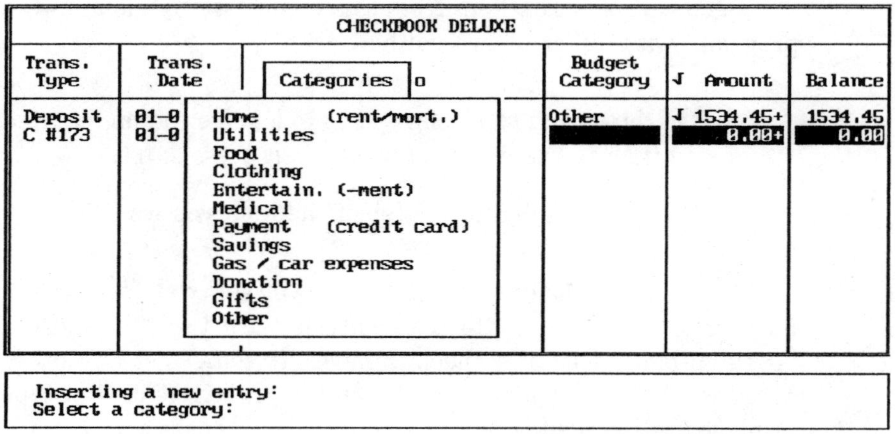

```
                           CHECKBOOK DELUXE
┌──────────┬──────────┬─────────────────────────┬──────────┬─────────────┬─────────┐
│ Trans.   │ Trans.   │                          │ Budget   │             │         │
│ Type     │ Date     │  Categories        □     │ Category │ √  Amount   │ Balance │
├──────────┼──────────┼──────────────────────────┼──────────┼─────────────┼─────────┤
│ Deposit  │ 01-0     │ Home        (rent/mort.) │ Other    │ √ 1534.45+  │ 1534.45 │
│ C #173   │ 01-0     │ Utilities                │          │      0.00+  │    0.00 │
│          │          │ Food                     │          │             │         │
│          │          │ Clothing                 │          │             │         │
│          │          │ Entertain. (-ment)       │          │             │         │
│          │          │ Medical                  │          │             │         │
│          │          │ Payment    (credit card) │          │             │         │
│          │          │ Savings                  │          │             │         │
│          │          │ Gas / car expenses       │          │             │         │
│          │          │ Donation                 │          │             │         │
│          │          │ Gifts                    │          │             │         │
│          │          │ Other                    │          │             │         │
└──────────┴──────────┴──────────────────────────┴──────────┴─────────────┴─────────┘

┌────────────────────────────────────────────────────────────────────────────────────┐
│ Inserting a new entry:                                                               │
│ Select a category:                                                                   │
└────────────────────────────────────────────────────────────────────────────────────┘
```

Figure 20-3.   The Budget Categories menu

kind of information—see the last section of this chapter.) Select a Category in the same way that you chose a Transaction Type.

The last field you can enter is the Amount. Enter the transaction amount in dollars and cents. You do not need to make the number positive or negative because the program will do that automatically. The program makes all debits negative values and all credits positive values. For this reason make sure that you enter the proper Transaction Type. Once you enter the Amount, the program recalculates the balances for each entry and displays them.

The Edit Entries mini-menu also lets you change and delete entries. If you made a mistake and need to change any field in an existing entry, you must first make that line the selected entry by using the arrow keys. Then press **C** for Change. You will be taken to each field in the entry and given an opportunity to change it. The current value of each field will appear in the Prompt/Menu window. If you press ENTER for a field, the current value will remain.

If you insert a certain transaction by accident, you can delete the entire entry. Simply select the entry and press **D** for

Delete. You will get an "Are you sure?" message in the Prompt/ Menu window. This keeps you from deleting an entry when you press **D** by mistake. If you are sure that you want to remove the entry, press **Y** followed by ENTER. The entry will disappear, and the entries below the deleted entry will move up one line.

If you have never used this program, start with the following practice run. Invoke the program and enter the filename **sample.fil**. When you get to the Checkbook Deluxe screen, use the UP ARROW to make the first entry the selected entry. Now press **C** to change the entry. Keep the current Transaction Type, change the date to "01-01-89," and keep the current Memo and the current Budget Category. Finally, enter an amount of **1534.45**.

Now move the selected entry to the "bottom of file" line and press **I** to add a new entry. Enter the following values:

Transaction Type: Check, #173
Transaction Date: Jan. 2, 1989
Memo: Best Mortgage
Budget Category: Home
Amount: $ 823.82

If you entered everything correctly, your screen should look exactly like Figure 20-4. If there is a difference, use the Change command to make the correction.

Balancing the Checkbook

Next to the Amount field, you should see a checkmark in the field headings and in the initial deposit entry. This mark shows which entries appear on your bank statement. The program will automatically balance your checkbook, displaying both the actual account balance and the balance that should appear at the bottom of the bank statement.

When the monthly bank statement arrives in the mail,

CHECKBOOK DELUXE						
Trans. Type	Trans. Date	Memo	Budget Category	√	Amount	Balance
Deposit C #173	01-01-89 01-02-89	Initial File Balance Best Mortgage (bottom of file)	Other Home	√	1534.45+ 823.82-	1534.45 710.63

Change current line: <UP> <DOWN> <PGUP> <PGDN>
Command options: **C**hange **I**nsert **D**elete **B**alance **Q**uit

Figure 20-4.   Sample entries

invoke the Checkbook Deluxe program, and select the B option
from the Edit Entries mini-menu. The Prompt/Menu window
will now show you a value for the Bank Balance, and it will
display new commands available from this mini-menu.

To mark an entry, all you have to do is make that entry the
selected entry and press the + key. This key will toggle the
checkmark in the selected entry: if the mark was there, it will
disappear; if the mark was not there, it will appear. The selected
entry automatically moves down after you press the + key.
Thus, if you start at the first entry appearing on the bank
statement you can mark off all the entries in just a few moments. Every time you mark an entry, notice that the Bank
Balance updates in the Prompt/Menu window.

As an example, study the screen in Figure 20-5. This
screen shows the entries checked off after the January statement came in the mail. Check numbers 178, 179, and 180 did not
appear on the statement, but all the other entries did. All screen
entries were therefore checked off except the three outstanding
checks. The Bank Balance in the lower right of the screen
should reflect the balance on the bank statement.

```
                            CHECKBOOK DELUXE
 ┌──────────┬──────────┬──────────────────────┬──────────┬───┬─────────┬────────┐
 │  Trans.  │  Trans.  │                      │  Budget  │ √ │ Amount  │Balance │
 │  Type    │  Date    │         Memo         │ Category │   │         │        │
 ├──────────┼──────────┼──────────────────────┼──────────┼───┼─────────┼────────┤
 │ C #174   │ 01-03-89 │ Ohio Edison          │ Utilities│ √ │  63.22- │ 647.41 │
 │ Deposit  │ 01-05-89 │ Paycheck             │ Other    │ √ │ 734.89+ │1382.30 │
 │ Withdraw │ 01-05-89 │ Cash for movie (ATM) │ Entertain.│ √ │ 60.00- │1322.30 │
 │ C #175   │ 01-10-89 │ Phone company        │ Utilities│ √ │  29.63- │1292.67 │
 │ Loan pmt │ 01-15-89 │ Car payment          │ Gas / car│ √ │ 210.00- │1082.67 │
 │ C #176   │ 01-17-89 │ VISA bill            │ Payment  │ √ │ 632.20- │ 450.47 │
 │ Deposit  │ 01-20-89 │ Paycheck             │ Other    │ √ │ 734.89+ │1185.36 │
 │ C #177   │ 01-22-89 │ Groceries            │ Food     │   │  63.77- │1121.59 │
 │ C #178   │ 01-24-89 │ Water company        │ Utilities│ √ │  25.60- │1095.99 │
 │ C #179   │ 01-27-89 │ K-mart               │ Clothing │   │ 143.27- │ 952.72 │
 │ Interest │ 01-31-89 │ Monthly interest     │ Other    │ √ │   5.21+ │ 957.93 │
 │ C #180   │ 02-02-89 │ Best Mortgage        │ Home     │   │ 823.82- │ 134.11 │
 │          │          │    (bottom of file)  │          │   │         │        │
 └──────────┴──────────┴──────────────────────┴──────────┴───┴─────────┴────────┘
 ┌─────────────────────────────────────────────────────────────────────────────┐
 │ Change current line:  <UP>  <DOWN>   <PGUP>   <PGDN>   Bank balance: 1164.97 │
 │ Mark outstanding entries with ⬚      Press ⬚ when finished                    │
 └─────────────────────────────────────────────────────────────────────────────┘
```

Figure 20-5.   Screen for balancing checkbook

How the Program Works

Now that you understand what the program does, you can take any of three options:

1. You can study this section to learn how the program works. Pay close attention to the program documentation.

2. You can spend the next several hours typing the program exactly as it appears in this chapter, and for the time being not worry about how the program works.

3. You can send for a copy of the program from the author, filling out the form found in the Preface.

The rest of this section is the actual code to make the Checkbook Deluxe program work. It relies heavily on the routines covered in the previous chapter. Each subprogram is preceded by a short discussion on the purpose of that particular subprogram.

The Data Structure

The first step in creating a program like this one is to determine the structure of the data, both when it is used in the program and when it is stored on disk. This particular program is well suited for QuickBASIC's record structures (or user-defined types) and random-access files. Here is the record definition used by this program:

```
TYPE CheckRec
    transtype AS STRING * 8
    transdate AS STRING * 8
    memo AS STRING * 25
    category AS STRING * 10
    outstanding AS STRING * 1
    amount AS LONG
    balance AS LONG
END TYPE
```

The *amount* field was chosen to be a LONG integer for several reasons. First, SINGLE numbers are accurate only to seven digits, which means that the program would show bad data if you had amounts of $100,000 or more. Second, although DOUBLE numbers are accurate enough, they take up twice as much file space. By using the LONG data type, you can store money values in cents, and display them in dollars and cents by dividing by 100.

As part of the main program (given later), the array *checks* is dimensioned as an array of type *CheckRec*. This array always contains the current page of entries.

Drawing the Spreadsheet

As covered in the previous section, the majority of the program requires a two-part display of a data window and a prompt/ menu window. The data window is loosely referred to as a spreadsheet, since it manipulates data in tabular form. Three subprograms are used to draw the data window: *DisplayCheck-Template, DisplayChecks*, and *Display1Check*.

The subroutine *DisplayCheckTemplate* draws all the lines that make up the data window. It requires no parameters because it always displays the same lines. The actual ASCII characters for the lines appear inside the PRINT statements. To learn how to enter these characters, study Chapter 15.

```
***
SUB DisplayCheckTemplate

',',',',',',',',',',',',',',',',',',',',',',',',',',',',','
'
'   Purpose:  displays the template that includes
'      all the graphic lines for the spreadsheet
'
'   Other routines called:
'      DisplayDoubleBox - draws a double-line box
'
'   Local variables:
'      linenum% - loop counter
'
',',',',',',',',',',',',',',',',',',',',',',',',',',',',','
CLS

COLOR 6, 8
CALL DisplayDoubleBox(1, 1, 3, 80)

LOCATE TopLine% - 5, 31
PRINT "CHECKBOOK DELUXE"
PRINT "||                                              ";
PRINT "                                            ||"
PRINT "|| Trans.     Trans.                          |";
PRINT "   Budget                          "
PRINT "|| Type       Date               Memo         |";
PRINT "  Category  ✓ Amount   Balance  "
PRINT "||                                            +";
PRINT "                                 ||"

FOR linenum% = TopLine% TO bottomline%
    PRINT "||                                          |";
    PRINT "                                 ||"
NEXT linenum%

PRINT " ||                                          |";
PRINT "                                 ||"

END SUB
***    ***
```

The *DisplayChecks* subroutine fills the data window with a page of entries. The routine that calls *DisplayChecks* must provide both the current size of the *checks* array and the index of the selected entry. Primarily, *DisplayChecks* does little more than call *Display1Check* for each entry.

```
SUB DisplayChecks (curindex%, numindices%)

',',',',',',',',',',',',',',',',',',',',',',',',',',',',',',',',',',',',','
'
'  Purpose:  displays all lines on the spreadsheet
'
'  Parameters:
'      curindex% - the current index to the checks array
'      numindices% - the number of valid indices in the
'          checks array
'
'  Other routines called:
'      Display1Check - displays one spreadsheet line
'
'  Local variables:
'      idx% - loop counter
'
',',',',',',',',',',',',',',',',',',',',',',',',',',',',',',',',',',',',',
'  update each line, even if it has no entry
FOR idx% = 1 TO ArraySize%
   IF idx% = curindex% THEN
       highlight% = True%
   ELSE
       highlight% = False%
   END IF
   CALL Display1Check(idx%, numindices%, highlight%)
NEXT idx%

END SUB
```

Display1Check will display one entry on a given line. The line number is computed by adding the array index with the number of the top line. This routine will highlight an entry if the calling routine sets the *reverse%* flag in the argument list. *Display1Check* also blanks out a line if that line is not used.

```
SUB Display1Check (arrayidx%, numindices%, reverse%)

',',',',',',',',',',',',',',',',',',',',',',',',',',',',',',',',',',',',','
'
'  Purpose: displays one line of the spreadsheet,
'      highlighting if required
'
'  Parameters:
'      arrayidx% - the index to the checks array
'      numindices% - the number of valid indices in the
'          checks array
'      reverse% - flag that determines if the entry
'          is highlighted
'
'  Global variables used:
'      checks() - the array containing the entries
```

```
'         shown on the screen
'
',',',',',',',',',',',',',',',',',',',',',',',',',',',',',',',',',
'  set the proper color
IF reverse% THEN
   COLOR 0, 7
ELSE
   COLOR 7, 0
END IF

'  move to the current screen line
LOCATE TopLine% + arrayidx% - 1

'  if current line is an entry, display it
IF arrayidx% <= numindices% THEN
   LOCATE , 3: PRINT checks(arrayidx%).transtype;
   LOCATE , 13: PRINT checks(arrayidx%).transdate;
   LOCATE , 24: PRINT checks(arrayidx%).memo;
   LOCATE , 50: PRINT checks(arrayidx%).category;
   LOCATE , 61: PRINT checks(arrayidx%).outstanding;
   PRINT USING "#####.##+"; checks(arrayidx%).amount / 100;
   LOCATE , 72
   PRINT USING "#####.##"; checks(arrayidx%).balance / 100;

'  display "Bottom line" entry or blank out line
ELSE
   IF arrayidx% = numindices% + 1 THEN
      LOCATE , 24: PRINT "    (bottom of file)        ";
   ELSE
      COLOR 7, 0
      LOCATE , 24: PRINT SPACE$(25);
   END IF

   COLOR 7, 0
   LOCATE , 3: PRINT SPACE$(8);
   LOCATE , 13: PRINT SPACE$(8);
   LOCATE , 50: PRINT SPACE$(10);
   LOCATE , 61: PRINT SPACE$(10);
   LOCATE , 72: PRINT SPACE$(8);
END IF

END SUB
```

Moving Around the Spreadsheet

To change the selected entry, four subroutines are required to process each of the four available move commands. These routines are *ProcessUp*, *ProcessDown*, *ProcessPgUp*, and *ProcessPgDn*.

ProcessUp moves the selected entry up one line. If the current line is not the top line, the routine can make the change in three steps: call *Display1Check* to display the current line in normal video, change the current line, and then call *Display1Check* to display the new current line in reverse video. If the current line is the top line, *ProcessUp* has the entire *checks* array reloaded with the new first entry, and then has the entire data window redisplayed.

```
SUB ProcessUp (curindex%, numindices%, topentry%, _
                                        filesize%)

',',',',',',',',',',',',',',',',',',',',',',',',',',',',',',',',
'
'   Purpose:  moves up one line in the spreadsheet.
'       If already at the top line, the routine "scrolls"
'       one line.
'
'   Parameters:
'       curindex% (in/out) - the current index to the
'           checks array
'       numindices% (in/out) - the number of valid indices
'           in the checks array
'       topentry% (in/out) - the file record number of the
'           first element in the checks array
'       filesize% (in) - the size of the file containing
'           the transaction records
'
'   Other routines called:
'       Display1Check - updates one entry line
'       LoadChecks - reloads the checks() array
'           from the entry file
'       DisplayChecks - redisplays the entire spreadsheet
'
',',',',',',',',',',',',',',',',',',',',',',',',',',',',',',',',
'   move up one line
IF curindex% > 1 THEN
    CALL Display1Check(curindex%, numindices%, False%)
    curindex% = curindex% - 1
    CALL Display1Check(curindex%, numindices%, True%)

'   scroll one line
ELSEIF topentry% > 1 THEN
    topentry% = topentry% - 1
    CALL LoadChecks(topentry%, numindices%, filesize%)
    CALL DisplayChecks(curindex%, numindices%)

'   can't scroll past first record
ELSE
    BEEP
END IF

END SUB
```

ProcessDown works in a way exactly opposite to
ProcessUp:

```
SUB ProcessDown (curindex%, numindices%, topentry%, _
                                         filesize%)

',',',',',',',',',',',',',',',',',',',',',',',',',',',',',',',',
'
'   Purpose:  moves down one line in the spreadsheet.
'       If already at the bottom, "scrolls" the screen
'       one line
'
'   Parameters:
'       curindex% (in/out) - the current index to the
'           checks array
'       numindices% (in/out) - the number of valid indices
'           in the checks array
'       topentry% (in/out) - the file record number of the
'           first element in the checks array
'       filesize% (in) - the size of the file containing
'           the transaction records
'
'   Other routines called:
'       Display1Check - updates one entry line
'       LoadChecks - reloads the checks() array
'           from the entry file
'       DisplayChecks - redisplays the entire spreadsheet
'
'
',',',',',',',',',',',',',',',',',',',',',',',',',',',',',',',',
IF curindex% < ArraySize% THEN

    ' if there's room, move down one line
    IF curindex% <= numindices% THEN
       CALL Display1Check(curindex%, numindices%, False%)
       curindex% = curindex% + 1
       CALL Display1Check(curindex%, numindices%, True%)

    ' can't move past "Bottom of file" line
    ELSE
       BEEP
    END IF

' if already at the bottom, "scroll" one line
ELSEIF topentry% + ArraySize% <= filesize% + 1 THEN
    topentry% = topentry% + 1
    CALL LoadChecks(topentry%, numindices%, filesize%)
    CALL DisplayChecks(curindex%, numindices%)

' can't scroll past bottom of file
ELSE
    BEEP
END IF

END SUB
```

The easiest job for *ProcessPgUp* is when the current page is already the first page. In this case, the routine works similarly to the previous two: dehighlighting the current line, changing the current line, and highlighting the new current line. If a new page needs to be displayed, however, the *checks* array must be reloaded and redisplayed.

```
SUB ProcessPgUp (curindex%, numindices%, topentry%, _
                                          filesize%)

'''''''''''''''''''''''''''''''''''''''''''''''''''''''''''
'
'   Purpose:  displays the previous page of entries.
'       If the current page is the first page, the routine
'       moves to the top of the first page.
'
'   Parameters:
'       curindex% (in/out) - the current index to the
'           checks array
'       numindices% (in/out) - the number of valid indices
'           in the checks array
'       topentry% (in/out) - the file record number of the
'           first element in the checks array
'       filesize% (in) - the size of the file containing
'           the transaction records
'
'   Other routines called:
'       Display1Check - updates one entry line
'       LoadChecks - reloads the checks() array
'           from the entry file
'       DisplayChecks - redisplays the entire spreadsheet
'
'''''''''''''''''''''''''''''''''''''''''''''''''''''''''
'   move back one page
IF topentry% > 1 THEN
    topentry% = topentry% - ArraySize + 1
    IF topentry% < 1 THEN topentry% = 1
    CALL LoadChecks(topentry%, numindices%, filesize%)
    CALL DisplayChecks(curindex%, numindices%)

'   if already at first page, move to top
ELSEIF curindex% > 1 THEN
    CALL Display1Check(curindex%, numindices%, False%)
    curindex% = 1
    CALL Display1Check(curindex%, numindices%, True%)

'   can't move past top of first page
ELSE
    BEEP
END IF

END SUB
```

ProcessPgDn follows the same rules as *ProcessPgUp*:

```
SUB ProcessPgDn (curindex%, numindices%, topentry%, _
                                    filesize%)

',',',',',',',',',',',',',',',',',',',',',',',',',',',',',',',',',',',',',','
'
'   Purpose:  displays the next page of entries.
'      If the current page is the last page, the current
'      entry becomes the last entry.
'
'   Parameters:
'      curindex% (in/out) - the current index to the
'         checks array
'      numindices% (in/out) - the number of valid indices
'         in the checks array
'      topentry% (in/out) - the file record number of the
'         first element in the checks array
'      filesize% (in) - the size of the file containing
'         the transaction records
'
'   Other routines called:
'      Display1Check - updates one entry line
'      LoadChecks - reloads the checks() array
'         from the entry file
'      DisplayChecks - redisplays the entire spreadsheet
'
'
',',',',',',',',',',',',',',',',',',',',',',',',',',',',',',',',',',',',','
'   if there is another page left, display it
IF topentry% + ArraySize < filesize% + 2 THEN
    topentry% = topentry% + ArraySize - 1
    CALL LoadChecks(topentry%, numindices%, filesize%)
    IF curindex% > numindices% + 1 THEN
        curindex% = numindices% + 1
    END IF
    CALL DisplayChecks(curindex%, numindices%)

'   if the current page is the last, move to bottom
ELSEIF curindex% <= numindices% THEN
    CALL Display1Check(curindex%, numindices%, False%)
    curindex% = numindices% + 1
    CALL Display1Check(curindex%, numindices%, True%)

'   can't move past the bottom of the last page
ELSE
    BEEP
END IF

END SUB
```

Manipulating Entries

The *ChangeEntry* routine includes the code for changing each field in the selected entry. It includes the calls to *DisplayMenu* and *GetMenuChoice* for the two menus. To make the menus appear and disappear, *ChangeEntry* copies the screen to another page in memory before displaying the menu. When the menu is no longer needed, *ChangeEntry* copies the old screen back to the current visual page, page 0. For some CGA users, this may momentarily cause a "snow" effect.

```
SUB ChangeEntry (curindex%, currentrec%)

','','','','','','','','','','','','','','','','','','','','','','','
'
'   Purpose:  allows the user to change each field in
'       the current entry
'
'   Parameters:
'       curindex% (in) - the current index to the checks
'           array
'       currentrec% (in) - the file record number of the
'           current entry
'
'   Global variables used:
'       checks() - the array containing the entries
'           shown on the screen
'       checkfile% - the current open file number
'       tranmenu, tranitems - menu data for the tranaction
'           type menu
'       catmenu, catitems - menu data for the categories
'           menu
'
'   Other routines called:
'       DisplayMenu - displays a menu on the screen
'       GetMenuChoice - allows user to select a menu item
'       GetLong - gets a LONG number from the user
'       GetDate - gets a valid date from the user
'       GetString - gets a limited-length string from
'           the user
'       GetDouble - gets a DOUBLE number from the user
'       DisplayEditOptions - displays the EditChecks
'           mini-menu
'
'   Local variables:
'       linenum% - the actual line of the current entry
'       choice$ - the menu character chosen by the user
'       itemnum% - the number of the item chosen
'       cnt% - loop counter
'       checknum& - the check number entered by user
'
','','','','','','','','','','','','','','','','','','','','','','',
SHARED checkfile%
SHARED tranmenu AS MenuInfoRec, tranitems() AS MenuItemsRec
SHARED catmenu AS MenuInfoRec, catitems() AS MenuItemsRec

linenum% = curindex% + TopLine% - 1
```

```
LOCATE 23, 4: PRINT "Select a transaction type: "

'   save the screen on another page
PCOPY 0, 1

'   let user select a transaction type
CALL DisplayMenu(tranmenu, tranitems())

'   determine current type, if any
choice$ = "C"
FOR cnt% = 1 TO tranmenu.numitems
   IF checks(curindex%).transtype = _
                 LEFT$(tranitems(cnt%).itemname, 8) THEN
      choice$ = tranitems(cnt%).cmdkey
      EXIT FOR
   END IF
NEXT cnt%

CALL GetMenuChoice(tranmenu, tranitems(), choice$, _
                                            itemnum%)


'   restore saved screen (or, erase menu)
PCOPY 1, 0

'   if current entry is a check, get the number
IF choice$ = "C" THEN
   checknum& = VAL(MID$(checks(curindex%).transtype, 4))
   LOCATE 23, 4
   PRINT "Enter the check number: (default="; checknum&
   LOCATE linenum%, 3: PRINT "C #";
   CALL GetLong(checknum&, 5)
   checks(curindex%).transtype = "C #" + _
                                 LTRIM$(STR$(checknum&))
ELSE
   checks(curindex%).transtype = _
                 LEFT$(tranitems(itemnum%).itemname, 8)
END IF
LOCATE linenum%, 3
PRINT checks(curindex%).transtype

'   get the transaction date from the user
LOCATE 23, 4
PRINT "Enter the transaction date: (default=";
PRINT checks(curindex%).transdate; ")"; SPACE$(20)
LOCATE linenum%, 13
CALL GetDate(checks(curindex%).transdate)

'   get the memo from the user
LOCATE 23, 4: PRINT "Enter a memo: (default = ";
PRINT checks(curindex%).memo; ")"
LOCATE linenum%, 24
CALL GetString(checks(curindex%).memo, 25)

'   get the budget category from the user
LOCATE 23, 4: PRINT "Select a category: "; SPACE$(50)

'   save the screen
```

```
PCOPY 0, 1
CALL DisplayMenu(catmenu, catitems())

'   determine the default choice
choice$ = "0"
FOR cnt% = 1 TO catmenu.numitems
   IF checks(curindex%).category = _
               LEFT$(catitems(cnt%).itemname, 10) THEN
      choice$ = catitems(cnt%).cmdkey
      EXIT FOR
   END IF
NEXT cnt%

CALL GetMenuChoice(catmenu, catitems(), choice$, _
                                        itemnum%)

'   restore the screen
PCOPY 1, 0
checks(curindex%).category = _
               LEFT$(catitems(itemnum%).itemname, 10)
LOCATE linenum%, 50
PRINT checks(curindex%).category;

'   get the transaction amount
tempdbl# = checks(curindex%).amount / 100
LOCATE 23, 4: PRINT "Enter the amount:  (default = ";
PRINT USING "######.##)                 "; ABS(tempdbl#)
LOCATE linenum%, 62
CALL GetDouble(tempdbl#, 8, 2)

'   make deposits, interest always positive (credits)
IF checks(curindex%).transtype = "Deposit " THEN
   checks(curindex%).amount = ABS(tempdbl#) * 100
ELSEIF checks(curindex%).transtype = "Interest" THEN
   checks(curindex%).amount = ABS(tempdbl#) * 100

'   make other entries negative (debits)
ELSE
   checks(curindex%).amount = -ABS(tempdbl#) * 100
END IF

'   save the current record
PUT #checkfile%, currentrec%, checks(curindex%)
CALL DisplayEditOptions

END SUB
```

When any entry is changed, all of the balance fields for every record after the current one must be updated. The *UpdateBalances* subroutine changes the balances in both the file and the *checks* array. Anytime a change is made to the *checks* array, the file is updated at the same time. This way you will not lose any data if the user presses CTRL-BREAK somewhere in the middle of the program.

```
SUB UpdateBalances (curindex%, numindices%, topentry%, _
                              filesize%)

',',',',',',',',',',',',',',',',',',',',',',',',',',',',',',',',',',',','
'
'  Purpose:  recalculates balances starting with the
'     current entry.  Calculates both the entries that
'     are displayed, and the ones that are on future
'     pages on the spreadsheet.
'
'  Parameters:
'     curindex% (in) - the current index to the checks
'        array
'     numindices% (in) - the number of valid indices
'        in the checks array
'     topentry% (in) - the file record number of the
'        first element in the checks array
'     filesize% (in) - the size of the file containing
'        the transaction records
'
'  Global variables used:
'     checks() - the array containing the entries
'        shown on the screen
'     checkfile% - the number of the open file
'        containing the entries
'
'  Local variables:
'     temprec - temporary file record
'     oldbal& - holds previous balance
'
',',',',',',',',',',',',',',',',',',',',',',',',',',',',',',',',',','
SHARED checkfile%
DIM temprec AS CheckRec


' get previous balance
IF curindex% = 1 THEN
    IF topentry% = 1 THEN
        oldbal& = 0
    ELSE
        GET #checkfile%, topentry% - 1, temprec
        oldbal& = temprec.balance
    END IF
ELSE
    oldbal& = checks(curindex% - 1).balance
END IF


' update balances that are displayed
COLOR 7, 0
FOR idx% = curindex% TO numindices%
    checks(idx%).balance = oldbal& + checks(idx%).amount
    LOCATE idx% + TopLine% - 1, 72
    oldbal& = checks(idx%).balance
    PRINT USING "#####.##"; oldbal& / 100
    PUT #checkfile%, topentry% + idx% - 1, checks(idx%)
NEXT idx%
```

```
'   update balances that are not displayed
FOR entry% = topentry% + numindices% TO filesize%
   GET #checkfile%, entry%, temprec
   temprec.balance = oldbal& + temprec.amount
   oldbal& = temprec.balance
   PUT #checkfile%, entry%, temprec
NEXT entry%

END SUB
```

When the user wants to insert a new entry, the *InsertEntry* routine is called. This routine must shift down all the records in the file to make room for the new entry. Some programmers would be tempted to implement a linked list to avoid all the file I/O associated with a record shift. In this application, however, the file should never be longer than a few hundred entries, so the record shift takes little time. Also, the vast majority of the time the user will insert records either at the very end of the file or very close to the end.

After the records are shifted in the file, the *checks* array is reloaded and redisplayed. Then *InsertEntry* calls *ChangeEntry* to change each of the fields in the new entry. The final job of *InsertEntry* is to call *ProcessDown* to save the user from having to use the DOWN ARROW key to insert multiple entries.

```
SUB InsertEntry (curindex%, numindices%, topentry%,_
                                          filesize%)

',',',',',',',',',',',',',',',',',',',',',',',',',',',',',',',',',',',',',',',',','
'
'   Purpose:  inserts a blank record just before the
'       current entry, then allows the user to change
'       each field.  After the changes, it automatically
'       moves down to the next entry.
'
'   Parameters:
'       curindex% (in/out) - the current index to the
'           checks array
'       numindices% (in/out) - the number of valid indices
'           in the checks array
'       topentry% (in/out) - the file record number of the
'           first element in the checks array
'       filesize% (in/out) - the size of the file
'           containing the transaction records
'
'   Global variables used:
'       checks() - the array containing the entries
```

```
'          shown on the screen
'        checkfile# - the file number of the entry file
'
'  Other routines called:
'        ClearEditOptions - clears the mini menu
'        LoadChecks - reloads the checks() array
'        DisplayChecks - redisplays the spreadsheet
'        ChangeEntry - allows user to change each
'            field in the current entry
'        UpdateBalances - updates the balance for
'            each entry after the one that changed
'        ProcessDown - moves down one entry
'
'  Local variables:
'        temprec - a temporary file record
'        rec% - loop counter
'
'
','','','','','','','','','','','','','','','','','','','','','','','','','','
SHARED checkfile%
DIM temprec AS CheckRec

CALL ClearEditOptions
PRINT "Inserting a new entry:"

'  move the records down in the file
currentrec% = topentry% + curindex% - 1
FOR rec% = filesize% TO currentrec% STEP -1
    GET #checkfile%, rec%, temprec
    PUT #checkfile%, rec% + 1, temprec
NEXT rec%
filesize% = filesize% + 1

'  create and save a default entry
checks(curindex%) = blankcheck
IF curindex% > 1 THEN
    checks(curindex%).transdate = _
                    checks(curindex% - 1).transdate
END IF
PUT #checkfile%, currentrec%, checks(curindex%)

'  reload and display the entries in the spreadsheet
CALL LoadChecks(topentry%, numindices%, filesize%)
CALL DisplayChecks(curindex%, numindices%)

'  allow user to change each field
CALL ChangeEntry(curindex%, currentrec%)
CALL UpdateBalances(curindex%, numindices%, topentry%, _
                                        filesize%)

'  move down to the next entry
CALL ProcessDown(curindex%, numindices%, topentry%, _
                                        filesize%)

END SUB
```

The *DeleteEntry* subroutine also does a record shift in the check file. When the unwanted entry is gone, the *checks* array must be reloaded and redisplayed. Some programmers might be tempted to use the textbook method of shifting the array as well as the file. However, the code to load a new entry at the bottom of the window would have to be repeated, and the reloading takes minimal time.

When *DeleteEntry* eliminates an entry, it lowers the value of the variable *filesize%*. This is somewhat of a lie, because you cannot decrease the size of a random-access file. The variable *filesize%* thus becomes the total number of useful records in the file. The *CloseFile* routine given later will resolve this anomaly.

```
SUB DeleteEntry (curindex%, numindices%, topentry%, _
                                          filesize%)

',',',',',',',',',',',',',',',',',',',',',',',',',',',',',',',',
'
'   Purpose:   deletes the current entry from the entry
'       file.  Makes sure user did not hit "D" by accident.
'
'   Parameters:
'       curindex% (in) - the current index to the checks
'           array
'       numindices% (in/out) - the number of valid indices
'           in the checks array
'       topentry% (in/out) - the file record number of the
'           first element in the checks array
'       filesize% (in/out) - the size of the file contain-
'           ing the transaction records
'
'   Global variables used:
'       checkfile% - the number of the open entry file
'
'   Other routines called:
'       ClearEditOptions - clears the mini-menu
'       GetString - gets a limited-length string from
'           the user
'       LoadChecks - reloads the checks() array from
'           the entry file
'       DisplayChecks - redisplays the spreadsheet
'       DisplayEditOptions - displays the EditChecks
'           mini-menu
'
'   Local variables:
'       doit$ - makes sure user really wants to delete
'           the entry
'       rec% - loop counter
'
',',',',',',',',',',',',',',',',',',',',',',',',',',',',',',',
```

```
DIM temprec AS CheckRec
SHARED checkfile%

CALL ClearEditOptions

'   make sure user is sure
PRINT "Deleting this entry:"
LOCATE , 4
PRINT "Are you sure you want to delete this (Y/N)? ";
doit$ = "N"
CALL GetString(doit$, 1)

IF UCASE$(doit$) = "Y" THEN

    'move the others up in the file
    currentrec% = topentry% + curindex% - 1
    FOR rec% = currentrec% TO filesize% - 1
        GET #checkfile%, rec% + 1, temprec
        PUT #checkfile%, rec%, temprec
    NEXT rec%
    filesize% = filesize% - 1

    '   reload and display spreadsheet
    CALL LoadChecks(topentry%, numindices%, filesize%)
    CALL DisplayChecks(curindex%, numindices%)
END IF

CALL DisplayEditOptions

END SUB
```

Manipulating the File

Although many of the subroutines use GET# and PUT# to perform file I/O, three routines are responsible for the majority: *GetCheckFile, LoadChecks,* and *CloseFile.*

GetCheckFile must be called to get a filename and open the file. This routine displays the screen shown in Figure 20-1. It also creates a default first record in newly created files.

```
SUB GetCheckFile (topentry%, filesize%)

','','','','','','','','','','','','','','','','','','','','','
'
'   Purpose:  gets the name of the entry file from the
'       user.  If the user gives no name, the routine
'       uses "check.fil".  The user can choose to leave
'       the program by typing "QUIT".
'
'   Parameters:
'       topentry% (out) - the file record number of the
```

```
'              first element in the checks array
'        filesize% (out) - the size of the file containing
'              the transaction records
'
'  Global variables used:
'     checkfile% - the number of the open entry file
'     checkfilename$ - the name of the chosen file
'
'  Other routines called:
'     GetString - gets a limited-length string from
'              the user
'
'  Local variables:
'     temprec - a temporary file record
'     answer$ - string to see if program should
'              create a new file
'
'
',','','','','','','','','','','','','','','','','','','','','','','','','','
SHARED checkfile%, checkfilename$
DIM temprec AS CheckRec

checkfile% = FREEFILE

'  loop until user has entered a valid filename
DO

    '  get the name of the file
    CLS
    LOCATE 10, 10
    PRINT "Enter name of check file or QUIT to quit: ";
    checkfilename$ = "check.fil"
    CALL GetString(checkfilename$, 12)

    '  if user wants out, get out
    IF checkfilename$ = "QUIT" THEN END

    OPEN checkfilename$ FOR RANDOM AS #checkfile% _
                                    LEN = LEN(temprec)
    filesize% = LOF(checkfile%) / LEN(temprec)

    '  if the file is empty, see if the user still wants
    '  to use it
    IF filesize% = 0 THEN
        PRINT "File does not exist.  Create one? (Y/N): ";
        answer$ = "N"
        CALL GetString(answer$, 1)

        '  place an initial record in the file
        IF UCASE$(answer$) = "Y" THEN
            temprec = blankcheck
            temprec.transtype = "Deposit "
            temprec.transdate = LEFT$(DATE$,6) + RIGHT$(DATE$,2)
            temprec.memo = "Initial File Balance"
            temprec.category = "Other"
            temprec.outstanding = "{"
```

```
            PUT #checkfile%, 1, temprec
            filesize% = 1

        '   if the user made a mistake, delete the file
        ELSE
            CLOSE #checkfile%
            KILL checkfilename$
        END IF
    END IF
LOOP UNTIL filesize% > 0

'   start by displaying the last page of entries
topentry% = filesize% - ArraySize% + 2
IF topentry% < 1 THEN topentry% = 1

END SUB
```

The *LoadChecks* routine is called anytime the *checks* array must be reloaded. This routine requires a value in *topentry%* for the record number to be placed in the first element of the *checks* array. Often there are not enough records to fill the entire array, so *LoadChecks* assigns the actual array size to the variable *numindices%*.

```
SUB LoadChecks (topentry%, numindices%, filesize%)

'''''''''''''''''''''''''''''''''''''''''''''''''''
'
'   Purpose:  fills the checks() array from the
'       transaction file
'
'   Parameters:
'       numindices% (out) - the number of valid indices
'           in the checks array
'       topentry% (in) - the file record number of the
'           first element in the checks array
'       filesize% (in) - the size of the file containing
'           the transaction records
'
'   Global variables used:
'       checks() - the array containing the entries
'           shown on the screen
'       checkfile% - the number of the open entry file
'
'   Local variables:
'       idx% - loop counter
'       entry% - the record number being read
'
'
'''''''''''''''''''''''''''''''''''''''''''''''''''
SHARED checkfile%

numindices% = 0
```

```
'  try to fill the entire array
FOR idx% = 1 TO ArraySize%
   entry% = topentry% + idx% - 1

   '  get a record from the file
   IF entry% <= filesize% THEN
      numindices% = numindices% + 1
      GET #checkfile%, entry%, checks(idx%)

   '  if no more records, stop
   ELSE
      EXIT FOR
   END IF
NEXT idx%

END SUB
```

Normally, the *CloseFile* subroutine will close only the current entry file. If the user finishes the current session with fewer records than there were at the start of the session, *CloseFile* must eliminate the extra records. It accomplishes this by copying the good records into a temporary file, deleting the original file, and renaming the temporary file to be the same as the original file.

```
SUB CloseFile
','','','','','','','','','','','','','','','','','','','','
'
'  Purpose:  cleans up the file if there are fewer
'     actual entries than there are file records,
'     and closes the file
'
'  Global variables used:
'     checkfile% - the number of the open file
'     checkfilename$ - the name of the open file
'
'  Local variables:
'     temprec - temporary file record
'     idx% - loop counter
'     newsize% - the size of the new file
'
','','','','','','','','','','','','','','','','','','','','
SHARED checkfile%, checkfilename$
DIM temprec AS CheckRec

'  if there are blank entries in the file, eliminate them
IF LOF(checkfile%) / LEN(blankcheck) > filesize% THEN
   LOCATE 22, 4: PRINT "Cleaning Up. . ."; SPACE$(45)
```

```
'   create a temporary file and write all records to it
tempfile% = FREEFILE
OPEN "temp.tmp" FOR RANDOM AS #tempfile% _
                                    LEN = LEN(blankcheck)
FOR idx% = 1 TO filesize%
    GET #checkfile%, idx%, temprec
    PUT #tempfile%, idx%, temprec
NEXT idx%
CLOSE #checkfile%
newsize% = LOF(tempfile%) / LEN(blankcheck)
CLOSE #tempfile%

'   destroy current file and rename temporary file to
'   be the new current file
KILL checkfilename$
IF newsize% > 0 THEN
    NAME "temp.tmp" AS checkfilename$

'   if file has no entries, delete it
ELSE
    KILL "temp.tmp"
END IF

ELSE
    CLOSE #checkfile%
END IF

END SUB
```

The Mini-Menu Drivers

The two subroutines that have mini-menus are *EditChecks* and
BalanceCheckbook. Both of these have essentially the same
structure: a giant SELECT-END SELECT structure within a
DO-LOOP that calls the appropriate subroutine based on the
selected command.

Here is the *EditChecks* subroutine:

```
SUB EditChecks (curindex%, numindices%, topentry%, _
                                    filesize%)

',',',',',',',',',',',',',',',',',',',',',',',',',',',',',',',',',',','
'
'   Purpose:  this is the driver for the transaction
'       spreadsheet.  It gets a key from the user and
'       calls the appropriate routine to handle the action.
'
'   Parameters:
'       curindex% (in/out) - the current index to the
'           checks array
'       numindices% (in/out) - the number of valid indices
'           in the checks array
```

```
'        topentry% (in/out) - the file record number of the
'            first element in the checks array
'        filesize% (in/out) - the size of the file containing
'            the transaction records
'
'    Global variables used:
'        checks() - the array containing the entries
'            shown on the screen
'
'    Other routines called:
'        DisplayEditOptions - displays the mini menu at
'            the bottom of the screen
'        ClearEditOptions - clears the mini menu
'        ChangeEntry - allows the user to change each
'            field in a transaction entry
'        UpdateBalances - recomputes the balances for
'            each entry after the one that changed
'        Display1Check - displays one entry line in the
'            transaction spreadsheet
'        InsertEntry - inserts a blank entry just before
'            the current entry, then allows the user to
'            change the fields in the new entry
'        DeleteEntry - deletes the current entry
'        BalanceCheckbook - allows the user to mark which
'            entries appear on the bank statement to help
'            balance the checkbook
'        GetString - gets a limited-length string from
'            the user
'        ProcessUp - moves the current entry up one line
'        ProcessDown - moves the current entry down one line
'        ProcessPgUp - displays the previous screen of entries
'        ProcessPgDn - displays the next screen of entries
'
'    Local variables:
'        quit$ - makes sure the user really wants to quit
'        onechar$ - the key pressed by the user
'        currentrec% - the position in the transaction file
'            of the current entry
'
'
',',',',',',',',',',',',',',',',',',',',',',',',',',',',',',',',',',',
' display the mini menu at the bottom part of the screen
CALL DisplayEditOptions
quit$ = "N"

' loop until the user is sure about quitting
DO

    ' get a key from the user
    COLOR 3, 1
    DO
        onechar$ = INKEY$
    LOOP WHILE onechar$ = ""

    ' call the proper routine based on the key pressed
```

```
SELECT CASE UCASE$(onechar$)

    ' change the current entry
    CASE "C"

        ' the user cannot change the bottom line
        IF curindex% > numindices% THEN
            BEEP
        ELSE
            CALL ClearEditOptions
            PRINT "Changing an existing entry:"

            ' determine which file is being modified
            currentrec% = topentry% + curindex% - 1

            ' allow user to change each field
            CALL ChangeEntry(curindex%, currentrec%)

            ' recompute all balances below this one
            CALL UpdateBalances(curindex%, numindices%, _
                                topentry%, filesize%)
            CALL Display1Check(curindex%, numindices%, _
                                True%)
        END IF

    ' insert blank record just before the current one
    CASE "I"
        CALL InsertEntry(curindex%, numindices%, _
                        topentry%, filesize%)

    ' delete the current entry
    CASE "D"
        IF curindex% > numindices% THEN
            BEEP
        ELSE
            CALL DeleteEntry(curindex%, numindices%, _
                            topentry%, filesize%)
        END IF

    ' allow the user to mark the entries
    ' that were verified by the bank statement
    CASE "B"
        CALL BalanceCheckbook(curindex%, numindices%, _
                            topentry%, filesize%)

    ' leave the program
    CASE "Q"
        CALL ClearEditOptions
        PRINT "Quit program:"
        LOCATE , 4
        PRINT "Are you sure you want to quit (Y/N)? ";
        CALL GetString(quit$, 1)

    ' move up one line
    CASE CHR$(0) + CHR$(&H48)
```

```
              CALL ProcessUp(curindex%, numindices%, _
                                     topentry%,  filesize%)
          '   move down one line
          CASE CHR$(0) + CHR$(&H50)
              CALL ProcessDown(curindex%, numindices%, _
                                     topentry%,  filesize%)

          '   move up one page
          CASE CHR$(0) + CHR$(&H49)
              CALL ProcessPgUp(curindex%, numindices%, _
                                     topentry%,  filesize%)

          '   move down one page
          CASE CHR$(0) + CHR$(&H51)
              CALL ProcessPgDn(curindex%, numindices%, _
                                     topentry%,  filesize%)

          CASE ELSE
              BEEP

      END SELECT

  LOOP UNTIL UCASE$(quit$) = "Y"

  END SUB
```

Two small subroutines are included because many of the routines use the mini-menu window to display prompts. The *DisplayEditOptions* routine will redisplay the mini-menu when the other routine is finished using the window.

```
SUB DisplayEditOptions

',',',',',',',',',',',',',',',',',',',',',',',',',',',',',',',',',',',',',',',',',',',',',',
'
'   Purpose:  displays the EditChecks mini-menu
'
'   Other routines called:
'       DisplayBox - draws a single-line box
'
'
',',',',',',',',',',',',',',',',',',',',',',',',',',',',',',',',',',',',',',',',',',',',',',',
COLOR 3, 1
CALL DisplayBox(21, 1, 24, 80)
LOCATE 22, 4
PRINT "Change current line:  <UP>  <DOWN>  <PGUP>  <PGDN>"
LOCATE 23, 4
PRINT "Command options:  Change   Insert";
PRINT "   Delete   Balance   Quit"

COLOR 1, 3
LOCATE 23, 22: PRINT "C";
LOCATE , 31: PRINT "I";
```

```
LOCATE , 40: PRINT "D";
LOCATE , 49: PRINT "B";
LOCATE , 59: PRINT "Q"
COLOR 3, 1

END SUB
```

The *ClearEditOptions* subroutine has only a few lines of executable code, but many routines call it to clear out the mini-menu window.

```
SUB ClearEditOptions

',',',',',',',',',',',',',',',',',',',',',',',',',',',',',',',',
'
'  Purpose:  clears the current mini-menu
'
'
',',',',',',',',',',',',',',',',',',',',',',',',',',',',',',',','
LOCATE 22, 4:   PRINT SPACE$(60);
LOCATE 23, 4:   PRINT SPACE$(60);
LOCATE 22, 4

END SUB
```

The checkbook-balancing mini-menu is driven by the routine *BalanceCheckbook:*

```
SUB BalanceCheckbook (curindex%, numindices%, topentry%, _
                                              filesize%)

',',',',',',',',',',',',',',',',',',',',',',',',',',',',',',','
'
'  Purpose:  displays a mini-menu that allows the user
'     to update the entries that are listed on the bank
'     statement.  Constantly outputs the bank balance
'     based on outstanding entries.
'
'  Parameters:
'     curindex% (in/out) - the current index to the
'        checks array
'     numindices% (in/out) - the number of valid indices
'        in the checks array
'     topentry% (in/out) - the file record number of the
'        first element in the checks array
'     filesize% (in) - the size of the file containing
'        the transaction records
'
'  Global variables used:
'     checks() - the array containing the entries
'        shown on the screen
```

```
'      checkfile% - the number of the open entry file
'
'   Other routines called:
'      ComputeBankBalance - computes the initial
'         bank balance based on file entries
'      ClearEditOptions - clears the mini menu
'      ProcessUp - moves the current entry up one line
'      ProcessDown - moves the current entry down one line
'      ProcessPgUp - displays the previous screen of entries
'      ProcessPgDn - displays the next screen of entries
'
'   Local variables:
'      bankbal& - the number that should appear at the
'         bottom of the bank statement
'      onechar$ - the key pressed by the user
'
','','','','','','','','','','','','','','','','','','','','','','
SHARED checkfile%

'   initialize the bank balance
bankbal& = ComputeBankBalance&(filesize%)

'   display mini-menu
LOCATE 23, 4: COLOR 3, 1
PRINT "Mark outstanding entries with +      ";
PRINT "Press Q when finished   "
LOCATE 22, 57: PRINT "Bank balance: "
COLOR 1, 3
LOCATE 22, 70: PRINT USING "######.##"; bankbal& / 100
LOCATE 23, 34: PRINT "+";
LOCATE , 46: PRINT "Q"
COLOR 3, 1

'   loop until user wants to leave menu
DO

    '   get a key
    DO
        onechar$ = INKEY$
    LOOP WHILE onechar$ = ""

    SELECT CASE UCASE$(onechar$)

        '   toggle outstanding entry mark and update balance
        CASE "+"
            IF curindex% <= numindices% THEN
                IF checks(curindex%).outstanding = "{" THEN
                    checks(curindex%).outstanding = " "
                    bankbal& = bankbal& -_
                                    checks(curindex%).amount
                ELSE
                    checks(curindex%).outstanding = "{"
                    bankbal& = bankbal& + checks(curindex%).amount
                END IF
                PUT #checkfile%, topentry% + curindex% - 1, _
                                    checks(curindex%)

                COLOR 1, 3
```

```
        LOCATE 22, 70
        PRINT USING "######.##"; bankbal& / 100

        '  move down one line
        CALL ProcessDown(curindex%, numindices%, _
                              topentry%, filesize%)
    ELSE
       BEEP
    END IF

'  quit (return to EditChecks mini-menu)
CASE "Q"
   CALL ClearEditOptions
   CALL DisplayEditOptions

'  move up one line
CASE CHR$(0) + CHR$(&H48)
     CALL ProcessUp(curindex%, numindices%, _
                         topentry%, filesize%)

'  move down one line
CASE CHR$(0) + CHR$(&H50)
     CALL ProcessDown(curindex%, numindices%, _
                           topentry%, filesize%)

'  move back one page
CASE CHR$(0) + CHR$(&H49)
     CALL ProcessPgUp(curindex%, numindices%, _
                           topentry%, filesize%)

'  move forward one page
CASE CHR$(0) + CHR$(&H51)
     CALL ProcessPgDn(curindex%, numindices%, _
                           topentry%, filesize%)

    CASE ELSE
       BEEP

 END SELECT

LOOP UNTIL UCASE$(onechar$) = "Q"

END SUB
```

Before *BalanceCheckbook* can allow the user to mark entries, it must compute an initial bank balance. The *Compute-BankBalance* function takes the final account balance, and takes out the amounts from the entries in the file that are not checked off. This function need only be called at the start of the *Balance-Checkbook* routine, because the Bank Balance can be updated after an entry is checked off by simply adding that value to the current balance.

```
FUNCTION ComputeBankBalance& (filesize%)

',',',',',',',',',',',',',',',',',',',',',',',',',',',',',',',',',',',
'
'   Purpose:  computes the balance that should appear
'      on the bank statement, based on which entries
'      are marked as outstanding
'
'   Parameters:
'      filesize% (in) - the size of the file containing
'         the transaction records
'
'   Global variables used:
'      checkfile% - the number of the open entry file
'
'   Local variables:
'      temprec - temporary file record
'      bankbal& - temporary variable for bank balance
'      entry% - loop counter
'
',',',',',',',',',',',',',',',',',',',',',',',',',',',',',',',',',',',
SHARED checkfile%
DIM temprec AS CheckRec

'   compute balance only for checked entries
bankbal& = 0
FOR entry% = 1 TO filesize%
   GET #checkfile%, entry%, temprec
   IF temprec.outstanding = "{" THEN
      bankbal& = bankbal& + temprec.amount
   END IF
NEXT entry%

ComputeBankBalance& = bankbal&

END FUNCTION
```

The Main Program

The main program is cluttered with DECLARE statements, constant declarations, and menu declarations. Beyond these, the main program does little beside call the routines to get a filename, load the *checks* array for the first time, display the spreadsheet, and call the *EditChecks* routine.

```
DECLARE SUB LoadChecks (topentry%, numindices%, _
                                   filesize%)
DECLARE SUB BalanceCheckbook (curindex%, numindices%, _
                        topentry%, filesize%)
DECLARE FUNCTION ComputeBankBalance& (filesize%)
DECLARE SUB UpdateBalances (curindex%, numindices%, _
                        topentry%, filesize%)
```

```
DECLARE SUB ChangeEntry (curindex%, currentrec%)
DECLARE SUB DeleteEntry (curindex%, numindices%, _
                            topentry%, filesize%)
DECLARE SUB GetCheckFile (topentry%, filesize%)
DECLARE SUB EditChecks (curindex%, numindices%, _
                            topentry%, filesize%)
DECLARE SUB InsertEntry (curindex%, numindices%, _
                            topentry%, filesize%)
DECLARE SUB DisplayCheckTemplate ()
DECLARE SUB DisplayChecks (curindex%, numindices%)
DECLARE SUB Display1Check (arrayidx%, numindices%, reverse%)
DECLARE SUB DisplayEditOptions ()
DECLARE SUB ClearEditOptions ()
DECLARE SUB CloseFile ()
DECLARE SUB ProcessDown (curindex%, numindices%, _
                            topentry%, filesize%)
DECLARE SUB ProcessUp (curindex%, numindices%, _
                            topentry%, filesize%)
DECLARE SUB ProcessPgUp (curindex%, numindices%, _
                            topentry%, _filesize%)
DECLARE SUB ProcessPgDn (curindex%, numindices%, _
                            topentry%, filesize%)

' $INCLUDE: 'TOOLS.INC'

',',',',',',',',',',',',',',',',',',',',',',',',',',',',',',',',',',',',',',',',',',',',',',',

'
'   Program:  CHECK.BAS
'
'   Required module:  TOOLS.BAS
'
'   Purpose:  acts as an electronic checkbook.
'       It allows the user to enter checks, deposits,
'       withdrawals, and so forth.  It automat-
'       ically computes the actual account balance
'       as well as the bank statement balance (for
'       balancing the checkbook).
'
'   Routines called:
'       LoadMenu - loads interactive menus
'       GetCheckFile - gets a filename from the
'          user and opens the file
'       LoadChecks - loads the checks() array from
'          the file
'       DisplayCheckTemplate - displays the lines of
'          the spreadsheet
'       DisplayChecks - displays the entries in the
'          spreadsheet
'       EditChecks - allows user to add, change, and
'          delete entries
'       CloseFile - cleans up and closes file
'
'
',',',',',',',',',',',',',',',',',',',',',',',',',',',',',',',',',',',',',',',',',',',',',',',',
```

```
TYPE CheckRec
    transtype AS STRING * 8
    transdate AS STRING * 8
    memo AS STRING * 25
    category AS STRING * 10
    outstanding AS STRING * 1
    amount AS LONG
    balance AS LONG
END TYPE

CONST TopLine% = 7
CONST bottomline% = 19
CONST ArraySize% = 13

DIM SHARED checks(1 TO ArraySize%) AS CheckRec
DIM SHARED blankcheck AS CheckRec
DIM checkfile%, checkfilename$
DIM tranmenu AS MenuInfoRec, tranitems(10) AS MenuItemsRec
DIM catmenu AS MenuInfoRec, catitems(15) AS MenuItemsRec

''''''''' executable code starts here  '''''''''''

'   load interactive menus
CALL LoadMenu(tranmenu, tranitems(), "trantype.mnu")
CALL LoadMenu(catmenu, catitems(), "category.mnu")

'   get filename from user
CALL GetCheckFile(topentry%, filesize%)

'   load checks array
CALL LoadChecks(topentry%, numindices%, filesize%)

'   display spreadsheet
CALL DisplayCheckTemplate
curindex% = numindices% + 1
CALL DisplayChecks(curindex%, numindices%)

'   allow user to add/change/delete/balance
CALL EditChecks(curindex%, numindices%, topentry%, _
                                        filesize%)

CALL CloseFile
```

Possible Enhancements

There are many possible ways to expand on this version of the Checkbook Deluxe program. A few enhancements are listed here, but you are sure to discover your own as you run the program for yourself.

1. Display a menu at the start of the program showing all the checkbook files in the current directory. Allow the user to choose one of these or to create a new file.

2. Provide a Utilities menu to make backup copies of the checkbook files, change disks and directories, and so forth.

3. Allow the user to enter a word or phrase, then search for that word or phrase among all the Memos in the file. This would help the user to find a particular entry quickly.

4. The Budget Category can be used in many different ways. You could write a routine that prints a report of all the entries for each month divided into budget categories. You could even create a separate budgeting tool.

A Data Plotting Package

Graphics Tools
What the PLOTDATA Program Does
How the PLOTDATA Program Works
Possible Enhancements

If you work in the business world, you understand the importance of pictures. If you are giving a presentation, your audience will understand your point much better if you show a graph instead of a numeric table. This chapter provides a package that lets you see data in graphic form. It gives you the ability to alter both axis parameters and data parameters. From the programmer's point of view, this package demonstrates how to create an effective user interface in a graphics screen mode.

The routines in this chapter assume that the program will run in screen mode 9. This means that you must have an EGA or VGA card with the appropriate monitor to run the software. Mode 9 is required because the program relies heavily on both high resolution and multiple colors. If you have a CGA, you can modify the program to work in mode 2, but the menus will be confusing when drawn in only one color. If you use mode 1, you are limited to 40 characters on each line.

Before getting to the PLOTDATA program, this chapter devotes a section to an additional set of tools not found in Chapter 19. These subprograms can be called by any program running in graphics mode. The second section of this chapter explains what you can do with the PLOTDATA program. Finally, you will see the entire source code, which shows you how PLOTDATA works.

Graphics Tools

This section contains a group of subroutines and functions that are used by the PLOTDATA program but are generic in form. Each routine in this module, called GTOOLS.BAS, can be called by any other module. The module-level code follows:

```
DECLARE FUNCTION FindMin! (anyarray!(), first%, last%)
DECLARE FUNCTION FindMax! (anyarray!(), first%, last%)
DECLARE FUNCTION Smaller% (first%, second%)
DECLARE SUB RestoreGWindow (x1%, y1%)
DECLARE FUNCTION ComputeArraySize% (x1%, y1%, x2%, y2%)
DECLARE SUB SaveGWindow (x1%, y1%, x2%, y2%)

',',',',',',',',',',',',',',',',',',',',',',',',',',',',',',',','
'
'   Module:   GTOOLS.BAS
'
'   Purpose:  provides support tools for programs that
'       run in graphics modes
'
'   Global variables:
'       gwindow!() - dynamic array containing the current
'           graphics window
'
'
',',',',',',',',',',',',',',',',',',',',',',',',',',',',',',',','
'   declare the dynamic array used by the window routines
' $DYNAMIC
DIM SHARED gwindow!(10)
' $STATIC
```

This code defines a global, dynamic array called *gwindow!,* which will be used by several subroutines to store window data.

Graphics Text I/O

The *GetInput* routine used extensively in the two previous chapters is perfect for getting data from the user while in screen mode 0. However, this routine cannot be used in any of the graphics modes because it uses background colors and blinking characters to show size and to create a cursor. In all graphics modes, there can be only one background color for the entire screen. If you called *GetInput* in a graphics mode, the routine would attempt to set a blinking attribute to a character, and it would give you an error message.

The subroutine *GetAnyInput* modifies *GetInput* slightly to account for these problems. It shows the current cursor location by drawing a thick line under the character. It also sets no background colors.

```
SUB GetAnyInput (instr$, maxlen%)

',',',',',',',',',',',',',',',',',',',',',',',',',',',',',',',',',',',',',',',',','
'
'   Purpose:  allows the user to enter a string, but
'       limits the length of the string.  Most cursor
'       movement commands are handled.  The cursor is
'       imitated by drawing two lines below the current
'       position.
'
'   Parameters:
'       instr$ (out) - the value entered by user
'       maxlen% (in) - the maximum length of the string
'
'   Local variables:
'       firstcol% - the starting column of the input
'       insertmode% - the insert mode (insert or overstrike)
'       curpos% - the current string index
'       onechar$ - the key pressed by user
'
',',',',',',',',',',',',',',',',',',',',',',',',',',',',',',',',',',',',',',',',','
CONST insert% = 1, overstrike% = 2

'   make required initializations
instr$ = ""
firstcol% = POS(0)
insertmode% = overstrike%
curpos% = 1

'   process characters one at a time
DO
    '   show cursor
    x% = (firstcol% + curpos%) * 8 - 15
    y% = CSRLIN * 14 - 1
    LINE (x%, y%)-(x% + 8, y% + 1), 15, B

    '   get a character
    DO
        onechar$ = INKEY$
    LOOP WHILE onechar$ = ""

    '   eliminate cursor
    LINE (x%, y%)-(x% + 8, y% + 1), 0, B

    '   check for special characters
    IF LEFT$(onechar$, 1) = CHR$(0) THEN
```

```
'   check for <RIGHT>
IF RIGHT$(onechar$, 1) = CHR$(77) THEN

    '   if before last character, move right one
    IF curpos% <= LEN(instr$) THEN
        curpos% = curpos% + 1
    END IF

'   check for <LEFT>
ELSEIF RIGHT$(onechar$, 1) = CHR$(75) THEN

    '   if past first character, move left one
    IF curpos% > 1 THEN
        curpos% = curpos% - 1
    END IF

'   check for <DEL>
ELSEIF RIGHT$(onechar$, 1) = CHR$(83) THEN

    '   if before last character, remove one
    IF curpos% <= LEN(instr$) THEN
        instr$ = LEFT$(instr$, curpos% - 1) + _
                            MID$(instr$, curpos% + 1)
        PRINT MID$(instr$, curpos%); " ";
    END IF

'   check for <INS>
ELSEIF RIGHT$(onechar$, 1) = CHR$(82) THEN

    '   toggle insert mode
    IF insertmode% = overstrike% THEN
        insertmode% = insert%
    ELSE
        insertmode% = overstrike%
    END IF

END IF

'   check for <BACKSPACE>
ELSEIF onechar$ = CHR$(8) THEN

    '   if past first character, remove one
    IF curpos% > 1 THEN
        IF curpos% > LEN(instr$) THEN
            PRINT CHR$(29); " "; CHR$(29);
        ELSE
            PRINT CHR$(29); MID$(instr$, curpos%);
            PRINT " "; CHR$(29);
        END IF
        instr$ = LEFT$(instr$, curpos% - 2) + _
                            MID$(instr$, curpos%)
        curpos% = curpos% - 1
    END IF

ELSEIF onechar$ = CHR$(13) THEN
```

```
     '  no special character, so check for overstrike mode
     ELSEIF insertmode% = overstrike% THEN

        '  if overstrike, replace that character or add to end
        IF curpos% <= LEN(instr$) THEN
           MID$(instr$, curpos%, 1) = onechar$
           PRINT onechar$;
           curpos% = curpos% + 1
        ELSEIF curpos% <= maxlen% THEN
           instr$ = instr$ + onechar$
           PRINT onechar$;
           curpos% = curpos% + 1
        ELSE
           BEEP
        END IF

     '  insert mode must be in insert
     ELSEIF curpos% <= maxlen% THEN

        '  insert character, move rest of string over
        instr$ = LEFT$(instr$, curpos% - 1) + onechar$ + _
                                     MID$(instr$, curpos%)
        PRINT MID$(instr$, curpos%);
        curpos% = curpos% + 1

     ELSE
        BEEP
     END IF

LOOP UNTIL onechar$ = CHR$(13)

END SUB
```

When you output a character to the screen, QuickBASIC displays the character using the current foreground and background colors. If you wanted to display a string with another background color, you would have a problem. At first, you could try drawing a box filled with the desired background color, and then printing the character on top of the box. Unfortunately, when you print the character, the box disappears.

The subroutine *InvertText* is one solution to displaying a different background color. This routine uses GET and PUT to display an inverted image over the characters you want to change. It uses *ComputeArraySize* to determine the minimum size of an array that could store the information. Then *Invert-Text* declares a dynamic array with that size, inverts the image, and erases the array from memory.

```
FUNCTION ComputeArraySize% (x1%, y1%, x2%, y2%)

',',',',',',',',',',',',',',',',',',',',',',',',',',',',',',',',',',',',',',',
'
'   Purpose:  computes the minimum size of a four-
'      byte array for storing a window with the
'      given coordinates (in screen mode 9)
'
'   Parameters:
'      x1% (in) - the leftmost x-coord of the window
'      y1% (in) - the topmost y-coord of the window
'      x2% (in) - the rightmost x-coord of the window
'      y2% (in) - the bottommost y-coord of the window
'
'
',',',',',',',',',',',',',',',',',',',',',',',',',',',',',',',',',',',',',',',',
'   compute the size based on the proper formula
ComputeArraySize% = 1 + INT((x2% - x1% + 8) / 8) * _
                                           (y2% - y1% + 1)


END FUNCTION
```

```
SUB InvertText (lin%, col%, nchars%)

',',',',',',',',',',',',',',',',',',',',',',',',',',',',',',',',',',',',',',',
'
'   Purpose:  inverts a window that contains a
'      given part of a line of text
'
'   Parameters:
'      lin% (in) - the line containing the text
'      col% (in) - the leftmost column of text
'      nchars% (in) - the number of characters
'          to invert
'
'   Other routines called:
'      ComputeArraySize% - computes the minimum
'          array size to save a window in mode 9
'
'   Local variables:
'      x1% - the leftmost x-coord of the window
'      y1% - the topmost y-coord of the window
'      x2% - the rightmost x-coord of the window
'      y2% - the bottommost y-coord of the window
'      arraysize% - the size of the window array
'      myarray!() - a temporary, dynamic array
'          containing the window contents
'
'
',',',',',',',',',',',',',',',',',',',',',',',',',',',',',',',',',',',',',',',
'   compute the corresponding graphics coordinates
x1% = col% * 8 - 8
x2% = (col% + nchars% - 1) * 8
```

```
yl% = lin% * 14 - 14
y2% = lin% * 14 - 1

arraysize% = ComputeArraySize%(x1%, y1%, x2%, y2%)

'   define a temporary array to contain the characters
'   to be inverted
' $DYNAMIC
REDIM myarray!(arraysize%)
' $STATIC

'   save the characters, then restore them inverted
GET (x1%, y1%)-(x2%, y2%), myarray!
PUT (x1%, y1%), myarray!, PRESET

'   eliminate the temporary array
ERASE myarray!

END SUB
```

Using Windows

The PLOTDATA program needs to be able to display a window of information on top of the current screen, and to restore the screen when the window is no longer needed. The *SaveGWindow* routine stores the contents of the screen where the window will go before it is displayed. Then the *RestoreGWindow* subroutine places the original screen contents over the unwanted window information. For an example of how these work together, see the next section.

```
SUB SaveGWindow (x1%, y1%, x2%, y2%)

',',',',',',',',',',',',',',',',',',',',',',',',',',',',',',',',',',',',',',',',
'
'  Purpose:  saves the contents of a portion of
'     the graphics screen in a dynamic array
'
'  Parameters:
'     x1% (in) - the leftmost x-coord of the window
'     y1% (in) - the topmost y-coord of the window
'     x2% (in) - the rightmost x-coord of the window
'     y2% (in) - the bottommost y-coord of the window
'
'  Global variables used:
'     gwindow!() - the dynamic array that holds
'        the window contents
'
'  Other routines called:
'     ComputeArraySize% - determines the size of
```

```
'            array required to save the window
'
'   Local variables:
'       arraysize% - the size required to save the
'          window
'
',',',',',',',',',',',',',',',',',',',',',',',',',',',',',',',
arraysize% = ComputeArraySize%(x1%, y1%, x2%, y2%)

'   define an array of just the right size
REDIM gwindow!(arraysize%)

'   store the window in the array
GET (x1%, y1%)-(x2%, y2%), gwindow!

END SUB
```

```
SUB RestoreGWindow (x1%, y1%)

',',',',',',',',',',',',',',',',',',',',',',',',',',',',',',
'
'   Purpose:  restores an area of the screen that
'      was saved by SaveGWindow
'
'   Parameters:
'       x1% - the leftmost x-coord of the window
'       y1% - the topmost y-coord of the window
'
'   Global variables used:
'       gwindow!() - the array containing the window
'          contents
'
'
',',',',',',',',',',',',',',',',',',',',',',',',',',',',',',',
'   restore the window
PUT (x1%, y1%), gwindow!, PSET

'   eliminate the window array
ERASE gwindow!

END SUB
```

The *SaveGWindow* and *RestoreGWindow* routines require parameters given in screen coordinates. When you want to display a text window, however, it is more convenient to use text coordinates (25 lines by 80 characters). The *SaveTextWindow* and *RestoreTextWindow* subroutines convert text coordinates to screen coordinates before calling their graphics counterparts.

```
SUB SaveTextWindow (leftcol%, topline%, rightcol%, _
                                        bottomline%)

',',',',',',',',',',',',',',',',',',',',',',',',',',',',',',',',

'
'   Purpose:  saves a window defined with text line
'      numbers and column numbers
'
'   Parameters:
'      leftcol% (in) - the left text column of window
'      topline% (in) - the top text line of window
'      rightcol% (in) - the right text column of window
'      bottomline% (in) - the bottom text line of window
'
'   Other routines called:
'      SaveGWindow - saves a window using graphics
'         coordinates
'
'   Local variables:
'      x1% - the x-coord based on the text column
'      y1% - the y-coord based on the text line
'      x2% - the rightmost x-coord of the text window
'      y2% - the bottommost y-coord of the text window
'
',',',',',',',',',',',',',',',',',',',',',',',',',',',',',',',',
'   determine the corresponding graphics coordinates
'   for each text coordinate (in mode 9)
x1% = leftcol% * 8 - 8
x2% = rightcol% * 8

y1% = topline% * 14 - 14
y2% = bottomline% * 14 - 1

'   save the window
CALL SaveGWindow(x1%, y1%, x2%, y2%)

END SUB
```

```
SUB RestoreTextWindow (leftcol%, topline%)

',',',',',',',',',',',',',',',',',',',',',',',',',',',',',',',',

'
'   Purpose:  restores a window saved by the routine
'      SaveTextWindow
'
'   Parameters:
'      leftcol% (in) - the left text column of window
'      topline% (in) - the top text line of window
'
'   Other routines called:
'      RestoreGWindow - restores a window using
'         graphics coordinates
'
```

```
'   Local variables:
'       x1% - the x-coord based on the text column
'       y1% - the y-coord based on the text line
'
',',',',',',',',',',',',',',',',',',',',',',',',',',',',',
'   determine the graphics coordinates of where the
'   window is located
x1% = leftcol% * 8 - 8
y1% = topline% * 14 - 14

'   restore the window
CALL RestoreGWindow(x1%, y1%)

END SUB
```

Other Tools

The last routines in this section are not limited to graphics programs, but are listed here because they were not used in the previous applications. You might consider including these routines in the TOOLS.BAS module from Chapter 19.

The *Smaller%* function is a simple routine that determines which of two INTEGER values is the smaller. It is placed in a subprogram because it is required by several other routines.

```
FUNCTION Smaller% (first%, second%)

',',',',',',',',',',',',',',',',',',',',',',',',',',',',
'
'   Purpose:   determines which is the smaller of
'       two numbers
'
'   Parameters:
'       first% - the first number
'       second% - the second number
'
',',',',',',',',',',',',',',',',',',',',',',',',',',',',
IF first% < second% THEN
   Smaller% = first%
ELSE
   Smaller% = second%
END IF

END FUNCTION
```

The *FindMin!* and *FindMax!* subroutines search a SINGLE array for the minimum and maximum values.

```
FUNCTION FindMax! (anyarray!(), first%, last%)

',',',',',',',',',',',',',',',',',',',',',',',',',',',',',',',',
'
'   Purpose:  determines the largest value in a
'      subset of an array
'
'   Parameters:
'      anyarray!() - the array to search
'      first% - the first element to search
'      last% - the last element to search
'
'   Local variables:
'      maximum! - the current maximum value
'      cnt% - loop counter
'
'
',',',',',',',',',',',',',',',',',',',',',',',',',',',',',',',',',
'   set max to the first element
maximum! = anyarray!(first%)

'   check the rest of the elements
FOR cnt% = first% + 1 TO last%
   IF anyarray!(cnt%) > maximum! THEN
      maximum! = anyarray!(cnt%)
   END IF
NEXT cnt%

FindMax! = maximum!

END FUNCTION
```

```
FUNCTION FindMin! (anyarray!(), first%, last%)

',',',',',',',',',',',',',',',',',',',',',',',',',',',',',',',',
'
'   Purpose:  determines the smallest value in a
'      subset of an array
'
'   Parameters:
'      anyarray!() - the array to search
'      first% - the first element to search
'      last% - the last element to search
'
'   Local variables:
'      minimum! - the current minimum value
'      cnt% - loop counter
'
'
',',',',',',',',',',',',',',',',',',',',',',',',',',',',',',',',',
'   set min to the first element
minimum! = anyarray!(first%)
```

```
'   check the rest of the elements
FOR cnt% = first% + 1 TO last%
    IF anyarray!(cnt%) < minimum! THEN
        minimum! = anyarray!(cnt%)
    END IF
NEXT cnt%

FindMin! = minimum!

END FUNCTION
```

What the PLOTDATA Program Does

Before showing you the QuickBASIC code for PLOTDATA, this section describes the capabilities of the program. It can be considered a user manual for the program.

When you start the PLOTDATA program, you will see the screen shown in Figure 21-1. Along the top line of the screen are the main program options. Pressing **D** will display the Dataset menu, **A** gives you the Axis Parameters menu, and **P** is for the

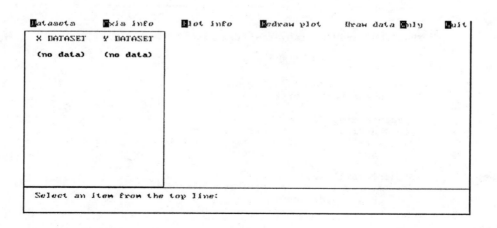

Figure 21-1.   The initial PLOTDATA screen

Plot Parameters menu. To plot the data you use **R** to draw the entire plot with the axes, and you use **O** to plot just data (for multiple-dataset plots). The final option is to use **Q** to leave the program.

The PLOTDATA screen is divided into three sections:

- The *data window* is on the left side of the screen, where the first page of data to plot is displayed.

- The *plot window* is on the right side of the screen, where the plot appears.

- The bottom two lines on the screen represent the *prompt window*, where you will see current instructions.

Loading Data

To load data into the system, you must select the D option from the top line. The Dataset menu will appear in the center of the screen, as shown in Figure 21-2. This menu allows you to load data from a file into the X dataset, the Y dataset, or both. When

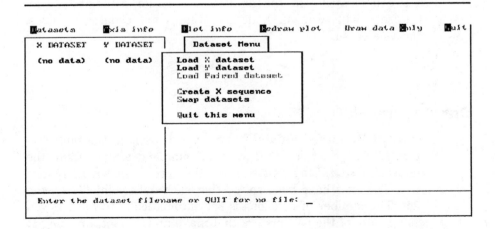

Figure 21-2.   The Dataset menu

you select any of the load options, you will be prompted for a filename. This file must contain the same number of elements as the first line. The file used as the example throughout this section, called *sample.fil,* looks like this:

```
6
1.0      34.5
2.0      33.1
3.0       5.3
4.0      67.2
5.0      50.2
6.0      20.1
```

This file contains two datasets. To load this file properly, you must select the Load Paired Dataset menu option. Once you load the file, the data window will contain the first page of each dataset.

There are two other commands on the Dataset menu. The Create X Sequence command allows you to create a dataset that contains a given sequence. You will be prompted for the first number in the dataset, the size of the dataset, and the increment between elements in the dataset. The other command, Swap Datasets, will swap all X dataset values for Y dataset values, and vice versa.

Drawing the Plot

Once you've loaded a dataset, you can draw it in the plot window. If you select the Redraw Plot command after loading the dataset in *sample.fil,* you will see the screen shown in Figure 21-3. The axes have been set so that each data point fits on the plot. The number of divisions is set automatically to four. If you change any of the parameters that make up this plot, pressing **R** will clear the current plot and redraw it using the new parameters.

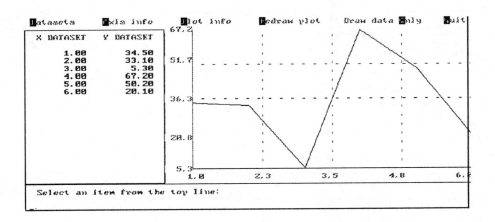

Figure 21-3.   The default plot

Changing Axis Parameters

The Axis Parameters menu, given in Figure 21-4, enables you to change the limits and divisions of both axes. The program automatically computes the values to display at each division. To make these values even integers, you can select five divisions on the x-axis, and axis limits of 0.0 and 80.0 with four divisions on the y-axis.

The Autoscale command recomputes the default axis minimums and maximums. If you load a paired dataset from the Dataset menu, these values will be computed automatically. If you go back and load a different X or Y dataset, the axis limits are not reset.

Changing Plot Parameters

The Plot Parameters menu lets you change information about the data being plotted. This menu should appear if you select P from the top line, and is shown in Figure 21-5. The first two

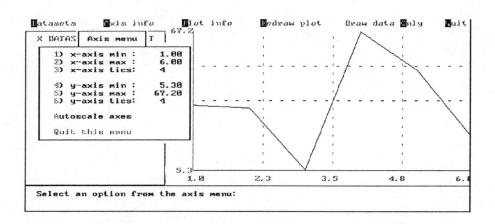

Figure 21-4.   The Axis Parameters menu

options on this menu allow you to plot only a subset of each dataset. You can select a new First Index and a new Last Index.

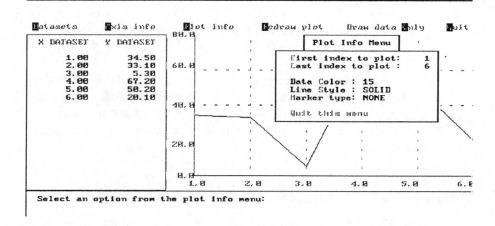

Figure 21-5.   The Plot Parameters menu

The other three options on this menu refer to the plot itself. The Data Color is the color of the data the next time you select Redraw Plot or Draw Data Only. This must be a number between 1 and 15. The Line Style option lets you switch among the following styles: solid, dotted, dashed, and none. The Marker type will draw a symbol at each data point. This type can be an X, a plus sign, a small box, or nothing.

Drawing Multiple Plots

The PLOTDATA program gives you the ability to place more than one plot on the same set of axes. To do this, you must follow this sequence:

1. Load the first set of data in the Dataset menu.

2. Select axis parameters that will fit both sets of data.

3. Select plot parameters for the first set.

4. Use Redraw to draw the first set.

5. Load the second set of data.

6. Select plot parameters for the second set.

7. Use Plot Data Only to draw the second set of data on top of the first set.

Figure 21-6 shows two sets of data on the same plot. The first set of data, from *sample.fil*, is drawn in a solid line with no marker. The second set is shown in the data window. This set is drawn with a dashed line and an X marker on each data point.

How the PLOTDATA Program Works

Now that you know what the PLOTDATA program is designed to do, you are ready to study the QuickBASIC code that makes it work.

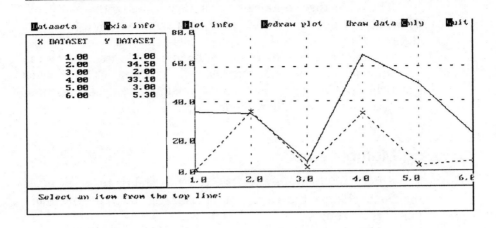

Figure 21-6. A multiple-dataset plot

Drawing the Screen

The subroutine *DrawPlotDataScreen* is called only once at the start of the program. The top menu line and the window lines are never erased during program execution. This routine calls *DisplayData* to initialize the data window display, and *Invert-Text* to highlight the command keys for the top-line menu.

```
SUB DrawPlotDataScreen

','','','','','','','','','','','','','','','','','','','','','','','
'
'   Purpose:  displays the main screen for the
'       PLOTDATA program.  Includes three windows:
'       a data window, a plot window, and a prompt
'       window.  The top line of the screen contains
'       the main menu.
'
'   Other routines called:
'       DisplayData - displays the data in the
'           data window
'       InvertText - inverts the colors of a word of
'           text on a line
'
'
','','','','','','','','','','','','','','','','','','','','','','','
```

```
'   draw the window boundaries
LINE (0, 21)-(199, 299), 7, B
LINE (0, 300)-(639, 349), 1, B
LINE (200, 21)-(639, 299), 5, B

'   initialize the data window
COLOR 3
LOCATE 3, 3
PRINT "X DATASET    Y DATASET";

CALL DisplayData(xdata!(), 0, 1)
CALL DisplayData(ydata!(), 0, 2)

'   draw the top-line menu with proper highlights
COLOR 3
LOCATE 1, 2
PRINT "Datasets      Axis info      Plot info      ";
PRINT "Redraw plot    Draw data Only    Quit";
CALL InvertText(1, 2, 1)
CALL InvertText(1, 15, 1)
CALL InvertText(1, 29, 1)
CALL InvertText(1, 43, 1)
CALL InvertText(1, 68, 1)
CALL InvertText(1, 76, 1)
END SUB
```

```
SUB DisplayData (array!(), arraysize%, side%)

','','','','','','','','','','','','','','','','','','','','
'
'   Purpose:  displays one side of the dataset window.
'      After displaying the entire array, this routine
'      blanks out the rest of the lines in the window.
'
'   Parameters:
'      array!() (in) - the array to display
'      arraysize% (in) - the size of the dataset
'      side% (in) - the side of the window to display
'         the data (1 - left, 2 - right)
'
'   Local variables:
'      col% - column to display data
'      i% - loop counter
'
'
','','','','','','','','','','','','','','','','','','','','
COLOR 7

'   set the column for display
IF side% = 1 THEN
   col% = 2
ELSE
   col% = 14
```

```
END IF

'  loop through each line in data window
FOR i% = 1 TO 17
    LOCATE i% + 4, col%

    '  if there is data, display it
    IF i% <= arraysize% THEN
        PRINT USING "###,###.##"; array!(i%);

    '  if not, clear that line
    ELSE
        PRINT SPACE$(11);
    END IF
NEXT i%

'  if array is empty, say so
IF arraysize% = 0 THEN
    LOCATE 5, col% + 1
    PRINT "(no data)"
END IF

END SUB
```

The Dataset Menu

Each time a menu is displayed, the area behind the window is saved in a temporary array by *SaveGWindow*. When the user selects the Q command from a menu, the menu disappears, and the former screen contents are replaced. This gives the impression of having pop-up menus.

The *DatasetMenu* routine is responsible for allowing the user to load data into the two datasets. If the user wants to load one dataset, this subroutine calls *LoadSingleDataset*. If the user has a file that contains both datasets, the *LoadPairedDataset* routine is called.

```
SUB DatasetMenu (xsize%, ysize%)

','','','','','','','','','','','','','','','','','','','','
'
'  Purpose:  displays the menu that allows the
'      user to enter data for plotting from a text
'      file, or create a data sequence
'
'  Parameters:
'      xsize% (out) - the size of the x dataset
'      ysize% (out) - the size of the y dataset
'
```

```
'   Global variables used:
'       xdata!() - the x-axis dataset
'       ydata!() - the y-axis dataset
'       axisinfo - the axis minimums, maximums, and
'           number of divisions
'       plotinfo - the plot start and end indices,
'           color, linestyle and markertype
'
'   Other routines called:
'       SaveTextWindow - saves the area where a menu
'           will go
'       DisplayMenu - displays a menu stored by the
'           MENUS program
'       GetMenuChoice - allows the user to select an
'           item from the menu
'       LoadSingleDataset - loads a single dataset from
'           a text file
'       DisplayDataset - displays the loaded dataset
'       LoadPairedDataset - loads a paired dataset from
'           a text file
'       GetAnyInput - inputs a string when in screen
'           mode 9
'       Smaller% - determines the smaller of two values
'       RestoreTextWindow - restores the menu area
'
'   Local variables:
'       firstline% - the first menu line
'       datachoice$ - menu item selected by user
'       tempstr$ - a temporary string
'       cnt% - loop counter
'       firstval! - first data value in a created sequence
'       incr! - increment for the created sequence
'
'
',',',',',',',',',',',',',',',',',',',',',',',',',',',',',',',',',',
SHARED datamenu AS MenuInfoRec, dataitems() AS MenuItemsRec

'   save the window and display the menu
LOCATE 24, 3: PRINT SPACE$(60);
CALL SaveTextWindow(datamenu.leftcol, datamenu.topline - 2, _
 datamenu.rightcol, datamenu.topline + datamenu.numitems + 1)
CALL DisplayMenu(datamenu, dataitems())

'   get a menu choice from the user
datachoice$ = "Q"
DO
    LOCATE 23, 3: PRINT SPACE$(60);

    LOCATE 23, 3: COLOR 7
    PRINT "Select an option from the dataset menu: ";

    CALL GetMenuChoice(datamenu, dataitems(), datachoice$, _
                                                    dummy%)
    LOCATE 23, 3: PRINT SPACE$(60);

    SELECT CASE datachoice$
```

```
'   allow user to enter new X dataset
CASE "X"
   CALL LoadSingleDataset(xdata!(), xsize%)
   plotinfo.last = Smaller%(xsize%, ysize%)
   CALL DisplayData(xdata!(), xsize%, 1)

'   allow user to enter new Y dataset
CASE "Y"
   CALL LoadSingleDataset(ydata!(), ysize%)
   plotinfo.last = Smaller%(xsize%, ysize%)
   CALL DisplayData(ydata!(), ysize%, 2)

'    allow user to enter new paired dataset
CASE "P"
   CALL LoadPairedDataset(xsize%, ysize%)
   CALL DisplayData(xdata!(), xsize%, 1)
   CALL DisplayData(ydata!(), ysize%, 2)

'    allow user to create a sequence
CASE "C"

   '   get first value, increment, number of values
   LOCATE 23, 3: COLOR 3
   PRINT "Enter first value: ";
   CALL GetAnyInput(tempstr$, 8)
   firstval! = VAL(tempstr$)
   LOCATE 23, 3
   PRINT "Enter number of values: ";
   CALL GetAnyInput(tempstr$, 4)
   xsize% = VAL(tempstr$)
   LOCATE 23, 3
   PRINT "Enter constant increment:   ";
   CALL GetAnyInput(tempstr$, 8)
   incr! = VAL(tempstr$)

   '   create the new dataset
   ERASE xdata!
   REDIM xdata!(xsize%)
   FOR cnt% = 1 TO xsize%
      xdata!(cnt%) = firstval! + (cnt% - 1) * incr!
   NEXT cnt%
   CALL DisplayData(xdata!(), xsize%, 1)

'   allow user to swap the datasets
CASE "S"
   IF xsize% <> ysize% THEN
      LOCATE 24, 3: COLOR 14
      PRINT "You cannot swap different size datasets!";
      BEEP

   ELSE
      FOR cnt% = 1 TO xsize%
         temp! = xdata!(cnt%)
         xdata!(cnt%) = ydata!(cnt%)
         ydata!(cnt%) = temp!
```

```
             NEXT cnt%
             temp! = axisinfo.xmin
             axisinfo.xmin = axisinfo.ymin
             axisinfo.ymin = temp!
             temp! = axisinfo.xmax
             axisinfo.xmax = axisinfo.ymax
             axisinfo.ymax = temp!
             temp! = axisinfo.xdivs
             axisinfo.xdivs = axisinfo.ydivs
             axisinfo.ydivs = temp!
             CALL DisplayData(xdata!(), xsize%, 1)
             CALL DisplayData(ydata!(), ysize%, 2)
          END IF

       CASE ELSE

    END SELECT

LOOP UNTIL datachoice$ = "Q"

CALL RestoreTextWindow(datamenu.leftcol, datamenu.topline - 2)

END SUB


────────────────────────────────────────────────────


SUB LoadPairedDataset (xsize%, ysize%)

','','','','','','','','','','','','','','','','','','','','','
'
'   Purpose:  loads a paired dataset from a text
'      file.  The first line of the file must
'      contain the number of array elements.
'
'   Parameters:
'      xsize% (out) - the size of the x dataset
'      ysize% (out) - the size of the y dataset
'
'   Global variables used:
'      xdata!() - the x-axis dataset
'      ydata!() - the y-axis dataset
'      axisinfo - the axis minimums, maximums, and
'         number of divisions
'      plotinfo - the plot start and end indices,
'         color, linestyle and markertype
'      axesrescaled% - determines if the user can use
'         the Plot Data Only command
'      badopen% - set by error handler
'
'   Other routines called:
'      GetAnyInput - gets a fixed-length string
'         from the user
'
'   Local variables:
'      datafile% - the number of the text file
```

```
'       filename$ - the name of the text file
'       cnt% - loop counter
'
',',',',',',',',',',',',',',',',',',',',',',',',',',',',',',','
'  get a filename from the user
DO

    LOCATE 23, 3: COLOR 3
    PRINT "Enter the dataset filename or QUIT for no file: ";
    CALL GetAnyInput(filename$, 12)

    '  allow the user to get out without loading anything
    IF filename$ = "QUIT" THEN EXIT SUB

    datafile% = FREEFILE

    '  attempt to open the file
    ON ERROR GOTO OpenError
    badopen% = False%

    OPEN filename$ FOR INPUT AS #datafile%
    ON ERROR GOTO 0

    '  if open unsuccessful, try again
    IF badopen% THEN
        LOCATE 24, 3: COLOR 14
        PRINT "Error opening file.   ";
        PRINT "Please enter another filename!";
    END IF
LOOP WHILE badopen%

LOCATE 24, 3: PRINT SPACE$(60);

'  define new arrays and load the datasets
INPUT #datafile%, xsize%
ysize% = xsize%
ERASE xdata!, ydata!
REDIM xdata!(xsize%), ydata!(ysize%)

FOR cnt% = 1 TO xsize%
    INPUT #datafile%, xdata!(cnt%), ydata!(cnt%)
NEXT cnt%

'  set the appropriate default values
axisinfo.xmin = FindMin!(xdata!(), 1, xsize%)
axisinfo.xmax = FindMax!(xdata!(), 1, xsize%)
axisinfo.ymin = FindMin!(ydata!(), 1, ysize%)
axisinfo.ymax = FindMax!(ydata!(), 1, ysize%)
axesrescaled% = True%

plotinfo.first = 1
plotinfo.last = xsize%

CLOSE #datafile%

END SUB
```

```
SUB LoadSingleDataset (anyarray!(), arraysize%)

',',',',',',',',',',',',',',',',',',',',',',',',',',',',',',',',',',',',
'
'  Purpose:  loads a single dataset from a text
'     file.  The first line of the file must
'     contain the number of array elements.
'
'  Parameters:
'     anyarray!() - the dataset being loaded
'     arraysize% (out) - the size of the dataset
'
'  Global variables used:
'     badopen% - set by error handler
'
'  Other routines called:
'     GetAnyInput - gets a fixed-length string
'        from the user
'
'  Local variables:
'     datafile% - the number of the text file
'     filename$ - the name of the text file
'     cnt% - loop counter
'
'
',',',',',',',',',',',',',',',',',',',',',',',',',',',',',',',',',',',
'  get a valid filename from the user
DO

    LOCATE 23, 3
    COLOR 3
    PRINT "Enter the dataset filename or QUIT for no file: ";
    CALL GetAnyInput(filename$, 12)

    '  allow the user to quit without loading
    IF filename$ = "QUIT" THEN EXIT SUB

    datafile% = FREEFILE

    '  attempt to open the file
    ON ERROR GOTO OpenError
    badopen% = False%

    OPEN filename$ FOR INPUT AS #datafile%
    ON ERROR GOTO 0

    '  if open failed, get a new filename
    IF badopen% THEN
        LOCATE 24, 3: COLOR 14
        PRINT "Error opening file.  ";
        PRINT "Please enter another filename!";
    END IF
LOOP WHILE badopen%
```

```
LOCATE 24, 3: PRINT SPACE$(60);

'   define a new array and load it
INPUT #datafile%, arraysize%
ERASE anyarray!
REDIM anyarray!(arraysize%)

FOR cnt% = 1 TO arraysize%
   INPUT #datafile%, anyarray!(cnt%)
NEXT cnt%

CLOSE #datafile%

END SUB
```

The Axis Menu

The subroutine *AxisParametersMenu* displays the menu that allows the axis limits and divisions to be changed. If the user wants the axes scaled automatically, this routine calls the functions *FindMin!* and *FindMax!* to determine the new default values.

```
SUB AxisParametersMenu (xsize%, ysize%)

',',',',',',',',',',',',',',',',',',',',',',',',',',',',',',',',',',',',',',',',','
'
'   Purpose:  displays a menu that allows the user
'      to alter axis parameters:  minimum, maximum,
'      and number of divisions for each axis.  Also
'      included is the ability to "autoscale" the
'      axes by searching for the minimum and maximum
'      values in the arrays.
'
'   Parameters:
'      xsize% (in) - the size of the x dataset
'      ysize% (in) - the size of the y dataset
'
'   Global variables used:
'      xdata!() - the x-axis dataset
'      ydata!() - the y-axis dataset
'      axisinfo - the axis minimums, maximums, and
'         number of divisions
'      plotinfo - the plot start and end indices,
'         color, linestyle and markertype
'
'   Other routines called:
'      SaveTextWindow - saves the area where a menu
'         will go
'      DisplayMenu - displays a menu stored by the
'         MENUS program
```

```
'       GetMenuChoice - allows the user to select an
'           item from the menu
'       GetAnyInput - inputs a string when in screen
'           mode 9
'       FindMin! - finds the minimum value in an array
'       FindMax! - finds the maximum value in an array
'       Smaller% - determines the smaller of two values
'       RestoreTextWindow - restores the menu area
'
'   Local variables:
'       firstline% - the first menu line
'       axischoice$ - menu item selected by user
'       tempstr$ - a temporary string
'
',',',',',',',',',',',',',',',',',',',',',',',',',',',',',',',
SHARED axismenu AS MenuInfoRec, axisitems() AS MenuItemsRec

'   save the window and display the menu
LOCATE 24, 3: PRINT SPACE$(60);
CALL SaveTextWindow(axismenu.leftcol, axismenu.topline - 2, _
 axismenu.rightcol, axismenu.topline + axismenu.numitems + 1)
CALL DisplayMenu(axismenu, axisitems())

'   display data on the menu
firstline% = axismenu.topline
LOCATE firstline% + 1, 21
PRINT USING "#####.##"; axisinfo.xmin
LOCATE firstline% + 2, 21
PRINT USING "#####.##"; axisinfo.xmax
LOCATE firstline% + 3, 21
PRINT USING "#####"; axisinfo.xdivs
LOCATE firstline% + 5, 21
PRINT USING "#####.##"; axisinfo.ymin
LOCATE firstline% + 6, 21
PRINT USING "#####.##"; axisinfo.ymax
LOCATE firstline% + 7, 21
PRINT USING "#####"; axisinfo.ydivs

'   get a choice from the user
axischoice$ = "Q"
DO
    LOCATE 23, 3: PRINT SPACE$(60);
    LOCATE 23, 3: COLOR 7
    PRINT "Select an option from the axis menu: ";
    CALL GetMenuChoice(axismenu, axisitems(), axischoice$, _
                                                    dummy%)
    LOCATE 23, 3: PRINT SPACE$(60);

    SELECT CASE axischoice$

        '   allow user to change x-axis minimum
        CASE "1"
            LOCATE 23, 3
            PRINT "Enter the new x-axis minimum value  : "
            LOCATE firstline% + 1, 21
            CALL GetAnyInput(tempstr$, 8)
```

```
      IF tempstr$ <> "" THEN
         axisinfo.xmin = VAL(tempstr$)
      END IF

      LOCATE firstline% + 1, 21
      PRINT USING "#####.##"; axisinfo.xmin

'  allow user to change x-axis maximum
CASE "2"
      LOCATE 23, 3
      PRINT "Enter the new x-axis maximum value  : "
      LOCATE firstline% + 2, 21
      CALL GetAnyInput(tempstr$, 8)
      IF tempstr$ <> "" THEN
         axisinfo.xmax = VAL(tempstr$)
      END IF

      LOCATE firstline% + 2, 21
      PRINT USING "#####.##"; axisinfo.xmax

'  allow user to change number of x-axis divisions
CASE "3"
      LOCATE 23, 3
      PRINT "Enter the number of x-axis divisions: "
      LOCATE firstline% + 3, 21
      CALL GetAnyInput(tempstr$, 2)
      IF tempstr$ <> "" THEN
         axisinfo.xdivs = VAL(tempstr$)
      END IF

      LOCATE firstline% + 3, 21
      PRINT USING "#####"; axisinfo.xdivs

'  allow user to change y-axis minimum
CASE "4"
      LOCATE 23, 3
      PRINT "Enter the new y-axis minimum value  : "
      LOCATE firstline% + 5, 21
      CALL GetAnyInput(tempstr$, 8)
      IF tempstr$ <> "" THEN
         axisinfo.ymin = VAL(tempstr$)
      END IF

      LOCATE firstline% + 5, 21
      PRINT USING "#####.##"; axisinfo.ymin

'  allow user to change y-axis maximum
CASE "5"
      LOCATE 23, 3
      PRINT "Enter the new y-axis maximum value  : "
      LOCATE firstline% + 6, 21
      CALL GetAnyInput(tempstr$, 8)
      IF tempstr$ <> "" THEN
         axisinfo.ymax = VAL(tempstr$)
      END IF
```

```
                    LOCATE firstline% + 6, 21
                    PRINT USING "#####.##"; axisinfo.ymax

             '   allow user to change number of y-axis divisions
             CASE "6"
                    LOCATE 23, 3
                    PRINT "Enter the number of y-axis divisions: "
                    LOCATE firstline% + 7, 21
                    CALL GetAnyInput(tempstr$, 2)
                    IF tempstr$ <> "" THEN
                        axisinfo.ydivs = VAL(tempstr$)
                    END IF

                    LOCATE firstline% + 7, 21
                    PRINT USING "#####"; axisinfo.ydivs

             '   autoscale both axes
             CASE "A"
                    axisinfo.xmin = FindMin!(xdata!(), 1, xsize%)
                    axisinfo.xmax = FindMax!(xdata!(), 1, xsize%)
                    axisinfo.ymin = FindMin!(ydata!(), 1, ysize%)
                    axisinfo.ymax = FindMax!(ydata!(), 1, ysize%)
                    axesrescaled% = True%
                    plotinfo.first = 1
                    plotinfo.last = Smaller%(xsize%, ysize%)
                    LOCATE firstline% + 1, 21
                    PRINT USING "#####.##"; axisinfo.xmin
                    LOCATE firstline% + 2, 21
                    PRINT USING "#####.##"; axisinfo.xmax
                    LOCATE firstline% + 5, 21
                    PRINT USING "#####.##"; axisinfo.ymin
                    LOCATE firstline% + 6, 21
                    PRINT USING "#####.##"; axisinfo.ymax

           CASE ELSE

        END SELECT

   LOOP UNTIL axischoice$ = "Q"

   CALL RestoreTextWindow(axismenu.leftcol, axismenu.topline - 2)

   END SUB
```

The Plot Menu

When the user needs to change plotting parameters, PLOT-DATA calls the subroutine *PlotParametersMenu*. One interesting part of this routine is the code that changes line styles and marker types. When the user selects the Line Style option, the style automatically moves to the next style in the list. The user is never allowed to type the name of the line style. This method has the dual purpose of saving the user keystrokes and preventing the user from making a mistake.

```
SUB PlotParametersMenu (xsize%, ysize%)

','','','','','','','','','','','','','','','','','','','','','','
'
'  Purpose:  displays the menu that allows the
'      user to limit the data to a subset, and to
'      change the color, line style, and marker
'      type of the data to plot
'
'  Parameters:
'      xsize% (in) - the size of the x dataset
'      ysize% (in) - the size of the y dataset
'
'  Global variables used:
'      xdata!() - the x-axis dataset
'      ydata!() - the y-axis dataset
'      axisinfo - the axis minimums, maximums, and
'          number of divisions
'      plotinfo - the plot start and end indices,
'          color, linestyle and markertype
'
'  Other routines called:
'      SaveTextWindow - saves the area where a menu
'          will go
'      DisplayMenu - displays a menu stored by the
'          MENUS program
'      GetMenuChoice - allows the user to select an
'          item from the menu
'      GetAnyInput - inputs a string when in screen
'          mode 9
'      RestoreTextWindow - restores the menu area
'
'  Local variables:
'      firstline% - the first menu line
'      plotchoice$ - menu item selected by user
'      tempstr$ - a temporary string
'
'
','','','','','','','','','','','','','','','','','','','','','','
SHARED plotmenu AS MenuInfoRec, plotitems() AS MenuItemsRec

'  save the window and draw the menu
LOCATE 24, 3: PRINT SPACE$(60);
CALL SaveTextWindow(plotmenu.leftcol, plotmenu.topline - 2, _
  plotmenu.rightcol, plotmenu.topline + plotmenu.numitems + 1)
CALL DisplayMenu(plotmenu, plotitems())

'  display the data user can change with this menu
firstline% = plotmenu.topline
LOCATE firstline% + 1, 69
```

```
            PRINT USING "####"; plotinfo.first
            LOCATE firstline% + 2, 69
            PRINT USING "####"; plotinfo.last
            LOCATE firstline% + 4, 61
            PRINT USING "##"; plotinfo.colr
            LOCATE firstline% + 5, 61
            PRINT plotinfo.style
            LOCATE firstline% + 6, 61
            PRINT plotinfo.marker

        '   get a menu choice from the user
        plotchoice$ = "Q"
        DO
            LOCATE 23, 3: PRINT SPACE$(60);
            LOCATE 23, 3: COLOR 7
            PRINT "Select an option from the plot info menu: ";

            CALL GetMenuChoice(plotmenu, plotitems(), plotchoice$, _
                                                        dummy%)

            LOCATE 23, 3: PRINT SPACE$(60);

            SELECT CASE plotchoice$

                '   allow user to change first element plotted
                CASE "F"
                    LOCATE 23, 3
                    PRINT "Enter the first element number to plot: "
                    LOCATE firstline% + 1, 69
                    CALL GetAnyInput(tempstr$, 4)
                    IF tempstr$ <> "" THEN
                        plotinfo.first = VAL(tempstr$)
                    END IF

                    LOCATE firstline% + 1, 69
                    PRINT USING "####"; plotinfo.first

                '   allow user to change last element plotted
                CASE "L"
                    LOCATE 23, 3
                    PRINT "Enter the last element number to plot: "
                    LOCATE firstline% + 2, 69
                    CALL GetAnyInput(tempstr$, 4)
                    IF tempstr$ <> "" THEN
                        plotinfo.last = VAL(tempstr$)
                    END IF

                    LOCATE firstline% + 2, 69
                    PRINT USING "####"; plotinfo.last

                '   allow user to change data color
                CASE "C"
                    LOCATE 23, 3
                    PRINT "Enter the color to plot the data: "
                    LOCATE firstline% + 4, 61
                    CALL GetAnyInput(tempstr$, 2)
                    IF tempstr$ <> "" THEN
```

```
            plotinfo.colr = VAL(tempstr$)
         END IF

         LOCATE firstline% + 4, 61
         PRINT USING "##"; plotinfo.colr

    '    allow user to toggle through line styles
    CASE "S"
         SELECT CASE plotinfo.style
            CASE "SOLID "
               plotinfo.style = "DOTTED"
            CASE "DOTTED"
               plotinfo.style = "DASHED"
            CASE "DASHED"
               plotinfo.style = "NONE  "
            CASE ELSE
               plotinfo.style = "SOLID "
         END SELECT

         LOCATE firstline% + 5, 61
         PRINT plotinfo.style

    '    allow user to toggle through marker types
    CASE "M"
         SELECT CASE plotinfo.marker
            CASE "NONE  "
               plotinfo.marker = "X     "
            CASE "X     "
               plotinfo.marker = "PLUS  "
            CASE "PLUS  "
               plotinfo.marker = "BOX   "
            CASE ELSE
               plotinfo.marker = "NONE  "
         END SELECT

         LOCATE firstline% + 6, 61
         PRINT plotinfo.marker

    CASE ELSE

  END SELECT

LOOP UNTIL plotchoice$ = "Q"

CALL RestoreTextWindow(plotmenu.leftcol, plotmenu.topline - 2)

END SUB
```

Drawing the Plot

Three routines are used to draw the plot on the screen: *Label-Axes*, *DrawAxes*, and *DrawPlot*. The *LabelAxes* routine places the text labels on the plot. Because there are only 25 lines on the screen, a text line may not match up directly to a division mark. *LabelAxes* makes sure that the label goes on the closest line. The numbers are displayed to the nearest tenth due to space limitations.

```
SUB LabelAxes

',',',',',',',',',',',',',',',',',',',',',',',',',',',',',',',',',',',',',',',',',',',',',',',',',',',',',',',',','
'
'    Purpose:  places text labels on both axes with
'        values for each division.  Label locations
'        are estimated to the nearest line number or
'        column number.
'
'    Global variables used:
'        axisinfo - the axis minimums, maximums, and
'            number of divisions
'
'    Local variables:
'        topy% - the top line that can contain a label
'        bottomy% - the bottom line that can have a label
'        yval! - the current y-axis division value
'        ydiff! - the size of each y-axis division
'        leftcol% - the left column that can contain
'            a label
'        rightcol% - the rightmost column that can
'            have a label
'        xval! - the current x-axis division value
'        xdiff! - the size of each x-axis division
'
'
',',',',',',',',',',',',',',',',',',',',',',',',',',',',',',',',',',',',',',',',',',',',',',',',',',',','
topy% = 2
bottomy% = 20

'   label each y-axis division
yval! = axisinfo.ymin
ydiff! = (axisinfo.ymax - axisinfo.ymin) / axisinfo.ydivs

FOR cnt% = 0 TO axisinfo.ydivs

    '   find the nearest line to the division boundary
    labelline% = bottomy% - (bottomy% - topy%) * cnt% / _
                                        axisinfo.ydivs
    LOCATE labelline%, 26
    PRINT USING "###.#"; yval!
    yval! = yval! + ydiff!
NEXT cnt%

leftcol% = 28
rightcol% = 76

'   label each x-axis division
xval! = axisinfo.xmin
```

```
xdiff! = (axisinfo.xmax - axisinfo.xmin) / axisinfo.xdivs

FOR cnt% = 0 TO axisinfo.xdivs

    ' find the nearest column to the division boundary
    labelcol% = leftcol% + (rightcol% - leftcol%) * cnt% / _
                                         axisinfo.xdivs
    LOCATE 21, labelcol%
    PRINT USING "###.#"; xval!
    xval! = xval! + xdiff!
NEXT cnt%

END SUB
```

The *DrawAxes* routine draws the dotted lines that separate the divisions on the plot. The subroutine creates a temporary viewport and window, so that the axes limits match the world-coordinate system. This allows QuickBASIC to do the mapping for you. The window and viewport are restored at the end of the routine to allow graphics I/O on other areas of the screen.

```
SUB DrawAxes

',',',',',',',',',',',',',',',',',',',',',',',',',',',',',',','
'
' Purpose:  draws the axes of the plot on the
'     screen, including the dotted lines for the
'     divisions
'
' Global variables used:
'     axisrescaled% - determines whether the user
'         can use the Plot Data Only command
'     axisinfo - the axis minimums, maximums, and
'         number of divisions
'
' Other routines called:
'     LabelAxes - places numeric labels at each
'         division on each axis
'
' Local variables:
'     xval! - the x-coord for an x-axis division
'     xdiff! - the distance between x-axis divisions
'     yval! - the y-coord for an y-axis division
'     ydiff! - the distance between y-axis divisions
'
'
',',',',',',',',',',',',',',',',',',',',',',',',',',',',',',',','
axesrescaled% = False%

' clear the area and draw a border
LINE (200, 21)-(639, 299), 0, BF
LINE (200, 21)-(639, 299), 5, B
```

```
'   label the axes
CALL LabelAxes

'   create a window and viewport for the data area
VIEW (241, 22)-(638, 271), 0, 5
WINDOW (axisinfo.xmin, axisinfo.ymin)-(axisinfo.xmax, _
                                       axisinfo.ymax)

'   draw a dotted line up from each x-axis division
xval! = axisinfo.xmin
xdiff! = (axisinfo.xmax - axisinfo.xmin) / axisinfo.xdivs
FOR cnt% = 1 TO axisinfo.xdivs - 1
    xval! = xval! + xdiff!
    LINE (xval!, axisinfo.ymin)-
    (xval!, axisinfo.ymax), 5,, &HF
NEXT cnt%

'   draw a dotted line across each y-axis division
yval! = axisinfo.ymin
ydiff! = (axisinfo.ymax - axisinfo.ymin) / axisinfo.ydivs
FOR cnt% = 1 TO axisinfo.ydivs - 1
    yval! = yval! + ydiff!
    LINE (axisinfo.xmin, yval!)-
    (axisinfo.xmax, yval!), 5,, &HF
NEXT cnt%

'   restore the window and viewport
WINDOW
VIEW

END SUB
```

When the *DrawPlot* subroutine is called to draw the data, it must first set the line styles and marker types based on the user input. The QuickBASIC LINE and DRAW statements take care of the rest automatically.

```
SUB DrawPlot

',',',',',',',',',',',',',',',',',',',',',',',',',',',',',',','
'
'   Purpose:  draws the lines and markers for the
'       current datasets.  This routine can be
'       called alone, or just after a call to
'       DrawAxes.
'
'   Global variables used:
'       xdata!() - the x-axis dataset
'       ydata!() - the y-axis dataset
'       axisinfo - the axis minimums, maximums, and
'           number of divisions
'       plotinfo - the plot start and end indices,
```

```
'           color, linestyle and markertype
'
'  Local variables:
'      cnt% - loop counter
'      linestyle% - the line style to draw the data with
'      drawstr$ - the DRAW macro for displaying a marker
'
',',',',',',',',',',',',',',',',',',',',',',',',',',',',',',',',',',
'  define the proper window and viewport
VIEW (241, 22)-(638, 271)
WINDOW (axisinfo.xmin, axisinfo.ymin)-(axisinfo.xmax, _
                                        axisinfo.ymax)


'  determine the proper line style
SELECT CASE plotinfo.style
   CASE "SOLID "
      linestyle% = &HFFFF
   CASE "DOTTED"
      linestyle% = &H303
   CASE "DASHED"
      linestyle% = &HFOFO
   CASE "NONE  "
      linestyle% = 0
END SELECT

'  draw each line
FOR cnt% = plotinfo.first TO plotinfo.last - 1
   LINE (xdata!(cnt%), ydata!(cnt%))-(xdata!(cnt% + 1), _
            ydata!(cnt% + 1)), plotinfo.colr, , linestyle%
NEXT cnt%

'  determine the proper marker type
SELECT CASE plotinfo.marker
   CASE "X     "
      drawstr$ = "NE3 NF3 NG3 NH3"
   CASE "PLUS  "
      drawstr$ = "NU3 NL3 ND3 NR3"
   CASE "BOX   "
      drawstr$ = "BH2 R4 D4 L4 U4 BF2"
   CASE ELSE
      drawstr$ = "BNU0"
END SELECT

'  draw each marker
FOR cnt% = plotinfo.first TO plotinfo.last
   PSET (xdata!(cnt%), ydata!(cnt%)), plotinfo.colr
   DRAW drawstr$
NEXT cnt%

'  restore the window and viewport
WINDOW
VIEW

END SUB
```

The Main Program

The main program, PLOTDATA.BAS, is essentially a menu driver. It calls the appropriate subroutine based on the menu selection from the top-line menu. It also has the mundane job of declaring all records, global variables, and menus.

```
DECLARE SUB DrawPlotDataScreen ()
DECLARE SUB AxisParametersMenu (xsize%, ysize%)
DECLARE SUB DrawPlot ()
DECLARE SUB PlotParametersMenu (xsize%, ysize%)
DECLARE SUB DrawAxes ()
DECLARE SUB LoadSingleDataset (anyarray!(), arraysize%)
DECLARE SUB LabelAxes ()
DECLARE SUB LoadPairedDataset (xsize%, ysize%)
DECLARE SUB DisplayData (array!(), arraysize%, side%)
DECLARE SUB DatasetMenu (xsize%, ysize%)
DECLARE SUB GetAnyInput (instr$, maxlen%)
DECLARE SUB SaveTextWindow (leftcol%, topline%, rightcol%, _
                                          bottomline%)
DECLARE SUB RestoreTextWindow (leftcol%, topline%)
DECLARE SUB InvertText (lin%, col%, nchars%)
DECLARE FUNCTION FindMin! (anyarray!(), first%, last%)
DECLARE FUNCTION FindMax! (anyarray!(), first%, last%)
DECLARE FUNCTION Smaller% (first%, second%)

',',',',',',',',',',',',',',',',',',',',',',',',',',',',',',',',',',',',',',',',',',',',',',
'
'  Program:  PLOTDATA.BAS
'
'  Purpose:  allows the user to display numerical
'     data on a line graph.  The user can alter the
'     axes definitions as well as line style, data
'     color, and other parameters.  User can plot
'     more than one dataset on the same graph.
'
'  Primary global variables:
'     xdata!() - the x-axis dataset
'     ydata!() - the y-axis dataset
'     axisinfo - the axis minimums, maximums, and
'        number of divisions
'     plotinfo - the plot start and end indices,
'        color, linestyle and markertype
'
'  Other routines called:
'     LoadMenu - loads a menu from a file created
'        by the MENUS program
'     DrawPlotDataScreen - draws the screen for
'        this program
'     DatasetMenu - displays menu for allowing user
'        to change the datasets
'     AxisParametersMenu - displays menu for
'        allowing user to change axis parameters
```

```
'       PlotParametersMenu - displays menu for
'          allowing user to change plot parameters
'       DrawAxes - draws the axes and labels
'       DrawPlot - draws the dataset lines and markers
'
'   Local variables:
'       onechar$ - the key pressed by user
'
'
',',',',',',',',',',',',',',',',',',',',',',',',',',',',',',',',

'  $INCLUDE: 'TOOLS.INC'

'  $DYNAMIC
DIM SHARED gwindow!(10), xdata!(10), ydata!(10)
ERASE gwindow!
'  $STATIC

DIM datamenu AS MenuInfoRec, dataitems(10) AS MenuItemsRec
DIM axismenu AS MenuInfoRec, axisitems(10) AS MenuItemsRec
DIM plotmenu AS MenuInfoRec, plotitems(10) AS MenuItemsRec

TYPE AxisRec
    xmin AS SINGLE
    xmax AS SINGLE
    xdivs AS INTEGER
    ymin AS SINGLE
    ymax AS SINGLE
    ydivs AS INTEGER
END TYPE

TYPE PlotRec
    first AS INTEGER
    last AS INTEGER
    colr AS INTEGER
    style AS STRING * 6
    marker AS STRING * 6
END TYPE

DIM SHARED axisinfo AS AxisRec
DIM SHARED plotinfo AS PlotRec
DIM SHARED badopen%
DIM SHARED axesrescaled%

',',',',',',',',',' executable code starts here  ',',',',',',',',',',

'  set initial default values
axisinfo.xdivs = 4
axisinfo.ydivs = 4

plotinfo.first = 1
plotinfo.last = 0
plotinfo.colr = 15
plotinfo.style = "SOLID"
plotinfo.marker = "NONE"
```

```
axesrescaled% = True%

SCREEN 9

'   load the menus
CALL LoadMenu(datamenu, dataitems(), "dataset.mnu")
CALL LoadMenu(axismenu, axisitems(), "axis.mnu")
CALL LoadMenu(plotmenu, plotitems(), "plotinfo.mnu")

CALL DrawPlotDataScreen

'   get a menu selection from the user
DO
    LOCATE 23, 3: COLOR 3
    PRINT "Select an item from the top line: ";

    DO
        onechar$ = UCASE$(INKEY$)
    LOOP WHILE onechar$ = ""
    LOCATE 24, 3: PRINT SPACE$(60);

    SELECT CASE onechar$

        'dataset menu
        CASE "D"
            CALL DatasetMenu(xsize%, ysize%)

        'axis info menu
        CASE "A"
            CALL AxisParametersMenu(xsize%, ysize%)

        'plot info menu
        CASE "P"
            CALL PlotParametersMenu(xsize%, ysize%)

        'redraw plot
        CASE "R"
            IF plotinfo.last = 0 THEN
                LOCATE 24, 3: COLOR 14
                PRINT "You have no data to plot!";
                BEEP

            ELSE
                CALL DrawAxes
                CALL DrawPlot
            END IF

        'draw data only
        CASE "O"
            IF plotinfo.last = 0 THEN
                LOCATE 24, 3: COLOR 14
                PRINT "You have no data to plot!";
                BEEP

            ELSEIF axesrescaled% THEN
                LOCATE 24, 3: COLOR 14
```

```
           PRINT "Axes are improperly scaled!";
           BEEP
       ELSE
           CALL DrawPlot
       END IF

   CASE "Q"

   CASE ELSE
       BEEP

   END SELECT

LOOP UNTIL onechar$ = "Q"

END

'  error for LoadPairedDataset and LoadSingleDataset
OpenError:
   badopen% = True%
   RESUME NEXT
```

Possible Enhancements

This program is really a skeleton for you to adapt to fit your particular application. There are hundreds of different things you could do to enhance the program. Here are just a few:

• Create a command that erases the screen and draws only the plot in the center of the screen. Then copy the screen contents to a file for later retrieval for presentations.

• Allow the user to edit individual dataset elements. The user could page through the data window, and then alter specific elements. The new dataset could be saved to a file.

• Save the last set of axis parameters and plot parameters in a file, and load these as defaults during the next session. This way the user does not have to reset these each time.

• Allow the x-axis dataset to be string data. This data would act as labels along the x-axis. The y-axis data would be spaced evenly across the plot. A typical example might be the months of the year.

• QuickBASIC is in desperate need of a graphics text font that could be written at any angle. If you wrote such a font, along with the supporting software, you could label the axes or tilt the axis labels at an angle.

Appendixes

This part contains a few lists and tables that you will need to reference fairly often. They are grouped here in the back of the book so you can find them more easily.

Appendix A is the list of reserved words. Use this list when the QuickBASIC editor disallows a variable name. If a word is in this list, you cannot use it as a procedure or variable name.

Appendix B contains the table of ASCII codes. These codes are especially useful when you need to display a special character, such as a musical note or a happy face.

Appendix C includes all of the keyboard scan codes. You will need these tables when you want to process special input, such as arrow keys and function keys.

QuickBASIC Reserved Words

ABS	CLEAR
ACCESS	CLNG
ALIAS	CLOSE
AND	CLS
ANY	COLOR
APPEND	COM
AS	COMMAND$
ASC	COMMON
ATN	CONST
BASE	COS
BEEP	CSNG
BINARY	CSRLIN
BLOAD	CVD
BSAVE	CVDMBF
BYVAL	CVI
CALL	CVL
CALLS	CVS
CASE	CVSMBF
CDBL	DATA
CDECL	DATE$
CHAIN	DECLARE
CHDIR	DEF
CHR$	DEFDBL
CINT	DEFINT
CIRCLE	DEFLNG

DEFSNG	INPUT$
DEFSTR	INSTR
DIM	INT
DO	INTEGER
DOUBLE	IOCTL
DRAW	IOCTL$
ELSE	IS
ELSEIF	KEY
END	KILL
ENDIF	LBOUND
ENVIRON	LCASE$
ENVIRON$	LEFT$
EOF	LEN
EQV	LET
ERASE	LINE
ERDEV	LOC
ERDEV$	LOCAL
ERL	LOCATE
ERR	LOCK
ERROR	LOF
EXIT	LOG
EXP	LONG
FIELD	LOOP
FILEATTR	LPOS
FILES	LPRINT
FIX	LSET
FOR	LTRIM$
FRE	MID$
FREEFILE	MKD$
FUNCTION	MKDIR
GET	MKDMBF$
GOSUB	MKI$
GOTO	MKL$
HEX$	MKS$
IF	MKSMBF$
IMP	MOD
INKEY$	NAME
INP	NEXT
INPUT	NOT

OCT$	SEEK
OFF	SELECT
ON	SETMEM
OPEN	SGN
OPTION	SHARED
OR	SHELL
OUT	SIGNAL
OUTPUT	SIN
PAINT	SINGLE
PALETTE	SLEEP
PCOPY	SOUND
PEEK	SPACE$
PEN	SPC
PLAY	SQR
PMAP	STATIC
POINT	STEP
POKE	STICK
POS	STOP
PRESET	STR$
PRINT	STRIG
PSET	STRING
PUT	STRING$
RANDOMIZE	SUB
READ	SWAP
REDIM	SYSTEM
REM	TAB
RESET	TAN
RESTORE	THEN
RESUME	TIME$
RETURN	TIMER
RIGHT$	TO
RMDIR	TROFF
RND	TRON
RSET	TYPE
RTRIM$	UBOUND
RUN	UCASE$
SADD	UEVENT
SCREEN	UNLOCK

UNTIL
USING
VAL
VARPTR
VARPTR$
VARSEG
VIEW
WAIT
WEND
WHILE
WIDTH
WINDOW
WRITE
XOR

ASCII Codes for the IBM PC

ASCII Value	Character	ASCII Value	Character
0	Null	12	Form-feed
1	☺	13	Carriage return
2	☻	14	♫
3	♥	15	☼
4	♦	16	►
5	♣	17	◄
6	♠	18	↕
7	Beep	19	!!
8	◘	20	π
9	Tab	21	§
10	Linefeed	22	▬
11	Cursor home	23	↨

Table B-1.   ASCII Codes for the IBM PC

ASCII Value	Character	ASCII Value	Character
24	↑	58	:
25	↓	59	;
26	→	60	<
27	←	61	=
28	Cursor right	62	>
29	Cursor left	63	?
30	Cursor up	64	@
31	Cursor down	65	A
32	Space	66	B
33	!	67	C
34	"	68	D
35	#	69	E
36	$	70	F
37	%	71	G
38	&	72	H
39	'	73	I
40	(	74	J
41	)	75	K
42	*	76	L
43	+	77	M
44	,	78	N
45	-	79	O
46	.	80	P
47	/	81	Q
48	0	82	R
49	1	83	S
50	2	84	T
51	3	85	U
52	4	86	V
53	5	87	W
54	6	88	X
55	7	89	Y
56	8	90	Z
57	9	91	[

Table B-1. ASCII Codes for the IBM PC *(continued)*

ASCII Value	Character	ASCII Value	Character
92	\	126	~
93	]	127	⌂
94	^	128	Ç
95	—	129	ü
96	'	130	é
97	a	131	â
98	b	132	ä
99	c	133	à
100	d	134	å
101	e	135	ç
102	f	136	ê
103	g	137	ë
104	h	138	è
105	i	139	ï
106	j	140	î
107	k	141	ì
108	l	142	Ä
109	m	143	Å
110	n	144	É
111	o	145	æ
112	p	146	Æ
113	q	147	ô
114	r	148	ö
115	s	149	ò
116	t	150	û
117	u	151	ù
118	v	152	ÿ
119	w	153	Ö
120	x	154	Ü
121	y	155	¢
122	z	156	£
123	{	157	¥
124	¦	158	Pt
125	}	159	f

Table B-1.   ASCII Codes for the IBM PC *(continued)*

ASCII Value	Character	ASCII Value	Character
160	á	194	┬
161	í	195	├
162	ó	196	─
163	ú	197	┼
164	ñ	198	╞
165	Ñ	199	╟
166	a̲	200	╚
167	o̲	201	╔
168	¿	202	╩
169	⌐	203	╦
170	¬	204	╠
171	½	205	═
172	¼	206	╬
173	¡	207	╧
174	«	208	╨
175	»	209	╤
176	░	210	╥
177	▒	211	╙
178	▓	212	╘
179	│	213	╒
180	┤	214	╓
181	╡	215	╫
182	╢	216	╪
183	╖	217	┘
184	╕	218	┌
185	╣	219	█
186	║	220	▄
187	╗	221	▌
188	╝	222	▐
189	╜	223	▀
190	╛	224	α
191	┐	225	β
192	└	226	Γ
193	┴	227	π

Table B-1.   ASCII Codes for the IBM PC *(continued)*

ASCII Value	Character	ASCII Value	Character
228	Σ	242	≥
229	σ	243	≤
230	μ	244	⌠
231	τ	245	⌡
232	φ	246	÷
233	θ	247	≈
234	Ω	248	°
235	δ	249	•
236	∞	250	·
237	∅	251	√
238	∈	252	^{n}
239	∩	253	^{2}
240	≡	254	■
241	±	255	(blank 'FF')

Table B-1.   ASCII Codes for the IBM PC *(continued)*

Scan Codes

Key	Scan Code	Key	Scan Code
a or A	30	0 or)	11
b or B	48	1 or !	02
c or C	46	2 or @	03
d or D	32	3 or #	04
e or E	18	4 or $	05
f or F	33	5 or %	06
g or G	34	6 or ^	07
h or H	35	7 or &	08
i or I	23	8 or *	09
j or J	36	9 or (	10
k or K	37		
l or L	38	– or _	12
m or M	50	= or +	13
n or N	49	[or {	26
o or O	24	] or }	27
p or P	25	; or :	39
q or Q	16	; or "	40
r or R	19	' or ~	41
s or S	31	\ or		43
t or T	20	, or <	51
u or U	22	. or >	52
v or V	47	/ or ?	53

Table C-1.   Keyboard Scan Codes

Key	Scan Code	Key	Scan Code
w or W	17	* or PRTSC	55
x or X	45		
y or Y	21		
z or Z	44		

Table C-1.   Keyboard Scan Codes *(continued)*

Key	Normal Code	code with ALT	code with CTRL	code with SHIFT
F1	59	104	94	84
F2	60	105	95	85
F3	61	106	96	86
F4	62	107	97	87
F5	63	108	98	88
F6	64	109	99	89
F7	65	110	100	90
F8	66	111	101	91
F9	67	112	102	92
F10	68	113	103	93
HOME	71		119	55
UP	72			56
PGUP	73		132	57
LEFT	75		115	52
(5)	76			53
RIGHT	77		116	54
END	79		117	49
DOWN	80			50
PGDN	81		118	51
INS	82			48
DEL	83			46
Grey +	78			43
Grey −	74			45

Table C-2.   Scan Codes and Extended ASCII Codes for Function Keys and Keypad Keys

CodeView®	Microsoft Corporation
IBM®	International Business Machines, Corporation
WordStar®	MicroPro International Corporation

T
R
A
D
E
M
A
R
K
S

The manuscript for this book was prepared and submitted to Osborne/McGraw-Hill in electronic form. The acquisitions editor for this project was Jeff Pepper, the technical reviewer was Bud Aaron, and the project editor was Nancy Beckus.

Text design by Judy Wohlfrom, using Century Expanded for text body and Eras Demi for display.

Cover art by Bay Graphics Design Associates. Color separation and cover supplier, Phoenix Color Corporation. Screens produced with InSet, from InSet Systems, Inc. Book printed and bound by R.R. Donnelley & Sons Company, Crawfordsville, Indiana.